A History of Ayutthaya

For early centuries, Ayutthaya ranked alongside China and India as one of the three great powers of Asia. This is the first English-language study of Ayutthaya's emergence in the late thirteenth century to the city's destruction in 1767. Drawing on chronicles, accounts by Europeans, Chinese, Persians, and Japanese, law codes, visual culture, literature, and language, Baker and Phongpaichit offer a vivid and original view of early modern Siam. Ayutthaya emerged as an aggressive port that became China's major trading partner. Its society and kingship were shaped in an era of warfare. From 1600, peace paved the way for Ayutthaya to prosper as Asia's leading entrepot under an expansive mercantile absolutism. Siam was an urban, commercial, and extraordinarily cosmopolitan society. The city's dramatic fall resulted not from social or political decline but a failure to manage the consequences of prosperity. Focusing on commerce, kingship, Buddhism, and war, this book offers new perspectives on Southeast Asia in the early modern world.

Chris Baker is an independent scholar. Pasuk Phongpaichit is Professor of Economics at Chulalongkorn University, Bangkok. Together they have written eight books and over thirty articles on Thailand's history, literature, and political economy; have translated key historical sources, pioneering works by Thai historians, and literary classics, including the epic poem *The Tale of Khun Chang Khun Phaen* (2010) which won the AAS translation prize; and have held visiting posts at universities in the USA, Japan, and Australia.

A History of Ayutthaya

Siam in the Early Modern World

Chris Baker

Pasuk Phongpaichit

CAMBRIDGE
UNIVERSITY PRESS

CAMBRIDGE
UNIVERSITY PRESS

University Printing House, Cambridge CB2 8BS, United Kingdom

One Liberty Plaza, 20th Floor, New York, NY 10006, USA

477 Williamstown Road, Port Melbourne, VIC 3207, Australia

4843/24, 2nd Floor, Ansari Road, Daryaganj, Delhi – 110002, India

79 Anson Road, #06-04/06, Singapore 079906

Cambridge University Press is part of the University of Cambridge.

It furthers the University's mission by disseminating knowledge in the pursuit of education, learning, and research at the highest international levels of excellence.

www.cambridge.org
Information on this title: www.cambridge.org/9781107190764
DOI: 10.1017/9781108120197

First published 2017

Printed in the United Kingdom by Clays, St Ives plc

A catalog record for this publication is available from the British Library.

ISBN 978-1-107-19076-4 Hardback
ISBN 978-1-316-64113-2 Paperback

Contents

Figures and Tables

Figures

Tables

Maps

Preface: Ayutthaya in History

European travelers in the sixteenth and seventeenth centuries placed Ayutthaya or Siam among the three great powers of Asia alongside China and India. They reckoned the city as large as London or Paris, and they marveled at the gold in the temples and treasuries. Later events have obscured this major part of the Southeast Asian past. In 1767, Ayutthaya was destroyed by Burmese armies. Much of its historical record was lost. As Siam avoided formal colonialism, it missed the data gathering and history writing by early colonial officers elsewhere. To this day, there is no academic study of the full four centuries of Siam in the Ayutthaya era.

Of course, Ayutthaya is covered in David Wyatt's *Thailand: a short history*, but within fifty pages, and in Baas Terwiel's *Thailand's political history* in even fewer. Popular histories of Ayutthaya succumb to fascination with the few years of French involvement in the late seventeenth century. In Thai-language scholarship, the situation is similar. There are several brilliant studies of themes and sub-periods, and many popular accounts, but only one academic overview, now over three decades old.[1]

The history of Southeast Asia was originally written from the post-colonial capitals. Its major theme was the commercial and cultural penetration of the west. Having no colonial ex-master, few spices, and even fewer converts to Christianity, Siam had a subdued role in this account. Ayutthaya's rise (and fall) belongs instead to an Asian story of Asian trading networks, cultural influence from China and India, and rivalries between regional neighbors. This Asian story is now coming into its own.

Within Thailand, the neglect of Ayutthaya is bound up with the role it was assigned in the national history. The early histories of Siam, compiled from the mid-nineteenth century, begin with the foundation of Ayutthaya in 1351 in the royal chronicles.[2] However, in a speech delivered in 1907

[1] Srisakara, *Krung si ayutthaya khong rao*; see below.
[2] See "Brief notices of the history of Siam," prepared by King Mongkut for Sir John Bowring in 1855, in Bowring, *Kingdom and people of Siam*, vol. 2, 341–5.

in the ruins of the grand palace at Ayutthaya, King Chulalongkorn called
for the construction of a new national history:

> Those many countries which have been formed into nations and countries
> uphold that the history of one's nation and country is an important matter to be
> known clearly and accurately through study and teaching. It is a discipline for
> evaluating ideas and actions as right or wrong, good or bad, as a means to incul-
> cate love of one's nation and land.

He noted that most countries had histories stretching over a thousand
years. He regretted that Siam's history extended back no further than
1351, and attributed this to over-reliance on the royal chronicles. He
urged the audience to use other sources, such as Pali chronicles and
archeology, to extend Siam's history further into the past.

> I'd like to persuade all of you to make up your minds that we will collect the his-
> torical materials of the country of Siam for every city, every race, every dynasty,
> and every era to compile a history of Siam over the past thousand years.[3]

In the following year, King Chulalongkorn's son, the future King
Vajiravudh, made an expedition to Sukhothai and nearby cities carrying
the text of an inscription found by King Mongkut at Sukhothai in 1833
and dated to 1292. His account of the tour, published in 1908 with many
photographs, showed that these cities had been significant in the past
and that their archeology could be cross-linked with information in the
inscription. He hoped that his book would "make the Thai more aware
that our Thai race is deep-rooted and is not a race of jungle-folk or, as
the English say, uncivilized."[4]

Between 1912 and 1917, Prince Damrong Rajanubhab, a half-
brother of King Chulalongkorn, compiled the first history based on
several sources including inscriptions, a collection of legends known
as the *Northern chronicles*,[5] the Ayutthaya royal chronicles, the work of
"European students of the antiquities of China,"[6] and translations from
the Tang annals. He found that the Thai had migrated from southern
China, occupied a first kingdom at Nanchao in Yunnan, and then displaced a former population of Khmer and Mon-Khmer speakers in
the Chaophraya Basin, where they created several small kingdoms. The
most important of these had its capital at Sukhothai, founded around
1238, where Buddhism flourished and "King Rāma Khamhaeng was a

[3] Baker, "Antiquarian Society of Siam," 95, 97, translation slightly modified.
[4] Vajiravudh, *Thieo mueang phra ruang*, 9.
[5] *Phongsawadan nuea.*
[6] In *Amongst the Shans* (1885), A. R. Colquhoun noted the large number of Tai-speakers
  in southern China, and the Sinologist Lacouperie linked Colquhoun's data to peoples
  named in Chinese annals of the second to fourth century CE.

very powerful monarch and is to be considered as one of the greatest of the Thai sovereigns."[7] Ayutthaya was founded later by the descendant of a "King Brahma" who had ruled one of the earliest Thai kingdoms on the Mekong River. Damrong announced: "The history of Siam may properly be divided into three periods, namely, (1) the period when Sukhothai was the capital, (2) the period when Ayuddhya was the capital, and (3) the period since Bangkok (Ratanakosindr) has been the capital."[8] Prince Damrong's work fulfilled King Chulalongkorn's criteria of being based on several sources and stretching back over a thousand years. It was also the history of a race, the Thai, which had become a nation.

Over the next decade, Prince Damrong compiled a core history of Ayutthaya. Again he used a range of sources including the Ayutthaya chronicles, excerpts from the Burmese chronicles, and records by western visitors. He enumerated twenty-four wars with Burma from 1539 to 1767, showing that Burma was the near-constant aggressor. He argued that the falls of Ayutthaya in 1569 and again in 1767 were caused by internal disunity among the Thai nobility, and he highlighted the heroism of King Naresuan who "proclaimed the independence" of Siam after the first fall. His *Thai rop phama* (Thai wars with Burma) has remained in print ever since.[9] A decade later, Damrong analyzed the social and political systems of Sukhothai and Ayutthaya respectively: at Sukhothai, "Thai values" had flourished, including a love of freedom, tolerance, peaceful co-existence, and the ability to progress, but in early Ayutthaya, the rulers had adopted Indian concepts and institutions from Angkor, including slavery.[10]

Prince Damrong's work was developed into a national history that occupied the textbooks and popular accounts for the rest of the twentieth century. In this history, Sukhothai is the "first capital of the Thai" and its era in the thirteenth and fourteenth centuries is the "Dawn of Happiness," a "Golden Age" marked by Buddhism, paternal kingship, and Damrong's "Thai values." During the Ayutthaya era, the Thai purity of Sukhothai is besmirched by Khmer influence; Buddhism is infected by Brahmanism; paternal kingship gives way to the idea of a *devaraja* god-king and royal absolutism; and the Thai freedoms are buried by slavery and monopoly. In this story of decline, Burma plays the role of nemesis,

---

[7] Damrong, "Story of the records of Siamese history"; Damrong, "Siamese history prior to the founding of Ayuddhyā," quote on 44; the latter is a translation of Damrong, "Phraniphon khamnam"; Charnvit, "From dynastic to 'national' history."
[8] Damrong, "Story of the records of Siamese history," 1.
[9] Damrong, *Our wars with the Burmese.*
[10] Damrong, *Laksana kan pokkhrong*, a lecture given in 1927.

and the fall of Ayutthaya in 1767 is a catharsis that prepares the way for revival and resurgence in the Bangkok era.[11]

This story is reflected in the first English-language history of Siam, published by W. A. R. Wood in 1924. Wood's account up to the foundation of Ayutthaya is taken directly from Damrong's work. On the Ayutthaya era, Wood added material from the Luang Prasoet chronicle of Ayutthaya, found in 1907, and from several European accounts, especially that of Van Vliet. Wood's chapters are divided by reigns, and the whole book is a story of kings fighting wars.[12]

After this narrative was set into the textbooks and Prince Damrong was canonized as the "father of Thai history," the story acquired a sacred quality. Over the next fifty years, several Thai and international scholars developed the histories of the Sukhothai and Bangkok eras, but Ayutthaya was neglected.[13]

Starting in the 1980s, an attack on this national history was mounted by a group associated with *Sinlapa watthanatham* (Art and Culture), a monthly cultural magazine and publishing house.[14] The group's most prominent members were Srisakara Vallibhotama, a pioneer of surface anthropology, and Sujit Wongthes, a prolific editor, publicist, and all-round litterateur. First, the school attacked the narrow focus on Thai ethnicity in the national history. As archeological research revealed the extent of settlement in prehistoric times, this school famously proclaimed "the Thais were always here," denying the importance of the Thai migrations, stressing the "diversity" of origins of Thailand's eventual population, and criticizing the ethnic chauvinism in the national history.[15]

Second, the school presented history as a process of increasing anthropological complexity in which kings and other hero figures were incidental. In Srisakara's master work, *Sayam prathet* (The country of Siam), the motors of history are the increasing ethnic complexity of society and the gradual extension of commercial networks and cultural exchanges. Through these processes, the basis of society evolves from village in the Bronze Age, to town (*mueang*) in the early first millennium CE, to state in the late first millennium, and finally to kingdom (*ratcha-anajak*) in the early Ayutthaya era. As ethnicity and monarchy no longer served as the focus of history, the *Sinlapa watthanatham* school needed a substitute.

[11] For a summary version in English, see *Thailand in the 80s*, 22–32.

[12] Wood, *History of Siam*.

[13] In the footnotes and further readings for the two chapters on Ayutthaya in his *Thailand*, published in 1984, David Wyatt cited only one secondary work (Smith, *Dutch in seventeenth-century Thailand*) and two very recent theses, by Charnvit and Busakorn, considered below.

[14] The group was also associated with another magazine, *Muang Boran* (Ancient City).

[15] Sujit, *Khon thai yu thini*.

Srisakara proposed a kind of geo-nationalism in which Thai history included anything which happened in the past within the boundaries that eventually defined the country.[16]

Srisakara's *Krung si ayutthaya khong rao* (Our Ayutthaya, 1984) placed the Ayutthaya era within this overall scheme: from the fifth century CE, two groups of towns appeared in the west and east of the lower Chaophraya Plain respectively; over the eighth to twelfth century, Suphanburi and Lopburi emerged as larger, dominant places in the two areas; in the fourteenth century, these two city-states allied to form Ayutthaya. Thus, in Sujit's summary of the book, "Ayutthaya did not appear like a miracle worked by the gods, but as an outgrowth of prior development."[17] After making a case for giving Ayutthaya more importance than Sukhothai in the national history, and presenting this view of its emergence, which was path-breaking for its time, the book followed the conventional story.

The *Sinlapa watthanatham* school is scarcely known outside Thailand because very little of its output appeared in English. Within the country, however, the school was influential, particularly in stressing the diversity (*khwam lak lai*) of the population.

In contrast to the inwardness of the *Sinlapa watthanatham* group, other Thai historians found a new perspective on Ayutthaya by venturing outside the country. In the 1970s and 1980s, four Thai scholars completed outstanding studies on Ayutthaya history for overseas doctorates: Charnvit Kasetsiri at Cornell University on the rise of Ayutthaya; Sunait Chutintaranond at Cornell University on Thai–Burmese warfare in the sixteenth century; Dhiravat na Pombejra at the School of Asian and African Studies (SOAS) on the Prasat Thong dynasty in the seventeenth century; and Busakorn Lailert at SOAS on the Ban Phlu Luang dynasty in the seventeenth to eighteenth century. The publication history of these four scholars is intriguing. Only one of these four pioneering dissertations became a "thesis book" in English. None of them was translated into Thai. Two of the scholars published excerpts of their thesis as well as later research in both Thai and English, but concentrated heavily on economic themes in contrast to the political focus of their dissertations. One of the theses was not only never published in full, but became rather difficult to access.

Even so, through this pioneering research, and through their teaching and advocacy, these scholars transformed the standing of Ayutthaya within Thai history. In an article first published in 1999, Charnvit began with a direct challenge to Sukhothai's premier role in the national history,

---

[16] Srisakara, "Nakhon si thammarat kap prawatisat thai," 78.

[17] Srisakara, *Krung si ayutthaya khong rao*, (14), preface by Sujit Wongthes.

stating: "Ayutthaya was the first major political, cultural and commercial center of the Thai."[18] These scholars established that Ayutthaya was a more complex and long-lasting state than Sukhothai, and had a much greater role in shaping Thailand of the present day. In mainstream history, the Ayutthaya era is no longer a low point in the national story but part of a continuous rise.

Charnvit and Dhiravat were central to the subsequent trend in the historiography of Ayutthaya. The early histories, such as those by Damrong and Wood, were about kings and wars because these are the subjects covered in the chronicles. By contrast, Charnvit, Dhiravat, and many international scholars presented Ayutthaya as one of the great commercial centers of Asia. They highlighted the enormous variety and complexity of Ayutthaya's trade, the special relationship with China, and the prominent role of the monarchy in commerce.[19]

By comparison, new work on the politics of the Ayutthaya era was more limited. Two contributions stand out. The first was by Nidhi Eoseewong, who belonged to the same generation as these four pioneers, but chose to write his Michigan doctoral thesis on Indonesia rather than Siam. After his return to Thailand, he wrote studies of the reigns of King Narai (1656–88) and King Taksin (1767–82),[20] using the language of modern politics (party, faction, coup) to remove the "sacred" aura that history writing copied from the chronicles. He also brought out the social shifts and social conflicts that lie behind the historical narrative. Second, Phiset Jiajanphong, who had a career in the archeology section of the Fine Arts Department, put his own re-readings of the inscriptions and other early sources, as well as an appreciation of landscape, into ingenious reinterpretations of Siam from the thirteenth to fifteenth century which challenged the progression from Sukhothai to Ayutthaya in the national history.[21]

Recent international scholarship has told the story of Ayutthaya within a regional framework. Anthony Reid's *Southeast Asia in the age of commerce* (1988, 1993) provided a Braudelian portrait of society in the region over four centuries, and argued that the region underwent a boom spurred by international commerce from the mid-fifteenth to mid-seventeenth century. In *Strange parallels* (2003), Victor Lieberman found a common rhythm in the political history of Mainland Southeast Asia from the ninth to nineteenth century, and a common trend of consolidation from many small states to a few large ones. These studies have drawn attention to many

---

[18] Charnvit, "Origins of a capital and seaport," 55.
[19] Several key works appeared in Kajit, *Ayudhya and Asia* (1995), and Breazeale, *From Japan to Arabia* (1999).
[20] Nidhi, *Kanmueang thai samai phra narai* (1980), and *Kanmueang thai samai phrajao krung thonburi* (1986).
[21] Phiset, *Phra maha thammaracha.*

factors (climate trends, bullion flows, religious changes) which are more visible within a regional and international perspective than a local one.

This book offers a history of Ayutthaya from its first appearance in the late thirteenth century to its fall in 1767, focusing on commerce, kingship, Buddhism, and war. For the story of commerce, which is a backbone of Ayutthaya's history, we rely on a large body of research published since the 1980s. For the artistic and religious aspects, we draw on a much smaller but still fascinating literature. For the political, social, legal, and literary history, we use principally the original sources.

These sources are famous for being sparse and problematic: chronicles are unreliable; laws cannot be dated; monuments have been destroyed; observations by Chinese and Western observers are filtered through a cultural lens; and so on. These problems are no different from those with historical sources everywhere. Over the last few years, much material has become newly available or more accessible. Richard Cushman's side-by-side translation of different versions of the royal chronicles has made this source much easier to use, while Thai editions of all the main chronicles have been published in affordable editions. The Thailand Research Fund's series of *100 ekkasan samkhan: sapphasara prawatisat thai* (One hundred key documents for Thai history) has brought to light several hidden sources as well as offering re-readings of major inscriptions. Geoff Wade's translation from the *Ming shi-lu* and Yoneo Ishii's extracts from Japanese sources provide new external views on Siam with reliable dating. Dhiravat and Anthony Farrington published the complete records of the English East India Company on Siam. Several foreign accounts, especially by Dutch, French, and Portuguese visitors, have recently been translated and published. Besides, there are many indigenous historical sources, particularly law, literature, art, and physical landscape, which have been little used.

Early literary works have posed special problems because they are difficult to date and difficult to read due to archaic poetic constructions and vocabulary not found in any dictionary. Recent annotated editions by the Royal Institute and individual scholars, especially Winai Pongsripian, have reduced these problems. There are similar issues of dating for visual material from art and architecture, but much more of this work is now readily available because of the revolutions in graphics and publishing. Ayutthaya-era murals are becoming less easy to see *in situ* because they are now closed up for their own protection, but many have been beautifully photographed and published, especially by the Muang Boran publishing house. Similarly, several late-Ayutthaya illustrated manuscripts have been published or made available on the net. We draw on a great many sources that were not available or not accessible two decades ago. At the back of the book, we provide a note on our approach to some of the controversial or "difficult" sources.

Acknowledgments

This book has developed over more than a decade and incurred many debts. In the early stages of the project, we were helped by two of the greats who have gone before, David Wyatt and Yoneo Ishii. We owe a special debt to Chatthip Nartsupha and Charnvit Kasetsiri, whose enthusiasm for Thai history and generosity of spirit have been a source of inspiration. We have been lucky to traipse round several sites listening to Piriya Krairiksh, and to have had the counsel of Niyada Lausoonthorn, to whom we are forever indebted. We owe a special thanks to Kaoru Sugihara, who hosted us in Kyoto, and exposed us to his world history seminar in Tokyo, where one key idea of the book took shape. We are grateful to Han ten Brummelhuis, who generously made available his unpublished translation of Van Neijenrode; to Bob Bickner who provided his working translation of *Lilit phra lo*; to Matt Gallon who allowed us to adapt a map he drew; to Paisarn Piemmettawat, Julispong Chularatana, Ananda Chuchoti, Baas Terwiel, Thavatchai Tangsirivanich, Ruth Bowler, and Sran Tongpan for help on the illustrations; and to Geoff Wade, Patrick Jory, Junko Koizumi, Davisakd Puaksom, Patrick Dumon, and Parkpume Vanichaka who responded to many queries. Special thanks to the Siam Society and the Center for Southeast Asian Studies in Kyoto.

We are especially grateful to friends who read all or part of the book in draft form and offered us corrections, suggestions, advice, and encouragement. These include Alan Strathern, Bhawan Ruangsilp, Chatthip Nartsupha, Craig Reynolds, Dhiravat na Pombejra, Hiram Woodward, Justin McDaniel, Kennon Breazeale, Matt Reeder, Nicolas Revire, Peter Skilling, Pimpraphai Bisalputra, Sun Laichen, Sunait Chutintaranond, Tamara Loos, and two anonymous readers.

Note on the Text

References to Richard Cushman, *Royal Chronicles of Ayutthaya*, are abbreviated as *RCA*. For early Ayutthaya, where the narrative is highly compressed, the page reference is supplemented by a line reference. An abbreviation in brackets denotes the edition: LP = Luang Prasoet; BM = British Museum; PC = Phan Chanthanumat; RA = Royal Autograph. Prior to the late seventeenth century, the various *phitsadan* chronicles (i.e., those other than LP) are not significantly different, and we use BM to indicate these chronicles in general for this period. We have read all chronicle references in the Thai originals, and we occasionally modify Cushman's translation (and indicate so).

References to Geoff Wade's online translations from the *Ming shi-lu* are given in the form: Wade, *Southeast Asia* online no.

Years in the form "1474/5" have been converted to CE from a calendar where the year crosses two CE years.

Names of Thai kings are spelled according to conventional forms. We generally follow the regnal names and dates chosen by Wyatt, and provide an appendix table showing other options. For Thai authors, we use their own preferred English spelling wherever possible. Otherwise Thai is transcribed using the Royal Institute system with the exception of using "j" for *jo jan*.

Pali-Sanskrit words are usually spelled in the Pali-derived form, hence *dhamma* rather than *dharma*.

We use "Chaophraya Basin" for the full area draining into the Chaophraya River (i.e., including Lanna), and "Chaophraya Plain" for the flat part below the hills.

The city's early name was Ayodhya, borrowed from Rama's city in the Indian *Ramayana*. Prasert na Nagara suggests that the form "Ayutthaya," meaning "invincible," was a defiant variant invented after the defeat by Pegu in 1569. To avoid confusion, Ayutthaya is here used throughout.

1   Before Ayutthaya

Ayutthaya looms into history from the late thirteenth century CE. Over the following two centuries it becomes the principal city of a territory known as Siam, occupying the deltaic plain of the Chaophraya River, the Central Plain of Thailand today. To west, north, and east, this plain is bounded by hill ranges straggling southwards from the Himalayas (see Map 1.1). Though the hills are not high, forest made them more forbidding. Within these boundaries, the territory is knitted together by water routes along rivers and coastal seas, the most convenient medium of transport prior to the modern era. As the Chaophraya Plain drops only 80 meters across 500 kilometers from the hills to the sea, rivers are sluggish and craft could be poled or paddled northward for most of the year. The hill boundaries and water communications resulted in Siam developing as a distinctive cultural zone.

Today around 1300 millimeters of rain fall on the 162,000 square kilometers of the Chaophraya River's catchment area from May to October, and most of the runoff is channeled down the Chaophraya. The flow is now controlled by dams and water gates, but earlier it would break the banks and flood the lower delta almost every year. Today the plain is a tessellated landscape of paddy fields. In the past, the ecology was very different. High heat and plentiful water generated a rich and varied biomass ranging from deciduous forest near the hills to tropical rainforest further south and mangroves along the coasts. For humans, this ecology supported both a rich economy of hunting and gathering and a productive agriculture, but also hosted many predators including carnivorous animals, poisonous reptiles, disease-carrying insects, and many germs, viruses, and parasites. Forests were seen as dangerous, especially for their fevers and other deadly diseases. Because of high mortality, the population of Mainland Southeast Asia remained small and sparse, with density between a fifth to tenth of the neighboring zones in China and India.[1]

---

[1] Population is discussed in more detail in Chapter 5.

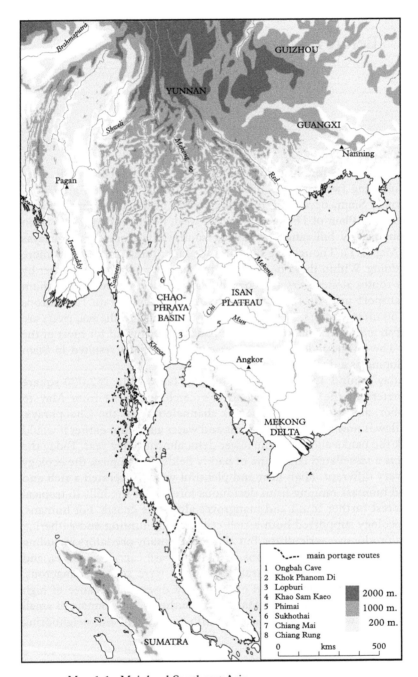

Map 1.1. Mainland Southeast Asia

This chapter traces the history of the Chaophraya Plain to the eve of Ayutthaya's foundation, using mainly secondary works. The historiography of this era has been transformed over recent years. The earlier version was a story of competing empires (Pagan, Srivijaya, Angkor, Dvaravati) and broad geopolitical conflict, reminiscent of the world in the twentieth century. With more digging, more inscriptions, more artifacts, new techniques, and more sensitive readings of sources, the story has become more fragmented, less violent, and more subtle.

Early Peoples

Man arrived rather late in Mainland Southeast Asia. Traces of human settlement in the region stretch back around 40,000 years, but these traces are faint. From about 11,000 BCE, when the climate became warmer and wetter, hunter-gatherers using tools made by flaking river pebbles became more common throughout the region. Along the hills that now divide Thailand and Burma are several caves and rock shelters where these Hoabinhian hunter-gatherers spent the rainy seasons.

Around 17,000 years ago, the sea was over 100 meters below the present level. The mainland and the islands of the western archipelago were connected in a single land mass. The sea rose gradually, reaching a maximum of around 4 meters above its present-level at around 6550 BCE, submerging the lower Chaophraya Plain. Thereafter, the sea dropped and the coastline moved south, reaching Bangkok between 3000 and 1000 BCE, and settling near its current site by 500 CE. Recent research shows the sea receded earlier than once thought, revising the long-held view that the lower gulf was underwater in the first millennium CE and that many Dvaravati sites were on the coast of the time.[2]

Few hunter-gatherer sites have been found in the lowland, probably because such sites are easily obliterated, but two are known on the estuary of the Bang Pakong River. These sites belie the image of hunter-gatherers as small and mobile groups. Khok Phanom Di was occupied for 500 years from around 2000 BCE by a community of several hundred people. At first, they visited temporarily and harvested a huge range of fish and shellfish, supplemented by game and vegetable products from the nearby forests. After settling, they fashioned bone into fish-hooks and other tools, made sea shells into jewelry, manufactured a large quantity and variety of pottery, and ate some rice, perhaps acquired through exchange. After perhaps ten generations of regular settlement, when the sea receded, they fashioned granite into hoes to till the ground, and shells

---

[2] Trongjai, "Reconsidering the palaeo-shoreline."

into knives to harvest plants. Several generations later, they began to make larger pots with a different technique and new decoration, hinting at an influx of new people. One woman, probably a master potter, was buried with 120,000 shell disc beads, her tools, and examples of her pottery skill. Around 1600 BCE, the site was abandoned.[3] This extraordinary excavation displays the strength and flexibility of the hunter-gatherer economy in this rich environment.

The earliest evidence for rice growing is around 2000 BCE. Some believe it developed locally since wild rice grows naturally in the area, but more likely it came from the mid-Yangzi valley, where domestic rice cultivation was well developed by the fourth millennium BCE, and spread along the coasts to Mainland Southeast Asia in a package with the keeping of cattle and dogs, a style of pottery with curved incisions, and a tradition of inhumation burial.[4] The researched sites in the Chaophraya Plain are all on the fringe of the western hills, or on the uplands in Lopburi, and may have developed from earlier forager settlements through an influx of new people. The early farmers still gained much of their food from hunting birds, deer, monkeys, crocodiles, rhinos, turtles, and other fauna, and from collecting frogs, fish, and shellfish from the waterways. As Bronson summarized, "No farmers in any region outside southern and eastern Asia could produce as much food with as little labor from the same amount of land."[5] In civilization models based on temperate zones, the coming of agriculture is a major disjuncture because agriculture supports larger and denser populations which in turn develop more complex hierarchies. Southeast Asia diverged from this model for the simple reason that the hunter-gatherer economy was so productive. Agriculture did not replace hunter-gathering, but supplemented it.

Bronze appeared around 1250 to 1000 BCE.[6] Again, the technology most likely arrived from southern China where a well-developed bronze industry using the same techniques flourished by 1500 BCE. A copper mining center has been discovered in the Khao Wong Prachan valley in Lopburi. Bronze was used to make some tools such as axe-heads and needles, but mostly for jewelry and ornaments. The settlements of this era were small, with a maximum of around 250 people, and scattered rather than clustered, possibly to preserve territories for hunting and gathering. After 1000 BCE, people were often buried with fine pots,

---

[3] Higham and Rachanie, *Early Thailand*, 46–75.
[4] Higham and Rachanie, *Early Thailand*, 77–105.
[5] Bronson, "Extraction of natural resources," 295.
[6] Some scholars argue for an earlier date around 2000–1800 BCE; see the discussion in Rispoli, Ciaria, and Pigott, "Establishing the prehistoric cultural sequence," 119–34, and Higham, Douka, and Higham, "New chronology for the Bronze Age."

tools, jewelry, animal parts, or clay figurines of domesticated animals. One site shows evidence of a dominant chiefly lineage, but at present it stands as an exception. What is truly striking is the variety – both within a single community, and between locations – on burial practices, pottery styles, taste in jewelry, and cultic objects. Two villages only 20 kilometers apart maintained completely different pottery traditions over several hundred years.[7]

Overall the archeological record to this point at present suggest a range of small local communities where the environment provided a good living, where neither economic monopoly nor armed political domination was creating any significant social division, where there was a high degree of local experimentation in cultural and ritual practices, and where intercommunity exchanges were common but socially neutral.

Around 500 BCE, communities began to make things from iron. While copper and tin for making bronze were found in only a few locations, the raw material for iron was widely available in laterite rocks. The technology may have evolved locally but again the date is late enough that diffusion from elsewhere is more likely, possibly from India as humped (zebu) cattle also appeared in the same era.[8] The first iron articles were decorative goods, mimicking bronze examples, but before long the main usage was to make implements for agriculture and hunting – knives, sickles, hoes, billhooks, digging sticks, and spades.[9] The impact of iron was much greater than bronze.

Population expanded. On the Isan Plateau, where the archeological work has been more intense, over 1,500 Iron Age sites have been counted. Some could have accommodated over 2,000 people.[10] In the Chaophraya Plain, many sites have been found around the old copper-working area in Lopburi, in the Lower Pasak valley, along the Maeklong and Bang Pakong rivers, and farther north along the Ping and Yom rivers. An increase in burials at the Lopburi sites suggests population growth.[11]

A distinctive form of settlement appeared – the moated mound. The original pattern for these may have been a natural landform, but it was improved by adding moats in concentric rings. The water may have been used for irrigation, but more likely they provided a secure domestic water

---

[7] Higham and Rachanie, *Early Thailand*, 130–55; Glover, Pornchai, and Villiers, *Early metallurgy*; Solheim and Ayres, "Late prehistoric and early historic pottery."

[8] Rispoli, Ciaria, and Pigott, "Establishing the prehistoric cultural sequence," 134–5.

[9] Higham and Rachanie, *Early Thailand*, 167–80; Glover, Pornchai, and Villiers, *Early metallurgy*.

[10] Srisakara, *Isan*, 37–60.

[11] Srisakara, "Early urban centres in the Chao Phraya valley"; Rispoli, Ciaria, and Pigott, "Establishing the prehistoric cultural sequence," 135–6

supply through the long dry season and periods of drought.[12] Graves suggest craft skills became more developed, more specialized, and more valued: metal-workers, potters, and textile makers were all buried with the tools of their trade. Burials show more clustering into what may be clans, with more variation by gender and age. A few sites show stronger evidence of chiefs or chiefly lineages. At Ongbah Cave on the Khwae Yai River, some men were buried in hardwood coffins carved with the images of bird's heads and filled with beads, bronze ornaments, iron tools, and weapons – lances, spears, and halberds.[13] Other sites have yielded arrowheads, projectiles for pellet bows, and spears which have been "killed," possibly in honor of a warrior.[14] But much of this could still come from a hunting culture. No arsenals have been found, and no definite proof of fortifications.

In the sites along the lower reaches of the rivers, exotic goods appear in the graves, including beads and figurines from India, and several high-tin bronze bowls decorated with vegetation, dwellings, the first pictorial representation of humans, along with images of sheep and horses, which are not native to Southeast Asia.[15] While sites on the west of the plain show linkage westward to India either by sea or over the portage routes, especially via the Three Pagodas Pass, sites on this western side have yielded glass beads also found down the Malay Peninsula, and green stone ear rings, bone combs, and ornaments found also in Vietnam, the Philippines, and southern China. Graves from this era contain more exotic status-defining goods, suggesting the emergence of "a farmer-warrior elite."[16] Fragments of pottery carry Indian religious symbols and excerpts of written scripts.[17]

Who were these early peoples? To date, the discussion of the early peopling of the region has been dominated by linguists using a model of languages developing by division and diffusion from a common core. Benedict traced all the major Southeast Asian language families back to a single root in southern China; the Austronesian family branched off first by ocean travel and developed into Malay and the related languages of the archipelago; the Austroasiatic or Mon-Khmer family passed by land or sea into Mainland Southeast Asia.[18] Bellwood and Blust proposed that Mon-Khmer moved with the spread of the new rice agriculture from the

---

[12] O'Reilly, "Increasing complexity."
[13] Sorensen, "Ongbah cave and its fifth drum."
[14] Higham and Rachanie, *Early Thailand*, 179–80.
[15] Higham and Rachanie, *Early Thailand*, 172–5; Glover and Bellina, "Ban Don Ta Phet and Khao Sam Kaeo."
[16] Rispoli, Ciaria, and Pigott, "Establishing the prehistoric cultural sequence," 136.
[17] Borell, Bellina, and Boonyarit, "Contacts between the upper Thai–Malay peninsula and the Mediterranean world"; Bellina, "Development of coastal polities."
[18] Benedict, *Austro-Thai language and culture.*

third millennium BCE. From eastern India through to Vietnam, the different Mon-Khmer languages share the same words for rice and bronze, and have similar words for millet, winnowing, transplanting, dogs, goats, bronze, and getting drunk on liquor – implying that these peoples knew about these things before they became scattered over a wide area.[19] Bellwood argues that rice agriculture was spread by waves of migration that superseded the hunter-gatherers, whose remnants are small negrito groups like the Senoi and Hlabri, still found in the depths of the forests.[20]

In this view, packages of peoples, languages, and technologies are layered onto the landscape like the layers in an archeological dig. But gene pools and various forms of knowledge (technology, ritual) may not have traveled together. Genes can be transmitted in small samples. Ideas, languages, and technologies may move with people or with artifacts. In the past, when rather little research was available, the archeological record suggested great discontinuities, occasioned by outside forces such as migration, but as the record has thickened, the continuities are more striking. The long-range studies of the hunter-gatherer settlements in the Bang Pakong estuary and the metal-working communities in Lopburi show people adjusting to successive changes in the environment, with some innovations brought by people from outside. Some elements of language may have arrived from southern China along with rice and bronze, but others may have come from India with the craftsmen and traders of exotic goods. The earliest representations of human faces in the Chaophraya Plain in stucco found at Nakhon Pathom and other sites are striking for the variety in shape and features.[21]

A DNA analysis of skeletons from sites in the Upper Mun Basin from 1500 BCE to 500 BCE showed that the people today who are most closely related to these ancient people are the Chao Bon or Nyah-Kur, a Mon-Khmer speaking group that still lives on the nearby hills.[22] Such small Mon-Khmer speaking communities are found from the Annamite cordillera to western India. In such a fragmented area, local languages would originally have been very diverse. The Mon-Khmer languages probably developed as lingua franca as trade and exchange increased, especially along the coasts.[23]

---

[19] Zide and Zide, "Cultural vocabulary"; Blust, "Beyond the Austronesian homeland"; Higham, "Archaeology, linguistics and the expansion of the East and Southeast Asian neolithic."

[20] Bellwood, "Southeast Asia before history," 91; Bellwood, "Cultural and biological differentiation."

[21] Best seen in the collection in the Phra Pathom Chedi National Museum, Nakhon Pathom.

[22] Patcharee et al., "Genetic history of Southeast Asian populations," 436–9.

[23] Bayard's comments on Shorto, "The linguistic protohistory," in Smith and Watson, *Early Southeast Asia*, 279–80.

In sum, nature provided very rich livelihoods for early peoples in the Chaophraya Plain, but also presented them with many threats from predators and disease. Life expectancy was low. The population increased slowly. Settlements were small and stayed mostly on the uplands on the edges of the plain. Perhaps the climate was wetter than today, the forest in the Chaophraya Plain denser, and the predators more prolific. Because the hunter-gatherer economy was so productive, the arrival of agriculture was much less of a revolution than in temperate zones. Bronze also had a limited impact, and was used mainly for personal ornamentation. Only with the arrival of iron was there more significant change – slightly larger settlements, some sign of social division, and more exchange, but no stark social division, no political integration, and very limited evidence of violence. From the early centuries CE, the pace of change picked up, in part because of influences arriving from outside, mainly from India.

Towns

In the early centuries CE, the region slips from prehistory to history, with the appearance of monumental buildings and inscriptions, and with records in the Chinese gazetteers. From the sixth or seventh century CE, larger settlements appear throughout the Chaophraya Plain. They are influenced by cultural imports from India, where urban societies had developed a thousand years earlier.

Contacts

In the last few centuries BCE, Mediterranean traders reached India, and Arab and Indian sailors mastered the technique of crossing the Indian Ocean using the rhythm of the monsoons.[24] Indian writings of this era mention Suvarnadvipa or Suvarnabhumi, a land of gold, which translated into the Golden Chryse or Golden Chersonese for Greek and Roman geographers, and Kimlin or Chinlin in Chinese. This term arose because of gold found in Sumatra and on the peninsula that served as both a bridge and a barrier between east and west, but also because of other economic opportunities. By the fourth or fifth centuries BCE, there were settlements on the middle peninsula using portage routes to connect the trade systems of the Indian Ocean and South China Seas. Between the fourth and second centuries BCE at Khao Sam Kaeo on the east coast of the peninsula, a large Indian-style settlement appeared making products

---

[24] Glover, "Early trade between India and South-East Asia"; Ray, "Early maritime contacts."

of stone, glass, ceramics, and metals – a relocation of Indian production to better access markets in the South China Seas. The settlement grew Japanese-style rice along with pulses, cotton, and sesame from India.[25] Short-range trading systems were now chained together from China to Europe. By the first century CE, European objects, especially Roman intaglios, coins, and medallions, had reached several sites on the middle and upper peninsula.[26] The first Chinese account of the portage routes dates to the first or second century BCE.

Early Arab and Chinese accounts record that Southeast Asians were great seafarers. A Chinese text from the third century CE described Southeast Asian ships with a sense of wonder: "The large ones are more than fifty meters in length ... they carry from six to seven hundred persons, with 10,000 bushels [c. 600 tons] of cargo." Archeologists have found remnants dated to the fourth century CE, and some images are known from carvings and murals. These ships were built with fiber-lashed planks, up to four masts, and heavy cladding. The Chinese had nothing to rival them until the ninth century CE, and European visitors were stunned by the size and sophistication of their later form.[27]

From the first century CE, the Han Chinese also became interested in the peninsula.[28] The growing power and profligacy of the Chinese imperial court created a demand for many exotic items from tropical and subtropical areas including kingfisher feathers, pearls, ivory, rhino horn, and precious stones, but especially perfumes of all kinds including aromatic woods. The peninsula became famed in the Chinese courts as the source of the best aloes wood: "It is like something belonging to the immortals ... Light one stick and the whole house is filled with a fragrant mist which is still there after three days."[29] From 240 CE the Chinese court developed the tribute system, under which local rulers gained access to trade with China, along with political recognition, by offering tribute. Between 600 and 850, the Chinese court received 110 tribute missions from thirty-four named places in Southeast Asia, of which half sent only one mission.[30] Many were probably on the peninsula, including five states that may have controlled portage routes across the peninsula (see Map 1.1).[31]

---

[25] Bellina et al., "Development of coastal polities"; Castillo, Bellina, and Fuller, "Rice, beans and trade crops."
[26] Borell, Bellina, and Boonyarit, "Contacts between the upper Thai–Malay peninsula and the Mediterranean world."
[27] Manguin, "Trading ships of the South China Sea," quote on 262.
[28] Wade, "Beyond the southern borders," 25.
[29] Wolters, "Tambralinga," 600.
[30] Smith, "Mainland Southeast Asia in the seventh and eighth centuries," 444.
[31] See also the speculative map in Wade, "Beyond the southern borders," 27.

Around 400 CE, a master mariner from the eastern coast of India left a carving of a Buddhist stupa near Kedah.[32] In the eighth century on the Takua Pa portage route there was a South Indian settlement, managed by a merchant guild and protected by a garrison of soldiers.[33] On the east coast around Nakhon Si Thammarat, around ninety sites have been found with Brahmanical artifacts including elaborate hilltop temple complexes, dating from the fifth century CE onwards.[34] The Chinese records describe local communities adopting Indian religious practice, including at Panpan in the seventh century:

> In the country are numerous Brahmans come from India in search of wealth. They are in high favour with the King ... There are ten monasteries where Buddhist monks and nuns study their canon ... the King of P'an-p'an sent accredited envoys to present, among other things, a tooth of the Buddha, painted stupas and ten varieties of perfume.[35]

The Gods Came

According to legend, in the mid-third century BCE during the time of the emperor Asoka, monks were sent to carry Buddhist teachings to Suvarnabhumi. The Ceylonese *Mahavamsa* chronicle describes the travels of two Buddhist monks to Suvarnabhumi in what may be the same era.[36] In the first century CE, Chinese monks came in the other direction, crossing Mainland Southeast Asia to find teachings, texts, and relics in India and Sri Lanka. Religious objects from India, probably carried by merchants, reached Southeast Asia by the early centuries CE. A sixth-century CE Chinese record of Dunxun states,

> there are five hundred families of *hu* [maybe merchants] from India, two *fo-t'u* [maybe Buddhists] and more than a thousand Indian Brahmans. The people of Tun-sun practise their doctrine and give them away their daughters in marriage; consequently many of the Brahmans do not go away.[37]

According to Piriya Krairiksh, Vishnu images and Shiva-*linga* appeared on the peninsula from the fourth century CE, and in the Chaophraya Plain from the sixth, while the first Buddha image from the peninsula dates to the fifth century, and the earliest representation of the Buddha

[32] Ray, "Early maritime contacts," 53.
[33] Christie, "Medieval Tamil-language inscriptions."
[34] Wannasarn, *Tambralinga and Nakhon Si Thammarat*, ch. 3.
[35] Wheatley, *Golden Khersonese*, 48–9.
[36] Wheatley, *Golden Khersonese*, 181.
[37] Wheatley, *Golden Khersonese*, 17; Wade, "Beyond the southern borders," 28; Prapod, *Ascendancy of Theravāda Buddhism*, 67.

from the Chaophraya Plain to the early sixth.[38] Other historians differ somewhat in the dating. The first inscriptions date to the sixth century. They are written in Mon and Sanskrit, with terms or quotations from the Buddhist scriptures rendered in Pali, using a script developed from a south Indian type once called Pallava but now Late Southern Brahmi.

Between the seventh and twelfth centuries, a large number of images and other religious artifacts were produced in the Chaophraya Plain. They include various representations of the major Hindu gods, many minor Hindu deities, and Buddha images in various poses. Art historians have traced the stylistic influences on this corpus to Sri Lanka, Pallava southern India, Ellora, and Amaravati in the Krishna-Godavari delta area, but also in some cases to the Ganges valley, and even parts of western India. This wide range of geographical origins suggests the complexity of trade and cultural contacts. The variety in the iconography suggests many sects and schools, but how they were divided is unknown. In an early relief in the Saraburi Bodhisattva Cave, where the Buddha is depicted preaching to Shiva and Vishnu in the heavens, the Buddha is higher and larger, but the two Hindu gods are shown in regal rather than votive poses, and are only slightly deferential, while a Hindu-style rishi kneels in worship (Figure 1.1). At another cave near Ratchaburi, an inscription records that the Buddhist image was "the pious work of a holy rishi."[39] A Chinese report on Panpan (probably on the peninsula) noted, "The people all learn the Brahminical writings and greatly reverence the law of the Buddha."[40] At Si Thep, Buddhism seems to have co-existed with worship of the Hindu sun-god.[41] From this early period, Hindu gods seem to have been accommodated with the Buddha.

Many images follow classic Indian iconography, but others have variations which show local influence. Only four three-dimensional versions of wheels of the law have been found in South Asia, compared to over forty in and around the Chaophraya Plain.[42] Votive tablets with a haloed Buddha seated on a throne and flanked by two *bodhisattas* have been found in the Chaophraya Plain, peninsula, Java, Burma, and Vietnam, but are unknown in India.[43] The appearance of the earth goddess, Mae Thorani, in the legend of Buddha subduing Mara – one of the most popular representations of Buddha from the eleventh century onwards – is based on a text found only in Southeast Asia.

[38] Piriya, *Roots of Thai art*, 48–9, 54–5, 100–1.
[39] Brown, *Dvāravatī wheels of the law*, 30.
[40] Wheatley, *Golden Khersonese*, 48.
[41] Pattaratorn, "Transformation of Brahmanical and Buddhist imagery."
[42] Brown, *Dvāravatī wheels of the law*, 160.
[43] Skilling, "Buddhism and the circulation of ritual," 377–8; Skilling, "Dvaravati: recent revelations and research," 107.

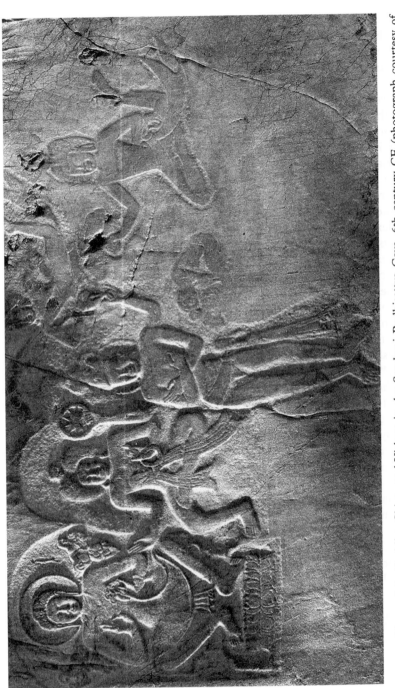

Figure 1.1. Buddha, Shiva, and Vishnu in the Saraburi Bodhisattva Cave, 6th century CE (photograph courtesy of Paisarn Piammettawat, River Books, Bangkok)

The Buddha and the Hindu gods were dovetailed with local religious practices including ancestor worship, fertility ceremonies, and spirit cults. This was nothing new. These religions had triumphed on the Indian subcontinent through their ability to coexist with earlier beliefs. The *naga*, probably the most widespread local spirit in Mainland Southeast Asia, was folded effortlessly into both the Hindu and Buddhist traditions. Buddha is sometimes found standing on a strange mythical animal, dubbed Panaspati. Several figurines have been found of a nude boy leading a monkey. The stucco and carvings from the earliest Hindu and Buddhist temples in the region include pot-bellied dwarfs, grinning lions, monsters, and mutated animals, as well as scenes probably portraying fertility rituals. Early Buddhist practice focused greatly on relics of the Buddha and the erection of reliquary stupas to house them. Buddhist monks from China traveled to the region in part because of its rising fame as a source of relics. Buddha may have been initially accepted as "the great ancestor." At some places, relic stupas were built over earlier graveyards.[44] Early religious sites were often outside the towns: in caves, on mountain tops, at river confluences – probably places already sacred and now redefined as the residence of a Hindu god or stopping place of the journeying Buddha.

As Robert Brown summarizes, "it was the gods themselves who came to South East Asia and were embraced."[45] How they were represented and worshipped was often a local affair.

Buddhist Beginnings

Older historiography was intent on showing that the Buddhism found in the Chaophraya Plain from the fifth to seventh centuries onwards was the Theravada form found in modern Thailand. More recently scholars have noted that the vocabulary of sectarian affiliations, including the term "Theravada" (way of the elders), is a modern invention.[46] Early Buddhism in the Chaophraya Plain seems to have had seeds of the practice later termed "Theravada," but also other tendencies.

From the first two Buddhist Councils after the death of Gotama Buddha, debates arose over the interpretation of his teachings and the development of his legacy. Several schools appeared. Anuradhapura in Sri Lanka emerged as an important center, where monks committed

---

[44] Winai, "Jaruek dong mae nang mueang," 21–2.
[45] Brown, *Dvāravatī wheels of the law*, 99.
[46] Skilling et al., *How Theravāda is Theravāda?*

the Buddha's teachings to writing using the Pali language, rather than Sanskrit favored elsewhere. These scriptures included a seven-book section known as the Abhidhamma with a distinctive system of metaphysics. While the Lanka school accepted that there had been Buddhas before Gotama, they argued that the teachings were constant and they focused on Gotama. The Lanka monks also compiled a chronicle of Buddhism which claimed an uninterrupted linear descent from the Buddha through the first disciples and Emperor Asoka to their lineage at Anuradhapura. Over time the Lankan practice was identified as those following the way of the *sthavira* or *thera*, Sanskrit and Pali respectively for "elders."[47] As Buddhism faded in its original homeland, these distinctive features gave the Lankan center a strong appeal to monastic communities and political leaders elsewhere.

The early Buddhist texts and objects from the Chaophraya Basin clearly show influence from this center in Sri Lanka, though probably transmitted via India. Inscriptions use Pali for Buddhist terms and repeatedly quote three scriptural extracts. The first is the *Ye dhamma* verse, found in twenty-six of the forty-two known inscriptions. On hearing this alone, the two early disciples, Sariputta and Moggallana, were converted to Buddhism and set on the path to enlightenment.

> The states that have arisen from a cause
> Their cause the Tathāgata proclaims,
> As well as their cessation.
> This is the teaching of the Great Ascetic. (tr. Peter Skilling)

The second is the *Paticcasamuppada* or theory of dependent origination. In the days immediately after enlightenment, the Buddha gave this explanation of the causes underlying human suffering. The third is the first sermon in which he presented the Four Noble Truths for overcoming this suffering.[48] These are key texts for Theravada but also for other schools of Buddhism.

Among the many variations within Buddhism in the first millennium CE was a different stream of thought and practice dubbed Mahayana or the "Great Vehicle." Its distinctive features included a belief in the realization of Buddhahood by all beings, and its development of a more varied iconography featuring *bodhisattas* in pursuit of Buddhahood, historical Buddhas other than Gotama, and ancillary gods and goddesses. In early images from Southeast Asia, the most common pose is Buddha

---

[47] Gethin, "Was Buddhagosa a Theravādin?"
[48] Revire, "Glimpses of Buddhist practices and rituals," 253–7; Skilling, "Precious deposits," 59–60.

subduing Mara, which was popular also in Lanka and became a classic image of Theravada, but there are also many images of Avalokiteshwara, the Buddha of compassion, and of Prajnaparamita, the female deity and embodiment of perfect wisdom, both of which would be classified as Mahayana in today's vocabulary. Inscriptions were made in Sanskrit as well as Pali. The visiting Chinese monk Yijing in the late seventh century noted that Hinayana and Mahayana approaches "are practiced in a mixed way" in Southeast Asia.[49]

As it later developed, Theravada Buddhism in Southeast Asia was defined not only by doctrine but also by practice, especially the role of a community of renunciant monks dependent on support from the laity. There are faint signs of such practice in this era. Early inscriptions show the importance of earning merit, in order to achieve a better rebirth, by offering charity to monks or constructing religious buildings. Yijing mentioned that monks in Dvaravati performed "the begging *dhuta*," and a terracotta fragment from U Thong appears to show three monks on almsround.[50]

The practices known today, and the divisions between schools and sects, are the result of a long development, and cannot be assumed back into the past. Although some roots of Theravada Buddhism were present in this era, so too were other tendencies.

Riverside Towns

From around the sixth century, there was a shift to living in larger settlements. In India over the previous millennium, rules and conventions for urban living had been built into custom and law. People lived longer if they were careful about their food, washed often, had good drinking water, and follow some social restrictions. Some of these rules and customs may have arrived with the gods. Perhaps the first of these towns, U Thong, was built in a bow of a river in the shape of a conch shell, measuring 1.7 by 0.8 kilometers, far larger than any earlier site. Along the riverbanks nearby there were other settlements connected by roads and waterways.[51] The largest of these early towns, Nakhon Pathom, measuring 3.7 by 2.0 kilometers, had a moat, canals running through the town, and over a hundred buildings with brick bases. At its center was the Phra Pathon Stupa, founded possibly in the late seventh century and massive for its time.[52] Other major religious

---

[49] Deeg, "Sthavira, Thera," 154; Skilling, "Buddhism and the circulation of ritual."
[50] Revire, "Glimpses of Buddhist practices and rituals," 241–52.
[51] Boisselier, *Nouvelles connaissances archéologiques*; Wheatley, *Nāgara and commandery*.
[52] Piriya, "Phra Pathon Chedi," esp. 233–4.

monuments were outside the city wall, hinting at a division between town-dwellers and forest-dwellers in the monkhood. Canals ran out into the surrounding countryside, where there was a penumbra of smaller settlements.[53] Towns also appeared at Ratchaburi and around Phetchaburi.

To the east of the Chaophraya River, conch-shaped towns measuring around 1.4 by 0.8 kilometers appeared at Mueang Phra Rot and Dong Si Mahosot, each with a penumbra of satellite settlements, similar to Nakhon Pathom.[54] Lopburi is probably the site of Lavapura mentioned in inscriptions, but its early form has been obscured by later development. The second largest town may have been Si Thep, a moated site in the Pasak River valley, which was occupied from the sixth century, expanded many times, and embellished with several large monuments, including Khao Klang Nok, 64 meters square and around 20 meters high, built with large laterite blocks in a unique design.[55] Sap Champa, another important site, lay close by. Another group is found on the lower Ping River above Nakhon Sawan.[56] Around thirty-five to forty of these town sites are known (see Map 1.2). Others may have been effaced by later development. The Chinese records of this era mention several places, but the names are difficult to match with the sites.[57] Early inscriptions from these towns are in Mon and Indian languages, suggesting Mon became a lingua franca as people congregated in towns and trading networks thickened.[58]

Dvaravati, Trade, and Rule

In the early seventh century, a traveler from Annam sailed with his parents to Duoluobodi (To-lo-po-ti) where he "renounced the world and became a monk," before traveling further to China, Sri Lanka, and India. Two other monks, Xuanzang (Hsüang-tsang) and Yijing (I-tsing), heard of the place and located it between Srikshetra (Prome, now in Burma) and Isanapura (Sambor Prei Kuk, now in Cambodia), but paid no visit. These fragmentary accounts found their way into a Tang encyclopedia. Duoluobodi sent three tribute missions to China in 638, 640, and 649. George Coedès identified Duoluobodi with a name found on

---

[53] Dupont, *L'archéologie mône de Dvāravatī*, 20–1; Dhida, "State formation in the lower Tha Chin-Mae Khong basin"; Piriya, *Roots of Thai art*, 54–5.
[54] Srisakara, "Political and cultural continuities at Dvaravati sites."
[55] Skilling, "L'énigme de Si Thep."
[56] Murphy and Pimchanok, "Fifty years of archeological research"; Winai, "Jaruek dong mae nang mueang."
[57] Wheatley, *Golden Khersonese.*
[58] Bauer, "Notes on Mon epigraphy."

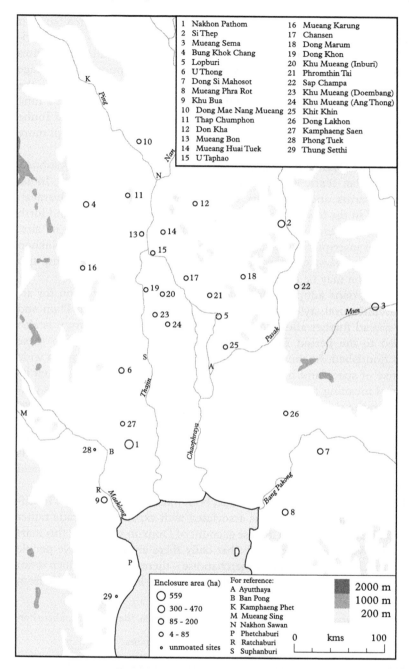

1	Nakhon Pathom	16	Mueang Karung
2	Si Thep	17	Chansen
3	Mueang Sema	18	Dong Marum
4	Bung Khok Chang	19	Dong Khon
5	Lopburi	20	Khu Mueang (Inburi)
6	U Thong	21	Phromthin Tai
7	Dong Si Mahosot	22	Sap Champa
8	Mueang Phra Rot	23	Khu Mueang (Doembang)
9	Khu Bua	24	Khu Mueang (Ang Thong)
10	Dong Mae Nang Mueang	25	Khit Khin
11	Thap Chumphon	26	Dong Lakhon
12	Don Kha	27	Kamphaeng Saen
13	Mueang Bon	28	Phong Tuek
14	Mueang Huai Tuek	29	Thung Setthi
15	U Taphao		

Enclosure area (ha)

For reference:
A Ayutthaya
B Ban Pong
K Kamphaeng Phet
M Mueang Sing
N Nakhon Sawan
P Phetchaburi
R Ratchaburi
S Suphanburi

○ 559
○ 300 - 470
○ 85 - 200
○ 4 - 85
○ unmoated sites

2000 m
1000 m
200 m

0   kms   100

Map 1.2. Town sites in the Chaophraya Plain in the first millennium (based, with permission, on an original by Matt Gallon)

medallions first discovered at Nakhon Pathom, inscribed with a Sanskrit phrase "sridvaravatisvarapunya," meaning "merit of the lord of glorious Dvaravati." Similar medallions were found in around ten other sites around the Chaophraya Plain. A fragmentary inscription on an image base found near Khorat reads "daughter of the Lord of Dvaravati ... the queen set up this image ... this of the Tathagata."[59] The Tongdian, a Tang encyclopedia compiled over 766–801 CE, describes a state called Touhe (T'ou-ho) which has sometimes been identified with Dvaravati but more likely was in the archipelago.[60]

The name Dvaravati, meaning "possessing gates," appears as Krishna's city in Indian texts, and was used as a place-name in ancient India, Arakan, Burma, and Cambodia. Coedès proposed there was a "Dvaravati kingdom" in the lower Chaophraya Plain.[61] Debate went back and forth on Dvaravati's location, with Nakhon Pathom favored due to its size. Sukhothai inscriptions 2 and 11 refer to a city that is probably Nakhon Pathom as *nakhon phra krit*, the city of Lord Krishna, suggesting this identification may be right.[62]

Art historians adopted Dvaravati as the catch-all description for art and architectural styles which developed in the Chaophraya Plain and later spread further afield to north, east, and south. The term was also applied to the period from the sixth to eleventh century when these styles flourished. As the term "Dvaravati" was thus stretched over a wide expanse of space and time, there was a strong temptation to stretch its political meaning too. Yet the sum total of sources on Dvaravati is presented in the single paragraph at the start of this section. Dvaravati was probably one of many city-states that appeared in this era and had a handful of mentions in Chinese sources over a brief span of years. The appearance of "Dvaravati" in the official city titles of the future capitals of Ayutthaya and Bangkok suggests some larger importance, but could be an invention of tradition.

This was a time of increasing trade, both internal and external. The diffusion of "Dvaravati" style was associated with expansion of trade rather than political power. The Chinese account of Dunxun states, "At this mart East and West meet together so that daily there are innumerable people there. Precious goods and rare merchandise – there is nothing which is not there."[63] Chinese records mention the use of seed-like coinage made from

[59] Skilling, "Dvaravati: Recent revelations and research"; Wade, "Beyond the southern borders," 27.
[60] Yamamoto, "East Asian historical sources for Dvāravatī studies."
[61] Coedès, *Indianized states of Southeast Asia*, 76–7.
[62] Winai, "Silajaruek wat si chum," 43, 79–80; *Pramuan jaruek samai phraya lithai*, 153–8.
[63] Wheatley, *Golden Khersonese*, 16.

a metal such as silver or lead.[64] The towns of this era were sited on trade routes by river and land. Phong Tuek lay on the way to the Three Pagodas Pass, and outposts have been found further up this route with remains of trade goods.[65] Dong Mae Nang Mueang straddled the route leading up the Chaophraya river system to the north. Beyond Si Mahosot lay a route towards the Tonle Sap and the Lower Mekong. Si Thep and Mueang Sema lay on routes from the Chaophraya Plain to the long-standing areas of settlement on the Isan Plateau. Exotic goods arrived along these routes. A Roman-style lamp, probably made in the eastern Mediterranean between the fifth and seventh century CE, was found at Phong Tuek.[66] A third-century Roman coin, images of Sogdian traders, and pottery from India and Tang China were found at U Thong. Even the inland site of Chansen has turned up a wide range of exotic goods from east and west, while Phromthin Tai near Lopburi has yielded hoards of coins as well as trading goods, suggesting a major commercial center, and Dong Mae Nang Mueang had remains of both Persian and Chinese pottery.[67]

Chiefs began to call themselves with Indic-influenced names, especially the suffix -varman meaning the protégé of a god, and Sanskrit titles meaning king or ruler (isvara). In one inscription from U Thong, the grandson of a former ruler claims to have "obtained the lion throne through regular succession."[68] Terracotta trays found at Nakhon Pathom were decorated with Indic symbols of royalty such as fly-whisks, parasols, conches, turtles, thunderbolts, and elephant goads.[69] Most of these places, however, were modest trading towns and the Indic ideas and symbols may represent more pretension than reality. Relatively few inscriptions have been found – a tiny fraction of the number found in the Khmer country from the same period. Many are in vernacular languages, especially Mon, and a large proportion were authored by commoners, suggesting there was no monopoly on this technique held by a royal elite. Coins and medallions are not stamped with the royal symbols likely to be favored by rulers, but with religious symbols (conch, Om), or images of prosperity (pots-of-plenty, cow-and-calf) likely to appeal to merchants. The most common symbol – the srivatsa or abode of the fertility goddess – seems to combine both these possibilities.[70] The biggest project of sculpture from this era – on the laterite wall of a water tank

[64] Wicks, "Ancient coinage of Mainland Southeast Asia," 209–10.
[65] Dhida, (Sri) Dvaravati, 116.
[66] Borell, "Early Byzantine lamp from Pong Tuk."
[67] Wicks, Money, markets, and trade, 165.
[68] Brown, Dvāravatī wheels of the law, 49.
[69] Boeles, "King of Śri Dvāravatī," 107–9; Higham, Early cultures, 257.
[70] Wicks, "Ancient coinage of Mainland Southeast Asia," 211–12.

at Si Mahosot – portrays animals rather than gods or kings. The cultural
material shows great local variety.[71]

Indian concepts, words, and symbols may have served to strengthen
rulers, but Buddhism may have imposed some constraints. An inscription from the Pasak basin records that a king must "have formidable
power feared by all the enemies from nearby towns," but also must "have
integrity … have wisdom" and "be benevolent." Another inscription
from Sap Champa states that the ruler is "a follower of Buddhism …
a great king and leader … who practises dharma, gives alms, and has
compassion." A seventh-century ruler of Si Thep claimed to be "powerful and the terror of his enemies" but also possessing "renowned moral
principles." In two legends about Nakhon Pathom, the ruler accidentally
kills his own father and must redeem himself by religious devotion and
patronage, including building the great stupa.[72]

There may have been a state of Dvaravati and it may have enjoyed
prominence for a short time, but this was an era of many independent
towns. Srisakara suggests there may have been several loose confederations along different river courses.[73]

The Influence of Angkor

Over this same era, a different society and culture developed to the east.
Around the Tonle Sap, farmers developed techniques for storing water,
which enabled production of a large agricultural surplus supporting a
dense population. Local chiefs gained control over land, extracted a surplus of rice and manpower, and invested these in military might and
ritual display. By the ninth century, they had built a capital at Angkor
that surpassed in splendor anywhere else in the region, before or since.[74]

Provincial lords beyond the Angkor heartland built towns and temples
which copied Angkor styles, including symmetrical plans for towns and
temples, rectangular *barai* ponds, laterite for building, and respect for
the Hindu gods. This trend flowed northwards across the Dangrek range
onto the Isan Plateau. Many small *wat* were built in the center of old
moated settlements, copying Angkor styles but also showing local indi-
viduality through animal imagery, rustic scenes, and humorous touches
in the decoration. In the eleventh century, a local family that adopted

---

[71] Phiraphon, *Mueang si mahosot*; Pattaratorn, "In search of Maitreya," esp. 98–9.
[72] Dhida, *(Sri) Dvaravati*, 77, 206; Higham, *Early cultures*, 261; Woodward, "Studies in the
art of Central Siam," 155–6; Woodward, "What there was before Siam," 25.
[73] Srisakara, "Political and cultural continuities at Dvaravati sites," 233–5.
[74] Vickery, *Society, economy and politics*; Vickery, "Reign of Sūryavarman I."

the Sanskrit name Mahidharapura built a temple at Phimai with a pre-cisely symmetrical layout and a main tower with a unique curved lotus shape. Around 1112, a sixteen-year-old descendant of this family killed his great-uncle to seize the Angkor throne and become Suryavarman II. He built Angkor Wat with the same precision and same lotus towers as Phimai, only on a colossally greater scale. The twelfth and thirteenth cen-turies saw a much wider spread of Angkor-style urban sites and religious monuments on the Isan Plateau.[75]

From the late ninth century onwards, Angkor's magnetism was also felt in the Chaophraya Plain. Angkor-style temples were built at the passes on the three main routes from the east down into the plain, and at the three major settlements along this cultural border – Si Thep, Muang Sema, and Si Mahosot. One temple at Muang Sema was converted from Buddhism to Saivism. An 868 Khmer-language inscription about Si Canasa records the erection of a Shiva-*linga*.[76] In this same era, the pat-tern of settlement shifted again. Several places founded around the sixth century declined or were abandoned. In the case of U Thong, the river shifted, cutting off easy access to the gulf. In the other cases, there may have been epidemics, or other places became more attractive. Some sites, particularly Nakhon Pathom and Si Thep, seem to have been enlarged.

Possibly there were migrations from the Khmer country. Along the Suphan-Thachin and Maeklong rivers, new places appeared with some of the distinctive features of Angkorian town-planning – squarish plans roughly aligned to the compass, central monuments, a surrounding moat or earthwork, ponds or *barai* outside, and dykes built across the slope of the land to catch the runoff for irrigation. Along the Maeklong River, the ruins are mainly laterite and the sites have yielded images of the radiat-ing Avalokiteshwara and other trace of Mahayanist Bayon style. Along the Thachin River, the ruins are mainly clay bricks and the sites have yielded images of Buddha under *naga*. Perhaps there were two groups of migrants.[77] Elsewhere Angkorian-style temples were built in existing towns, such as Nakhon Pathom, Lopburi, Ratchaburi, and Phetchaburi. These places tended to be the towns of the future, perhaps because Khmer-style water management supported a larger and healthier popu-lation. The people of U Thong may have moved 30 kilometers northeast to Suphanburi where the town's design is a fascinating hybrid. In the

[75] Srisakara, *Isan*, 236–7.

[76] Mayuri, "Si janasa rue janasapura," 108–9; Chalit, "Mueang sema khue sun klang si janasa," 129, 139–46.

[77] Podjanok et al., "Tracing post-Dvaravati culture from space"; Woodward, "Studies in the art of Central Siam," 116–24.

"Dvaravati" style, the city was sited in a bend of the river closed by a moat measuring 1.9 by 0.7 kilometers, and had a major forest temple outside the walls, but the moat is a strict rectangle rather than the usual conch shape, and a relic stupa was built at the city center in Angkorian style. Both the walls and the stupa may date to the twelfth century.[78] Phetchaburi, legendarily founded or refounded in 1157/8, was also sited in a bend of a river with a wall and moat roughly 1 kilometer square, a Bayon-style temple, and possibly a relic stupa at the center.[79] Also at the same time, Angkor-influenced settlements appeared in frontier areas around the Chaophraya Plain – especially at Mueang Sing on the Three Pagodas route to the west, and at Sukhothai and Si Satchanalai on the river systems stretching to the north.

Some historians have assumed this extension of Angkorian styles across the Chaophraya Plain represents waves of conquest and domination, and have drawn maps showing boundaries of a "Khmer Empire" pushed gradually westwards over the centuries. Over the nineteenth and twentieth centuries the term "empire" has acquired some baggage. It implies conquest, administration, and extraction of resources. But there is little evidence to support the application of this model to Angkor and the Chaophraya Plain. While there are many inscriptional records and bas-reliefs about Angkor's military expeditions to the east, there is only a single ambiguous reference to a military expedition in the west by Jayavarman VII.[80] From the Chaophraya Plain, there are none of the characteristic Angkorian inscriptions about official temple endowments, and only sparse references to Khmer-titled administrators.[81] The Angkor records deal in detail with resource transfers, yet have nothing on flows from the provinces. Kulke argues that the Angkor heartland was self-sufficient, and its rulers had no need to look far afield for resources.[82]

In the Chaophraya Plain, the adoption of Angkorian styles was patchy. Most likely, some local rulers chose to associate themselves with Angkor – by forming marriage connections with the Angkor rulers, sending symbolic tribute, building derivative monuments, even participating in the dynastic politics – while others did not.[83] Those that did make this association

---

[78] Manat, *Prawatisat mueang suphan*, esp. 77–86, 271–9; Julathat, "Bot-rian: rueang jedisathan nai suphanburi."

[79] Smithies and Dhiravat, "Instructions given to the Siamese envoys," 127; Muang Boran, *Chabap phetchaburi*.

[80] The Banteay Chhmar inscription (K.227) mentions Jayavarman VII and his son resisting an army in the west, but does not specify how far west, allowing the imagination free rein.

[81] Vickery, "Cambodia and its neighbours," 274.

[82] Kulke, "The early and the imperial kingdom," 13–14.

[83] Srisakara, *Isan*, 176–7.

presumably felt that they gained advantages – for the ruling family and for the town as a whole – by association with the most powerful and magnificent ritual center in the region. What was spreading was not Angkor's military power and bureaucratic reach, but its ritual magnetism.

At one place Angkorian influence was significantly stronger. Lopburi (Lavo, Lavapura) was sited on a slightly raised terrace which had been settled for over a millennium, and was connected by river to the gulf. It came under Angkor influence from the tenth century: a Buddha image found at the city's relic stupa has an inscription fragment that dates to 923 CE and may have been authored by Jayavarman IV of Angkor. Shortly after becoming ruler at Angkor in 1002, Suryavarman I commanded that anyone in Lavo disturbing the Buddhist monks and rishis who "offered their ardour" to him should be "seized and brought before a tribunal to hear their case." Another undated inscription entrusts three Khmer-titled officials to oversee offerings to a Vishnu image. Elsewhere there is a reference to "*sruk* Lavo," using the usual term for an Angkorian province. In 1191, a son of Jayavarman VII may have held an official position at Lopburi.[84] Over these three centuries, three large Khmer-style temples were built in the town. Prang Khaek, the earliest, may date to the tenth century. Wat Mahathat displays obvious homage to the towers at Phimai and Angkor Wat. Phra Prang Sam Yot copied the style of triple sanctuaries favored by Jayavarman VII.

Lopburi was clearly a political and cultural outpost of Angkor for two centuries or more, but the relationship was not a simple hierarchy. In Suryavarman II's procession sculpted in bas-relief in the southern gallery of Angkor Wat, Jayasinhavarman of Lavo is portrayed almost as grandly as Suyavarman himself, and his troops are distinctively dressed in elaborate helmets with animal heads. Suryavarman II patronized Buddhism at Lopburi, rather than the Saivism of his capital. A fragmentary inscription possibly shows an Angkor king honoring a local tutelary spirit.[85] The Lopburi rulers contracted marriage connections not only with Angkor but also with Pagan. Lavo sent many embassies to China, beginning in 1115. In 1155, the missions from Lohu (Lopburi) and Chenla (Angkor) arrived together. In 1225 a survey of ports sending ships to Guangzhou records Lohu as a tributary of Chenla. Between 1289 and 1299 Lohu sent five missions independently.[86]

---

[84] See Sak-Humphry, *Sdok Kak Thom inscription*, 49 (Khmer text, 39–40); Vickery, "Reign of Sūryavarman I," 240; inscription 19 and 20, Sāl sūṅ, in Coedès, *Recueil des inscriptions de Siam*, vol. 2, 23, 26–9 and Winai and Trongjai, *Moradok khwam songjam haeng nopphaburi*, 20–2, 294–303; K.285, Phimeankas, see Vickery, "Cambodia and its neighbours," 278.

[85] K.410, Winai and Trongjai, *Moradok khwam songjam haeng nopphaburi*, 296–303.

[86] Suebsang, "Sino-Siamese tributary relations," 1289–99; Winai and Trongjai, *Moradok khwam songjam haeng nopphaburi*, 25–7.

Some historians argue that Lavo was under Angkor control from the tenth to thirteenth centuries, but sent independent missions to China when Angkor was distracted by succession disputes, and finally spun free before 1289. More likely, the relationship was always somewhat flexible.

According to the eulogy by his son, Jayavarman VII built 107 hospitals (*arogyasala*) and another 121 "fire houses" (*vahnigrha*) ranged along roads from the capital, but none lie further west than Prachin at the edge of the Chaophraya Plain. Jayavarman VII also sent an image named Jayabuddhamahanatha, possibly his likeness, more likely a radiating Avalokiteshvara, to twenty-five cities, six of which were in the Chaophraya Plain: "Lavodayapura [Lopburi], Svarṇapura [Suphanburi], Sambūkapura [maybe Ban Pong], Jaya-Rājapuri [Ratchaburi], Jaya-Siṃhapuri [Mueang Sing], Jaya-Vajrapuri [Phetchaburi or Kamphaeng Phet]."[87] The presentation of these statues is sometimes read as evidence of rule, but without corroborating evidence of military or administrative power, a better characterization is cultural diplomacy.

Summary on the Growth of Towns

From the sixth to twelfth centuries, towns and small-scale polities spread across wide areas of the peninsula, the Isan Plateau, the lower Mekong basin, and the Chaophraya Plain. On the Chaophraya Plain, some forty moated towns developed, mostly alongside rivers. They exchanged more goods with one another, and with places farther afield to both east and west. Their rulers adopted Indic titles, marshaled labor for building moats, dykes, and temples, and patronized craftsmen with expertise in metalwork, stucco, and terracotta. These towns shared religious practice, art styles, and the Mon language (at least for inscriptions), but they do not seem to have been politically integrated, except perhaps in local confederations.

As the Angkor region developed into a magnificent capital, from the tenth century, its influence flowed into the Chaophraya Plain. Architecture, town planning, political vocabulary, and religious trends arrived, along with much else that cannot be seen. Possibly these transfers were the result of people migrating away from the Angkor heartland, carrying new ideas and expertise, and of local city lords drawing on Angkor's power and magnificence for their own benefit.

---

[87] Woodward, "Jayabuddhamahānātha images of Cambodia"; Maxwell, "Stele inscription of Preah Khan," 81–2, 95.

The Tai

Towards the end of the first millennium, settlement spread northward from the lower Chaophraya Plain. A Khmer-influenced town appeared at Sukhothai, perhaps in the tenth or eleventh century. Several small sites have been found in the upper reaches of all the main Chaophraya tributaries. In the legend of Chamadevi, a Mon princess from Lavo-Lopburi goes to found a new city of Hariphunchai (Lamphun). She travels north with 500 monks, 500 scholars, and a caravan of sculptors, painters, jewelers, goldsmiths, and other craftsmen. She provides areas in the new city for those born from the footprints of elephants, rhinos, and wild buffaloes – interpreted to mean the local hunter-gatherer population. This is a story of bringing civilization to a remote area. One chronicle dates this migration to 663 CE, but archeological evidence favors the eleventh or twelfth century.[88]

In this same era, people speaking languages from the Tai family began moving into the upper reaches of the Chaophraya river system from the north. The first records are in old poems, stories, and chronicles.[89]

The Tai have roots in southern China. When the Han Chinese moved southwards across the Yangzi in the last few centuries BCE, they found the region populated by many different peoples they described as "barbarians," collectively termed as the Yue or Bai-yi. Chinese observers recorded how these people cultivated rice, built stilt houses without nails, tattooed their bodies, decorated their teeth, cultivated silkworms, used bronze drums in rituals, adopted snakes, frogs, and birds as totems, divined with chicken bones, liked antiphonal singing, and put women to work. They also spoke many tonal languages, likened to birdsong: "all twitter like birds and call like animals and their languages are not the same; they are as different from each other as are monkeys, snakes, fish, and tortoises."[90] Several of these languages belonged to a grouping now known as Tai-Kadai or Kra-Dai. Originally found in central southern China, the speakers were pushed gradually south and then west, and fragmented into several groups living along the southern coast by the start of the Common Era.[91]

Over the next millennium, as the Han Chinese gradually occupied the south, most of the Yue or Bai-yi were sinicized, creating the hybrid cultures now found in southern China and their languages which retain traces of tonality.[92] But not all were compliant. Around 220 BCE, "Yüeh

[88] Srisakara, *Mueang boran nai anajak sukhothai*; Swearer and Sommai, *Legend of Queen Cāma*, 55–62.
[89] Sarassawadee, *History of Lan Na*, 17.
[90] Barlow, *Zhuang*, ch. 4, from the *Man Shu*.
[91] Chamberlain, "Kra-Dai."
[92] Holm, "Layer of Old Chinese readings," 29–30.

people fled into the depths of the mountains and forests, and it was not possible to fight them."[93] People resisting integration moved into the high valleys among the mountains in the interior of the southwest. The Chinese sent garrisons to impose control, but faced constant resistance. The ancestor of the Tai languages probably took shape among the remnants of many Yue peoples thrown together in these hills.

In the early seventh century, the Tang court resolved to pacify the area by force. In 722, 400,000 rose in revolt behind a leader who declared himself king of the Nan Yue. Some 60,000 were beheaded after his defeat. In 756, another revolt attracted 200,000 followers and lasted four years. In the 860s, many local people sided with attackers from Nanchao, and in the aftermath some 30,000 of them were beheaded. In the 1040s, a powerful matriarch-shamaness, her chiefly husband, and their son, Nong Zhi-gao (Nung Tri Cao), raised a revolt, took Nanning, besieged Guangzhou for fifty-seven days, and slew the commanders of five Chinese armies sent against them before they were defeated, and many of their leaders killed.[94] Over these three bloody centuries, some people began to migrate westward. Linguistic evidence suggests these movements began between the eighth and tenth centuries.[95]

There are only fragmentary records of this movement, which was not a mass migration at a single time, but many small groups scattered across many decades. The Vietnamese recorded groups of two to three thousand "Mang savages" passing by.[96] In the chronicle of the Tai-Ahom, the pioneers arrive in Assam with 9,000 people, eight nobles, two elephants, and 300 horses.[97] Some legendary accounts talk of a single pioneer, a couple, a pair of brothers, or a handful of families. Map 1.3, which overlays the linguists' family tree on the geography, shows the general pattern not the specific routes, which would have snaked along the rivers and over the lower passes. The early migrants may have moved north into upper Guangxi and Guizhou. A second stream crossed the Vietnamese cordillera into the Mekong valley. The third and major stream started along old trade routes up the Black and Red rivers, then branched westward through the hills.

[93] Taylor, *Birth of Vietnam*, 18, quoting the *Huai nan tzu*; Holm, "Layer of Old Chinese readings," 33–4.

[94] Taylor, *Birth of Vietnam*, 245–7; Evans, "Tai original diaspora"; Barlow, *Zhuang*; Anderson, *Rebel den of Nung Tri Cao*.

[95] The southwestern Tai languages had absorbed many words from Late Middle Chinese, dated to the seventh century; see Pittayawat, "Layers of Chinese loanwords," 63–4; Chamberlain, "Kra-Dai," 69–71.

[96] Gait, *History of Assam*, 73; Kelley, "Tai words and the place of the Tai in the Vietnamese past," 143; Baker, "From Yue to Tai," 9–10.

[97] Gait, *History of Assam*, 73.

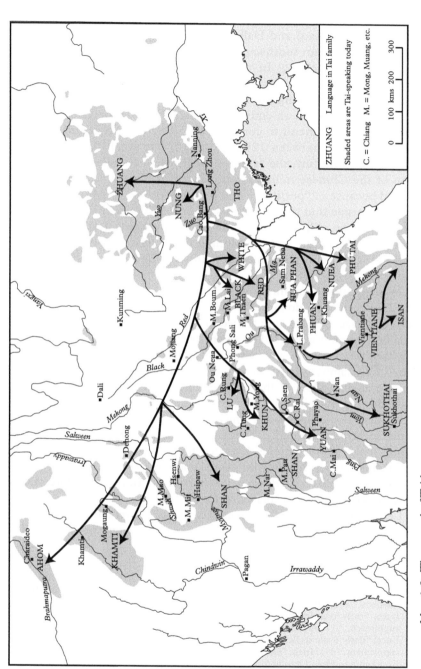

Map 1.3. The spread of Tai languages

In the thirteenth century, raids by the Chinese frontier states of Nanzhao (Nanchao) and Dali and by the Mongols may have pushed some of this stream southward along the rivers, especially the Shweli, Salween, and Mekong. In the 1250s, the Mongol leader Khubilai Khan attacked south towards Pagan. In the 1290s, Mongol forces attacked Ch'eli (Chiang Rung) and Chiang Mai, subdued "over twenty kingdoms," and sent an embassy to Angkor.[98] But the area remained rebellious and difficult to control. The Mongol court ordered armies south six times between 1297 and 1312, but the 1301–2 campaign resulted in a mutiny, the "ruin of the army," and subsequent execution of the Chinese military commander, while the 1312 effort collapsed because of "pestilence and other hardships."[99] Mongol officials began to argue that the mountains, forests, fevers, and supply difficulties meant the military losses outweighed any gains. Local chiefs sent tribute of elephants, and the Mongol threat passed, but this pressure had probably deflected some Tai southward into Mainland Southeast Asia.[100]

In many sites along this 1,000-kilometer arc from Guangxi to Assam, the Tai became the dominant community and their language the dominant language. Condominas argued that the Tai diffusion was "the work of small groups of warriors led by an aristocracy which succeeded in imposing itself on numerous and varied groups of people covering vast territories."[101] Certainly, the struggle with the Han Chinese had created a warrior culture in the valleys of the Guangxi interior. Their armies were based on a three-man unit which farmed together and also fought as a team: "One man carried the shield which covered the body and the other two threw spears from behind ... They came on like a southern fire." The Nong group, which rebelled in the eleventh century, bred horses for cavalry, tattooed their bodies, fought with swords and crossbows, built hill-top forts for defense, and recruited women as warriors.[102] But military force alone may not be a sufficient explanation for the spread of Tai languages.

Legendary accounts of these migrations share several themes, particularly the search for good rice land. The *Khwam to muang* of the Black Tai relates:

---

[98] Luce, "Early Syam in Burma's history: a supplement," 72; Flood, "Sukhothai-Mongol relations," 221; Zhou, *Record of Cambodia*.

[99] Luce, "Early Syam in Burma's history," 165–6, and "Early Syam in Burma's history: a supplement," 77–80; Chen, *Frontier land systems*, 9.

[100] Luce, "Early Syam in Burma's history," 164–71 and "Early Syam in Burma's history: a supplement," 79; Hsieh, "On the dynamics of Tai/Dai-Lue ethnicity," 308–9.

[101] Condominas, *From Lawa to Mon*, 73.

[102] Barlow, "Zhuang minority peoples," 253, 257–8; Schafer, *Vermilion bird*, 50, 56.

This last child had no ricefield...
He set forth to establish a territory of his own ...
Muang Theng was round like a winnowing basket,
A valley gently curved as a buffalo horn.
It was a good place, wide, with ricefields on either side,
A desirable place where thousands could live.
The Ancestors founded Muang Theng.[103]

Languages often become dominant in an area because their speakers have some economic asset. The Tai did not bring rice, which had long been present in these hills, but they may have brought techniques for a higher and more secure yield, developed during their sojourn in the hills of southwest China. The Chinese observed that the people in these hills grew rice watered by the run-off from karst outcrops, using dikes, retention dams, bamboo pipes, stone-lined ditches, and lifting devices.[104] Across the hills, the sites chosen by Tai settlements have a distinctive topography: a large basin, often at a confluence where the rivers had created a broad alluvial plain, with streams flowing from the surrounding hills that can be tapped for irrigation.

These sites were not empty and the Tai had to confront earlier populations. In some legends there is conflict. The Black Tai find an excellent valley by the Red River but the resident Laha are fierce and initially unwelcoming. When the Black Tai leader asks to marry the chief's daughter, the chief brings fifty bodyguards to the wedding feast, displaying a conspicuous lack of trust, but these guards are persuaded to stack their weapons and proceed to get drunk. The Tai kill the Laha chief, his daughter is rendered speechless by this treachery, and the other Laha run away in fright.[105] At the end of such tales, the Tai take possession of the valley, and their predecessors retreat to the hills.

In some places the Tai may have triumphed by bringing diseases for which the isolated local communities had no defensive immunity. At Hariphunchai, there is a devastating epidemic:

Those who lived in houses with a cholera victim contracted the disease in such increasing numbers that none of them survived ... the remaining population of Haripuñjaya, in order to save their own lives, fled to a city named Sudhamma and settled there.[106]

---

[103] Chamberlain, "Black Tai chronicle," 45, 49. Muang Theng is modern Dien Bien Phu.
[104] Barlow, *Zhuang*, ch. 2.1.
[105] Phatthiya, *Prawattisat sipsong chuthai*, 147–52; Chamberlain, "Black Tai chronicle," 67–8.
[106] Swearer and Sommai, *Legend of Queen Cāma*, 105–6.

In the foundation story of Chiang Saen, a flood carries away the total population except one old woman, the sole person not to eat a huge albino eel on the previous day – a story which may combine both flood and epidemic.[107]

Other tales tell of fraternity and compromise. In the *Suwanna khamdaeng* story, the Tai pioneer who is led to the new city by a golden deer announces, "It is necessary to obey the people who were born and live at that place." He raises the Lawa chief to a high official rank and marries two of his daughters. The chief then teaches the Tai people how to live without theft, lying, adultery, drunkenness, or drugs. Both Lawa and Tai are happy. The rains are good. One year of cultivation yields seven harvests. People multiply and new settlements proliferate.[108] At the end of some such stories, the local people begin to imitate the "language and customs" of the Tai, and are eventually absorbed.[109]

From the Mekong River, one of the main arteries of the Tai migrations, the headwaters of the Chaophraya tributaries are only a short distance to the south, separated by low ridges (see Map 2.2). Possibly the Tai made this crossing from the late twelfth century. In the *Sinhanavati* legend, the son of a Tai chief comes from the north, displaces some Lawa, and founds a town called Yonok, probably Chiang Saen. His descendants, harried by people who might be Mongols, are forced to flee south, first down the Kok River, where they found Fang, then across a low watershed into the Ping valley, where they found Chiang Rai in 1263. Towards the end of the century, they move further south to the Chiang Mai area, and the losing son in a succession dispute flees further south to found Kamphaeng Phet. Another stream branches south from the Mekong down the Ing River, founds Phayao, and then moves on to Chaliang (Si Satchanalai). In the Nan chronicle, the founders begin from the Mekong, settle first near the headwaters of the Nan River, and gradually shift south to found Nan in 1368.[110]

Warriors and Settlements

By the end of the thirteenth century, there were Tai settlements along the Middle Mekong and on the upper reaches of the Chaophraya river system down to the points where the rivers emerged from the hills. At

---

[107] Notton, *Annales du Siam*, vol. 1, Sinhanavati.
[108] Notton, *Annales du Siam*, vol. 1, 7–11.
[109] Wade, "*Bai-yi zhuan*," 7.
[110] Notton, *Annales du Siam*, vol. 1, Sinhanavati; Penth, "On the history of Chiang Rai"; Wyatt, *Nan chronicle*, 37–53.

these points, such as Sukhothai, Si Satchanalai, and Kamphaeng Phet, there were still hills that could be home to a guardian spirit as well as retaining water to irrigate the rice fields. Looking south, however, the landscape was irredeemably flat and hence alien. Only down the Ping River, where there are several hilly outcrops, did the settlements drift further south, to its juncture with the Nan River (modern Nakhon Sawan).

The legends and early inscriptions describe a culture dominated by warriors. The Chiang Mai chronicle describes one successful warrior thus:

Some [domains] he conquered and some he did not, taking one domain in some years and nine in others; sometimes taking two or three years for one; sometimes taking one without a battle. Those he took, he ruled, killing the rulers he conquered. When he killed the rulers, he would have one of his officers govern there, and sometimes he would maintain [the previous ruler] in charge.[111]

Mangrai, the founder of Chiang Mai and perhaps the greatest chief of the era, had his thirteen-year-old son assassinated by a poisoned arrow for threatening revolt.[112] Fa Ngum, the founder of Lanxang (Lanchang), may have arranged the death of his own father to clear his way to the throne.[113] Ramaraja (Ramkhamhaeng) of Sukhothai described how in his youth he often "raided a town or village and captured elephants, men and women, silver or gold," and later as a ruler, he raided over a wide area and helped other warriors to establish their own *mueang*.[114] Another Sukhothai noble described how, in his youth, he "knew the qualities of elephants, he knew the qualities of horses ... he knew the qualities of lions." Between the ages of seventeen and twenty-six he fought three great duels with other nobles. In the last of these, he won even though his mount was female and his opponent was "riding a huge male war elephant, which was in rut... dripping oil [so abundantly] that it soaked his feet." The clash of the two beasts, the stabbing of the great tusker, and the final pursuit are described in graphic and gory detail.[115] These chiefs spent much of their reigns in the saddle, living in "improvised bamboo palaces and field camps."[116] They rewarded their valiant generals with command of outlying settlements, and showered them with gifts of gold, titles, regalia, and women. In laws ascribed to Mangrai, ordinary soldiers

---

[111] Wyatt, "Relics, oaths, and politics," 46, quoting *Tamnan mangrai chiang mai chiang tung.*
[112] Wyatt and Aroonrut, *Chiang Mai chronicle*, 20–1.
[113] Stuart-Fox, *Lao kingdom of Lān Xāng*, 57.
[114] Chulalongkorn University, *Inscription of King Ramkamhaeng*; Griswold and Prasert, "Inscription of King Rāma Gaṃhèn," 203–8.
[115] Inscription 2, Griswold and Prasert, "King Lōdaiya of Sukhodaya," 115, 117; Winai, "Silajaruek wat si chum," 70–4.
[116] Tambiah, *World conqueror*, 89.

who take an enemy head are rewarded with promotion, land, money, regalia, and women, while failed warriors are liable to be killed.[117]

The warriors were at the peak of a steep social pyramid. In the Mangrai laws, people were organized under officials with decimal titles, a system probably inherited from the Han Chinese or the Mongols.[118] The nobility was divided into at least three groups: the ruler's own family; other nobles who participated in the ruler's coronation; and the sub-rulers of outlying settlements and their family members.[119] Ordinary people are described with many terms (*phrai fa, phrai tai, phrai fa na sai, phrai fa na pok*) which suggest a complex system of labor control, though the meanings are elusive. At Sukhothai, an officer with the title of *nai sayotha* was probably in charge of marshaling manpower, and people were bought and sold in the market alongside various animals.[120]

By describing the virtues of good rulers, the inscriptions and law codes hint at the vices of bad ones. Lithai of Sukhothai (see below) is lauded because he refrained from killing people for minor crimes, subjecting weak people to heavy corvée, appropriating the property of nobles and commoners at death, seizing women at will, and interfering with people who trade. Mangrai's laws describe "Mara [demon] lords," epitomes of bad rulership, who "subject their citizens to extortion, flog them and tie them up with fetters or rope, bully or oppress them, seize their goods, cohabit with their daughters and nieces, or force their wives to sleep with them." Ramaraja of Sukhothai proclaims that he does not "connive with thieves or favor concealers of stolen goods," covet the wealth of others, or kill or beat enemy captives.[121] These homilies would lack their moral force if the descriptions of misrule were unrealistic.

The Tai were not only pushed south by the Chinese, but also pulled south by commerce. All the main Tai towns were on rivers which served as routes between southwestern China and the sea. From Sukhothai, a land-based route also led down to the port of Martaban. When Mangrai shifted his capital to Chiang Mai, he began building the market "at the same time" as the palace.[122] His decision to capture Hariphunchai (Lamphun) was motivated by trade:

---

[117] Griswold and Prasert, "Judgments of King Măn Răy," 148.
[118] Griswold and Prasert, "Judgments of King Măn Răy," 147–8.
[119] Vickery, "Piltdown 3," 167–8.
[120] Nidhi, "Sangkhom lae watthanatham samai sukhothai," 99–100; Inscription 2, Griswold and Prasert, "King Lödaiya of Sukhodaya," 120.
[121] Inscription 4, Griswold and Prasert, "Epigraphy of Mahādharmarāja of Sukhodaya, part 1," 221–3; Trongjai, *Pramuan jaruek phraya lithai*, 195–6; Griswold and Prasert, "Judgments of King Măn Răy," 154; Chulalongkorn University, *Inscription of King Ramkhamhaeng the Great*; Griswold and Prasert, "Inscription of King Rāma Gaṃhèn," 207–10.
[122] Wyatt and Aroonrut, *Chiang Mai chronicle*, 45.

Commerce was thriving. At that time, many parties of traders from Hariphunjai came to conduct commerce in Fang. King Mangrai therefore summoned the traders and asked them, "This Hariphunjai where you live: How prosperous is it?" A trader replied, "The Hariphunjai where I live is ... replete with all kinds of goods things. Traders of all countries frequent it both by land and by water to trade ..." King Mangrai upon hearing that Hariphunjai was wealthy was consumed with a desire to obtain it.[123]

Sukhothai Inscription I vaunts the attractions of the city by stating: "whoever wants to trade in elephants does so; whoever wants to trade in horses does so; whoever wants to trade in silver and gold does so."[124] Another Sukhothai inscription from around 1360 recounts that "The people go by boat to trade or ride their horses to sell" under the protection of the ruler.[125] The story of Makadu hints at the close relationship of traders and rulers. Makadu comes from Martaban to trade at Sukhothai, where he rises to be governor of the palace. While the king is away at war, Makadu seduces the king's daughter, then persuades her to elope to escape retribution. Makadu returns to Martaban and grows so wealthy that the town's ruler plots to kill him, but Makadu acts first, killing the ruler and taking over the town. He then formally submits to the authority of Sukhothai. Rather than being angered at the elopement, the Sukhothai king welcomes the connection with such a wealthy and dutiful colleague. He sends a bunch of regalia and a golden inscription conferring on Makadu the title of *chao fa ruea* (prince of ships).[126] The story suggests great intimacy between trade and rule.

The legends and chronicles portray the warrior chiefs making alliances for mutual benefit, particularly at times of pressure from the Chinese or Mongols to the north. In the Chiang Mai chronicle, Ramaraja of Sukhothai and Ngam Mueang of Phayao decide they are fictive brothers.[127] In 1393, Nan and Sukhothai agreed to help one another in case of "trouble" or attack, and to return people, animals, and fleeing criminals who crossed their mutual border. This agreement was written on stone, and subject to a moral community of supernatural forces including the ancestral spirits of both ruling lines, of all their deceased rulers, of the major rivers, caves, and mountains in the region, of other noble lines, and a list of Indic deities.[128] The negotiation of friendship between

---

[123] Wyatt and Aroonrut, *Chiang Mai chronicle*, 18–19.
[124] Chulalongkorn University, *Inscription of King Ramkhamhaeng the Great*.
[125] Inscription 3, Griswold and Prasert, "Epigraphy of Mahādharmarāja of Sukhodaya, part 1," 109; Trongjai, *Pramuan jaruek phraya lithai*, 181.
[126] Griswold and Prasert, "King Lödaiya of Sukhodaya," 41–7; Guillon, *Mons*, 156–7.
[127] Wyatt and Aroonrut, *Chiang Mai chronicle*, 25–7.
[128] Griswold and Prasert, "Pact between Sukhodaya and Nān."

Phayao and Sukhothai is told by the Chiang Mai chronicle with a little more spice. Ngam Mueang of Phayao slights one of his beautiful wives by criticizing her cooking, and then leaves town. The ruler of Sukhothai passes by and, taking his opportunity, "seduced her many times." When Ngam Mueang finds out, he launches into a pursuit told with as many magical transformations as a Chinese movie, and finally locks up his rival in a cage. Soon after, he relents and calls on Mangrai to arbitrate. The Sukhothai ruler agrees to apologize and pay an indemnity, following which the three rulers drink their mingled blood to seal an oath of life-long friendship.[129]

Through such alliances, three loose confederations of towns formed in the interior between the end of the thirteenth century and the mid-fourteenth. Lanna emerged on the upper reaches of the Chaophraya tributaries, put together by Mangrai with a capital at Chiang Mai, legendarily founded in 1296. Lanxang was formed around the middle Mekong in the mid-fourteenth century. The third, at the fringe of the hills, acquired no name but was seen from Ayutthaya as the *mueang nuea* or Northern Cities. With the lingering warrior ethic, and a splintered geography of river valleys divided by hill ridges, these confederations were always loose and fractious, occasionally united by a strong leader through conquest, alliance, and marriage ties, but soon after torn apart by feuds.

Sukhothai

At the end of the thirteenth century, Sukhothai emerged as the chief place in the Northern Cities. Its population seems to have come from both south and north. In the plain around the town are some thirty moated sites which resemble those found in the Chaophraya Plain and Isan Plateau over the previous five centuries, so they may be part of a drift northward captured in the Chamadevi story. To the west of the town, there are earthworks to direct water flowing down from the hills in the characteristic style of Tai settlements.[130] A Khmer-style town appeared, probably around 1200. Later in the thirteenth century, a much larger walled and moated town measuring 1.9 by 1.4 kilometers was built immediately to the south, suggesting an influx of people. The new town had the classic Angkor-influenced design with a square shape, a relic stupa near the center, and a *barai* outside the walls. In the earliest Sukhothai inscription, dated to 1292, the titles used are by origin Khmer

---

[129] Wyatt and Aroonrut, *Chiang Mai chronicle*, 23–5.
[130] Srisakara, *Mueang boran nai anajak sukhothai.*

(*kamraten an, somdet*), Mon (*phra, phraya*), general Indic (*rajakumar*), Chinese (*khun*), Tai (*chao, thao*), and various combinations of these.[131] Sukhothai was a cosmopolitan settlement.

According to a later inscription, a warrior chief named Si Nao Nam Thum, who had raided all around the upper Chaophraya Basin in the early thirteenth century, gained control of Sukhothai by an elephant duel with a Mon. He ruled both Sukhothai and nearby Si Satchanalai, and built a great stupa, but then seems to have lost the two towns. His son Pha Mueang, who ruled a place called Mueang Rat, had "a thousand elephants, his country was girt about by areca palms, and countless cities paid him homage."[132] From the Khmer ruler at Angkor, he received a title (*kamraten an*), a regalia sword, and a princess in marriage. Another local chief called Bang Klang Hao rounded up some troops and captured both Sukhothai and Si Satchanalai from a "valiant" person holding a Khmer-style title (*khom sabatkhlon lamphong*). Bang Klang Hao formally offered the towns to Pha Mueang who declined, and instead invested Bang Klang Hao as the new ruler, and transferred to him his Khmer-bestowed title of Si Indra(patindra)dit.

In the old reading of this story, the "valiant" person is transformed into the "commander of the Khmer garrison," suggesting a prior military occupation, and this event represents "the liberation of Sukhodaya from Khmer suzerainty and the establishment of the independent kingdom under a *Tai* dynasty."[133] The ethnic framing and concept of "liberation" have been imported from another era. In the modern reading, the inscription tells of victory by one local lord associated with Angkor over another warrior with a Khmer title. The story of the foundation of Lanxang (Luang Prabang) is similar: a local chief, Fa Ngum, travels to Angkor, returns with a Khmer wife, and proceeds to subdue other local chiefs. In this era, local chiefs drew legitimacy from association with distant but resplendent Angkor.

By raiding and marriage alliance, Bang Klang Hao's son Ramaraja dominated a territory which his grandson Lithai described as "vast, extending in every direction."[134] As elsewhere in this era, such warrior

---

[131] Vickery, "Piltdown 3," 167.

[132] Mueang Rat may have been Thung Yang. Phiset, *Phra maha thammaracha*, 11, 16–17; Winai, "Silajaruek wat si chum," 41; Inscription 2, Griswold and Prasert, "King Lödaiya of Sukhodaya," 109.

[133] Inscription 2, Griswold and Prasert, "King Lödaiya of Sukhodaya," 85, 110 fn. 37.

[134] The fourth face of Sukhothai Inscription 1 contains a long list of dependents, but the text on this face is generally believed to be a late addition. Ramaraja's expeditions probably extended over a similar area as those of his grandson, Lithai, described later in this paragraph.

dominance was ephemeral. Under his successor in the early four-teenth century "the country was torn ... into many fragments and pieces" as nine or ten local chiefs broke away.[135] Lithai had to attack Sukhothai and break down its gates to regain control. Through the 1350s, Lithai mounted a series of expeditions to demand submission from surrounding rulers – along the Ping, Yom, and Pasak rivers; up through Phrae to Nan – and concluded marriage alliances with the most important. In inscriptions made around 1361, Lithai alluded to "poison in the fish, potions in the rice" and repeatedly cited his compassion towards "people who cheated or betrayed him, or people who tried to poison him," suggesting another time of turmoil and fragmentation.[136]

Lithai took the title Phra Maha Thammaracha which was adopted as the royal title by his descendants. The clan remained *primus inter pares* in the Northern Cities but no more than that. Branches of the family broke away to rule at other cities, and at times there was more than one town ruler holding the Phra Maha Thammaracha title. Other clans also developed their own ruling title, particularly at Phichai and Kamphaeng Phet.[137] This was an era of city-states, not larger kingdoms.

In the mid-fourteenth century, the political center of the Northern Cities shifted to Phitsanulok, perhaps for strategic or commercial rea-sons, perhaps because the agricultural hinterland of Sukhothai could not support a large population.[138] Sukhothai's prominence as a political cen-ter had lasted less than a century. In religion and art, however, the city's importance was greater and more long-lasting.

Lankan Buddhism

In the twelfth century, the king of Sri Lanka unified the monkhood under the Mahavihara temple in Anuradhapura. Over the twelfth and thirteenth centuries, a network was created linking this center to Buddhist com-munities in Arakan, Thaton, Pagan, Martaban, Nakhon Si Thammarat, Sukhothai, Chiang Mai, and Ayutthaya. Aided by the increase in marine

[135] Inscription 3, Griswold and Prasert, "Epigraphy of Mahādharmarāja of Sukhodaya, part 1," 106–7; Trongjai, *Pramuan jaruek phraya lithai*, 180.
[136] Inscription 5, Griswold and Prasert, "Epigraphy of Mahādharmarāja of Sukhodaya, part 1," 155, fn. 21, translation modified in line with Trongjai, *Pramuan jaruek samai phraya lithai*, 195–6.
[137] Phiset, *Phra maha thammaracha*, 79–86.
[138] Srisakara, *Mueang boran nai anajak sukhothai*; Piriya, *Sinlapa sukhothai lae ayutthaya*, 98.

trade, monks traveled between these centers, exchanging texts, rituals and portable artifacts like cloth paintings and molded tablets. These exchanges helped to develop distinctive practices in which the renunciant monk had a leading role. These practices have often been shorthanded as "Lankan" but were the product of exchange between several centers.

In the early fourteenth century, the Martaban ruler sent twelve monks to Sri Lanka to be reordained at the monastery of Udumbaragiri near Polonnaruwa. On their return in 1331, they established a new order which became known as the Aranyavasin or "forest monks," practicing a more rigorous form of monastic discipline, including a refusal to reside at monasteries in towns, long spells wandering in the forests, and ascetic practices for self-purification. The new order rapidly attracted followers.

Probably in the late thirteenth century, a monk came to Sukhothai from Nakhon Si Thammarat, and Ramaraja built a forest monastery for him outside the city.[139] In the early fourteenth century, a Sukhothai monk, Sujato, went to study in Sri Lanka for five years and Pagan for another five before establishing himself at Ayutthaya. In the 1330s, two monks from Sukhothai went to study for five years at Martaban where they were reordained according to Lankan practice. They returned to Sukhothai for another five years, then traveled again to Martaban to gain their Thera (elder) qualification and to bring eight other monks for reordination. The original two then settled at forest monasteries at Sukhothai and Si Satchanalai.[140]

These monks brought from Lanka new "teachings and disciplinary rules." They claimed the authenticity of being ordained in the Lankan lineage which stretched back to the Buddha and his disciples, and of following correct practice on wording of ordination, wearing of the robe, chanting, and so on. This authenticity was a source of great authority.[141] Their arrival seems to have combined with a social upheaval. When the Sukhothai monks traveled north to Lanna, the *wat* chronicles describe a frenzy, with people flocking to be ordained "each day ten men, twenty men, thirty men, forty men, fifty men, a hundred men, numerous in number until living quarters could not be found." The monks founding new *wat* "each year ten monasteries, twenty monasteries, thirty, forty, fifty monasteries ... totaling five hundred, all exceedingly prosperous."[142] In the 1430s, another Chiang Mai monk, Nanagambhira, returned from

---

[139] Griswold and Prasert, "Inscription of King Rāma Gaṃhèn," 212.
[140] Sommai and Swearer, "Translation of *Tamnān mūlasāsanā*," 80–1; Ratanapanna Thera, *Sheaf of garlands*, 117.
[141] Sommai and Swearer, "Translation of *Tamnān mūlasāsanā*," 77, 80, 87–92; Prapod, *Ascendency of Theravāda Buddhism*, 176.
[142] Mangrai, *Pādaeng chronicle*, 111–12.

Sri Lanka to Sukhothai where he reordained 7,520 monks, after which "The king had his ministers and the citizens of Sukhōdaya, numbering 1,000, ordained into the new order."[143] Many new *wat* were built in Sukhothai at this time, both inside the walls and in the surrounding area. New designs and building techniques were employed to build preaching halls that were larger and could accommodate more people, suggesting increased numbers of devotees.[144]

The popularity of these monks was part of a transition in these warrior-dominated societies, visible in stories of dramatic religious awakening. Pha Mueang, the warrior who relinquished his rule of Sukhothai to Bang Klang Hao, retired to a life of religious zeal: "he caused cetiyas to be built, he earned the gratitude of many kings, he was the teacher and protector of a whole throng of monarchs ... he bestowed alms ... on venerable persons in enormous quantity."[145] Ramaraja's Inscription I, of 1292, tells a similar story, first recording his youthful exploits as a warrior, then boasting of the Buddhist features of his Sukhothai: "there are viharas, there are golden statues of the Buddha, and eighteen-cubit statues; there are big statues of the Buddha and medium-sized ones, there are big viharas and medium-sized ones; there are senior monks, nissayamuttakas, theras and mahatheras."[146]

The epitome of this transition from warlordism to devotion is the story of Pha Mueang's grandson who had spent his youth in elephant duels. He was disturbed so much by the death of a young son that he "saw that this world of rebirths is impermanent ... He destroyed all his weapons ... He longed to live in the forest ... renounce his [princely] caste and leave his home." He became a monk under the name Si Sattha (in full, Si Sattharajachulamani), and wandered around the neighboring region, performing good works, and establishing or restoring religious sites. "At one place he went through the market buying up all the living creatures and setting them free ... such as human beings, goats, pig, dogs, ducks, chickens, geese, birds, fish, deer."[147] He traveled via Martaban to India, where he was again active in restoring religious sites, and then to Sri Lanka. After ten years, in the mid-1340s, he returned to Sukhothai with two relics and a group of Sinhalese craftsmen, and was probably instrumental in the construction of Wat Si Chum, the largest monument apart

---

[143] Sommai and Swearer, "Translation of *Tamnan mūlasāsanā*," 92–3.
[144] Gosling, *Chronology of religious architecture*, 93–5, 126–9. Some of Gosling's work dating of styles has been challenged, but her correlation of epigraphic data and groundplans is more secure.
[145] Inscription 2, Griswold and Prasert, "King Lödaiya of Sukhodaya," 112.
[146] Chulalongkorn University, *Inscription of King Ramkamhaeng the Great*, side 2 (translation slightly modified).
[147] Inscription 2, Griswold and Prasert, "King Lödaiya of Sukhodaya," 117–18, 120; Winai, "Silajaruek wat si chum," 74, 78.

from the central relic stupa. The *jataka* illustrations enshrined within the *wat*'s walls show traces of Lankan style.[148] The inscription found at the *wat* portrays Si Sattha as a model of monastic devotion:

He likes to observe the precepts and meditate in the depths of woods and forests, absorbed in thought, forgetting to eat ... His daily routine is like [that of] Sinhala in every way. He likes to wander about the country in search of wisdom ... He likes to practice asceticism. He is not idle by day or by night, because he earnestly desires to accumulate the requisites of Buddhahood.[149]

The inscription stresses Si Sattha's role as the initiator and executor of this immense construction project, while the reigning king (Ramaraja's son, Lithai's father) receives only a perfunctory mention. Si Sattha's Lankan artisans also worked on expansion of Wat Mahathat, the city's central, grandest, and most distinctive monument. The iconography emphasized the life of the Buddha and the stature of the *sangha* (monkhood). The surrounding towers were probably decorated with a series of bas-reliefs depicting the biography of the historical Buddha, while the base of the main stupa was ringed with a frieze of walking monks, which became a popular motif in Sukhothai architecture.

In the early 1340s, the king's son and heir, Lithai, went to reside in Si Satchanalai, where he devoted himself to religious study and patronage. He is accredited with composing the *Traiphum phra ruang*, a massive Buddhist cosmology, with the help of two teachers and seven monks, one of whom had traveled to Sri Lanka.[150] He repaired Si Satchanalai's Wat Mahathat, and built several other new temples, with inscriptions recording the people's joy at these acts of devotion.

This religious enthusiasm had political implications which surface in stories about relics. Believed to be ashes and fragments retrieved after the Buddha's cremation, relics had been brought to the region over several centuries. Their arrival and enshrinement were one of the several ways in which a locality was brought into the sacred geography of a Buddhist universe. Some relics were brought from Sri Lanka. Others traveled to the region by their own power and were discovered by monks with the help of revelation and insight. Relics proved their authenticity by performing magic acts, especially whizzing about in the air and emitting colorful rays. The ability to find such hidden relics, and to provoke these authenticating performances, implied a high degree of religious merit.

Stories about relics hint at the tension between rulers and religion. According to two *wat* chronicles, Si Sattha discovered a relic while

---

[148] Pattaratorn, "Illustrating the lives of the bodhisatta," 28–39.
[149] Inscription 2, Griswold and Prasert, "King Lödaiya of Sukhodaya," 113–14; Winai, "Silajaruek wat si chum," 66–7.
[150] Reynolds and Reynolds, *Three worlds*, 46.

traveling from Sukhothai to Si Satchanalai. At Lithai's invitation, Si
Sattha brought the relic to Si Satchanalai and kept it in Wat Mahathat.
He and Lithai together made offerings to the relic, which shot up into
the air "like a dancing hamsa bird" and emitted six-colored rays. "All the
people saw this stupendous miracle, which quickly made them rejoice
even more than before." The king sent for the relic to be brought to
Sukhothai. The chronicle relates in dramatic detail that the king honored and beseeched the relic but "it did not perform a single miracle ...
because that city was not the place where the Lord Buddha's relic would
remain."[151] Such stories, repeated elsewhere, emphasize that religious
power was contained within the *sangha* and not available to the king.

From Lanna, the *wat* chronicles describe a long struggle between monks
and kings, depicting an axial period for the transformation of warrior chiefs
into Buddhist kings. At Sukhothai, from where no *wat* chronicle is known,
this struggle can be seen less dramatically in the inscriptions. Rulers tried
to bring this new force under control by ordaining into the monkhood in
order to share in the institution's moral power, lavishing patronage, and
claiming the authority to appoint or approve a religious hierarchy.

After Lithai succeeded his father as ruler at Sukhothai in the mid-fourteenth century, he continued his good works, building and repairing several temples, and installing replicas of the Buddha's footprint, based on
a model he had seen from Sri Lanka, on four nearby hills (another technique of sacred geography). In an inscription commemorating the installation of another relic brought from Sri Lanka in 1357 Lithai set out a
manifesto of Buddhist rulership. As background he notes the decline of an
old order: since the early thirteenth century, "the princes, Brahmins and
wealthy merchants deteriorated from then on; those learned in astrology
and medicine deteriorated from then on, and did not behave correctly."[152]
Then he presents a justification of his right to rule. First of all he is a
devout Buddhist, who "follows the five precepts at all times," painstakingly
conducts ceremonies, gives alms, and studies the texts. Second, he has an
extraordinary range and depth of knowledge covering calendrical astronomy, weather forecasting, geography, religious practice, medicine, curative
magic, and elephant lore. Third, he delivers fair judgments, and refrains
from killing people for minor crimes, subjecting weak people to heavy corvée, appropriating the property of nobles and commoners at death, or seizing women at will. Fourth, he promotes agricultural expansion and trade
by clearing forest, building irrigation works, planting "coconuts and jack-
fruits everywhere," and protecting traders. He sums up: "Any ruler who

---

[151] Griswold and Prasert, "King Lödaiya of Sukhodaya," 63, 65.
[152] Inscription 3, Griswold and Prasert, "Epigraphy of Mahādharmarāja of Sukhodaya,
part 1," 96–7, translation modified in line with Trongjai, *Pramuan jaruek phraya lithai*, 175.

acts in accordance with these principles ... will rule this *muang* for a very long time; any (ruler) who acts in violation of them will not last long."[153]

Through a mixture of patronage and religious devotion, Lithai endeavored to gain power of appointment over monastic posts. In 1359, he went to Wat Padaeng, a forest monastery in Si Satchanalai, to preside over its abbot's funeral, and to formally appoint the successor. Two years later in 1361, Lithai had the Mango Grove monastery enlarged and beautified, and imported another Lanka-trained monk from Martaban to head it. He cast a massive Buddha image for Wat Mahathat, and had himself ordained into the monkhood there. In the four commemorating inscriptions, Lithai claimed, "I do not wish for the treasure of a *cakkavattin* or of Indra or of Brahma. I wish only to free myself, to become a Buddha in order to lead all creatures to cross these three realms" – upon which, the earth quaked and various other miracles occurred.[154] In the 1410s, a Sukhothai ruler was able to appoint the heads of religious orders and preside over an ecclesiastical court, and there were officials who looked after relations between ruler and *sangha*.[155]

Although Sukhothai faded as a political center in the late fourteenth century, it expanded as a religious center. Several large standing *attharasa* or "18-cubit" Buddha images were created, based on the Buddha's legendary height, and also large footprints. As commonly happens, the religious enthusiasm of this period found expression in striking works of artistic creativity, especially Buddha images cast in bronze or carved in stone for *wat* decoration. The distinctive Sukhothai images of the walking Buddha and the seated Buddha touching the earth radiate a combination of moral strength, compassion, and calm. Perhaps these reflect the hope invested in Buddhism in a time of great social change.

Summary on the Tai and Sukhothai

The Tai who arrived in the Chaophraya Plain were product of a turbulent history. In the society that developed in Sukhothai and other Northern Cities by the thirteenth century, the Tai and their warrior chiefs were thrown together with older Mon-Khmer residents, often generically termed Lawa, and people who had drifted north from the city-states of

---

[153] Inscription 3, Griswold and Prasert, "Epigraphy of Mahādharmarāja of Sukhodaya, part 1," 103–10; Trongjai, *Pramuan jaruek phraya lithai*, 176–82.

[154] Inscription 4, Griswold and Prasert, "Epigraphy of Mahādharmarāja of Sukhodaya, part 1," 142–3, translation modified in line with Trongjai, *Pramuan jaruek phraya lithai*, 223.

[155] Griswold and Prasert, "Epigraphic and historical studies, no. 12," 95–6, 108–12; Griswold and Prasert, "Declaration of independence," 236–42; Ishii, *Sangha, state and society*, 62.

the lower Chaophraya Plain and perhaps from Angkor too. Sukhothai's art, architecture, water management, and language show that the place was a cultural crossroads, absorbing influences from Angkor, Pagan, the Mon country, Lanna, and the peninsula. The ex-warrior Si Sattha's description of his own apotheosis – destroying his weapons, freeing people in the markets, taking up the robe – can be read as metaphor for a broader social crisis in which a warrior ethic was challenged by the humanism of resurgent Buddhism. The cultural innovation of Sukhothai was not the work of "Tai genius" but the product of a collision of different peoples, a social crisis, and the influx of new ideas.

Conclusion

In the old historiography, the main driver of the early history of the Chaophraya Basin was the arrival of the Tai into a seemingly almost empty space. This interpretation has been supplanted as a result of a generation of work by archeologists and cultural historians, who have written a four-millennium story of hunter-gatherers, agriculturists, and metal-workers. While outside influences – cultural from India, economic from China – played a large role, the main theme is gradual, long-term, local evolution with successive shifts to larger settlements, resulting in a society of riverside towns in the last half of the first millennium.

Because this story has been built from cultural material much more than written sources, there has been a tendency to imagine the political history from the cultural one. The idea of a major "Dvaravati kingdom" has taken shape as a by-product of the art historian's adoption of "Dvaravati" as the convenient tag for a set of styles. The reach of a "Khmer Empire" has been imagined from the spread of fashions in sculpture and architecture. Sources may yet emerge to ground these concepts, but until then it is safer to let the cultural remain cultural. The Chaophraya Plain in the second half of the first millennium CE was a society of small and medium-sized towns, rather remote from each other, probably independent, and rather varied in their town plans, monuments, and artifacts.

The emergence of confederations of towns in Lanna, Lanxang, and the Northern Cities over the twelfth to fourteenth centuries was a product of many causes, not only the arrival of the Tai, but also a northward drift of people from the lower plain, intermittent pressure from China, and perhaps also developments in trade. The arrival of reformed Buddhist practice from Sri Lanka and Burma combined with some kind of social upheaval to force a transition from warrior dominance to Buddhist-influenced kingship.

In the same era, a similar confederation developed to the south, near the coast of the gulf, under the influence of similar factors, but also of the sea.

> In 686 of the lesser era, a year of the rat, the Buddha image of Lord
> Phananchoeng[1] was established. In 712, a year of the tiger, on Friday,
> the sixth waning day of the fifth month at three hours and nine segments,
> the great city of Si Ayutthaya was established. In 731, a year of the cock,
> Wat Phra Ram was established. At that time, King Ramathibodi died.[2]

Thus begins the Luang Prasoet chronicle of Ayutthaya, compiled in
1681 from "documents written by astrologers, documents from the
library, and events in the royal chronicles." What is fascinating in this
extract is what is missing. About the city's founder, all the chronicle
records is his death. At Ayutthaya, in contrast to Sukhothai and Lanna,
there are no inscriptions telling of warrior glory, and no ballads or legends securely dated to the city's early years.[3] Ayutthaya was a different
kind of place.

The date of establishing the city in the chronicle is equivalent to
March 4, 1351. Ayutthaya existed before this official foundation – as an
ambitious port-city. From the late thirteenth century, it sent expeditions
south down the peninsula and across to Sumatra, to extract resources
and gain a share of the coastal trade. It became China's major trading
partner in Southeast Asia. In the Thai chronicles, the story of this trade-
and-raid port-city is invisible. Here it is told through outside sources,
mainly Chinese records, Arabic texts, annals from the Malay world, and
early Portuguese reports.

From the late fourteenth century, Ayutthaya expanded its influence
into the interior, mainly northwards up the Chaophraya river system.
In the old historiography, it absorbed Sukhothai and the Northern
Cities through military might. That interpretation is based on a
model of military subjection and territorial control, borrowed from

---

[1] A massive Buddha image, now in Wat Phananchoeng to the southeast of the island.
[2] *Phraratcha phongsawadan krung kao chabap luang prasoet*, 12. This translation is slightly
different from *RCA*, 10, ll. 32–6; 11, ll. 34–5. The "segment" (*bat*) in the time was later
equivalent to six minutes.
[3] Many legends appeared later, as discussed below. See Charnvit, *Rise of Ayudhya*, ch. 4.

the modern European state system. Rereading the sources against a different model of political power produces a different result. The key political unit is the city-state. Broader structures are formed by relations among rulers. Sukhothai and other places remained as largely independent city-states for much longer than usually imagined. The emergence of Siam came about through a merger between the ruling families, peoples, cultures, and practices of Ayutthaya and the Northern Cities over two centuries. The port-city of Ayutthaya was gradually transformed by administrative systems, artistic taste, religious practice, and much else originating from its northern neighbors. At the climax of this process in the mid-sixteenth century, northern nobles took power in Ayutthaya.

Xian and the Peninsula

Ayutthaya sits at the center of the lower Chaophraya deltaic plain. In the era before modern engineering, the rivers rose for around three months during the monsoon to a maximum of 4 meters above their dry-season level, flooding most of the lower plain.[4] Settlements in the floodplain were confined to riverside levees, created by the deposit of silt, or some slightly elevated areas. Ayutthaya lies at the southern tip of one such area. The site flooded most years by a meter, turning the city into "islands in the middle of a sea ... Along the shoreline of the city, which remains above the waterline of the rising river, the land is higher. The river does overflow here, but not as much as elsewhere."[5]

The fall from Chainat to the sea, a distance of 200 kilometers, is just 15 meters. Crossing this gently sloping plain, the rivers snake and occasionally shift course. Early settlements in this landscape were often located in meanders converted to a moated site by a canal.[6] Ayutthaya today is at the junction of the Pasak and Chaophraya Rivers, but in earlier times neither of these rivers came close, only the Lopburi River, which splits from the Chaophraya at Singburi, and would have carried much more water in the past than today. On reaching the elevated land around Ayutthaya, it twisted like a snake, creating an exaggerated meander easily converted into a moat by a canal on the eastern side, possibly following the course of the Nai Kai Canal today (see Map 2.1).[7]

---

[4] Takaya, *Agricultural development*, 133–4.
[5] Diogo da Couto around 1600 in Breazeale, "Portuguese impressions of Ayutthaya," 53.
[6] Pornpun, "Environmental history," 6–20.
[7] The old course of the Pasak, now obliterated, was traced by Phraya Boranratchathanin; see Wansiri and Pridi, *Krung kao lao rueang*, 127–30.

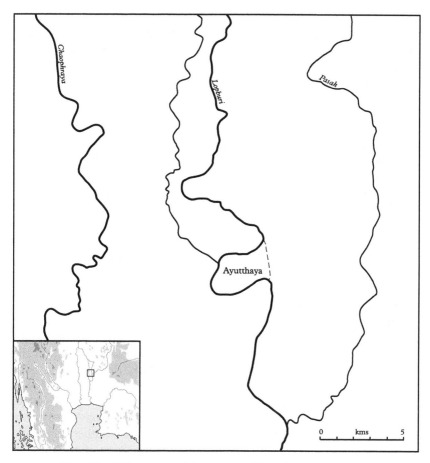

Map 2.1. Old courses of rivers around Ayutthaya

Emergence

In 1282/3, a Chinese official fled to a port named "Xian."[8] In early scholarship Xian was identified as Sukhothai, but this is unlikely. The Chinese court included Xian on a list of *maritime* kingdoms from which it demanded submission.[9] The Guangzhou gazetteer from 1297 to 1307 recorded that the "Country of Xian controls Shang-shui Su-gu-di,"[10]

---

[8] Wade, "*Ming shi-lu* as a source," 257, fn. 13. The Chinese term is sometimes rendered as Hsien or Sien.

[9] Luce, "Early Syam in Burma's history," 61, 76.

[10] Yamamoto, "Thailand as it is referred to in the Da-de Nan-hai Zhi."

where Su-gu-di is clearly Sukhothai, and Shang-shui may be another place-name, or may indicate that Su-gu-di was "upriver" from Xian. By the mid-fourteenth century, the Chinese records clearly use Xian to mean Ayutthaya. Maybe the Chinese originally used the term for a different place,[11] but most likely Xian meant Ayutthaya from the start.

Xian sent a mission to China in 1292, and China sent a return mission in the following year, suggesting Xian was already a port of some status. In 1296, the Chinese envoy to Angkor, Zhou Daguan, recorded that Cambodia imported cloth and silkworms from Xian, and suffered from repeated attacks by its people.[12] The early history of Xian, however, is unknown. Some historians have proposed that there was an earlier Khmer-style settlement to the east of the later city, where there are old *wat* and traces of *barai*.[13] More likely, the old settlement was in the meander. At Wat Mahathat, which would have been roughly at the center of such a settlement, there are distinctive Khmer motifs carved on stones believed to have been taken from an earlier structure. Under this *wat* and nearby Wat Khun Mueang Jai there are traces of pre-twelfth century buildings.[14] Old *wat* in the area to the east may have been forest monasteries, similar to the pattern of other early towns. Digs have yielded pottery shards dateable back to the 1270s.[15]

Other evidence suggests Ayutthaya was a substantial place before its "foundation" in 1351. According to the Luang Prasoet chronicle, the Phananchoeng image was established in 1324/5, possibly as a large free-standing Buddha outside the city, similar to the Palelai image at Suphanburi.[16] The *Tamnan mulasasana*, a Buddhist chronicle, relates that the Sukhothai monks Sumana and Anomadasi visited Ayutthaya in search of Buddhist scriptures in the 1320s, and that another monk had earlier been honored on return from Lanka by the "king of Ayōdhiyā."[17] On his return from Sri Lanka around 1344, the Sukhothai monk Si Sattha visited "Ayodhya Si Ramathepnakhon, the place of the pond of Virunasa of Patala."[18] "Si Ramathepnakhon" means the city of the god Rama. In the *Ramayana*, Viruna is the *naga* king of Patala, who gives refuge to

---

[11] Rungrot ("Lum maenam chaophraya," 135–8) suggests that Xian was originally Suphanburi, but has no evidence.

[12] Zhou, *Record of Cambodia*, 50, 76, 79, 82.

[13] Srisakara, *Krung si ayutthaya khong rao*, foreword.

[14] Polkinghorne et al., "One Buddha can hide another," 586; *Borannasathan nai jangwat phranakhon si ayutthaya*, vol. 2, 51–2.

[15] Pricha, *Set phachana din phao*.

[16] *RCA*, 10, ll. 32–3 (*LP*).

[17] Sommai and Swearer, "Translation of *Tamnān mūlasāsanā*," 80–1; Griswold and Prasert, "King Lödaiya of Sukhodaya," 24, 59.

[18] Translation adapted from Griswold and Prasert, "King Lödaiya of Sukhodaya," 137–8, 143; Trongjai, *Pramuan jaruek samai phraya lithai*, 153–8.

Rama's wife, Sita. The pond may be the Sano Pond which figures in other legends of the city's foundation and is probably the lake in the middle of the island now known as *bueng ram*, Rama's Pond. Damaged words in the inscription may refer to a palace beside the pond.[19] By the early fourteenth century, a town already existed on the site, had a significant Buddha image, and had been named through references to the *Ramayana*.

Xian possibly began as an offshoot from the long-established city at Lopburi (Lavo) on the same river. The *Ming shi-lu* reports:

> Xian was later divided in two countries, Lavo and Xian. In Xian the soil is barren and not suitable for agriculture. The terrain of Lavo is a fine, level plain and most of the plantations yield good crops, and Xian depended on them for supplies.[20]

Xian may have been "barren" because the lower Chaophraya delta was marshy or saline. Ma Huan, the recorder of the Zheng He voyages, reported in 1433 that Xian was poor for agriculture because the land was "wet and swampy."[21] Xian/Ayutthaya seems to have risen to overshadow Lopburi and other cities in the lower Chaophraya Plain by exploiting opportunities created by the decline of the Srivijaya trading network in the thirteenth century.

Xian After Srivijaya

From the tenth to thirteenth centuries, the population of southern China increased by migration and the economy grew on agricultural innovation. To promote trade as a revenue source, the Sung rulers invested in harbors, rewarded successful local merchants with high ranks, set up rest-houses for foreign merchants "who were welcomed on arrival by a banquet and the favors of female entertainers,"[22] and intermittently allowed the export of large volumes of copper cash. Wade suggests these measures created the demand and the liquidity for an "early age of commerce in Southeast Asia," which resulted in the rise of many port cities around the region.[23] A confederation of ports in southern Sumatra became rich and powerful by monopolizing the flow of Chinese trade through the Melaka Straits. Although often termed an "empire," Srivijaya was a trading network.

[19] Baker, "Final part of the *Description of Ayutthaya*," 187; *Van Vliet's Siam*, 104–5, 200–1; Charnvit, *Rise of Ayudhya*, 61.
[20] Adapted from Wicks, *Money, markets, and trade*, 177–8, and Grimm, "Thailand in the light," 2.
[21] Ma Huan, *Ying-yai Sheng-lan*, 103.
[22] Wheatley, "Geographical notes," 25.
[23] Wade, "Early age of commerce."

Srivijaya's success attracted rivals. A raid on Srivijaya in 1025 by the Chola king from southern India began a phase of fragmentation and decline.[24] At the same time, new shipping technologies and more open markets in China increased the volume of the region's maritime trade. In the late thirteenth and early fourteenth century, several port centers, including some on the upper gulf coast, competed to gain a share. Between 1200 and 1205 the Chinese received three missions from a state they called Chen-li-fu, probably located in the upper gulf and some way up a river, but not identified.[25] The ruler, who had a Khmer title (*kamretan an*) and Indic name (Sri Mahidharavarman), "administers over sixty settlements," and "lives in a palace resembling a Buddhist temple. All his utensils are of gold."[26] He sent elephants, ivory, rhino horn, and cloth as tribute to the Chinese court. The Chinese officials ridiculed the memorial as "a comic affair," and Chen-li-fu was gently "excused from giving tribute" in the future. Chinese records also mention Possulan, which was five days sailing away from Chen-li-fu. By this era there were ports on the upper gulf with rulers interested to become part of the trading world supplying Chinese demand.

From the end of the thirteenth century, Xian contested for a share of post-Srivijaya regional trade. Its fleets operated down the peninsula and across the straits to Sumatra. They were so aggressive that other port polities repeatedly pressed China to restrain them.

In 1295, China forbade Xian to attack Malayu and Jambi.[27] Northern Sumatra chronicles report that Xian sent "some hundred boats large and small" to attack the pepper entrepot at Samudra-aroon in the early fourteenth century, and describe a battle lasting two months and ending with a massacre of the Xian army. In the *Sejarah Melayu*'s version, the Xian forces arrived "in the guise of traders," and abducted the Pasai ruler to their capital where he was put to work "to tend the palace fowls" until a Pasai noble negotiated his release.[28] Shortly before 1332 Xian attacked Temasek (modern Singapore) and then plundered the straits.[29] Arab geographers describe Temasek as the southern extent of the coast of Xian.[30] In 1349, the Chinese traveler Wang Ta-yuan reported on Xian that:

[24] Wolters, *Fall of Srivijaya*; Wang, "Nanhai trade"; Wheatley, "Geographical notes"; Hall, *Maritime trade*, 232–4.
[25] Rungrot ("Lum maenam chaophraya," 134–5) suggests it may be Suphanburi.
[26] Wolters, "Chên-li-fu," 1.
[27] Flood, "Sukhothai-Mongol relations," 224; Coedès, *Indianized states of Southeast Asia*, 204–7; Luce, "Early Syam in Burma's history: a supplement," 90.
[28] Hill, "Hikayat Raja-Raja Pasai," 127; Brown, "Malay annals," 45–7.
[29] Wolters, *Fall of Srivijaya*, 79.
[30] Tibbetts, *Study of the Arabic texts*, 240; Hall, *Maritime trade*, 240.

The people are much given to piracy; whenever there is an uprising in any other country, they at once embark in as many as a hundred junks ... and by the vigour of their attack they secure what they want.[31]

In 1392, a ruler imposed by Xian was thrown out of Temasek, but Xian's influence remained. A Malay prince, Parameswara, settled at Melaka (Malacca), but had to flee north from a Xian attack. In 1404, his son Iskander sent tribute to Xian. In 1407 Xian again raided Sumatra, Pahang, and Melaka, and "sent troops to take away their [Chinese] seals and patents" – a way to disrupt a rival trading with China.[32] The Chinese set up a stone tablet defining Melaka's status after which Xian "did not dare to disturb" Melaka, according to Fei Hsin, but Xian does not seem to have been deterred much. In 1419, the Chinese again warned Xian against sending troops to Melaka with "dangerous weapons." In 1421, the Xian ruler "offered tribute of local products in contrition for the crime of having attacked Malacca."[33]

Ma Huan, who may have visited Xian in 1421/2, recorded: "They like to practise fighting on water, [and] their king constantly despatches his commanders to subject neighbouring countries." Fei Hsin, another scribe on the Zheng He voyages, wrote "The customs are violent and fierce: they particularly respect bravery. They invade and despoil neighbouring regions ... and are practised and skilful at fighting on water." Ma Huan also noted that Melaka "paid an annual tribute of forty *liang* of gold; [and] if it were not [to pay], then Xian-luo would send men to attack it."[34] In 1431, Melaka complained to the Chinese court that Xian "had long wanted to invade their country ... They requested that the Court send persons to instruct the king of Siam to no longer oppress or mistreat their country."[35] In the same year, a Ryukyu ship reported that "the King [of Siam] had punished the previous chief [of Palembang] and had put a new chief in power."[36]

Reports of Ayutthaya's activities on the peninsula fade from the Chinese records after the 1430s, but other sources show Ayutthaya continued to raid. In 1445/6, Ayutthaya demanded Melaka submit tribute, and responded to its refusal by sending "a vast army" overland. The Malay annals describe the attack on Melaka as a failure, with the

[31] Rockhill, "Notes on the relations and trade of China," 100.
[32] Wolters, *Fall of Srivijaya*, 109, 154–5; Brown, "Malay annals," 55; Wade, "Melaka in Ming Dynasty texts," 43; Wade, "*Ming shi-lu* as a source," 273; Wade, *Southeast Asia* online no. 1070.
[33] Fei Hsin, *Hsing-ch'a Sheng-lan*, 53–4; Wade, *Southeast Asia* online no. 2608; Wade, "*Ming shi-lu* as a source," 273.
[34] Ma Huan, *Ying-yai Sheng-lan*, 107–8; Fei Hsin, *Hsing-ch'a Sheng-lan*, 42–3.
[35] Wade, "*Ming shi-lu* as a source," 273–4; Wade, *Southeast Asia* online no. 1296.
[36] Kobata and Matsuda, *Ryukyuan relations*, 65.

Ayutthayan forces abandoning wooden items of baggage which sprouted to form forests north of the city.[37] In 1455/6, the Ayutthaya chronicle states "an army was assembled and sent to seize Malacca,"[38] but the Malay annals claim the force retreated after the Melakans started fires to simulate a much larger number of defending troops. Immediately after, Melaka sent a tribute mission to China, and a mission of peace to Ayutthaya. Ayutthaya's reply pointedly addressed the Melakan ruler as a subordinate, but in the Malay annals, peace is made: the Melaka envoy helps Ayutthaya in a war on a neighboring country, is rewarded with the gift of a princess, and returns to Melaka with a Siamese envoy who is warmly received.[39] From this point, the Ayutthayan attacks appear to have ceased.[40] Writing in the 1510s, Tomé Pires noted that Melaka and Pahang had thrown off Ayutthayan domination twenty-two years earlier.[41]

It is often assumed that Ligor (Nakhon Si Thammarat) was a southern ally or agent of Sukhothai and Ayutthaya from an early time. Yet Ligor does not figure in the accounts of Ayutthaya's southern expeditions in the Malay, Arab, or Chinese records, and does not appear in the Thai royal chronicles until the late sixteenth century. Similarly, in the chronicles of Nakhon Si Thammarat there is no mention of any involvement with these forays from Ayutthaya.[42] In the early sixteenth century, Pinto and Pires list Ligor as a tributary of Ayutthaya, but there is no record of when this relationship was formed.

In sum, from the 1290s to the 1490s, Xian/Ayutthaya sent armies and fleets southward. In part, it was subjecting local rulers in order to extract resources, probably including people. In part, it was muscling in on the coastal trade. Pires' account from the end of this period indicates the scale and variety of the Siam–Melaka trade before the Portuguese arrival. "Up to thirty junks a year" carried Siamese rice, dried salted fish, arak, and vegetables to Melaka, along with "benzoin, brazil, lead, tin, silver, gold, ivory, cassia fistula … vessels of cast copper and gold, ruby and diamond rings … a large quantity of cheap coarse Siamese cloth." On the return journey to Siam, the junks carried "male and female slaves, which

---

[37] Brown, "Malay annals," 64–6; Marrison, "Siamese wars with Malacca," 61–3.
[38] *RCA*, 16, ll. 29–30 (*LP*).
[39] Brown, "Malay annals," 68, 70–2; Marrison, "Siamese wars with Malacca," 63–4; Salleh, "Ayudhya in Sejarah Melayu."
[40] Marrison, "Siamese wars with Malacca," 65.
[41] Pires, *Suma Oriental*, vol. 1, 108.
[42] The accounts of Ayutthaya kings' patronage of the stupa at Ligor are of uncertain date; see Wyatt, *Crystal sands*, 35–6, 124–9, 144–5; Munro-Hay, *Nakhon Si Thammarat*, 80–118. Ligor appears as a dependent on the fourth face of Sukhothai Inscription 1 and in clause 2 of the Ayutthaya Palace Law, but both these passages are later insertions.

they take in quantities ... wide and narrow muslins, and Kling cloths in the fashion of Siam, camlets, rosewater, carpets, brocades from Cambay, white cowries," various spices, and goods from China.[43] A handful of shipwrecks dated to the late fourteenth and early fifteenth century show that ceramics from kilns in Sawankhalok, Sukhothai, and Suphanburi were being exported, probably through Ayutthaya.[44] Siam was exporting mainly forest goods, foodstuffs, and ceramics, and importing mainly people and luxury goods such as spices and exotic textiles.

Xian and China

In parallel with its trading and raiding activities to the south, Xian developed a dominant position in the commerce between China and Southeast Asia. For an aspiring port capital in Southeast Asia, relations with China were paramount. China was not only a large market and a source of advanced manufactures, but also a fount of political legitimacy under the imperial tribute system. By agreeing to receive a tribute mission, China recognized the sender as a legitimate ruler of a "country."

Before the mid-fourteenth century, various cities around the upper gulf sent missions to China. Lavo/Lopburi sent four between 1289 and 1299, Phetchaburi one in 1294, and the story of Chen-li-fu is recounted above. Among these towns, the most active was Xian. A first mission was sent in 1292. In the following year, a Chinese emissary was sent to "summon and persuade" Xian to send tribute again. When this summons was ignored, another emissary arrived with a threat of taking "sons and brothers and vassal-retainers" as hostages, if no mission appeared. This insistence on the part of the Chinese court suggests that Xian was already an important place. In 1295, the ruler of Xian appeared at the Chinese court to present a golden plate. Further missions from Xian arrived in 1299, 1300, 1314, 1319, and 1323. In 1299, the Xian envoy petitioned for special marks of favor ("saddles, bridle-bits, white horses and golden-threaded garments") on grounds of earlier precedent. Except for the garments, the request was turned down, but it shows that Xian already had big ideas about itself.[45]

---

[43] Pires, *Suma Oriental*, vol. 1, 107–8.
[44] Brown, *Ming gap*, 38–41. Mysteriously, Chinese and European accounts of Ayutthaya do not mention ceramic exports.
[45] Luce, "Early Syam in Burma's history," 140, 143, 187; Wicks, *Money, markets and trade*, 178; Grimm, "Thailand in the light," 8–10; Wade, *"Ming shi-lu* as a source," 285–7; Charnvit, *Rise of Ayudhya*, 79–81, 111–3; Ishii, "Exploring a new approach," 38–9; Flood, "Sukhothai-Mongol relations," 225; Luce, "Early Syam in Burma's history: a supplement," 90.

In 1371 the Chinese authorities, concerned by an outflow of silver and difficulties controlling rich merchants and foreigners in the port cities, banned private commerce. Only tribute missions were allowed to trade, and only recognized states were permitted to offer tribute. Over the next century, Xian/Ayutthaya exploited these new arrangements to become the Chinese authorities' favorite trading partner in the southern seas. For centuries, China had looked to Southeast Asia for goods found in tropical forests. The *Ming shi-lu* lists forty-four "customary trading articles" from Xian, more than from any other port.[46] These included exotic animals (black bear, white monkey, six-legged tortoise, elephant), aromatic woods, textiles, pepper, colorful bird feathers, and medicinal ingredients. From the 1390s onwards, traders from the Ryukyu Islands also established trading relations with Ayutthaya in order to buy sappanwood and pepper for sending as tribute to the Chinese court. Ships from Xian visited Korea in 1391 and 1394.[47]

Xian sent sixty-eight tribute missions to China between 1369 and 1439, far more than the Chinese stipulation of one every three years, and more than any other port. Champa came second with fifty-eight.[48] The tribute vessels carried mainly forest goods, especially aromatics and exotic items, returning with luxury fabrics, porcelain, medicines, and currency (copper cash and paper money). The amounts were significant. In 1387, the Xian envoys took six tonnes of pepper and sixty tonnes of sappanwood.[49] So much sappanwood and pepper was imported to China that they became items of mass consumption and were used by government to pay officials and soldiers.[50]

Ayutthaya enjoyed privilege and favor from China. In 1377, a Chinese envoy brought to Ayutthaya the "seal of the king of the country," the same mark of recognition that had been bestowed on Srivijaya, and commented, "In terms of present-day *fan* [foreign] kings, it can be said that you are worthy and virtuous." In 1383, Ayutthaya was the first to be given a new Chinese certificates of trade, followed by fourteen other places. In 1396, an envoy came to "make sacrifices" at the funeral of the late Ayutthayan king, an unusual mark of recognition, repeated in 1416 and 1453. Ayutthayan traders were specifically exempted from prosecution, and the *Ming shi-lu* reported that "Xian-luo is the most familiar" of the 167 ports with which the Chinese transacted. Although the emperor

[46] Wicks, *Money, markets and trade*, 180; Charnvit, "Ayudhya: capital-port of Siam," 77.
[47] Ishii, *"Rekidai Hōan,"* 89–90; Kobata and Matsuda, *Ryukyuan relations*, 53–5; Piyada, "Relations between Ayutthaya and Ryukyu."
[48] Reid, "Documenting the rise and fall."
[49] Wade, *"Ming shi-lu* as a source," 270; Wade, *Southeast Asia* online no. 2818.
[50] Reid, *Southeast Asia in the age of commerce*, vol. 2, 12.

repeatedly warned other polities not to send tribute missions more frequently than once in three years, Ayutthaya often sent missions annually
without receiving a rebuke. Ayutthaya ships were regularly assisted when
they were blown ashore on the Chinese coast, attacked by robbers, or ran
out of money. The Tai-zu emperor (1370–98) considered only Ayutthaya
and the Khmer were well-behaved, and rejected missions from several
other ports.[51]

In the early fifteenth century, Ayutthaya asked to be supplied with the
Chinese new set of official weights and measures for local use. In 1480,
the emperor sent the ruler a set of red-dragon robes which, Wade notes,
"was very unusual in Ming foreign relations and suggests a relationship
of some closeness." The Chinese court occasionally welcomed missions
from females at Ayutthaya including a sister and consort of the king, a
departure from the usual Chinese practice and thus another mark of
favor.[52]

At the same time, Ayutthayan traders quietly developed business outside the tribute system. An Ayutthayan ship wrecked off Hainan in 1374
was "suspected to be (just) a foreign merchant" because there was no
official manifest and many of the items were not on the approved list. In
1457 and 1481 Ayutthaya traders were rebuked for privately purchas-
ing salt and children outside the tribute framework.[53] Yet Ayutthaya paid
enough attention to the niceties of official trade to ensure these mutually
profitable indiscretions were overlooked.

The first Zheng He voyage, in 1405, marked the renewal of China's
interest in the sea. Wade argues that Chinese emperors "intended to
bring the maritime world to submission,"[54] particularly by controlling
the straits of Melaka and countering the increased activity of Islamic
traders from the west. Through the mid-fifteenth century Chinese trade
contracted, due to government restrictions and economic factors.[55]
Other ports such as Ryukyu seized the opportunity to act as an entrepot
between China and Southeast Asia. Over 1430 to 1442 alone, at least
seventeen Ryukyu trade missions visited Ayutthaya.[56] From around

[51] Wade, *Southeast Asia* online nos. 1885, 2483, 3071, 2341, 963, 3103, 314, 410, 701, 732,
1385, 1004, 2000; Hamashita, "Ayudhya-China relations"; Grimm, "Thailand in the
light," 5–6; Wolters, *Fall of Srivijaya*, 66.
[52] Wade, "*Ming shi-lu* as a source," 272; Wade, *Southeast Asia* online nos. 2538,
3275, 3051.
[53] Wicks, *Money, markets and trade*, 181; Grimm, "Thailand in the light," 4; Wade, *Southeast
Asia* online nos. 1422, 247, 2650; Wade, "*Ming shi-lu* as a source," 270.
[54] Wade, "Southeast Asia in the 15th century," 28.
[55] Atwell, "Money, and the weather."
[56] Reid, "Documenting the rise and fall," 7; Kobata and Matsuda, *Ryukyuan
relations*, 67–78.

1487, the trading restrictions relaxed and "a great efflux of Chinese trading junks from ports in South China" began to arrive in Southeast Asian
ports.[57] By the 1490s, according to Wade, the private trade "appears ...
to have far outstripped the formal, official trade."[58] From 1511, tribute missions declined in importance, reduced to one per reign, but the
private trade compensated.[59] In the early sixteenth century, there was
another burst of trade between Ayutthaya and the Ryukyu Islands with
twenty-one voyages over 1509–64, with crews numbering from 112 to
232 persons.[60]

Through its deft exploitation of the Chinese official system and its
lacunae, Ayutthaya became the dominant trading center on the Southeast
Asian mainland.

Chinese Settlers

Chinese settlements appeared in most ports and political centers of
the region following the expansion of Chinese trade from the eleventh
century onwards. Zhou Daguan mentions Chinese at both Angkor and
Champa in 1296.[61] Skinner suggests there were Chinese settlements
in all the gulf ports before the thirteenth century.[62] In 1282, some 200
Sung refugees fled to the gulf and the Chinese sent a mission to Xian to
recover them.[63] In 1282/3, a Chinese official fleeing the Mongol army
took up residence at Xian, suggesting it was a known place of refuge.[64]
According to legend, the Phananchoeng image was erected in 1324/5
at the cremation site of a Chinese princess, who had been sent to the
Ayutthaya king and who had committed suicide. The image became a
place of pilgrimage for Chinese traders.[65]

From 1371, the Ming restrictions on Chinese traveling overseas or
transacting with foreign traders encouraged the development of Chinese
expatriate communities throughout Southeast Asia. Although the expatri-
ates were not officially allowed to return, they were in practice welcomed
as captains and traders on foreign ships. At Ayutthaya, some Chinese
became the king's agents in the tribute trade.[66] In 1412, a Chinese named

---

[57] Mills, "Arab and Chinese navigators," 9.
[58] Wade, "*Ming shi-lu* as a source," 271.
[59] Reid, *Southeast Asia in the age of commerce*, vol. 2, 15.
[60] Kobata and Matsuda, *Ryukyuan relations*, 96–9
[61] Zhou, *Record of Cambodia*, 51, 59, 67–8, 70–1, 81
[62] Skinner, *Chinese society in Thailand*, 1–2.
[63] Charnvit, *Rise of Ayudhya*, 66; Wade, "*Ming shi-lu* as a source," 257, fn. 1.
[64] Ishii, "Exploring a new approach," 38.
[65] Charnvit, "Origins of a capital and seaport," 66.
[66] Wade, "*Ming shi-lu* as a source," 283–4.

Qie Jiamei was given official appointment as an envoy from Ayutthaya to China.[67] In the 1420s, when the Ayutthaya ruler built Wat Ratchaburana, Chinese and Arabic merchants donated to the project, and deposited records and religious objects in the crypt hidden deep within the building. Several Chinese family names are found in the inscriptions, along with the phrase, "Great Ming Empire, donated by Buddhist followers." Murals on the crypt's walls depicted Chinese-style guardians, and a banner with Chinese script. Pattaratorn concludes these deposits demonstrate "the presence of Chinese traders and monks in Ayutthaya, the role of Chinese at court, and the influence of Chinese enterprises."[68]

The most elaborate of the several foundation myths of Ayutthaya, recorded by Van Vliet, concerns the son of a Chinese provincial ruler. Exiled from home for sexual misadventures, he travels with a fleet of junks to the peninsula; establishes first Langkasuka and then Ligor; achieves mercantile success; marries the Chinese emperor's daughter; and then moves gradually north founding Kui, Phetchaburi, Bangkok, and other places before establishing Ayutthaya. This story also has a Buddhist layer in which the Buddha visits Siam and predicts Ayutthaya's glory, and a Brahmanic layer in which a *rishi* identifies the city site, guides the founder through various rituals, and quells the local *naga* spirit. The Chinese layer can be read as a legendary account of the importance of the Chinese in the foundation and development of all the port-cities of the gulf, especially Ayutthaya. The son-in-law relationship to the Chinese emperor is invoked to explain "why the kings of Siam are singularly privileged in being allowed to send their junks to Canton and ambassadors to the Chinese kings."[69] The story has strong parallels with the foundation myths of many trading port-polities in the archipelago. In these, a Chinese or other merchant arrives in a "fully laden ship," establishes the polity, makes it prosper, and becomes ruler of a kingdom which "was, in the final analysis, a commercial venture."[70]

Founding Ayutthaya

The core of the early Ayutthaya kingdom was four towns in the lower Chaophraya Plain which had independently sent missions to China: Xian-Ayutthaya, Luohu-Lavo-Lopburi, Sumenbang-Suphanburi, and Pichaburi-Phetchaburi. Accounts dated 1349 variously record that

---

[67] Sng and Pimpraphai, *History of the Thai-Chinese*, 22.
[68] *Jittrakam lae sinlapawatthu nai kru phraprang wat ratchaburana*; Pattaratorn, "Wat Ratchaburana," 83–4, 88; Charnvit, *Rise of Ayudhya*, 81.
[69] *Van Vliet's Siam*, 103–5, 198–202.
[70] Manguin, "Merchant and the king."

"Xian submitted to Luo-hu" or "Xian brought Luo-hu to submission." The confusion is probably the result of copying error. The Thai chronicles report that Ayutthaya was founded two years later in 1351. Thereafter the Chinese records usually refer to Ayutthaya and Lopburi as a yoked pair, Xian-Luo(-hu), and sometimes include Suphanburi as Xian-Luohu-Sumenbang.[71]

The early dynastic history is very confused.[72] According to one version, the founder U Thong (Ramathibodi I) married into the ruling families of both Suphanburi and Lopburi. According to another, U Thong appointed his relatives to rule over these two towns. In both these versions, the late fourteenth century was marked by rivalry between two ruling families, one from Suphanburi and one from Ayutthaya-Lopburi. At U Thong's death, his son Ramesuan succeeded, but within a year Pha-ngua, U Thong's brother or brother-in-law, came down from Suphanburi, seized Ayutthaya, and sent Ramesuan to Lopburi. A week after Pha-ngua (Borommaracha I) died in 1388, Ramesuan marched down from Lopburi, killed Pha-ngua's son, and ruled for the next seven years. Ramesuan was succeeded by his son who ruled as Ramaracha until 1409, when a disaffected noble allied with the current Suphanburi ruler (either son or grandson of Pha-ngua) to capture Ayutthaya. Ramaracha may then have gone to the lower Khmer country and helped to build up the port-state later known as Lovek (Longvek, Lawaek, Lawaik).[73] This history shows that the ruling families of the two long-established cities in the area were both intent on controlling the newer center of Ayutthaya, presumably because of its growing wealth from maritime trade. However, in the *Sangitiyavamsa*, a chronicle compiled in the religious rather than royal tradition, and in the history of Siam that the Dutchman Van Vliet constructed from local sources in the seventeenth century, all the early kings appear to come from one family, though the conflicts are the same. The Chinese records also seem to confirm this, and suggest a chronology of kings different from that found in the chronicles (see Appendix: List of Kings).[74] Either way, by the early fifteenth century, Ayutthaya had become the seat of the ruler, while the Suphanburi family had become the ruling line.

There are at least seven different stories about U Thong, Ayutthaya's founder. These stories variously identify him as a Chinese adventurer,

---

[71] Wade, "*Ming shi-lu* as a source," 257, fn. 13; Ishii, "Exploring a new approach," 40.

[72] This topic is covered in Charnvit, *Rise of Ayudhya*, 106–9.

[73] Vickery, "Cambodia after Angkor," 491–2.

[74] *Van Vliet's Siam*, 202–6; *Wannakam samai rattanakosin lem 3: Sangkhittiyawong*, 220–3; Coedès, "Une recension Pālie des annnales d'Ayutthya," 18–19, 31; Wade, "*Ming shi-lu* as a source," 261–4.

as a ruler of one of the cities around the head of the gulf (Phetchaburi, Suphanburi, Lopburi), as a Tai prince or peasant migrating southwards from the hinterland, as a rich merchant, probably Chinese, who marries a local princess, or as an Angkorian Khmer noble or royal relative who marries a local princess.[75] Ma Huan adds another possibility by identifying the Xian ruler as "of the So-li race," possibly meaning a south Indian (Chola). Which of these stories has more truth is unknowable. The fact that there is no single well-attested foundation story suggests that Ayutthaya began as a trading power whose dominant figures had little interest in history, and that these stories accumulated later when rulers needed a history and genealogy. The inconsistencies in the early dynastic chronology also hint that this was reconstructed later when such matters became important. The variety of foundation stories reflects the city's cosmopolitan nature – with elements of Mon, Khmer, migrant Tai, Chinese, Malay, and Indian origin – and its varied economy, with the founder portrayed variously as a prince, a merchant, or a peasant's son.

From its early days, Ayutthaya was a cosmopolitan place. In the 1420s, Ma Huan noted there were "five or six hundred families of foreigners" in Shang-shui (which may be a place name, or may mean upriver).[76] A century later, Pires noted Ayutthaya was very cosmopolitan, with settlements of "Arabs, Persians, Bengalees, many Klings [south Indians], Chinese and other nationalities."[77] Ma Huan provided the first description:

The houses of the populace are constructed in storeyed form; in the upper [part of the house] they do not join planks together [to make a floor], but they use the wood of the areca-palm, which they cleave into strips resembling bamboo splits ... on [this platform] they spread rattan mats and bamboo matting, and on these they do all their sitting, sleeping, eating and resting ... The men dress their hair in a chignon, and use a white head-cloth to bind round the head [and] on the body they wear a long gown. The women also pin up their hair in a chignon, and wear a long gown ... It is their custom that all affairs are managed by their wives; both the king of the country and the common people, if they have matters which require thought and deliberation – punishments light and heavy, all trading transactions great and small – they all follow the decisions of their wives, [for] the mental capacity of the wives certainly exceeds that of the men ... The customs of the people are noisy and licentious.[78]

The description suggests a modest and slightly rowdy port town. The prominent role of women, which was noticed by other visitors through

---

[75] Charnvit, *Rise of Ayudhya*, ch. 4; Woodward, "Studies in the art of Central Siam," vol. 1, 165–7; Vickery, "Cambodia and its neighbours," 274; Smithies and Dhiravat, "Instructions given to the Siamese envoys," 127–8.

[76] Ma Huan, *Ying-yai Sheng-lan*, 106.

[77] Pires, *Suma Oriental*, 104.

[78] Ma Huan, *Ying-yai Sheng-lan*, 103, 104, 107.

to the nineteenth century, is an eloquent indicator of a society focused on commerce. The Chinese visitors noticed no impressive buildings. Both Ma Huan and Fei Hsin mention religious practice, but describe no imposing religious structure. Ma Huan's account of the ruler and his residence is also strikingly modest:

The house in which the king resides is rather elegant, neat and clean ... As to the king's dress: he uses a white cloth to wind round his head; on the upper [part of his body] he wears no garment; [and] round the lower [part he wears] a silk-embroidered kerchief, adding a waist-band of brocaded silk gauze. When going about [the king] mounts an elephant or else rides in a sedan-chair, while a man holds [over him] a gold-handed umbrella made of *chiao-chang* leaves, [which is] very elegant.[79]

Chinese descriptions of other peninsula states (and Zhou Daguan's description of the Angkor ruler) include great palaces, large processions, and much gold ornamentation. By contrast, the Xian ruler's abode is no more than "elegant, neat and clean," his clothing seems little different from the average, and the only touch of gold is the handle of his single umbrella made of *chiao-chang* (palm) leaves.

Ma Huan also recorded that "the country is a thousand *li* in circumference, the outer mountains steep and rugged, the inner land wet and swampy." An oval centered on Ayutthaya, stretching from the Chaophraya estuary up to Chainat, and including Suphanburi to the west and Lopburi to the east, would roughly match Ma Huan's 1,000 *li* (about 500–600 kilometers).

Early Ayutthaya was primarily a trading center oriented to the sea, probably similar to other new post-Srivijaya trading centers that appeared on the peninsula and around the archipelago.[80] The rulers of these centers were more likely to be merchants than warriors, and wealth rather than lineage was the key credential for claiming power. Their capitals were usually sited on the lower reaches of rivers where they could dominate the flow of trade goods from the interior. They lived from trade and showed little interest in controlling the land or peasantry except for an adjacent area needed for food supplies. They showed only limited interest in religious leadership, and invested little in resplendent monuments. They have left little or nothing to posterity as inscriptions. Hall summarizes how one such state, Samudra-Pasai in northern Sumatra, appears in its own chronicle as a "cosmopolitan urban centre on the edge of jungle."[81] Early Ayutthaya probably matched this pattern, though with more significance as a religious center (see below).

[79] Ma Huan, *Ying-yai Sheng-lan*, 103.
[80] Wolters, *Fall of Srivijaya*, ch. 1.
[81] Hall, *Maritime trade*, 215.

From Port-City to Territorial Power

From the 1370s, Ayutthaya sent armies north, pursuing the strategy adopted by many river-mouth states of exerting influence over the hinterland in order to secure flows of export goods, in this case the exotic items (aromatics, animals, ornaments) demanded in China's luxury market and possibly also ceramics.

At the beginning, Ayutthaya had no military advantage over the interior cities, which had a warrior heritage and probably access to larger reserves of manpower. A primary aim of Ayutthaya's earliest expeditions north was to acquire more people. In 1375/6 Ayutthaya armies "brought back a great many families" from Phitsanulok, and in the following year captured "many *thao, phraya*, troops, *khun* and *mün*."[82] Ayutthaya also brought back people from its raids down the lower peninsula, and traders on tribute missions were reported buying "the sons and daughters of impoverished people" from China in 1457 and again in 1481.[83]

The interior cities may also have had some advantage in weaponry. The use of gunpowder spread from China into Lanna and neighboring territories by the early fifteenth century. The first usage of small cannons, presumably Chinese, appear in the Chiang Mai chronicles in the 1440s.[84] Through maritime trade, however, Ayutthaya had access to weapons and manpower, and means to make the money to buy them. According to the Van Vliet Chronicle (see p. 285), King Intharacha (1409–24) "loved weapons so much that he sent various missions with junks to other countries to buy weapons."[85] Among the goods brought to Ayutthaya by the Ryukyu ships was sulfur for gunpowder.[86] Over time, access to the sea changed the military balance.

Ayutthaya and the Northern Cities

In the old historiography, Ayutthaya "conquered" or "absorbed" the kingdom of Sukhothai by the early fifteenth century. The chronicles report that when the Ayutthaya king's son visited Phitsanulok in 1438, "tears of blood were seen to flow from the eyes" of the Phra Jinaraja Buddha image, and this event has been read as sorrow at the Sukhothai

---

[82] *RCA*, 12, ll. 14, 20 (*LP*).
[83] Wade, *Southeast Asia* online nos. 247, 2650.
[84] Wyatt and Aroonrut, *Chiang Mai chronicle*, 86; Sun, "Military technology transfers from Ming China," 506–7, 512–13.
[85] *Van Vliet's Siam*, 206.
[86] Hamashita, "Ayudhya-China relations," 62.

kingdom's subordination.[87] But this interpretation assumes this passage uses a form of metaphor not found elsewhere in the chronicles. The relations between Ayutthaya and the old Sukhothai kingdom or Northern Cities were more subtle and complex than this story of conquest.

The Northern Cities were sited where the tributaries of the Chaophraya emerge from the hills onto the plain. Many were transition points between land and water transport. The exotic goods that were the mainstay of the China trade came from the hills beyond. Ma Huan recorded in the 1420s that there were trade routes that led north all the way into Yunnan "by a back entrance." Ralph Fitch in the 1580s noted that "to Iamahey [Chiang Mai] come many marchants out of China and bring great store of muske, golde, siluer and many other things of China works." According to Barros, "The little manufacture there is, such as silver and precious stones, comes from the Kingdom of Chiangmai."[88]

Over his reign from 1370 to 1388, King Borommaracha I (Pha-ngua of the Suphanburi line) made five military expeditions. In 1371/2, he "obtained all the northern cities," and two years later attacked Chakangrao (probably Phichai). Another two years later he took Phitsanulok, and captured the city's ruler. In 1378/9, he again attacked Phitsanulok and Phichai, and "Maha Thammaracha came forth to pay homage."[89] The repetitive nature of these expeditions hints that either Ayutthaya was not successful in imposing control, or that was not its aim. The term for "obtained" in the above quote is *ao*, "take" which can mean "attack" rather than capture or control. In part, these were raids to seize people and valuable Buddha images. In one account, Borommaracha I seized the Phra Sihing Buddha from Phitsanulok. Soon after, this image was legendarily taken from Ayutthaya to Kamphaeng Phet and then Chiang Mai, suggesting that Ayutthaya was not always dominant in these early years.[90]

The idea that Ayutthaya "absorbed" Sukhothai is based on a model of unique sovereignty and the Westphalia system of states in modern Europe. But these concepts were alien to this region in this era. Each city was largely independent. Power was not unique and sovereign but many-layered. One ruler might defeat another, demand homage, and extract some resources, but the subordinate was still a king and still ruled. Overlords did not impose any administrative control.

---

[87] *RCA*, 11, ll. 47; 15, ll. 43–4 (*LP*). Griswold and Prasert, "Fifteenth-century Siamese historical poem," 130.
[88] Ma Huan, *Ying-yai Sheng-lan*, 106; Ryley, *Ralph Fitch*, 171; *Thailand and Portugal*, 48, quoting *Da Ásia de João de Barros*.
[89] *RCA*, 11–12 (*LP*).
[90] Ratanapanna Thera, *Sheaf of garlands*, 123–4.

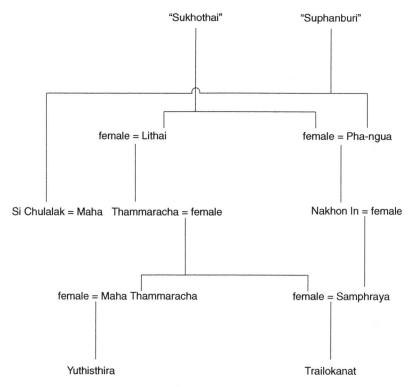

Figure 2.1. Marriage links between the Suphanburi and Sukhothai families (adapted from Phiset, *Phra maha thammaracha*, 90)

Phiset Jiajanphong has offered a more subtle interpretation of the relations between Ayutthaya and the Northern Cities. The Suphanburi family at Ayutthaya developed close marriage ties with the Sukhothai ruling clan, the descendants of Lithai, who had adopted Maha Thammaracha as their royal title (see Figure 2.1). Pha-ngua (Borommaracha I, 1370–88) took a daughter of Lithai as a consort. So also did the next two kings of Ayutthaya from the Suphanburi line, Nakhon In (Intharacha, 1409–24) and his son Samphraya (Borommaracha II, 1424–48). The exchange seems to have been reciprocated. Lithai's son and successor took as major queen a lady who carried an Ayutthaya title, who donated an Ayutthaya-style Buddha to a Sukhothai *wat*, and who was almost certainly from the Suphanburi family.[91]

---

[91] Phiset, *Phra maha thammaracha*, 48–9, 73–4, 78.

In these reciprocal marriage alliances, much more was exchanged between the two regions than royal women. The queens moved to their new homes with an entourage of nobles, monks, craftsmen, and retainers.[92] At the same time, northern nobles moved south to fulfill the aggressive merchant city's need for soldiery. The Portuguese a century later recorded that in Ayutthaya "the men who are knights and who are involved in warfare ... come mostly from the regions where can be found the cities of Sawankhaloke and Sukhothai."[93] Others probably migrated to a city of such evident wealth and opportunity. Climate may also have had a role. From the early fourteenth to early sixteenth century, rainfall was below average.[94] Food production may have been affected more in the Northern Cities, where agriculture depended on the immediate rainfall, than around Ayutthaya, where water was drawn from the rivers.

The Ayutthaya rulers helped their marital relatives in the Sukhothai family to dominate other cities. As part of this diplomacy, twin towns developed in the Northern Cities, best seen on the lower reaches of the Ping River. The town of Nakhon Chum on the west bank developed as a satellite of Sukhothai. The landscape has the main features of Tai settlements: a flat rice plain watered by streams from hills above, similar to Sukhothai itself. The town of Kamphaeng Phet was built on the opposite bank at the end of the fourteenth century to serve as the seat of an offshoot of the Suphanburi–Sukhothai marriage alliance. The town was sited on a raised bank of the river, and watered by channels leading river water into storage tanks, a practice found on the level coastal plain, particularly in towns built under Khmer influence. The configuration of the walls was similar to those at Suphanburi. The different landscapes of these two settlements, separated by only the width of a river, is a sketchy but eloquent glimpse of two cultures, originating from the hills and coastal plain respectively, coming into close contact. A law recorded in a local inscription hints at the interchange between the two cultures across the river. The law imposed penalties on slaves fleeing from one town to another, and on robbers taking slaves, livestock, or goods from one town to another. Phiset suggests the law was enacted because the twin towns were competitors for people. Similar twin towns appeared elsewhere in the Northern Cities, including Chainat opposite Song Khwae (Phitsanulok) and Yanyao opposite Phichit.[95] Ayutthaya's military forays into the Northern Cities, and

---

[92] Phiset, *Phra maha thammaracha*, 53–5.
[93] Barros quoted in *Thailand and Portugal*, 49.
[94] Lieberman and Buckley, "Impact of climate on Southeast Asia," esp. 1057, fig. 1.
[95] Phiset, *Phra maha thammaracha*, 42–7; Phiset, *Sasana lae kan mueang*, 151–66; Griswold and Prasert, "Law promulgated by the King of Ayudhyā," 109–39.

the creation of these twin towns, were designed to help their marital relatives in the contest between local families for dominance.

Phitsanulok became a second or twin capital. In 1374, 1379, 1388,
1396, and 1398, China had received missions from "the Su-men-bang
[Suphanburi] prince and heir to the king of the country of Siam,"[96] showing that the early Ayutthaya kings of the Suphanburi line sent a son as
uparaja or "deputy king" to preside at Suphanburi. In the early fifteenth
century, this practice was adjusted. Nakhon In, who was a product of
Suphanburi-Sukhothai parentage, sent a son to rule at Chainat, the twin
town of Phitsanulok.[97] This shift from Suphanburi to Phitsanulok began
a practice, continued intermittently for the next 150 years, whereby the
prospective heir at Ayutthaya first went to rule in Phitsanulok, which
became a second or twin capital, and sometimes the dominant place. In
1424, Nakhon In's son became ruler at Ayutthaya and in turn sent his son
to reside in Phitsanulok. It was at this visit that the Phra Jinaraja image
shed tears of blood. Rather than a metaphor of defeat, more likely this
was a supernatural event, attracting the prince as a pilgrim. Its recording
in the chronicles probably reflects that, while Ayutthaya had wealth and
military power through its access to maritime trade, Phitsanulok and
other Northern Cities had the stronger cultural tradition, epitomized by
such a beautiful, renowned, and powerful image.

The son, who was seven at the time, was descended on the paternal side from the Suphanburi lineage, now dominant at Ayutthaya, and
on the maternal side from the core Sukhothai lineage – his mother's
father, Lithai's son, had ruled at Phitsanulok with the title of Maha
Thammaracha. When this son succeeded to the Ayutthaya throne as
King Trailokanat in 1448, the possibilities of a merger between the two
dynasties may have seemed likely.

According to the Chiang Mai chronicle, Trailokanat had promised,
on accession, to give his childhood friend and maternal cousin, Phraya
Yuthisthira, the post of *uparaja* at Phitsanulok, but reneged on his promise; in pique, Phraya Yuthisthira transferred his allegiance to the king
of Lanna in Chiang Mai, departed north with many nobles, men, and
craftsmen, and persuaded the Lanna king to make a bid to control the
Northern Cities.[98] Perhaps this tale of bad faith between cousins is the
chronicle's way of recording an undercurrent of opposition within the
old Sukhothai nobility against Ayutthaya's growing influence.

---

[96] Wade, "*Ming shi-lu* as a source," 262–3; Wade, *Southeast Asia* online nos. 1428, 2112,
2917, 3969, 3119.
[97] *RCA*, 15, ll. 1–2 (*LP*); Phiset, *Phra maha thammaracha*, 72–4.
[98] Wyatt and Aroonrut, *Chiang Mai chronicle*, 82.

Yuthisthira's defection provoked almost a century of sporadic warring between Ayutthaya and Chiang Mai. Trailokanat made several expeditions to the Northern Cities, before moving permanently to Phitsanulok in 1463, and installing a son in Ayutthaya with the full title of king. Trailokanat either built or renovated Wat Chulamani at Phitsanulok, and was ordained there for eight months. He constructed a wall that enclosed Song Khwae and the twin town of Chainat, and probably gave the combined towns the new name of Phitsanulok.[99] He (or his father, Samphraya) may have built a palace there which was similar in design to the palace which he had rebuilt in Ayutthaya at the start of his reign.[100] In effect, Ayutthaya and Phitsanulok were twin capitals, with the senior king now at Phitsanulok.

Trailokanat's ordination in Phitsanulok in 1465 may have been a milestone in the cultural politics of the merger between Ayutthaya and the Northern Cities. Trailokanat was the first Ayutthaya king to be ordained while on the throne and was perhaps consciously following the earlier local example of Lithai of Sukhothai, but with added grandeur. He brought monks from Sri Lanka to perform the ordination, had five monks ordained before himself, perhaps a reference to the Buddha's five main disciples, and another 2,348 ordained after himself.[101] In 1482 he held a fifteen-day festival at Wat Phra Si Rattana Mahathat, Phitsanulok's most important *wat*, probably to mark a renovation that he had patronized.[102]

According to the chronicles, Trailokanat remained at Phitsanulok until his death in 1488. According to the *Sangitiyavamsa*, he abdicated in favor of his son Intharacha "after twenty years," meaning in 1468.[103] According to Chinese records, a king abdicated in 1482/3 because "he was very aged and had wearied of duties," and his successor was installed as "Krung Phra Nakhon Si Ayutthaya," signifying a return of the primary capital to Ayutthaya.[104] Whatever the dating, the primary capital returned to Ayutthaya but Phitsanulok continued in its secondary role. After Trailokanat's death, the new king's uncle remained at Phitsanulok, and although he is not designated *uparaja* in the chronicles, an inscription

---

[99] Griswold and Prasert, "Fifteenth-century Siamese historical poem"; Santi, *Prang lae lai punpan*, esp. 1–5.

[100] Baker, "Grand Palace," 76–7.

[101] Charnvit, "Buddhism and political integration," 170; Wat Chulamani inscription in *Phraratchaphongsawadan krung kao*, 37–9; McGill, "Jatakas, universal monarchs, and the year 2000."

[102] *RCA*, 18, ll. 1–3 (*LP*).

[103] *Wannakam samai rattanakosin lem 3: Sangkhittiyawong*, 222; Coedès, "Une recension Pālie des annales d'Ayuthya," 19.

[104] Wade, "*Ming shi-lu* as a source," 266–8. Wade, *Southeast Asia* online no. 2722, 3008. "Krung" comes from *kurung*, a Khmer word for ruler, later used to mean "city."

from Kampheng Phet in 1510 donates the merit to "the two kings."[105] In 1522, after reports of disorders and bad omens, the king again appointed a son as *uparaja* posted to Phitsanulok.[106]

Ayutthaya, Lanna, and Angkor

In the early fifteenth century, Ayutthaya armies ranged further afield – to Angkor in 1431/2, the west coast of the peninsula in 1441/2, and Chiang Mai in the early 1440s.[107] These expeditions may have been made possible by the greater use of elephants, mentioned in the account of the attack on Chiang Mai. The march northward required several months. Above the Northern Cities, the army had to travel by land, in part over difficult terrain. Because the journey would be extremely difficult in the rainy season, the window for campaigning was limited. The greater use of elephants extended Ayutthaya's military reach (see Chapter 3).

The first attack on Chiang Mai, in the early 1440s, falls into the old model of raiding for resources. According to the Chiang Mai chronicle, the Ayutthaya army, though large, was put to flight by a clever ruse, yet in 1445 Chiang Mai petitioned the Chinese court for new documents because the old ones "had been burnt and destroyed by bandit troops from the country of Siam,"[108] suggesting they may have burnt the Chiang Mai palace. After Yuthisthira's defection to Lanna in 1451, however, the fighting changed in purpose and nature. For almost a century, Ayutthaya and Lanna contested for influence over the Northern Cities, resulting in a new style of warfare with pitched battles, sieges, and espionage.

Tilokarat of Lanna was an ambitious dynast. He came to the throne in 1443 by usurping his father. He extended Chiang Mai's power eastward, taking Nan and Phrae, attempted to subdue Luang Prabang, and raided northwards, probably to seize people.[109] Just like the Suphanburi family at Ayutthaya, his Mangrai dynasty forged marriage alliances with the Sukhothai clans, and the two polities had probably sent a joint tribute mission to China in 1405.[110] After Yuthisthira transferred his allegiance to Tilokarat in 1451, the two attacked south in force and took control of the northern and western regions of the old Sukhothai domain, including

[105] Griswold and Prasert, "Inscription of the Śiva of Kāṃbèṅ Bejra," 233.
[106] *RCA*, 18, l. 27; 19, ll. 29–44 (*LP*).
[107] *RCA*, 16, ll. 1–6; Wyatt and Aroonrut, *Chiang Mai chronicle*, 78–80. An attack on Chiang Mai recorded in the later chronicles in the 1390s (*RCA*, 12–13) is almost certainly misplaced; the style of writing resembles the chronicles from the sixteenth century onwards.
[108] Wade, *Southeast Asia* online no. 1969.
[109] Wyatt and Aroonrut, *Chiang Mai chronicle*, 75–82.
[110] Wade, *Southeast Asia* online no. 517.

Sukhothai itself for a short time, and Phitsanulok briefly during 1459/60. Campaigns became almost annual events until an Ayutthaya victory at Chaliang in 1474/5, commemorated in the epic poem, *Yuan phai*.[111] After this, according to the Ayutthaya chronicle, Tilokarat of Chiang Mai "asked to establish friendly relations."[112] Yet the battle was not as decisive as the poem or chronicles claim. There were more skirmishes between Ayutthaya and Chiang Mai through to the 1540s.[113] Ayutthaya never succeeded in imposing its authority over Chiang Mai, but the 1474/5 battle ended the influence that Chiang Mai had established in the Northern Cities since 1451, and thus allowed the process of merger between Ayutthaya and Phitsanulok to continue.

While the main thrust of Ayutthaya's expansion was to the north, the same strategies of marriage alliance and military intervention were evident in other directions. At the time a royal son was first sent to Phitsanulok in the 1420s, two others were sent to Suphanburi and to Phraek Siracha (near modern Chainat). This reflected an old system, seen in the Sukhothai kingdom, of developing satellite cities in four cardinal directions from the capital, through various linkages including marriage alliances.[114] In the Ayutthaya Palace Law, possibly dated to 1468, there is a category of queen called *mae yua mueang*, which probably means royal ladies from the provincial cities. By the early sixteenth century, this arrangement had been formalized into a system of four queens with distinctive titles for the four cities.[115]

In the old historiography, Ayutthaya "sacked" Angkor. Yet Ayutthaya's relations with Angkor, as with Sukhothai, should not be portrayed in a modern framework of territorial conquest, but in a context of raiding for resources and shifting relations between ruling families.[116] There are references to Ayutthaya expeditions to Angkor in various sources from the 1350s onwards. Vickery argues that all the accounts of "conquest" or "occupation" through the fourteenth century are dubious. Wade and Wolters suggest that Ayutthaya may have had a presence in Angkor in the late 1360s and 1370s, but the evidence is inconclusive.[117] In 1431/2, an Ayutthayan army attacked Angkor, carried away people and religious treasures, and installed a son of the Ayutthayan king as ruler.[118] King

---

[111] Wyatt and Aroonrut, *Chiang Mai chronicle*, 85–90; Baker and Pasuk, *Yuan phai*; Griswold and Prasert, "Fifteenth-century Siamese historical poem."

[112] *RCA*, 17, ll. 40–1 (*LP*).

[113] *RCA* 20–1; Wyatt and Aroonrut, *Chiang Mai chronicle*, 102–12.

[114] Charnvit, *Rise of Ayudhya*, 127–8.

[115] Baker and Pasuk, *Palace Law of Ayutthaya*, 135; Phiset, *Phra maha thammaracha*, 48–9.

[116] As suggested by Vickery, "2/K.125 fragment," 61.

[117] Vickery, "Composition and transmission," 141–2; Wade, "Angkor and its external relations," 8–11; Wolters, "Khmer king at Basan."

[118] *RCA*, 15, ll. 31–9 (*LP*); Vickery, "Cambodia after Angkor," 491–2.

Borommaracha II led the expedition and was so pleased with its result that he conferred on its commanding general an elevated title and other honors.[119]

Ten years later, the Ayutthayan-installed ruler at Angkor was attacked by a rebel group, and in the following year he died. The rebel leader, Yat, who might have been an offshoot of the Suphanburi ruling family, came to control much of western Cambodia, but there is no record of him occupying Angkor. In 1443/4, a large group of Khmer, who had been brought from Angkor to Ayutthaya in 1431/2, including monks and astrologers, planned to take Ayutthaya by coup and then re-occupy Angkor. Their plot was discovered and over thirty were executed and impaled.[120] At the site of Angkor over forty Buddha images or fragments have been found carved in distinctly early-Ayutthaya style from local stone. Inscriptions from Angkor dated to the mid-sixteenth century and Chinese records use titles (*rajadhiraja, ramadhipati, cakrabartiraja*) not found earlier in Cambodia but common at Ayutthaya.[121] Ayutthaya monks, royalty, or nobility may have been present at Angkor for some years and have treated the site with some reverence.[122]

Over the remainder of the fifteenth century, there is no mention of Angkor in the Ayutthaya records, suggesting that Ayutthaya paid little further attention to this region, possibly because Angkor had been so conclusively abandoned that there was no benefit.

Political Geography

Although Ayutthaya gradually emerged as the dominant city in the Chaophraya Plain, the other centers, particularly in the Northern Cities, remained largely independent and still royal. The traditional royal titles of these cities' rulers were still in use through the fifteenth and early sixteenth centuries.[123] Phitsanulok was a sub-capital or capital for over a century. Pires recorded that the ruler of Kamphaeng Phet "has many fighting men. Inside his own territory he is like the King of this land."[124] A short inscription from 1510 shows him restoring the great relic

---

[119] Watanyu, "Jaruek khun si chaiyarat mongkhonthep"; Santi, "Silajaruek khun si chaiyarat mongkhonthep."

[120] Winai, "Phraratchaphongsawadan krung si ayutthaya chabap ho phra samut wachirayan," 73–7; Vickery, "Cambodia and its neighbours," 288–94.

[121] Vickery, "Cambodia and its neighbours," 281, 287.

[122] Polkinghorne et al., "One Buddha may hide another."

[123] Maha Thammaracha in Phitsanulok, Phaya Chaliang in Chaliang/Sawankhalok, Phaya Ramaraj in Sukhothai, Phaya Saen Soi Thao or Dhammasokaraja in Kamphaeng Phet, see Vickery, "2/K.125 fragment," 73–7.

[124] Pires, *Suma Oriental*, 101.

stupa, casting a Shiva statue, dredging a river, restoring a road, setting boundary markers, and repairing irrigation channels – all kingly activities.[125] Barros, who summarized Portuguese knowledge of Siam in the mid-sixteenth century, relayed that the largest cast image in Siam was at Sukhothai, that it was embellished with gold leaf on the upper section and colored decoration below, and that Ayutthaya had nothing to rival this in size or splendor.[126] On his visit to the Northern Cities in 1908, the future King Vajiravudh was surprised to find that the centers of Sukhothai, Si Satchanalai, Kamphaeng Phet, Phichai, and Phichit had been laid out like royal cities and sometimes had monuments as grand as those at Ayutthaya.[127]

These places disappear from the history, and hence seem crushed, because no chronicles or other written records have survived from this area other than some foundation legends,[128] but the places themselves tell a story. Chaliang-Satchanalai and Kamphaeng Phet were large and flourishing centers in the sixteenth century. Kamphaeng Phet was refortified with high brick walls and ramparts.[129] Chaliang was ringed with a laterite wall accommodating gun placements. Both cities were embellished with new complexes of temples in the style of a royal capital. Outside both places spread large areas which are now dotted with the ruins of small *wat*, which presumably were community temples and which suggest a large population. At Sukhothai, the walls were improved by adding two new rings. Piriya argues that many of the Sukhothai buildings attributed to the thirteenth and fourteenth centuries were built or substantially extended much later.[130]

Both Sukhothai and Chaliang-Satchanalai became large production centers for ceramics. At Satchanalai, production may have started from the tenth or eleventh century, and exports from the thirteenth. The kilns stretched over 10 kilometers along both banks of the Yom River, indicating usage over several centuries. Originally making mainly pipes for water supply and tiles and ornaments for temples and other buildings, these kilns later developed production of storage jars and household crockery. The design of the kilns, examples of Chinese pottery found on site, use of peony motifs, and other design elements all point to some influence from China. After Ming China restricted ceramic exports in the

---

[125] Griswold and Prasert, "Inscription of the Śiva of Kāṃbèṅ Bejra," 233.
[126] Campos, "Early Portuguese accounts," 12; *Thailand and Portugal*, 46.
[127] Vajiravudh, *Thieo mueang phra ruang*, 17, 59–60, 166–9.
[128] Collected in the *Phongsawadan nuea* (Northern chronicles) and partly reproduced in the royal chronicles, see *RCA*, 1–9.
[129] Breazeale, "Ayutthaya under siege," 46.
[130] Piriya, *Sinlapa sukhothai lae ayutthaya*, part I.

mid-fourteenth century, these kilns filled much of the resulting "Ming gap" in supply for overseas trade. In the mid-fifteenth century, the potters developed a distinctive green celadon glaze through better clay and hotter firing. The Sukhothai kilns turned out celadon plates with distinctive fish and floral designs from around 1400 to the 1480s. Chaliang-Satchanalai continued producing a darker celadon in bowls and jars, known as Sawankhalok ware, until the 1580s. The products went down river to the sea, but also by elephant down to Martaban. Celadon articles have been found in shipwrecks and archaeological sites all round Asia, down the east African coast, and in the Middle East. In the Ottoman Empire, celadon was valued higher than Chinese ware. After the Ming ban on ceramic exports from China ended in 1567, exports were competed out by a flood of cheap Chinese products.[131]

In the 1550s, João de Barros wrote a description of Siam based on reports of the traders, seamen, and mercenaries who had spent time there. He presented the core territory as two separate kingdoms. One he called "Chaumua" which seems to be *chao nuea*, the "northern people," equivalent to the Northern Cities, among which he specifically mentioned Sukhothai and Sawankhalok. The other, which included Ayutthaya and the gulf coast, Barros called "Muantay," glossed as *reyno de baixo*, the "kingdom below," hence *mueang tai*, the southern realm. He added that the latter was "more correctly speaking" called "Sião" or Xian/Siam, and that the two areas spoke different languages.[132] Some Portuguese maps from this era show Odia (Ayutthaya) and Sian (Siam) as separate places, with Odia by the gulf coast and Sian inland in the area of the Northern Cities.[133] The naming is muddled but the separation is clear.

The Early Ayutthaya Polity

In the late fifteenth century, Ayutthaya underwent a revolution in government as a consequence of the gradual merger between Ayutthaya and the Northern Cities. Society had become more complex. The structures and traditions of the two areas had to be deftly merged. These reforms are often attributed to Trailokanat (1448–88) but probably spread over several decades and reigns. His successor, Intharacha (1490–91) is credited

---

[131] Brown, *Ming gap*; Ho, "Export phases for Menam Basin ceramics"; Hein and Barbetti, "Si-Satchanalai and the development of glazed stoneware"; Gutman, "Martaban trade," 112; Piyada, "Relations between Ayutthaya and Ryukyu," 51–5; Peacock, "Ottomans and the Kingdom of Siam," 11; Natthapatra, *Khrueang thuai jin*, 229–31, 449.

[132] Villiers, "Portuguese and Spanish sources," 121; Campos, "Early Portuguese accounts," 11.

[133] Suárez, *Early mapping of Southeast Asia*, 141, 166–7.

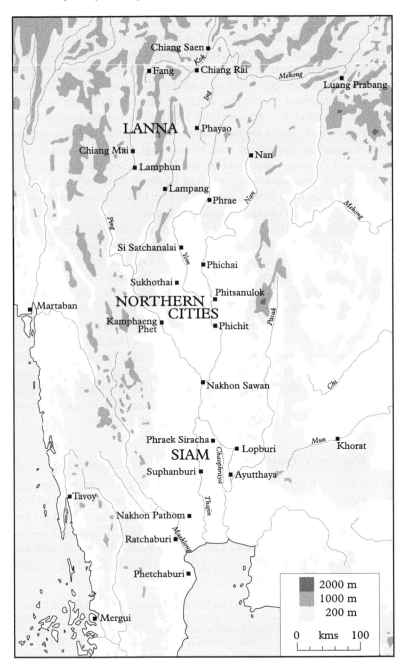

Map 2.2. Chaophraya Basin: principal places in the fifteenth century

with tax reforms, while Ramathibodi II (1491–1529) "imposed regulations and did not want them to be transgressed."[134]

Underpinning these changes were rising royal revenues, raised from trade through monopolies. The Ryukyuan traders who arrived in Xianluo in 1419 were told that their "porcelains ... traded only under government supervision, and no private purchase of sappanwood was permitted." Another mission in 1431 found that "the porcelains and other goods ... were mostly purchased under government control by local chiefs." The Ryukyuans complained bitterly that this monopoly system was new and detrimental to trade. The Ayutthayan officials ignored petitions to revoke the monopoly, but sent off presents of "red and white wine made from fragrant flowers" to mollify their Ryukyuan counterparts.[135] Perhaps because of these rising revenues, the Ayutthayan rulers could relax the demands on their own people. Trailokanat "demanded tribute, impost and gifts from no-one" and "used labourers as workers with daily wages and not as slaves as most Siamese kings have done."[136] Trade was the principal source of revenue. Ishii concluded, "The outstanding characteristic of the 'medieval' state [of Siam] is probably its commercial nature: the king strove exclusively through trade to increase the national wealth or more strictly, that of the royal household."[137]

The administrative machinery was expanded to handle new functions. The original administration, designed for a city-state, had four departments: *mueang* in charge of the city; *wang* in charge of the palace; *phaen* (*phaendin*) in charge of land and general administration; and *mahosoth* in charge of rites. The first expansion was to add a department to handle trade. The "four pillars" of government became *mueang, wang, na* (land), and *khlang*, meaning warehouse or treasury, in charge of trade. Whereas in 1419 the king himself had authored the missives sent to trading partners such as Ryukyu, by 1480 there was a hierarchy of officials who conducted trade negotiations. The titles appearing in missives to China hint that a department of trade had already been created under the Phrakhlang or royal warehouse, headed by a minister of Okphra rank, and including a *jao tha* or harbormaster and others with Chinese names.[138] Probably after 1490, when there was a major expansion in the westward arm of Ayutthaya's trade (see Chapter 3), the Phrakhlang developed separate departments to handle the eastward route, westward route, the warehouse, and general administration.[139]

---

[134] *Van Vliet's Siam*, 213.
[135] Hamashita, "Ayudhya-China relations," 61–3.
[136] *Van Vliet's Siam*, 207.
[137] Ishii, *Thailand*, 33.
[138] Hamashita, "Ayudhya-China relations," 65–9; Ishii, "*Rekidai Hōan*," 83–4.
[139] Breazeale, "Thai maritime trade"; Julispong, *Khunnang krom tha khwa*.

A second expansion was to add two new ministers, Kalahom and Chakri, to oversee Ayutthaya's increased influence beyond the *ratchathani* or inner realm. Later these posts acquired specific regions of responsibility, and later too became identified as heads of military and civil administration, but in this early period probably had parallel roles on the same principle of counter-balancing that created left and right divisions all the way down the official hierarchy.

In this era, law was increasingly used to manage a more complex society. Early law codes are known from Lanna and other Tai states. Our knowledge of law in the Ayutthaya era comes from the collection of old law texts known as the Three Seals Code, compiled in 1805. As Vickery has shown, the dates in the prefaces of these laws are unreliable, but the royal titles in the prefaces of many laws seem to match forms in use in the fifteenth century. By this time, law-making had begun on topics such as theft, marriage, kidnapping, treason, public disorder, and crimes against government as well as rules on legal procedure.[140] The Van Vliet chronicle confirms the importance of law in this era: under Ramathibodi II, "no theft was known and whoever was caught being unfaithful was punished with a severe death"; his successor Borommaracha IV "was a great enemy of bad judges and punished them with death"; while Chairacha was "a lover of good justice, he was not quick to punish but had all wrong-doers properly examined."[141] The Law on Theft, one of the longest codes, details a great variety of criminal practice, from petty theft to armed bandit gangs. The Law on Public Disorder, literally "on quarrelling, hitting, and cursing," describes many forms of personal dispute at different levels of violence. These two codes hint that law was being invented to combat the stresses of a more complex society.[142]

The *Kot monthianban* or Palace Law, tentatively dated to 1468, was effectively the law on government. Its major concern was the publication of hierarchy. The law sets out an elaborate structure of precedence within the royal family, along with means to display this precedence – through dress, regalia, stage directions – on public appearances at ceremonial events and during travel outside the palace. Further rules set out a similar structure for the higher nobility along with rules on dress, insignia, language, and behavior. Besides a way of imposing discipline on the elite, these rules were designed to embed hierarchy as a principle of social order. Everyone had to know their place.[143]

---

[140] Vickery, "Prolegomena," and "Constitution of Ayutthaya," 145–56.
[141] *Van Vliet's Siam*, 213–15. The laws are first mentioned in the chronicles in 1548, see *RCA*, 26.
[142] *Kotmai tra sam duang*, vol. 3, 184–302.
[143] Baker and Pasuk, *Palace Law of Ayutthaya*, 59.

In early Ayutthaya, the hierarchy was shallow, befitting a port polity, with only two titles. Ordinary officials had the title of *nai* while higher ranks, including generals and town governors, had the title of *khun*.[144] As the society became more complex, this hierarchy was stretched. At the start of his reign in 1448, King Trailokanat gave new titles to six ministers. The record of this event in the chronicles has often been interpreted as the invention of the whole *sakdina* system of ranking, but this is a misreading. It states:

> The king gave names, posts and *na* to officials … he had *thahan* be *samuha kalahom*, had *phonlaruen* be *samuha nayok*, had *khun wang* [palace] be *phra thammathikon*, had *khun mueang* [city] be *phra nakhonban mueang*, had *khun khlang* [treasury] be *kosathibodi*, had *khun na* [land] be *phra kasetra*, with 10,000 *na* …[145]

The titles of the four-pillar ministers were elevated from *khun* to *phra*, and they were given Sanskrit-derived official names describing their posts. The two new territorial ministers, possibly founded at this time, were also given Sanskrit-derived names. The fact that this renaming exercise appears among the first acts of a new ruler (which also included building a new palace) hints at its importance. Probably this was a critical stage in collating different administrative structures and ranking systems in the merging Ayutthaya-Phitsanulok polity. These senior officials received four marks of status: a *yot* or prefix of rank; a *rajathinanam*, or title, usually associated with a particular post; a *tamnaeng*, or job description; and a *sakdina* grade. The use of parallel ranking systems suggests a merger of multiple pre-existing practices. *Sakdina*, which may translate as "power over fields," was a numbered grade which ranged from 100,000 for the king through 10,000 for the highest officials down to five for the lowliest dependent. There is no evidence that the posts were accompanied by grants of land. The system of numerical ranking, which can be traced back through earlier Tai states to China,[146] was eventually extended right down through the administrative hierarchy, but when this happened is unknown. The introduction of the *phra* rank stretched the hierarchy from two levels to three. Another rank of *luang* between *khun* and *phra* seems to have appeared in the mid-sixteenth century, and *oya* or *okya* above *phra* by the late sixteenth.[147]

---

[144] Watanyu, "Jaruek khun si chaiyarat mongkhonthep," 43–4; Griswold and Prasert, "Law promulgated by the King of Ayudhyā"; Vickery, "Constitution of Ayutthaya," 161.

[145] *Phraratcha phongsawadan krung si ayutthaya chabap mo bratle*, 22; *RCA*, 16, ll. 17–20 (*BM*); Vickery, "Constitution of Ayutthaya," 162–3.

[146] Vickery, "Constitution of Ayutthaya," 177–82; Lemoine, "Thai Lue historical relations with China."

[147] Luang appears for the first time in the chronicles in 1548, and Okya in the 1590s; see *RCA*, 23, 159 (*BM*).

These changes in government have sometimes been linked to Ayutthaya's 1431/2 expedition to Angkor and a supposed absorption of Khmer practice, but there is little evidence of Angkor vocabulary in these reforms. Any Khmer element in Ayutthaya practice had longer roots, particularly through Lopburi. The roots of these changes are difficult to trace because scribes created new words for new titles and functions, sometimes blending a Sanskrit term with Khmer etymological principles and Thai pronunciation.[148] The changes in the late fifteenth century reflected the expansion of Ayutthaya, its growing wealth from trade, and the complex merger with the Northern Cities.

The Politics of Merger

This merger increased the complexity of Ayutthaya's politics. Two kinds of tension appear in the chronicles. The first was between crown and nobility. Both trade and warfare created opportunities for the emergence of powerful nobles. A noble official (Kalahom), rather than a member of the royal family, is mentioned as heading an army for the first time in 1462.[149] When warfare and the investment in palace, *wat*, and display raised the costs of royal government, nobles resisted attempts at increased taxation. Trailokanat's successor in the late fifteenth century

obtained large subsidies ... especially from the mandarins, but little from the community. In addition he introduced a practice in which, after the death of the mandarins, one tical of gold had to be paid for every ten measured lands from their estate.

As a result, his reign was "troubled" and his sudden death came "much to the joy of the mandarins."[150] In 1524, the chronicles for the first time mention a court purge: "people dropped anonymous messages. At that time the King had many of the nobility killed."[151] Immediately after, the kingdom was inflicted with all kinds of misfortune – too little water in the flood season, an earthquake, inflation – probably the chronicle's code for dissent and disorder. In 1529, the king died and his son succeeded. The Van Vliet chronicle reports that the new king began "merciful" but before long "ruled with a severe hand," and concludes that: "During his lifetime it was generally a troubled and never a fruitful time."[152]

---

148 Winai, "Rueang phasa tai thai," esp. 62.
149 *RCA*, 17, ll. 12–13 (*LP*).
150 *Van Vliet's Siam*, 208.
151 *RCA*, 19, ll. 32–3 (*LP*).
152 *Van Vliet's Siam*, 214.

The second form of tension was within the nobility, between those from Ayutthaya on the one hand and the Northern Cities on the other. In part this was simply a factional struggle for power, but in part it may also have involved a clash of political cultures. The nobility of the Northern Cities had a deeper historical tradition and a strong warrior ethic. The nobility of Ayutthaya had access to wealth from trade.

At the succession in 1529, a royal son who had been *uparaja* in Phitsanulok descended to assume the throne in Ayutthaya. Four years later he died from smallpox, and his five-year-old son was installed on the throne. Another member of the Suphanburi-Sukhothai family, possibly a brother of the previous king, who was resident in Phitsanulok and may have replaced his brother as *uparaja* there, came to Ayutthaya, had the young king executed, and ruled as King Chairacha. He brought with him from the Northern Cities a number of nobles, particularly a member of the old Sukhothai ruling family, probably married to his own daughter, who he appointed as head of the royal guard with the title of Khun Phirenthorathep.[153] Chairacha made two military expeditions to Lanna, both times using the Phraya of Phitsanulok, probably another member of the Sukhothai family, as his military commander.

At Chairacha's death in 1547/8, these tensions and intrigues were again present. Chairacha's brother fled into a monastery for "If I were to remain a layman at this moment, it appears that I would surely be in peril ... only the Holy Religion of the Buddha and the orange cloth ... can be relied upon to escape danger." Chairacha's eleven-year-old son was installed as king by a conclave of "monks, Brahmans, chief ministers, poets, sages, pundits, astrologers and priests," with his mother Thao Si Sudachan as regent. Portending the trouble to come, "the earth quaked."[154]

The story told by the chronicles of what followed has two themes. The first theme is about the danger of female power in royal politics. Si Sudachan gets pregnant by a lover, has her own son executed, and installs the lover as king. The second theme is about the tensions within the nobility. In 1529 and again in 1547/8, the nobles had attempted to install a young boy on the throne, a classic strategy of nobles hoping to limit the power of the throne. In both cases, too, the maneuver was designed to block succession by a powerful figure in the Suphanburi-Sukhothai clan. Si Sudachan may have been related to the Lopburi family which had contested with Suphanburi in the early years of the Ayutthaya kingdom. She held a consort title which suggests she came

[153] Phiset, *Phra maha thammaracha*, 97; *RCA*, 26, ll. 26–7.
[154] *RCA*, 21, ll. 34–5, 38–42 (*BM*).

from one of the four cardinal cities, but the identification with Lopburi
is speculative. Alternatively, her maneuver may simply have represented
an attempt by the Ayutthaya nobles to resist the growing power of those
from the Northern Cities. The chronicles report Si Sudachan justifying
her coup on grounds that "the northern provinces are in turmoil and
cannot be trusted on government matters," and her first move was an
attempted purge of the seven governors of the Northern Cities.[155]

The counter-coup that quickly followed consolidated the power of the
northern nobles. Within two months, Si Sudachan and her lover were
ambushed and killed. Chairacha's brother was brought out of the monkhood and installed as King Chakkraphat. This counter-coup was led by
Khun Phirenthorathep, the Sukhothai royal brought to Ayutthaya by
Chairacha. Among his allies were two other northern nobles, the lords of
Phichai and Chaliang, and possibly another from Nakhon Sawan.[156] As
reward, the governors of Phichai and Chaliang were raised in rank and
showered with presents. The rewards given to Khun Phirenthorathep were
much more striking. He was "created Prince Thammaracha [*somdetphra
maha thammarachathirat*], granted the right to issue royal commands,
and given Phitsanulok to rule." In addition, Chakkraphat presented him
with his own daughter and gave her the title of *mahesi*, the same as the
queens at Ayutthaya. To round it off, he added splendid presents including "a pair of barges and the insignia of royalty."[157]

Si Sudachan's attempted coup had clarified the realities of power
within the Ayutthaya kingdom. The Suphanburi-Sukhothai line still
supplied the king, but the northern nobles were the king-makers. The
old Sukhothai royal title of Maha Thammaracha had been revived, and
its holder ruled in Phitsanulok with power and splendor "as if he were
another king."[158]

The finale came twenty years later. The fall of Ayutthaya in 1569 is
traditionally portrayed as conflict between "Siam" and "Burma," and
this aspect is covered in the next chapter. But 1569 was also the final act
of the merger between Ayutthaya and the Northern Cities.

Peguan armies launched three attacks on Ayutthaya in 1548, 1563/4,
and 1568/9. On the first occasion, they abandoned the siege because of
the annual flooding in the monsoon; on the second, Ayutthaya capitulated but the Peguan king died soon after; and on the third, the city fell.
Maha Thammaracha of Phitsanulok was allied with Pegu, though the
details differ in various accounts. At the first attack, Maha Thammaracha

[155] *RCA*, 22, ll. 41–2 (*BM*); 23, ll. 7–9 (*BM*).
[156] Phiset, *Phra maha thammaracha*, 103–5; *RCA*, 23–5.
[157] *RCA*, 26, ll. 27–35 (*BM*).
[158] Phiset, *Phra maha thammaracha*, 105.

did not bring his troops from Phitsanulok to aid Ayutthaya until the siege had been lifted. Possibly he was playing a waiting game. In the Van Vliet chronicle's bucolic version of the second attack, Maha Thammaracha beat his wife in a quarrel and her father King Chakkraphat tried to kill him, so he fled to Burma and began "to beseech the King of Pegu to war with Siam."[159] The Burmese king's army approached Ayutthaya via Phitsanulok and Maha Thammaracha was made "field marshal of all of his foot soldiers."[160] After Ayutthaya had capitulated, according to the Burmese chronicles, Maha Thammaracha traveled to Pegu, submitted to the ruler, Bayin-naung, and was rewarded with a Burmese title and regalia.[161] In the Thai chronicles, however, Maha Thammaracha is shown to be on the side of Ayutthaya but holds himself strangely aloof.[162]

When Chakkraphat then tried to draw Lanxang into an alliance against Pegu, Maha Thammaracha disrupted the negotiations by capturing a Lanxang princess on her way to Ayutthaya. In the 1568/9 attack, according to the Van Vliet version, Maha Thammaracha again "advised the Peguan king to resume the war," led part of the Peguan army, and used Phitsanulok as a base. In the Thai chronicles' version, Maha Thammaracha starts out aligned to Ayutthaya but then defects to the Peguan side because of a desperately complex intrigue. Both accounts agree that Maha Thammaracha secured Ayutthaya's fall with the help of his wife's relatives and allied nobles inside the besieged city who opened the gates to the Pegu and Phitsanulok attackers.[163]

The northern nobles now took control at Ayutthaya. King Mahin, Chakkraphat's son, either died during the siege or was hauled away to Burma. The Peguan king "invited Prince Maha Thammaracha to ascend the throne of the Capital City of Ayutthaya."[164] In Van Vliet's version, Maha Thammaracha retained a reference to Phitsanulok in his royal title – Phra Maha Thammaracha Phrajao Song Khwae, where Song Khwae is the old name of Phitsanulok – and this title was used in missives to the Chinese court.[165] Maha Thammaracha appointed other northerners to senior positions, and revised all the appointments of provincial governors.[166] In 1584, his son, Naresuan, swept people down from the northern cities to populate Ayutthaya and its surrounding region.[167] On

---

[159] *Van Vliet's Siam*, 217–18.
[160] *Van Vliet's Siam*, 218.
[161] Aung Thein, "Burmese invasions of Siam," 50.
[162] *RCA*, 35–8 (*BM*).
[163] *RCA*, 71–4 (*BM*); *Van Vliet's Siam*, 220–2; Sunait, *Phama rop thai*, 16–17.
[164] *RCA*, 74, ll. 34–5 (*BM*).
[165] *Van Vliet's Siam*, 223, 227; Wade, *Southeast Asia* online no. 278.
[166] *RCA*, 75–6 (*BM*).
[167] *RCA*, 96, ll. 38–48 (*BM*).

his father's death in 1590, Naresuan ascended the throne. The Van Vliet chronicle's account of the coronation shows Naresuan importing a more militaristic kingship to Ayutthaya: he holds the ceremony of installation in the elephant enclosure, has 1,600 oarsmen burnt alive for making a mistake during the ceremony, and lectures the Ayutthaya nobles:

> This is the way you Siamese must be ruled because you are obstinate people of abominable nature and in a rotten state. But I shall do these things to you until I make you a respected nation. You are as grass on the fertile field; the shorter you are mowed, the more beautifully you grow. I will have gold strewn in the streets and let it lie there for months. Whoever looks at this gold with greed shall die.[168]

The temptation with gold perfectly expresses the contrast between the military ethic and the commercial impulse. The old Ayutthayan elite along with its gods and craftsmen had been hauled away to Pegu. The nobles of the Northern Cities moved in to supplant them. Ayutthaya became the sole capital, but the Sukhothai-Phitsanulok family occupied the throne. The hinterland came down to the center.

Merging Languages

The early inhabitants of the lower Chaophraya Plain probably spoke languages in the Mon-Khmer family. Until the eighth to ninth century CE, the only local language used in inscriptions in the Chaophraya Plain was Mon.[169] Khmer may have emerged as a more standardized language over the Angkorian period, and come into greater use in the Chaophraya towns which show other attachments to Angkorian culture (inscriptions, *barai*, town plans, temple styles). At what point Tai speakers arrived in the area is totally unknown. The word "Tai" appears in Cham records in the tenth century and Khmer records in the eleventh, but may be a proper name not an ethnonym. Some have detected Tai words or distinctive Tai dating systems in Khmer inscriptions of the twelfth and thirteenth centuries; but other scholars have argued this evidence is not conclusive. One of the earliest Thai-language inscriptions, related to the expedition to Angkor in 1431/2, has the text in Thai on one side and Khmer on the other.[170]

The first Ayutthaya kings used the title Somdet, adopted from Khmer. Later the favored form became "Somdet Chao Phraya" in which the three elements come from Khmer, Thai, and Mon, respectively. Of the

[168] *Van Vliet's Siam*, 228–9.
[169] Bauer, "Notes on Mon epigraphy." The possible exception is a set of inscriptions on silver sheets recovered from Wat Song Kop, Chainat; see *Prachum silajaruek phak thi 3*, nos. 44, 50, 51.
[170] Santi, "Silajaruek khun si chaiyarat mongkhonthep."

early terms for nobles, *nai* came from Mon, *khun* might be Khmer, Thai, or Chinese, and *phra* was Khmer.[171] One of the few collections of early Ayutthaya cultural material that can be securely dated is the cache of objects found in the crypt of Wat Ratchaburana, probably deposited in the 1420s. These included a miniature golden bell stupa which closely resembles similar objects from the Mon country, and 191 Khmer-style metal images and votive tablets, including images of the distinctive Angkorean Buddha-under-naga. Among a thousand votive tablets, nine have a dedication inscribed in Thai and three in Khmer. Tablets with an image of the distinctive Sukhothai walking Buddha were so numerous that they were probably being manufactured at Ayutthaya.[172]

Whatever languages the population of Ayutthaya spoke in the city's early years, Thai gradually came to dominate, but this language was also a product of merging traditions. The Thai language which evolved in Ayutthaya (and is the basis of modern Thai) differs greatly from other languages in the Tai linguistic family, including that of Lanna, because of the influence of Mon and Khmer. Mon contributed many basic words, including weights and measures, but also syntax, including particles to modify verbs, and stacking of relative clauses.[173] The influence of Khmer was deeper, more like a merger between the two tongues. Thai retains the tonality and uninflected grammar which are key characteristics of the Tai language family, but has absorbed from Khmer ways of constructing polysyllabic words, such as prefixes to convert adjectives to nouns, complex sentence structures, multiple pronouns to reflect status, as well as many basic function words (to be, or, by, but), and common terms (win, walk, sing, straight). Several everyday terms, especially adjectives, are compounds of a Thai and a Khmer word, or a Thai and a Mon word. This hybridized language must have evolved from three language communities living in close proximity over a long period. The process had begun at Sukhothai, as shown by the vocabulary in Sukhothai inscriptions, but intensified at Ayutthaya. The Khmer language was also affected by this contact, taking many features from Tai, and diverging from other languages in the Mon-Khmer family.[174] Research on DNA shows that today's Khmer-speakers are genetically more closely related to Thai-speakers than to others in the Austro-Asiatic (Mon-Khmer) language

---

[171] The contemporary terms are known from the Chinese records. See Wade, "*Ming shi-lu* as a source," 276–9.

[172] Piriya, *Roots of Thai art*, 302–4; Pattaratorn, "Wat Ratchaburana"; *Jittrakam lae sinlapawatthu nai kru phraprang wat ratchaburana.*

[173] Bauer, "Sukhothai Inscription II"; Vickery, "Some new evidence"; Winai, "Rueang phasa tai thai," 52–4, 70.

[174] Wilaiwan, "Khmero-Thai"; Huffman, "Thai and Cambodian"; Winai, "Rueang phasa tai thai," 44–76.

family, indicating that "genetic exchange between the Thai and Khmer groups was significant and truly reciprocal."[175] Early Ayutthaya was a melting pot.

Lankan Buddhism

Ongkan chaeng nam, believed to be an oath of loyalty to the king from early Ayutthaya, suggests the complexity of religious beliefs. To witness the oath, the text invokes the Hindu trinity, the Three Jewels of Buddhism, the gods in the Three Worlds cosmology, planets, spirits of the ancestors, spirits resident in nature, and various other spirit forces.[176] As at Sukhothai, however, the infusion of ideas and practices from Sri Lanka seems to have given Buddhism a dominant role.

At an early date, a "Maha Thera Saddhammalāṇkācarya of Ayōdhiya" studied in Sri Lanka and, after his return, "propagated Buddhism there until it flourished throughout Dvāravatī" and elsewhere. This might be the monk elsewhere called Dhammakitti, who spent a decade in Lanka before returning to "Ayodayapura," where he wrote a treatise, *Saddhamma saṅgaha*, summarizing the history of Buddhism from the early councils up to Lanka in the twelfth century.[177] In the early fourteenth century, the Sukhothai monk, Sujato, returned from Sri Lanka and established himself for a time at Ayutthaya where the king was "delighted with his virtue." Two other Sukhothai monks, Anomadasi and Sumana, also studied at Ayutthaya, and visited again after their sojourn in Sri Lanka. In the 1370s, a Lankan monk asked for help from the Ayutthaya king to send monks, 500 families, and texts to establish Buddhist teaching in Chiang Tung. In the 1420s, a Chiang Mai monk went to study in Ayutthaya with a teacher called Dhammagambhīra, before going on to Sri Lanka. When he returned to Ayutthaya in 1424, Dhammagambhīra persuaded King Borommaracha II to "abandon the old sāsana [religion], and invite all the monks to be reordained and study the [new] teachings and disciplinary rules." Six hundred monasteries accepted the invitation.[178] In the *Jinakalamalipakaranam* account, there were twenty-five Chiang Mai monks on this trip, they returned with a relic and two Sinhalese monks, and they stayed for four years in Ayutthaya where they re-ordained the preceptor of Borommaracha's queen and another senior monk.[179] Pattaratorn suspects their arrival

[175] Patcharee et al., "Genetic history of Southeast Asian populations," 439.
[176] *Wannakhadi samai ayutthaya*, vol. 1, 7–11.
[177] Penth, "Reflections"; San San Wai, "A study of Saddhama Saṅgaha treatise."
[178] Sommai and Swearer, "Translation of *Tamnān mūlasāsanā*," 77, 80, 87–92.
[179] Ratanapanna Thera, *Sheaf of garlands*, 129–31.

greatly influenced the building and dedication of Wat Ratchaburana, which incorporated a small Sinhalese-style bell-stupa in its design. King Borommaracha appears to have been an enthusiastic participant in the dedication as many gold articles of royal regalia were placed in the crypt.[180] From his visit in the same decade, the Chinese scribe Ma Huan recorded that the ruler of Xian-luo was "a firm believer in the Buddhist religion" and that "the people who become priests and nuns are exceedingly numerous."[181]

This religious enthusiasm was reflected in architecture. The reports of Chinese visitors in the 1420s suggest that the early rulers paid little attention to religious construction. Of the *wat* recorded as royal initiatives in the early reigns, only Wat Mahathat, built or rebuilt by Borommaracha I, was at the center of the city, while Wat Phutthaisawan, possibly built by U Thong, and Wat Phu Khao Thong, possibly built by Ramesuan,[182] were off the island, as was the older stupa of Wat Somonkot to the east. Central Ayutthaya had little to rival the splendid temples and famed Buddha images in the city centers of Sukhothai and Phitsanulok. The building of Wat Ratchaburana may have initiated a custom for kings at Ayutthaya to launch a major project of religious construction at the start of a reign. The next king, Trailokanat, built a new and larger palace, began the royal temple of Wat Phra Si Sanphet on the prior palace site, and restored Wat Phraram. Ramathibodi II built a preaching hall in Wat Phra Si Sanphet and installed there a Buddha image 16 meters tall, similar to the massive images of Sukhothai, plated with 350 kilograms of gold – an image which stunned European visitors two centuries later.[183] In the 1530s, Chairacha built Wat Si Chiang, considered perhaps the finest in Ayutthaya in its time, with a massive image.[184] By this time in the early sixteenth century the area around the Ayutthaya palace was as crowded with temples as any of the Northern Cities. The Buddha images made and honored in the city now included copies of the Sihing Buddha and the Sukhothai-style walking Buddha.[185]

From Ayutthaya of this era, no *wat* chronicle has survived, and there are no stories of relics and powerful monks who defy kings. In the royal chronicles, relics always appear in association with a king not a monk,

---

[180] Pattaratorn, "Wat Ratchaburana."
[181] Ma Huan, *Ying-yai Sheng-lan*, 103; see also Fei Hsin, *Hsing-ch'a Sheng-lan*, 105.
[182] Wat Phu Khao Thong is mentioned only in the later chronicles (*RCA*, 14, l. 17 (*BM*)), and may not have been at the current site.
[183] *RCA*, 19, ll. 6–13; Tachard, *Voyage to Siam*, 180–1.
[184] *Van Vliet's Siam*, 243–4; Wansiri and Pridi, *Krung kao lao rueang*, 226–8; McGill, "Art and architecture," 190–3.
[185] Piriya, "Prawatisat sinlapa ayutthaya," 54–6, 60–1, 150.

as omens.[186] Whether the *sangha* was docile, or memories have been suppressed, is unknown.

Sculpture reflected the rapprochement between Ayutthaya and Sukhothai. Representations of the Buddha in early Ayutthaya, often dubbed "U Thong style," followed earlier Angkorian traditions. The face is square, mouth wide and thin-lipped, eyes seemingly lidless and almost browless, and the body often broad-shouldered and rather robust. Buddha images made at Sukhothai in the same era, and sometimes copied in Ayutthaya workshops, had long oval faces, with a rather pointed chin, a narrow but full mouth, eyes lidded with a distinct brow, and a body slight and graceful, sometimes to the point of androgyny. Until the mid-fifteenth century, these two traditions remained distinct.[187] According to Woodward, however, in images produced around 1500 "the old dichotomy has been completely transcended. Here is a facial type that in its hauteur is intended to go beyond the old oval/square division and bear elements of both traditions."[188] The characteristic images of the middle Ayutthaya era, such as the many seated images modeled on the Sihing Buddha, are a compromise between the robustness of the Angkorian type and the gracefulness of the Sukhothai tradition.

The recording of history also changed. The accounts of the early reigns in the Luang Prasoet chronicle are very short and confined to matters of war, succession, royal construction, and omens, similar to the records kept by astrologers. There is none of the storytelling found in the Lanna chronicles or Sukhothai inscriptions. This begins to change during the Trailokanat reign, with colorful accounts of military events. It changes more decisively from the 1520s with detailed accounts of battles and a larger range of subject matter. The period from the 1470s to the 1520s is also the likely origin of the earliest works of literature in Siamese Thai. The composition of the *Mahachat khamluang*, the royal version of the *jataka* story of Phra Vessantara, is mentioned in the chronicles in 1482/3. The *Yuan phai* military epic dates to the same era. The love poem, *Thawathotsamat* (Twelve months) and the tales of *Samutthakot* and *Anirut* probably date to the early sixteenth century.

Across the late fifteenth and early sixteenth century, Ayutthaya became much more like an inland capital with splendid monuments and a reputation as a center of religion, learning, literature, and craftsmanship.

---

[186] *RCA*, 89, 94, 123, 126, 168, 213, 242, 331.
[187] McGill, "Jatakas, universal monarchs, and the year 2000," esp. 440–2.
[188] Woodward, "Thailand: Buddha images for worship," 5–6.

Conclusion

Xian/Ayutthaya in its first two centuries – beginning before the legendary foundation of 1351 – was a maritime power focused on becoming a dominant force in the trading world of the gulf and peninsula in the post-Srivijaya era. Who the people were and what craft they used in these maritime expeditions are unknown, but most likely they belonged to a shared culture of the Southeast Asian coasts. Over subsequent centuries, this strong orientation to the sea became less central to the economy and the culture. As Sumet Jumsai has shown, however, water symbolism is buried deep in the architecture, cosmology, ritual, myth, and literature of Siam. While this was obviously sustained by the continuing importance of rivers and canals for transport and residence, the origins lay in the sea.[189]

This maritime orientation is visible in the first direct records of the city (Ma Huan and Fei Hsin) and helps to explain the murky nature of its early history – no inscriptions, few monuments, Chinese involvement, a confusion of founder legends probably assembled later, and a shaky dynastic chronology. It was more a commercial port than a ritual capital.

Unlike most port-cities in the archipelago, Ayutthaya had a large hinterland, accessible by waterways. Driven by the commercial logic of controlling the trade routes and supply sources on which its commercial prominence depended, Ayutthaya set out to *become* a territorial power. This project drew Ayutthaya into a complex relationship with the Northern Cities in its immediate hinterland. Ayutthaya did not quickly conquer and absorb these cities in the early fifteenth century, as sometimes imagined. Rather, Sukhothai remained an important ritual center; Phitsanulok remained the key strategic center and for long periods the effective capital; and the northern armies remained critical for neutralizing the ambitious state of Lanna. The rulers of the Northern Cities retained their status, and their capitals became more splendid.

The merger of Ayutthaya and the Northern Cities was driven not so much by armed might as by the intertwining of the Suphanburi and Sukhothai families, and by Ayutthaya's gradual absorption of people, culture, language, aesthetics, and administrative practice from this northern region. In the early sixteenth century, northern nobles became kingmakers at Ayutthaya. In the 1560s, they allied with the Peguan ruler to dislodge the old elite and dominate the city. Administrative systems, religious sculpture, literary production, and the Thai language were shaped by this merger.

[189] Sumet, *Naga*.

Since the late thirteenth century, a settlement in a meander of the Lopburi River had become first a prospering port-city and then a religious, royal, and cultural center of growing power and splendor. The society of this city and its hinterland was shaped by a rising trend of warfare in the region.

3   An Age of Warfare

From the late 1300s there was a rise in warring across Mainland Southeast Asia. Many factors contributed to this increase in organized violence: new technologies of warfare, the ambitions of rulers, and competition over access to maritime trade, important to rulers both as a generator of wealth, and as a source of arms and other strategic goods.

For around two centuries, war had a significant role in shaping society. Success in war was the route to social advancement for both nobles and commoners. People were regimented under systems for conscription. A military ethos infused the practice of the court and the literary works of the era. Population probably declined, largely as a result of the disease and disruption attendant on war.

Around 1600, the incidence of warfare dropped sharply. Fighting did not disappear altogether, but it was reduced to a much lower level. People had begun to resist recruitment, partly through rebellion and partly through flight. Cities had invested in better forms of defense which resulted in many conflicts ending in stalemate.

The main sources for this era are the chronicles, both of Ayutthaya and of neighboring territories, and the reports of early European visitors, principally Portuguese. Some insights into the ideas that shaped society and institutions are found in a handful of surviving literary works, along with religious texts and law codes.

Rising Violence

Warring increased in several stages. In the first, from the 1380s onwards, Ayutthaya mounted expeditions into the Northern Cities. In the second, the armies ranged further afield – to Angkor in 1431/2 and to Chiang Mai for the first time in 1442/3. In the third stage from around 1450, Ayutthaya and Lanna clashed repeatedly in contest over the Northern Cities for almost a century. To the west, there was a similar pattern of conflict between the Shan regions to the north, Burmese towns in the

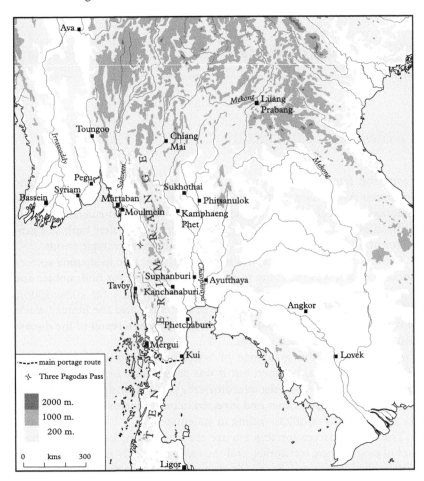

Map 3.1. Principal places in sixteenth-century wars in Mainland Southeast Asia

middle, and the Mon regions near the coast. To the east, on the lower reaches of the Mekong, rival Khmer dynasts first fought for precedence, and later these conflicts were complicated by intrusions of Vietnamese and Cham. In the fourth stage, from the 1540s, warring crossed the boundaries between these three basins (see Map 3.1). In 1548, a Peguan army crossed the Tenasserim range and attacked Ayutthaya. In 1551, an Ayutthaya army assaulted the new Khmer port capital of Lovek. Unlike earlier expeditions, these were direct attacks by one capital on another. Underlying this conflict lay the importance of maritime trade as a source of wealth, weaponry, and royal power.

Cross-Basin Warfare

The history of the Irrawaddy Basin over the fifteenth century runs strikingly parallel to that of the Chaophraya Basin. A new political center developed in the delta zone among a group of towns, including Pegu, Syriam, and Martaban, oriented to the rising trade in the Indian Ocean. A series of wars fought between this coastal zone and the historical center in the more heavily populated hinterland led eventually to the creation of a new state with its capital in the delta zone at Pegu. The major difference from the Chaophraya Basin was that this new state was dominated from the start by the Burmese warrior princes of the hinterland rather than the Mons of the delta zone.[1]

Within this similarity between the Irrawaddy and Chaophraya histories lay the seeds of conflict. The dynasts of both centers developed pretensions to extend their networks even wider, expressed in rival claims to the title of *cakkavattin* or universal emperor, the ideal of supreme rule described in the *Traiphum*, the Buddhist cosmology of the Three Worlds.[2] More concretely, the two centers clashed over possession of two areas of commercial and strategic significance: first, Chiang Mai, which commanded the trade route northward into China; second and more important, the neck of the peninsula with its portage routes between the Indian Ocean and South China Seas.

Between 1440 and 1490 Ayutthaya took control of this portage route. In 1441/2, Ayutthaya captured Thaithong, a town probably north of Tavoy (Tawai, Dawei).[3] By the 1460s, Ayutthaya controlled Tenasserim (Tanaosi, Tanintharyi) along with its twin port of Mergui (Marit, Myeik) which had the best natural harbor on this coast.[4] In 1488/9, an Ayutthayan army also captured Tavoy.[5] From Mergui a portage route led up the Tenasserim River, over a low pass down to the coast at Kui(buri), and onwards by water to Ayutthaya, taking ten to twenty days.[6] The value of this route increased after the Portuguese captured Melaka in 1511 and dominated the straits, inducing Asian traders to seek alternative routes.

With control of the portage route and coastal ports, Ayutthaya's westward trade increased. In the reign of Ramathibodi II (1491–1529),

[1] Lieberman, *Strange parallels*, vol. 1, 123–54.
[2] Sunait, "Cakravartin ideology."
[3] Winai, "Phraratchaphongsawadan krung si ayutthaya chabap ho phra samut wachirayan," 66–9.
[4] *RCA*, 18, l. 17 (*LP*); Vickery, "Khmer inscriptions of Tenasserim."
[5] *RCA*, 18, ll. 1720 (*LP*).
[6] *Travels of Ludovico di Varthema*, 197–8; Muhammad Rabi, *Ship of Sulaiman*, 46–7.

trade opened up with southern India, announced in the Van Vliet
chronicle with the tale of a king who threw a spear from India to Siam
in pique because the Ayutthaya king had adopted the same name of
Ram, but who then made friends. Thereafter, "Moorish traders from
the Coromandel Coast came with their cloth," and the king "was such
a great lover of foreign nations that he sent various missions to entice
them to his land."[7] Writing in the 1510s, Pires mentions "Kling cloths
in the fashion of Siam," showing that cloth was already being made
in southern India for export to Siam.[8] The fifteenth-century Persian
historian Abd-al Razzaq recorded that the traders of Ormuz visited
both Tenasserim and Shahr-i-nao, the "new city," meaning Ayutthaya.
A late fifteenth-century Arabic geography referred to the western
coast of the peninsula as *Barr al-Siam* or *Mul al-Siam*, meaning the
coast or mainland of Siam respectively.[9] Using information from the
Portuguese sea-captains and envoys sent to explore the region after
1511, Duarte Barbosa reported that the Ayutthaya ruler controlled
ports on both sides of the peninsula, especially Tenasserim, Mergui,
Kedah, and Selangor, to which ships from Arabia and Bengal brought
copper, quicksilver, vermilion, cloth, silk, saffron, coral, and opium.
In the 1550s, João de Barros included the west-coast ports of Tavoy,
Mergui, Tenasserim, Rey Tagala (near Martaban), and Cholom (possibly Salang, modern Phuket) among Ayutthaya's dependencies. He also
identified Ayutthaya along with China and Vijayanagar as the three
great powers of Asia.[10]

Ayutthaya's involvement on the upper peninsula brought it into conflict
with Pegu. Around the same time that Ayutthaya acquired Tenasserim,
the Burmese capital at Pegu took Martaban, and it later wrested control
of Tavoy. By the 1530s, Borommaracha IV of Ayutthaya "warred often
with Lan Chang and Pegu" and died from smallpox in 1533 on return
from a campaign in the border region. Six years later an Ayutthayan
army attacked Chiang Krai and Chiang Kran, the latter probably Gyaing
on the route to Martaban. In 1546, the Burmese chronicles record that
Ayutthaya sent a force of "200 elephants, 1,000 horse and 60,000 men"
to capture Tavoy.[11] In response, Tabinshweti of Pegu led an army to attack

[7] *Van Vliet's Siam*, 209–13.
[8] Guy, *Woven cargoes*, 122. Kling or Keling is a Malay term for Indian, adopted by the
Dutch to refer to south India.
[9] Tibbetts, *Study of the Arabic texts*, 99, 233; Tibbetts, *Arab navigation in the Indian
Ocean*, 477.
[10] Campos, "Early Portuguese accounts," 9.
[11] *Van Vliet's Siam*, 214; *RCA*, 20, ll. 24–5 (*LP*); Sunait, "Origins of Siamese–Burmese
warfare," 90.

Ayutthaya in 1548. The intensity of this conflict reflected how important the Indian Ocean trade and the portage route had become to the two main political centers.

While Ayutthaya was thus embroiled, a Khmer army raided into Siamese territory. Since its foray to Angkor in 1431/2, Ayutthaya had paid little attention to its eastern neighbor, except for some scrappy raids on border areas. The capital of the Khmer had shifted from inland Angkor to Lovek on the lower Mekong, pulled by the magnet of maritime trade. Lovek had become a rival to Ayutthaya for handling goods from the interior forests, especially musk, benzoin, and lac. The port had a settlement of 2,000 Chinese, and quarters for Japanese, Arabs, Spanish, Portuguese, and archipelago traders.[12] After the Peguan threat passed, an Ayutthayan army attacked Lovek in 1551.

These two expeditions – from Pegu to Ayutthaya, and from Ayutthaya to Lovek – transgressed the borders between spheres of influence, not by crossing lines on a map, but by marching armies across difficult tracts of hill and forest. These three centers had become not only rivals in the increasingly valuable maritime trade, but also prizes in themselves because of their wealth. Pinto claimed the Peguan nobles encouraged their ruler to attack Ayutthaya on cost-benefit grounds:

They all told him that under no circumstances should he allow this opportunity [to attack Siam] to escape him, since that kingdom was one of the best in the world, both for its riches and abundance of everything; moreover, the time and circumstances were all in his favor and gave promise of a victory so cheap that, to all appearances, its conquest could not possibly cost him more than a year's revenue, no matter how much of his treasure he was willing to spend.[13]

According to the Thai chronicles, Pegu announced its aggression against Ayutthaya with a letter explaining, "Naturally, in any Kingdom having beautiful women, white elephants, short-tusked elephants, jewel mines and gold mines, it is a rule that these will give rise to warfare."[14]

Elephants, Guns, and Mercenaries

The increase in the intensity of warfare ran in parallel with changes in military technology. The arrival of gunpowder has attracted most of the scholarly attention, but the increased use of elephants was more significant in the early phase.

---

[12] Puangthong, "War and trade," 34–9.
[13] Pinto, *Travels*, 411.
[14] *RCA*, 43, ll. 37–9 (*BM*).

Elephants

Yuan phai, "Defeat of the Yuan," an epic poem that describes a battle between Ayutthaya and Lanna in 1474/5, has a detailed, contemporary description of an army marching to battle. The most important division is the elephant brigade. The poem devotes 150 lines to around sixty individual elephants, with names and capsule descriptions: "Kaeo Jakrarat is skilled, adept, and strong ... Banphumi Monthon, safe from pike and gun ... Moen Monsak, shaped to fill a foe with fear."[15] The cavalry occupies only six verses with seventeen horses individually named, while only a handful of humans are granted the honor of a personal name in the whole poem, and none merits a description.

In the Sukhothai records and the early Lanna chronicles, rulers ride to war on elephants and fight elephant duels, but elephants are not used in large numbers. In 1498, Vasco da Gama reported that Ayutthaya could field 400 elephants, and in 1551 Barros raised this figure to ten thousand.[16] This increase, which probably occurred slightly earlier than these sources suggest, was a result of intense hunting. The first report of an Ayutthaya king leading an elephant hunt is dated to 1483/4,[17] and the reports increase in frequency from then onwards. Freelancing groups also hunted elephants to supply the king.[18] The discovery of many "white" elephants in the early sixteenth century was a result of the increased scale of hunting. Several were found in the foothills of the Tenasserim range to the west of Ayutthaya. The proximity of this rich hunting ground may have been an important factor in Ayutthaya's military dominance in the lower Chaophraya Plain. The hunting parties were massive. De Coutre described King Naresuan on a hunt in the 1590s with 20,000 men and 3,000 boats.[19]

Elephants transformed warfare in three main ways. They carried equipment, particularly the heavy gear needed in siege warfare, and were vital to the mobility of armies between river basins. They elevated the king and nobles above the fray of hand-to-hand fighting. In massed numbers at the charge, often primed with liquor, they were simply terrifying. Battle accounts such as *Yuan phai* dwell on the fearsomeness of elephants in musth – "leaking oil from cheeks back to the tail."[20] In the romance of

[15] Baker and Pasuk, *Yuan phai*, stanzas 211–48.
[16] *Travels of Ludovico di Varthema*, 198; Campos, "Early Portuguese accounts," 3, 11. Charney (*Southeast Asian warfare*, 137) notes that early European accounts exaggerated the numbers of elephants, but the increase is still evident.
[17] *RCA*, 18, ll. 5–6 (*LP*).
[18] Charney, *Southeast Asian warfare*, 139.
[19] Borschberg, *Memoirs and memorials*, 120.
[20] Baker and Pasuk, *Yuan phai*, stanza 232.

war in this era, the elephant duel has a role similar to the knightly joust in medieval Europe. Two opposing kings or princes contest, thus taking credit for the victory or loss, and showing Buddhist compassion by relieving their men from the need to fight and die. But while the horses are incidental to the tales of jousting, the elephants are heroes of the duel. The battle in *Yuan phai* is resolved by a duel in which the Ayutthaya elephant, rather than its rider, wins the day. In some versions of the most famous battle scene in Thai schoolbook history, Naresuan's elephant duel at Nong Sarai in 1593, the hero is not the king but his elephant which unbalances a much larger opponent, and is rewarded with the title of Chaophraya Prap Hongsa, Lord Crusher of Pegu.[21] These duel stories, along with the enthusiasm for naming the war elephants, attest to the importance of elephants in the warfare of this era. Among the elephants in *Yuan phai*, "some so superb surpass a city's worth."[22]

Knowledge of elephants was a branch of military science. Elephants were classified by physical characteristics and grouped into lineages associated with the gods of the Hindu pantheon. Elaborate *Tamra chang*, elephant manuals, described the mood and talents of different lineages. Surviving manuals date no earlier than the eighteenth century, but the vocabulary of elephant science is present in the *Yuan phai* poem and the chronicles.[23]

The use of horses also increased. Vasco da Gama reckoned Ayutthaya could field 4,000 horse-borne cavalry in 1498, and Barros put the figure at 25,000 in 1551. In the chronicles, the Pegu army in 1548 included 15,000 horse.[24] Locally bred horses were considered inferior in quality, and better stock was imported from India, Arabia, and later Japan.[25] *Sinthop*, meaning from Sind, became the conventional term for a good-quality horse in poetry. As with elephants, a science of classification was developed, based mainly on color of hide and shape of tail, and recorded in manuals.

Guns and Mercenaries

In the early sixteenth century there was an arms race, involving two main items: western gunpowder technology, which came with the arrival of the

---

[21] *Van Vliet's* Siam, 186–9; *RCA*, 130–1; Tun Aung Chain, *Chronicle of Ayutthaya*, 40–1; Terwiel, "What happened at Nong Sarai?"
[22] Baker and Pasuk, *Yuan phai*, stanza 238.
[23] *RCA*, 43 (*BM*); *Tamra chang*.
[24] Campos, "Early Portuguese accounts," 3; *RCA*, 44 (*BM*).
[25] Dhiravat, "Javanese horses for the court of Ayutthaya"; Satow, "Notes on the intercourse between Japan and Siam," 151, 159, 164, 170.

Portuguese in the region, and soldiers for hire, who increased in numbers with the appearance of Portuguese adventurers and many others.

The earliest gunpowder-using firearms were developed in China around the turn of the fourteenth century. Large quantities were manufactured by the 1380s and found their way to northern parts of Southeast Asia soon after. A copper-cast cannon is first mentioned in Chiang Mai in 1411.[26] The early weapons were mainly bombards or bazooka-like tube guns,[27] and probably few in number, but still had a special capacity to intimidate. In the 1440s, the Phrae ruler surrendered in terror after Chiang Mai besiegers shot the tops of sugar-palm trees, splitting them "from crown to root." In the 1440s, the Chiang Mai forces took Nan by using cannon to bombard the gates. In the fighting against Ayutthaya in the 1450s and 1460s, the Chiang Mai chronicles claim that southerners "died in great numbers," and a son of the Ayutthaya king may have been wounded by a bullet. In *Yuan phai*'s description of preparing the defenses of Chaliang in 1474/5, there are "guns installed at each defile and slit [and] cannons placed to best defend stockades."[28]

Though startling, this early ordnance was limited in range, accuracy, and efficacy. In the late fifteenth century, Europeans and Turks developed the technology of casting cannon, which soon arrived in the region. In 1511, a first Portuguese mission arrived in Ayutthaya from Melaka. In 1518, a third mission arrived with guns, munitions, and some Portuguese soldiers who immediately accompanied an army sent to repel a Lanna intrusion into the Northern Cities. In return, the Portuguese were granted permission to trade at Ayutthaya and for a short time were enthusiastic about sending ships from Melaka to Ayutthaya, but they lost interest after finding no spices and never established a factory. As suppliers of military expertise, however, the Portuguese played a major role. In the early 1520s, Domingo de Seixas was arrested for pirating a ship owned by the governor of Tenasserim, and he redeemed himself by offering his military services to the Ayutthaya king. Many Portuguese left the crown service and found employment with Siamese and other rulers because of their ability to cast cannons, teach others how to make and use them, and serve as artillerymen in the field. By the 1540s, there were 120 Portuguese in the personal guard of King Chairacha. Seixas and two Turks acted as field commanders on an expedition against Lanna

---

[26] Sun, "Military technology transfers from Ming China," 497–8, 507; Sun, "Saltpetre trade," 134; Wyatt and Aroonrut, *Chiang Mai chronicle*, 69–70.

[27] Charney, *Southeast Asian warfare*, 43–7; Sun, "Chinese-style gunpowder weapons in Southeast Asia."

[28] Wyatt and Aroonrut, *Chiang Mai chronicle*, 81, 86; Wyatt, *Nan chronicle*, 53; Baker and Pasuk, *Yuan phai*, stanza 160.

around 1540, after which Seixas left the region. By 1548, the number of Portuguese soldiers at Ayutthaya had dwindled to fifty, but they had already transferred some of their technology.[29] The first Portuguese visitors to Ayutthaya in the 1510s claimed there were few guns and no skills to manufacture them, but Diogo de Couto reported in 1548 that King Chakkraphat had "issued orders to found many pieces of bronze artillery, since he had excellent craftsmen and much copper, which comes there every year from China. It is said that there were 4,000 artillery pieces positioned on the walls [of Ayutthaya]." Portuguese friars in the 1590s reckoned there were "eight hundred pieces of artillery" on these walls.[30]

The supply of mercenaries increased in the same era. By the 1540s, the Ayutthaya army included not only Portuguese but also Luzons, Borneans, Chams, Javanese, and Minangkabauans. Pinto reckoned "foreign mercenaries from different nations" numbered 70,000 or a sixth of the army.[31] As Pinto tended to exaggerate numbers, the proportion is more significant than the total.

The Portuguese contribution to military strength was much greater in Burma. By 1519, the Portuguese had established a factory at Martaban which acquired rice to supply Melaka. The Pegu rulers bought Portuguese arms and hired Portuguese military experts, including Diego Soares de Melo, a renegade nobleman with a string of murders behind him in Europe and India, and a spell as a pirate in Goa. Arriving in 1538, he became the chief "field commander" of King Tabinshweti, was reputedly paid over ten times as much as Seixas at Ayutthaya, and was given a royal title and the governorship of Pegu. Soares was credited with directing the artillery which battered down the walls of Martaban in 1540–41, and with heading a band of 185 Portuguese in the 1548 attack on Ayutthaya. This siege was also prosecuted with "ingenious military devices invented daily ... by a Greek engineer."[32]

The artillery pieces that the Portuguese introduced in the early sixteenth century were clumsy and often dangerous, and their impact on warfare was limited. By mid-century, however, the Portuguese had begun to import hand-carried matchlock guns, particularly the arquebus, which had a larger impact. More of these weapons went to Pegu

---

[29] Bras de Albuquerque, "Beginning: Malacca and Ayutthaya"; Charney, "From merchants to musketeers," 73–8; Suthachai, "Portuguese lançados in Asia," 46–7; Pinto, *Travels*, 412–16; Trakulhun, "Suspicious friends," 182–4.
[30] Breazeale, "Ayutthaya under siege," 39; Ribadeneira, *Historia del archipelago*, vol. 1, 427.
[31] Pinto, *Travels*, 400.
[32] Trakulhun, "Suspicious friends," 15–16; Breazeale, "Ayutthaya under siege," 43; Pinto, *Travels*, 416.

than to Ayutthaya. Pinto estimated a thousand Portuguese gunners, a thousand cannon, and 60,000 arquebuses accompanied the 1563 attack on Ayutthaya. Cesare Frederike estimated the Peguan army had "80,000 arquebusses" as well as cannon.[33] The Peguan army also had foreign soldiers from all round the Indian Ocean and South China Sea: Turks, Abyssinians, Moors, Malabaris, Achinese, Javanese, Malays, "Luzons, Borneans, and Chams with some Menangkabowans among them."[34]

Pegu and Ayutthaya

The Peguan force may also have had an advantage in sheer numbers. Tabinshweti's early conquests had incorporated a broad area with a large population base for recruitment. Pinto estimated the invading force in 1548 as 800,000 men including 100,000 foreign mercenaries, 40,000 horse, 5,000 elephants, and 1,000 artillery pieces. Although these figures are inflated by Pinto's usual exaggeration, the army was probably enormous.

Ayutthaya had never been attacked before, and its defensive walls were inadequate. According to a Portuguese account, the city survived in 1548 because of the skill of the Portuguese gunners, who resisted attempts to bribe them to change sides. Part of the Burmese army detoured to besiege Kamphaeng Phet, where the desperate defenders "filled many jars with human excrement, diluted with urine, and hurled them down from the wall," a tactic which "stupefied" the Burmese sappers attempting to mine the defenses.[35] According to Pinto, a squad of Turks scaled the walls of Ayutthaya but were cut to pieces by "three thousand Javanese *amucks.*" The city survived because of massive human sacrifice – "the courtyard inside the city ... completely covered with dead bodies and rivers of blood" – and because Tabinshweti raised the siege after hearing of a revolt in his capital.[36]

After 1549, Ayutthaya's city walls were rebuilt with brick, and they were remodeled again after 1563. Elephants were hunted so intensively that some four to seven white elephants were discovered over eleven years.[37] More was invested in artillery so that by 1569 cannons were crucial to the city's defense.[38]

---

[33] Quoted in Reid, *Southeast Asia in the age of commerce,* vol. 2, 224.

[34] Suthachai, "Portuguese lançados in Asia," 46; Charney, "From merchants to musketeers," 77–8; Pinto, *Travels,* 412, 415.

[35] Breazeale, "Ayutthaya under siege," 47.

[36] Pinto, *Travels,* 414–8; *RCA,* 32–4 (*BM*). *Amuck* (amok) is a Malay word for a crazed warrior.

[37] From 1549 to 1560, see *RCA,* 28–31 (*LP*) and 42 (*BM*).

[38] Charney, *Southeast Asian warfare,* 93.

By 1560, Maha Thammaracha of Phitsanulok had openly aligned with Pegu (see Chapter 2). According to Van Vliet, Maha Thammaracha fled to Pegu after Chakkraphat tried to kill him, and "began to beseech the King of Pegu to war with Siam," but the king of Pegu was initially reluctant, until Maha Thammaracha provoked his jealousy of Chakkraphat's seven white elephants.[39]

The white or albino elephant had become a Palladium of monarchy across the Buddhist states of Mainland Southeast Asia. In the *Traiphum*, the "gem elephant" is one of the seven attributes of the *cakkavattin*, or universal emperor. As Sunait has shown, this image of an ideal emperor protecting the realm of Buddhism became part of the aspiration and legitimization of the expansionary dynasts of this era. The concept justified the increasing domination of the great centers over many lesser cities, and was invoked to justify aggression against rival rulers on grounds that they failed to nurture Buddhism.[40] In Southeast Asia, the *Traiphum*'s concept of a "gem elephant" was translated into a belief in the symbolic power of elephants with unusual characteristics, especially the white elephant. The capture of a white elephant is first reported in the Ayutthaya chronicles in 1471/2.[41] Under the Ayutthaya Palace Law, which dates from the same time, anyone discovering an auspicious elephant was bound to deliver it to the king and was richly rewarded.[42] The chronicles vaunt the connection between Chakkraphat's many white elephants and the glory of the city, particularly as a center of trade:

Ayutthaya was great and overflowing due to its possession of as many as seven white elephants. Its fame spread to all foreign countries and ships of French, English, Dutch and Surat merchants, as well as Chinese junks came to trade in vast numbers.[43]

Tabinshweti's brother-in-law and successor, Bayin-naung, requested Ayutthaya to send two white elephants. The request, interpreted as a demand for Ayutthaya to admit subordination to Pegu, was refused. In 1564 Bayin-naung marched an army through the Northern Cities to Ayutthaya, which capitulated after the Portuguese gunners in the Peguan army had mounted cannon on high platforms and "fired into the city, hitting many monasteries and houses of people and causing destruction every day."[44] Chakkraphat agreed to present the Burmese king with four

---

[39] *Van Vliet's Siam*, 218.
[40] Sunait, "Cakravartin ideology."
[41] *RCA*, 17, ll. 33–4 (*LP*).
[42] Baker and Pasuk, *Palace Law of Ayutthaya*, 92 (clause 43).
[43] *RCA*, 42, ll. 29–34 (*BM*). "French, English, Dutch" merchants were not present at this date. A later copyist has probably expanded the word "*farang*," meaning Portuguese in the original.
[44] Damrong, *Our wars with the Burmese*, 39.

white elephants, and to allow a royal son and two nobles to be taken away to Pegu as hostages. The Peguans carted away many skilled craftsmen and artists, but made no attempt to seize important ritual objects, to loot the city, or to remove people in large numbers.[45]

As Maha Thammaracha of Phitsanulok had sided with Pegu, Ayutthaya lacked the military resources of the Northern Cities, and could recruit troops only from the lower delta in an area bounded by Phetchaburi, Suphanburi, Chainat, and Nakhon Nayok.[46] In desperation, Chakkraphat looked further afield for allies. He called on the ruler of the port of Pattani to come with an armed force. Seeing Ayutthaya's weakness, this Pattani ruler attempted a coup of his own, attacking the palace with 300 men, but his troops were massacred.[47] Chakkraphat next enlisted Lanxang (Luang Prabang) as an ally, and agreed to the Lanxang ruler's request for his eldest daughter. A pact was negotiated by the *uparaja* of the two domains, consecrated by monks on both sides, inscribed on stone, and commemorated by a stupa.[48] Maha Thammaracha attempted to disrupt this Ayutthaya–Lanxang alliance by capturing Chakkraphat's daughter en route to Lanxang, and sending her off to Pegu. He also blocked the Lanxang army sent to aid Ayutthaya in 1568/9.

In 1569 Ayutthaya fell to the combined forces of Pegu and Phitsanulok, as related in Chapter 2. On this occasion, Peguan policy was very different from that of 1564, when it had been content to exert its superiority by the removal of white elephants, royal sons, and craftsmen. This time it aimed to undermine Ayutthaya's power as a rival political and trading center. The Peguan army was enormous – estimates range between 0.5 and 1.8 million – and like all armies of this era, incentivized by gain. From Pegu, Caesar Frederike reported:

I was at the coming home and returning from the warres was a goodly sight to behold, to see the Elephants come home in a square, laden with Gold, Silver, Jewels, and with Noble men and women that were taken Prisoners in that Citie.[49]

According to the Burmese chronicles,

there was not a single one in the whole of the fifty-four brigades who did not obtain one or two coolie loads of loot in the form of gold, silver, wearing apparel etc. Entertainments were held in every brigade for many days.[50]

---

[45] *RCA*, 44, 47–9; Than Tun, "Ayut'a men in the service of Burmese kings," 96–7.
[46] *RCA*, 60, ll. 32–6 (*BM*).
[47] *RCA*, 49 (*LP*); *Van Vliet's Siam*, 219; Teeuw and Wyatt, *Hikayat Patani*, vol. 2, 157–61, 231–5.
[48] Griswold and Prasert, "An inscription of 1563 A.D.," 60.
[49] Frederike, "Extracts of Master Caesar Frederike," 111.
[50] Aung Thein, "Burmese invasions of Siam," 67.

The Ayutthaya chronicles state that the Peguan army took away "all the statues," including those that had been taken from Angkor in 1431/2, along with "the royal adornments and the golden utensils reserved for reigning kings, and the concubines and attendants."[51] When Pegu attacked Lanxang two years later, the Pegu army included 200 elephants, 1,500 horse, and 30,000 men, all taken from Ayutthaya.[52] This was something new in the region – a massive transfer of the ingredients of royal power from one capital to another.[53]

The commercial consequences of the Pegu victory were great. Bayin-naung was now in command of all the ports on the upper western side of the peninsula. He appointed officials at Tavoy and Mergui to supervise merchant shipping, and built his own fleet to trade. He also controlled the sources of supply in the interior. In 1557–58, he marched an army into Lanna, and later sent his son to rule there. He imposed tribute quotas on the interior Tai states in luxury export products of musk, gold, and gems, formerly supplied by private traders.[54] Against this competition, Ayutthaya's prominence in regional trade declined dramatically. Of the eighty-eight licenses issued to junks by the Chinese port authorities over 1589 to 1592, only four were destined for Ayutthaya.[55] According to Faria y Sousa, Pegu "became the powerfullest Monarchy in Asia, except that of China."[56] A few years later, another Portuguese reckoned the ruler of Pegu had become "second [to China] in population and wealth in the East after he subdued the King of Siam, till then one of the three most powerful in that part of the world."[57]

War and Society

In recent centuries, war has been an enterprise conducted by states for the acquisition or defense of territory. The warring that is the subject of this chapter was different in several ways.

Victors were generally intent on acquiring resources, not territory. At its simplest, the object was simply loot – the gold, silver, and jewels kept in palace treasuries or made into religious objects. Also important were weapons, noble women to swell the numbers in the inner palace, and valuable people, including, craftsmen, entertainers, and other experts.

---

[51] *RCA*, 74, ll. 21–32 (*PC*).
[52] Than Tun, "Ayut'a men in the service of Burmese kings," 100.
[53] Ayutthaya took images from Angkor in 1431/2, but no source suggests a transfer on this scale.
[54] Lieberman, *Burmese administrative cycles*, 31.
[55] Reid, "Documenting the rise and fall," 8.
[56] Lieberman, *Burmese administrative cycles*, 32.
[57] Macgregor, "Brief account of the kingdom of Pegu," 108.

The list of those swept from Ayutthaya to Pegu in 1563/4 included artists, smiths, dyers, stone carvers, woodworkers, stucco molders, actors, dancers, doctors (experts) for elephants and horses, cooks, and hairdressers.[58] Many campaigns were conducted principally to seize people to become soldiers or slaves and enhance the population of the realm. The numbers involved were significant and often closely recorded. In one expedition to the Shan regions in the 1460s, Tilokarat of Chiang Mai hauled away "Shans as his subjects, both male and female, numbering 12,328 persons."[59]

Victors rarely dislodged or destroyed their rival rulers but rather brought them under their sway. Sometimes, as at Ayutthaya's capture of Angkor in 1431/2, a king might send a son or other relative to rule a defeated city, but history showed that blood was not a reliable guarantee of loyalty. More often, the defeated ruler would be left in place, made to swear an oath of fealty, required to provide a sister or daughter to become wife of his overlord, and perhaps also a son to serve as an additional hostage. Sometimes the overlord would provide the subordinate with resources including a royally gifted wife, regalia, weapons, and officials that made the subordinate a more effective ally, while the wife and officials could serve as informants. The subordinate ruler was not crushed out of existence, but strengthened so he could become a more stable and useful dependent. Condominas called this "emboxment."[60] In the political vocabulary of the time, kingship and sovereignty were relative rather than absolute. The terms *ekaraja* or *pathommaraja*, meaning "primary king," implied the existence of kings at lower levels. Similarly, the term *itsara* meant "supremacy" or "overlordship," the elevation of one king over another.

Another difference from modern practice was that war was not solely an enterprise of states or rulers, but was the ladder of success for all, from top to bottom of the social pyramid. For nobles, success in war was a way to gain royal favor, promotion up the hierarchy, and a share in the loot. Ordinary soldiers were also incentivized by shares in the rewards. Before battle, King Mangrai of Chiang Mai "distributed rewards of cowries and silver to them, for them to be his strength." In mid-battle rulers offered more funds to encourage their own troops, and to tempt enemy soldiers to defect. In the throes of an attack on Lamphun, Mangrai "bestowed lavish rewards upon every one of his troops" to persuade them to undertake

---

[58] Than Tun, "Ayut'a men in the service of Burmese kings," 96–7.
[59] Wyatt and Aroonrut, *Chiang Mai chronicle*, 99.
[60] Condominas, *From Lawa to Mon*, 35, 40, 79, 84. See also Tambiah, *World conqueror*, 111–15, 123–4.

the final assault.[61] In *Yuan phai*, the celebration of Ayutthaya's victory focuses on the capture of women, wealth, and people:

> Their ladies, lustrous skin and bosoms – lost!
> Their weapons, kit in no small measure – lost!
> Their countless bars of gold and children – lost!
> Their howdahs gilt and many tuskers – lost!
> …
> Our men, unstoppable, seize silver, gold.
> Their ladies, tuskers, horse are sent to Him [the king].
> We tie up prisoners, drag them round by horse.
> When tired, they're sold away or swapped for booze.[62]

The Palace Law of Ayutthaya, which may date to the 1460s, set out a graded scale of rewards for ordinary soldiers:

Anyone who rides a horse to battle and takes a head is rewarded with a golden bowl, cloth, and promotion … A *phrai* soldier or king's guard up to 400 *sakdina* who takes a lord is rewarded with good gold, good silver, appointment to eat [govern] a city, and a royally-presented wife.[63]

This last reward transported the receiver from the bottom of the social scale to near the top. Soldiers collected heads from the battlefield to claim their dues. In *Yuan phai*, the Ayutthaya troops "lop off heads and lug them back to give the king."[64] After a skirmish during the 1548 attack on Ayutthaya the chronicles report: "The [Peguan] cavalrymen who had taken heads from the men of the Capital constituted about four-fifths of his force." During the siege of Ayutthaya in 1563, skirmishing parties "killed the men of Hongsawadi, and captured many heads to present to the King."[65] The Palace Law also listed lesser rewards for capturing weapons, and even a prize for simply coming back alive and being available to fight again. From the king down to the lowliest foot soldier, warfare was probably the most important way to rise in wealth and status. This made war a collective enterprise.

Manning War

The size of the infantry forces put into the field seems to have increased sharply during these years. Vasco da Gama reckoned Ayutthaya had 20,000 infantry around 1500.[66] The army that is rather carefully

---

[61] Wyatt and Aroonrut, *Chiang Mai chronicle*, 46, 51–2.
[62] Baker and Pasuk, *Yuan phai*, stanzas 285–8.
[63] Baker and Pasuk, *Palace Law of Ayutthaya*, 93 (clause 46).
[64] Baker and Pasuk, *Yuan phai*, stanza 280.
[65] *RCA*, 34, ll. 41–2 (*BM*); 61, ll. 37–9(*BM*); 62, ll. 1–3 (*BM*).
[66] Campos, "Early Portuguese accounts," 3.

described in the *Yuan phai* epic had a total of 26,000 men contributed by three of the Northern Cities (Phitsanulok, Sukhothai, and Kamphaeng Phet).[67] According to the chronicles, Ayutthaya dispatched 50,000 plus a naval force to Cambodia in 1551, and another army of 30,000 in 1556.[68] Barros reckoned the full Ayutthaya army had 250,000 foot-soldiers. The Pegu forces attacking Ayutthaya from 1548 to 1569 were contributed by several Burmese cities and were reportedly enormous. Pinto estimated that Tabinshweti brought 800,000 troops in 1548, and Couto reported that Ayutthaya had 600,000 troops in defense.[69] Given the likely population figures of this time, these figures are clearly exaggerated, yet for observers who had seen warfare in Europe, these armies seemed colossal.

At the start of this era, traditional methods of recruitment may have sufficed – emptying the jails, seizing fierce people from the hills, and offering the incentives detailed in the Palace Law. But the increased scale of warfare required new methods. In 1518/9 the king "had the first official registers of each city compiled," and the Office of Registration within the Ayutthaya palace is first mentioned in 1548.[70] There is no description of how the system worked from this era. In seventeenth-century accounts, all able-bodied men were registered in an occasional census, placed under an overseer (*munnai*), and liable for military recruitment and other labor services. The chronicles' record of these first registers probably marks a significant stage in the elaboration of this system. Recruits were marshaled under officers whose titles included decimal numbers from ten to a hundred thousand. These titles appear in the Ayutthaya chronicles from the 1540s.[71] Possibly the introduction of these systems was part of the transfer of practices from the Northern Cities to Ayutthaya.

In 1518, the king "had the first Treatise on Victorious Warfare compiled."[72] Although Chinese and Indian manuals are sometimes thought to be the source, the surviving *Tamra phichai songkhram* from later eras have a distinctive form. They detail battle formations and list various ways to deceive the enemy, which are topics in the military segments of the Indian *Arthasastra*, but the major part is taken up with omens to predict the outcome of battle and supernatural methods to secure the result. The omens are read from astrological calculation or from observation of nature, particularly the shapes of clouds and appearance of the

---

[67] Baker and Pasuk, *Yuan phai*, stanzas 183–5.
[68] *RCA*, 29, ll. 3–4 (*BM*); 30, ll. 31–3 (*LP*).
[69] Pinto, *Travels*, 412; Breazeale, "Ayutthaya under siege," 42.
[70] *RCA*, 19, ll. 19–24 (*LP*); 22, l. 24 (*BM*).
[71] *RCA*, 26 (*BM*).
[72] *RCA*, 19, ll. 19–20 (*LP*).

sun and moon. The methods to achieve success include pre-battle rituals and means to make men and animals invulnerable to enemy weapons.[73] Similar omens and rituals are found in the contemporary sources, suggesting the early manuals were probably similar. In *Yuan phai*, the king waits for an omen read from the flight of birds before proceeding to the battlefield. Several of the elephants are described in the epic as invulnerable to weapons.[74] Rituals of cutting wood and cursing the enemy's name appear several times in the chronicles in the later sixteenth century.[75]

The weaponry of the elephant brigade, cavalry, and infantry was simple: swords, pikes, lances, and spears. Describing a Tenasserim force, Varthema wrote, "Their arms are small swords, shields of some sort of bark, a great quantity of bows and lances."[76] Archery was known, but little developed. Shields were generally made from plaited wood, and sometimes from hide. Armor was minimal or absent. In 1402/3 the Chiang Mai forces were so amazed when they confronted Ho (Yunnanese) troops clad in armor made from leather, copper, and iron that they asked a captive, "Why don't you die when slashed, shot with spears and swords and guns and arrows? How can we defeat you?" The helpful Ho told them to pour hot sand and pebbles down the neckline.[77]

Given the simplicity of the technology, success depended greatly on the comparative size of the army. The military manuals and battle stories in the chronicles are packed with ploys to fool the opponent on this point. Noise itself was a weapon. The Pasai chronicle describes the climax of a two-month battle between the Ayutthayan forces and the local troops on the seashore outside Pasai in the early fourteenth century as follows:

> The two armies were face to face when fighting broke out over the whole field. The uproar was deafening. A pall of dust rose to the sky, until the eye could no longer distinguish one person from another. Only the noise of the chiefs and the men shouting could be heard. The crash of arms echoed in the depths of the forest.[78]

One weapon used by the Ayutthayan army was massive bells designed to emit a "very fearful sound."[79] In *Yuan phai*, an orchestra accompanies the army marching into battle, and the poem emphasizes the uproar created by the instruments, the elephants' trumpeting, and "soldiers' lusty

[73] *Tamra phichai songkhram.*
[74] Baker and Pasuk, *Yuan phai*, stanzas 188, 211, 215.
[75] *RCA*, 98, 123, 129, 141, 143, 155.
[76] Guehler, "Travels of Ludovico di Varthema," 126–7.
[77] Wyatt and Aroonrut, *Chiang Mai chronicle*, 73.
[78] Hill, "Hikayat Raja-Raja Pasai," 128.
[79] Trakulhun, "Suspicious friends," 184.

cheers."[80] The initial impact of gunpowder may have come more from noise than killing power.

Fatality, Defence, and Resistance

By the mid-sixteenth century, the Portuguese had introduced not only deadlier technology but also a professional viciousness – they "fought dirty and they fought to kill."[81] Casualty rates undoubtedly increased. The Chiang Mai chronicle comments wearily on one of the smaller engagements from the end of this period, "both we and the Southerners had many troops killed."[82] Kengtung sent an army to assist in the Pegu assault on Ayutthaya where "a great many men, elephants and horses died."[83] A Portuguese account reckoned Tabinshweti lost 12,000 men in the assault on Martaban in 1544.[84] The idea that Southeast Asian armies did not try to kill their enemies is certainly misplaced.[85]

Because of the increasing use of cannon, cities invested constantly in bigger and better walls. Nan replaced its earthen walls with brick construction around 1400, and Kengtung sometime after 1416.[86] Trailokanat "built walls around and fortified many principal cities, such as Phitsanulok, Sawankhalok, Kamphaengphet, Sukhothai" in the mid-fifteenth century.[87] Chiang Mai remade its walls in the 1510s.[88] At Ayutthaya, the walls were improved after the attack in 1548 and again after the 1563 defeat, when a new channel was dug on the eastern side, several hundred meters to the east of the old location. After the fall of the city in 1569, this new eastern moat was enlarged to "ten *wa* wide and three *wa* deep" (20 meters and 6 meters), and the old walls on this eastern side were dismantled and rebuilt along the moat. Possibly at this time too, a canal was dug to supply the city moat with more water from the Pasak River.[89] Under attack, rulers would retreat behind these defenses, and use cannon and matchlocks to keep the attackers at a distance. Most engagements were sieges rather than field battles.

---

[80] Baker and Pasuk, *Yuan phai*, stanzas 258–9.
[81] Trakulhun, "Suspicious friends," 184–5.
[82] Wyatt and Aroonrut, *Chiang Mai chronicle*, 105.
[83] Mangrai, *Pādaeng chronicle*, 247.
[84] Trakulhun, "Suspicious friends," 185 from de Faria y Sousa.
[85] This idea was reported by Gervaise (*Natural and political history*, 95–6) and La Loubère (*New historical relation*, 90–2) and repeated by modern scholars, especially Reid (*Southeast Asia in the age of commerce*, vol. 1, 122), but convincingly rejected by Charney (*Southeast Asian warfare*, 17–22).
[86] Wyatt, *Nan chronicle*, 47; Mangrai, *Pādaeng chronicle*, 113.
[87] *Van Vliet's Siam*, 207.
[88] Wyatt and Aroonrut, *Chiang Mai chronicle*, 106.
[89] *RCA*, 82 ll. 18–21 (*LP*); ll. 21–3 (*BM*); Vandenberg, "Quest for the holy water."

The enemy was not the only threat to life and limb. Battle generals kept crack troops at the rear to scythe down deserters. The troops charged the enemy if only because this offered a better chance of survival. Besides the incentives for success in warfare, the Ayutthaya Palace Law also prescribed penalties for failure or desertion:

> Anyone in an elephant duel who uses the goad to make the elephant retreat, slash him down on the elephant's back, cut off his head, have him paraded, and give no support for his children and grandchildren in the future ... Anyone fighting on a boat who evilly retreats by one boat length is condemned to be placed in chains; if two boat lengths, [property] confiscated and demoted to cutting grass for elephants; if three boat lengths, execution.[90]

Deaths from disease also increased. Travel beyond the cities courted risks from forest fevers and wild animals. As armies ranged over wider distances, soldiers were more likely to meet diseases beyond their acquired immunities. Both of the Ayutthaya kings who led armies through the forests of the Tenasserim range in this era died from sickness on campaign (Borommaracha IV in 1533, Naresuan in 1605), as did Alaungpaya during the siege of Ayutthaya in 1560. Moving such vast forces across the landscape also left a trail of devastation, famine, and epidemic disease. On the march, armies had to live off the land. De Couto reported that "as soon as their [Pegu] forces reached a base, they immediately set out into the forests to hunt for snakes, lizards, monkeys, bears, tigers and all other venomous things."[91] Soldiers seized rice from villages, or commandeered land to plant their own. At the approach of an army, villagers gathered up their daughters and valuables and fled into the forest. By the late sixteenth century, rulers expecting a siege would devastate the food supplies in the surrounding area to deny them to the enemy.

Mobilizations resulted in shortages of rice and high prices.[92] The Kengtung chronicle reports that "a great number died of starvation" after Lanna began raiding the area for recruits in the early 1500s, and the Chiang Mai chronicles reports that "many died of smallpox."[93] The Peguan army arrived through the Three Pagodas Pass in 1548 but decided to return a different way since the "food supplies have already been totally devastated" along the inward route. When the Peguan army advanced through the Northern Cities in 1563, "in Phitsanulok rice was expensive ... everyone came down with smallpox and many died."[94] The Jesuit Nicolas Pimenta reported that one Pegu campaign in the late

[90] Baker and Pasuk, *Palace Law of Ayutthaya*, 93–4 (clause 48).
[91] Breazeale, "Ayutthaya under siege," 42.
[92] e.g., *RCA*, 15, ll. 35–9; 19, ll. 38–42 (*LP*).
[93] Mangrai, *Pādaeng chronicle*, 244–5; Wyatt and Aroonrut, *Chiang Mai chronicle*, 105.
[94] *RCA*, 37, ll. 1–3 (*BM*); 44, ll. 27–8 (*LP*).

sixteenth century ended "with the losse of more than halfe their Armie," while in another foray into foreign territory, "the aire not agreeing, they brake out in pushes [pustules] and diseases … that with some impatience of the torture [men] threw themselves into the River."[95] According to Pinto, Tabinshweti abandoned the siege of Ayutthaya in 1548 after discovering that "he had lost 140,000 men in the four and half months of the siege, most of them of disease."[96]

Conscription was feared, hated, and evaded. People bribed the recruiters, or fled to the forests or other towns. As the Peguan army approached Ayutthaya in 1548, recruiters sought people from the surrounding region but "for the most part they fled out to live in the wilderness and could not be rounded up."[97] According to Pinto, when Ayutthaya sent out twenty recruiters with headcount targets in 1545, the rich inhabitants of one port town clubbed together to give "a huge bribe" to the recruiting officers, who instead filled their targets with "all the sick, crippled, poor and aged." A later inspection of the recruiting rolls revealed "two hundred thousand armed men wrongly registered as exempt from government service."[98] A mobilization at Pegu failed in the 1590s because "some became Talapoies (Friers in their Ethnicisme) others hid themselves in Desarts, and Woods, and many sold themselves for Slaves."[99]

Recruitment became more difficult over time. The forces recorded in the wars and scuffles of the mid-sixteenth century seem small compared to earlier years. The Chiang Mai chronicle describes a battle in 1555 in which six elephants figured, and four persons were captured. Adventurers who rounded up people were richly rewarded. The ruler of a minor town who presented "a great many people, men and women, to be subjects of the king" of Chiang Mai in 1506 was rewarded with the rulership of Phrae. But sometimes these captives were hard to retain. In 1520, "all the Shans" in Chiang Mai fled to the north, killed the Chiang Saen ruler who was deputed to halt them, and escaped homewards across the Salween.[100] Chiefs in the Shan States responded to Pegu's conscription in 1570 with a world-weary defiance: "If we go with the king, we will die in a strange place. If we refuse to go with him he will certainly send an army to kill us. We choose to defy him and die in our own native place."[101]

---

[95] Pimenta, "Indian observations," 212–13.
[96] Pinto, *Travels*, 414–18; *RCA*, 32–4 (*BM*).
[97] *RCA*, 41, ll. 3–6 (*BM*).
[98] Pinto, *Travels*, 406; *RCA*, 41, ll. 13–16 (*BM*).
[99] Pimenta, "Indian observations," 212.
[100] Wyatt and Aroonrut, *Chiang Mai chronicle*, 104, 106, 116.
[101] The Mhannan (Glass Palace) Chronicle quoted in Than Tun, "Ayut'a men in the service of Burmese kings," 100.

Only occasionally does the scale of resentment surface in the historical record. In 1564 at Pegu, 20,000 Shan war captives rose in revolt, held off two armies, burnt down royal rest houses and monastery buildings, and almost frightened the court into headlong flight. An army of 50,000 had to be summoned from Syriam to restore control. Ten thousand rebels were captured and threatened with being burnt alive, but eventually only seventy leaders were executed, perhaps to conserve manpower, perhaps in fear of provoking more trouble.[102] The news of such an event must have rippled across the political centers of the region.

The Culture of a Warrior Court

Militarization bred a warrior court culture. The first presents sent by the Ayutthaya king to the Portuguese Estado included cane spears, iron weapons, a set of bells used in battle, and a scroll painting showing "scenes of Siamese wars" including "the King sitting in a grand wooden cabin, which he used when he went to war."[103] These martial artifacts were considered appropriate gifts from a king. A Portuguese visitor witnessed an Ayutthaya regatta with 3,000 warships:

after competing in a race in which they show the strength of their rowing, they start fighting one another. The festival consists in fighting, both on horseback and mounted on elephants, or on foot, with sword and shield and some wild beasts are brought in and those who are awaiting execution are thrown to the wild beasts.[104]

The annual cycle of royal ceremonies found in the Ayutthaya Palace Law included a grand military parade. It begins in the evening with a procession of every division of the military, featuring large numbers of elephants. Guards then "remove the elephants, and clear away elephant dung with water and sugarcane plants" before there are displays of "wrestling, boxing, polo tossing" and other skills. The ceremony resumes on the following morning with another grand military parade, followed by dances and various military displays:

luring elephants; bullock carriage fight; water buffalo fight; sheep fight; elephant fight; bald-headed people fight; chicken-flapping; polo tossing; wrestling; hitting shields; slashing; sword fight; tricks; horse polo.[105]

---

[102] Than Tun, "Ayut'a men in the service of Burmese kings," 97–9.
[103] *Thailand and Portugal*, 43, quoting Gaspar Correia, *Lendas da India*.
[104] *Thailand and Portugal*, 49, quoting *Da Ásia de João de Barros*.
[105] Baker and Pasuk, *Palace Law of Ayutthaya*, 116–18 (clauses 172–4).

Military displays of this kind are common in societies geared to war. So too are military epics, which have a social function in increasing the chances of military success, by promoting the values of a warrior elite, cultivating insensitivity to the taking of human life, romanticizing death, and glamorizing combat. The *Yuan phai* epic is the only martial poem in Thai prior to the nineteenth century. It opens with a long panegyric to King Trailokanat's mastery of knowledge of all kinds, including Buddhism, the arts of war, literary skill, and history. Almost half of the poem is taken up with a description of the army, celebrating the glamor of warring. Elephants are grand and beautiful, some with "tusks that curve to pierce the lofty sky." Weapons scintillate – "They lunge with lances, shift their shields to-fro, / send flashing light that seems to pierce the clouds." The army on the march is splendid and rousing, "with golden shades, umbrellas, flags above / and stirring sounds of music, drum and gong." At the climax of the battle, the royal elephant Songbun triumphs in a gory duel:

> Songbun retreats, returns in fierce attack.
> The Lao, in flight, head lopped, collapses down.
> Troops swirl with saber, goad and shield. Sparks fly!
> The pikemen cheer the tusker, "Thrust again!"
> The Lao hangs headless from the tusker's neck.
> His blood wells up and floods away till gone.

The foot-soldiers then proceed to massacre the enemy:

> Among dense tamarinds, the panicked Lao
> are knocked down to their tuskers' feet in droves,
> amid the din, are caught and slashed down dead,
> like row on row of felled banana trees.

The finale details the looting (excerpted above, p. 99), and celebrates the glory of the victorious king. He "wins more consorts beautiful ... More gold, more towns accrue ... His merit quells the age-destroying fire ... In hundreds come the lords to pay him court."[106]

Another early literary work, *Lilit phra lo*, is a romance but also has a strong military theme. The date is unknown but the language and meter place it prior to the seventeenth century. The plot is a classic of courtly love and revenge. One king kills another king in a battle. Using magic, the two granddaughters of the defeated king lure the victor's son and successor (Phra Lo) into a bout of intense love-making. Their grandmother discovers the lovers, and orders them all killed in revenge for her husband's death. After two maidservants and their lovers cling together

---

[106] Baker and Pasuk, *Yuan phai*, stanzas 272–95.

as they are cut to pieces by a hail or rocks, arrows, spears, and sword thrusts, the hero and the two princesses are dispatched in another hail of poisoned arrows. In anger over the deaths, the father of the two girls captures the executioners, ties them up, "and then they were sliced, as one slices the trunk of a banana tree ... And he had their officers boiled and flayed." Finally, the grandmother is "killed most painfully."[107]

Although *Yuan phai* vaunts Trailokanat's knowledge of Buddhism, and *Lilit phra lo* ends with grief-ridden scenes of merit-making, the plots of these two works show little evidence of the Buddhist values that inform many later literary works. *Yuan phai* is about loyalty and disloyalty between powerful men, martial skill, and winning loot and glory. The core of *Lilit phra lo* is about human passion, but the framing story of conflict, honor, and revenge determines the bloody ending.

The storytelling in the *phitsadan* or elaborate version of the royal chronicles also changes in this era.[108] Up to the mid-sixteenth century, this chronicle is a slightly embellished version of the Luang Prasoet original. Beginning with the story of Si Sudachan's failed coup in 1548, the elaborate chronicle is clearly a separate work. While the Luang Prasoet version has the style of a log or diary, this chronicle tells stories with characters, motives, and moral messages. The extant versions date from the late eighteenth century at the earliest, and have clearly been rewritten over the years, but were probably first composed near the events they record, as the style and content change greatly from reign to reign. Most likely this chronicle was compiled for use in educating royal princes on how to rule. The Palace Law has a slot in the king's daily timetable for listening to a reading from the chronicles.[109] For the second half of the sixteenth century, over nine-tenths of this chronicle is about war or the diplomatic maneuvers between rival rulers. There is virtually no mention of religious events such as building, repairs, or ceremonies over the whole half-century period. The royal chronicle in this era is a war story.

Kingship in Early Ayutthaya

Ma Huan's sketch of the Ayutthaya king in the 1420s suggested a rather simple style of kingship (see above, p. 58), but as Ayutthaya developed into a territorial power, the institution became grander and more complex.

---

[107] Bickner, *Lilit phra law*, stanza 599, 607.
[108] This chronicle has survived in many versions, but the differences in their accounts of the sixteenth and early seventeenth centuries are minor.
[109] Baker and Pasuk, *Palace Law of Ayutthaya*, 111–12 (clause 157).

In early Ayutthaya there were at least three theories on kingship. The first derived from the Aggañña (Akkhanya) Sutta, a text from the Pali canon about the origins of human society. Humans developed from divine beings (brahmas) who descended to live in the newly created world. Over time, their behavior deteriorated, especially after genders developed and lust arose. Amid a rising trend of wrongdoing, conflict, and violence, humans decided together to select from among themselves one person "who was the handsomest, the best favored, the most attractive, the most capable"[110] to serve as judge and ruler in return for food and other necessities. This ruler was called the *mahasommutirat* (Mahasammutiraja), often translated as the Great Elect but better rendered as the "ruler by general consent." This theory appears in the *Ongkan chaeng nam*, the text of an oath used in swearing allegiance to the king.[111]

A second theory is associated with the *jataka* tales of the Buddha's previous lives. The king is a *bodhisatta*, a Buddha-to-be, who is accumulating exceptional merit through right living and good deeds with the result that he will attain enlightenment and return to the human world as a Buddha in the future. This idea is evident in the name *no phutthangkun* (Buddhankura), "sprout of a future Buddha," a synonym for *bodhisatta*, used as a title for princes of the Ayutthaya royal line, and in the term *(trai)lokanat*, "refuge of the (three) worlds," an epithet of the Buddha, adopted as one of the titles of Ayutthaya kings.

The third theory appears in the opening stanzas of the *Yuan phai* epic, introducing King Trailokanat:

> Brahma, Vishnu, Shiva, golden Meru's lord,
> great Yama, fine Maruti on his horse,
> Varuna, Agni, demon-chief Kubera,
> the gods of shining sun and lustrous moon;
> these gods eleven joined with one resolve
> to make a holy Lord All-Knowing one
> to come, protect, sustain and feed this world.
> All gods vouchsafed to help Him to succeed.[112]

Eleven gods, including the Hindu trinity and the eight gods of the cardinal and sub-cardinal directions from Indian tradition, headed by Indra ("Meru's lord"), jointly create a king.

These three theories were not in conflict. All were different expressions of the idea that the king was a person of exceptional merit. The *bodhisatta* version was probably favored by the Buddhist monkhood as it implied

---

[110] Rhys Davids, *Dialogues of the Buddha*, 88; Collins, "Discourse on what is primary."
[111] *Wannakhadi samai ayutthaya*, vol. 1, 3–23, esp. 8.
[112] Baker and Pasuk, *Yuan phai*, stanzas 1–2.

a constraint on the king to rule well in accord with Buddhist principles, but appealed also to kings because it endowed them with moral authority. Trailokanat commissioned bronze images representing the 500 *bodhisatta* in the *jataka* tales, and composed a version of the *Mahachat*, the great birth story, about Phra Vessantara, the last *bodhisatta*.[113]

The eleven-god version may have been favored by the court because it associated the ruler with divinity. The theory appears in the chronicles' account of the ceremony of anointing Ekathotsarot as king in 1605. This account deftly blends Buddhist and Hindu elements by stating that the Hindu gods are "unceasingly manifested" in the king *because* he has the "magnificent and marvelous merit of a practicing Buddhist King" and because of "His immense penitential practices."[114] In short, the Hindu gods make him a king because he is a good Buddhist.

The eleven-god theory underlay the ceremony of anointment for creating a king. In the form known from late Ayutthaya, Brahmans pour sacred water over the king to symbolize his divine creation, after which the chief nobles present the new king with elements of the realm – the people, city, troops, treasury, and so on. The Indian-derived term for the anointing rite, *aphisek/abhiskheka*, appears for the first time in the Luang Prasoet chronicle in 1480.[115] The Palace Law also has descriptions of the royal anointing ceremony which suggest it had a similar form in early Ayutthaya.[116]

In this era, royal anointment was not confined to the start of a reign, but was repeated as part of the annual ritual calendar. The Palace Law lists no fewer than eighteen royal ceremonies involving anointment. In some, the bathing appears to be a simple blessing, but one annual ceremony, *butsayaphisek*, contains a full re-enactment of the king-making procedure with anointment by the Brahmans followed by presentation of the elements of the realm and ending with a feast.[117] Anointment is also part of ceremonies to mark stages in the life cycle of the king. The divine creation of the early Ayutthaya king seemed to need constant repetition.

The annual ritual cycle, known as the Royal Ceremonies of the Twelve Months, was a major part of the public role of royalty. This annual round is alluded to in a love poem, *Thawathotsamat*, "Twelve months," probably dating to the late fifteenth or early sixteenth century, and is described

---

[113] *RCA*, 16, ll. 40–2; 18, ll. 3–4; McGill, "Jatakas, universal monarchs, and the year 2000."
[114] *RCA*, 199, ll. 12–24 (*BM*).
[115] *RCA*, 17, l. 48 (*LP*); 18, l. 12 (*LP*).
[116] Clause 168 (Baker and Pasuk, *Palace Law of Ayutthaya*, 115) may be a fragmentary version of the bathing rite for creating a king, while clause 183 describes the presentation of the elements of the realm.
[117] Baker and Pasuk, *Palace Law of Ayutthaya*, 121–2 (clause 183).

in the Palace Law. The ceremonies had several purposes. Some were Buddhist, such as the start of the rains-retreat. Some aimed to ensure the productivity of agriculture, including a plowing ceremony and a rite to chase away the waters at the end of the rainy season. Some were about charity, including a rite to weigh the king and queen in gold for distribution as alms. Some were designed to bring about prosperity and well-being by propitiating the spirits and removing impurities. Some ensured the realm was properly aligned with universal forces by marking transitions in the calendar. Some displayed military might, as in the parade described above. As a whole, this round of ceremonial positioned the king as responsible for the prosperity, well-being, and security of the realm.

In the cycle described in the Palace Law, Buddhism has a rather limited role, while spirits and elemental forces are more prominent than in later versions of the cycle. The court Brahmans carried out rites of purification using the elements of fire and water, especially in the *Bophok* (pāvaka) ceremony, which propitiated a fierce water spirit in the river, and the spirit of a former queen. In the event of blood-letting within the palace compound, purification rites had to be performed both by Brahman priests and Buddhist monks, while pairs of chickens were propitiated at the four gates of the palace and then released "outside the city to take the inauspiciousness, evil, danger, and misfortune out beyond the King's capital."[118]

Kings accumulated wives and consorts for practical reasons of sustaining the lineage and building marriage alliances, but also as a symbolic display of the king's power. Pires reported in the 1510s that the Siamese king "has many wives, upwards of five hundred," probably an exaggeration but indicative of an impressive number.[119] In the Palace Law, queens were ranked by titles with the *akharamahesi* or primary queen at the summit, followed by other queens, consorts, female palace staff, and administrators of the inner palace who were often senior women of royal lineage. All these women were the exclusive property of the king. One clause dramatized this: the primary queen could not be touched, even to rescue her from drowning. Palace officials who disobeyed this rule faced the death penalty, and others faced death for their whole clan. The protection of royal women in general was specified in one of the most succinct statements in the whole law: "Anyone who is lover with a court lady or royal consort is executed to die over three days, and the woman is executed also." Another clause condemned to execution a man who "brings books of poetry into the palace to seduce palace maids and inner

---

[118] Baker and Pasuk, *Palace Law of Ayutthaya*, 108 (clause 149).
[119] Pires, *Suma Oriental*, 104.

palace servants." All women inside the palace counted as "royal ladies" to be protected.[120]

The Palace Law does not mention succession at all. The theories of kingship outlined above emphasize that the king becomes king because of his individual merit, and give no support for dynastic succession, though kings of course favored their sons on the instincts of paternity. The Palace Law set out a strict hierarchy among royal sons based on the status of the mother and the grant of titles by the king – in effect, a system of appointment. The title of *uparaja*, a deputy king who might have prior rights of succession, was present from the beginning of Ayutthaya.[121] In practice, most early successions were contests, trials of strength. This accorded both with the political theory, that the most meritorious should rule, and with the requirements of a society in which a major role of the king was as army chief.

Royal revenues came mainly from trade. Royal monopolies on major export items were in place by the early fifteenth century. Pires reported that "The foreign merchants in Siam pay two on every nine, and the Chinese pay two on every twelve."[122] By 1600 there was a customs post on the river below Ayutthaya. Despite the wars and the fall of the city, the royal treasuries seem to have been flush. An associate of De Coutre was shown "a chest of rubies" and allowed to select one estimated to be worth 70,000 *escudos*, and a 300-carat sapphire worth 8,000 *ducados*.[123]

The annual cycle of royal ceremonial and the Palace Law signify a transition in kingship from the simplicity of early Ayutthaya to a more majestic and more public style, underwritten by rising revenues. De Coutre described King Naresuan at audience and on an elephant hunt in the 1590s, showing more grandeur than Ma Huan's description of the Ayutthaya king 170 years earlier (see p. 58). In procession, Naresuan wore a gold headpiece studded with jewels, carried two golden crooks, had four large parasols, one of gold leaf and one gilded, and was surrounded by a large retinue. His palace was topped with five towers covered with gold leaf. He presided on an elevated throne, reputedly of solid gold, with two tigers chained at the base.[124]

Naresuan

The career of Maha Thammaracha's son Naresuan has become entwined with romantic legend. In the most likely version of his biography, he was

---

[120] Baker and Pasuk, *Palace Law of Ayutthaya*, 105–8 (clauses 128–48).
[121] *RCA*, 11, l. 6 (*BM*); 18, l. 12 (*LP*).
[122] Pires, *Suma Oriental*, 103.
[123] Borschberg, *Memoirs and memorials*, 114.
[124] Borschberg, *Memoirs and memorials*, 110, 112–13, 116–17, 130.

taken to Pegu as a hostage in 1569 or earlier, but escaped and established himself at Phitsanulok.[125] According to the *phitsadan* Ayutthaya chronicles, the Burmese became fearful of Naresuan's martial skills, plotted to kill him, and hence forfeited the right to his fealty. Naresuan abrogated any connection with Pegu, and drove the Burmese garrisons out of the Northern Cities.[126]

Naresuan first had to reestablish Ayutthaya's dominance within Siam. After Ayutthaya fell to Pegu, in 1569, other cities had pulled away. In 1570, the ruler of Phetchaburi "collected together many men, southerners all" and planned to attack the depleted Ayutthayan army, forcing the court to consider a retreat to the old strategic stronghold of Phitsanulok. The governors of Phichai and Sawankhalok took sides with Pegu but were eventually defeated and killed.[127] In 1581, one Yan Phichian, who "had studied weaponry," gathered a "rebellious rabble" of 3,000 men in Lopburi, marched on Ayutthaya, killed the Mahatthai minister, and began appointing his own high officials. Possibly this revolt, like Si Sudachan's failed coup in 1548, stemmed from the thwarted ambitions of the old Lopburi-Ayutthaya family. Yan Phichian was killed by one shot from a "triggered gun" of a "foreigner" named Amarawadi, and the revolt dispersed.[128]

In 1569, Pegu swept away a large number of people from Ayutthaya. Over each of the next three years, Lovek sent armies into the regions to the east and south of Ayutthaya to capture and carry away people.[129] Naresuan's early campaigns were aimed not only to crush these revolts and defections, but also to secure people to repopulate the capital and its environs. In the early 1580s, he brought back people from campaigns in the lower Irrawaddy; swept down 20,000 Tai Yai (Shan) from the north; accepted several influxes of Mon; and even had Yan Phichian's defeated rebels tattooed and drafted into the Ayutthaya forces. After restoring order in the Northern Cities, he sent many families down to the capital.[130] With these subtractions and additions, the people of Ayutthaya and its environs changed dramatically between the 1560s and 1580s.

From 1584 Pegu attempted to reassert its dominance over Ayutthaya. Against this threat, Naresuan proved to be a great military leader. He began by concentrating his forces, abandoning the Northern Cities,

---

[125] *Van Vliet's Siam*, 223–4; *RCA*, 78, ll. 1–5 (*LP*); Damrong, *Biography of King Naresuan*, 2–3, 25.
[126] *RCA*, 88–90 (*BM*).
[127] *RCA*, 77, 91–2 (*BM*).
[128] *RCA*, 82 (*BM*).
[129] *RCA*, 74, 76–8, 83–4 (*BM*).
[130] *RCA*, 83, 86, 90, 92, 94, 96.

sweeping all their people down to Ayutthaya, and recruiting troops from the area south and west of the city. He bought arquebusses from the European traders, and recruited a squad of Portuguese cannoneers as well as units of Japanese and Cham.[131] He introduced more armor, cladding his troops in "leather footwear, jackets and helmets," and equipping his elephants with "the face of Rahu and iron shoes" for greater protection against firearms.[132] Instead of allowing the Peguan forces to besiege Ayutthaya, he sent boats with small cannons and artillerymen to attack the enemy's forward camps. He strengthened Ayutthaya's walls for a third time, after which "All the way around [the city], the walls have beautiful bastions and many sentry posts, all furnished with many very large pieces of bronze artillery."[133] He depopulated the plain around Ayutthaya to deny supplies to the Peguan army which had to retire at the onset of the rains. He chose to ride a horse rather than an elephant, and made more use of cavalry, giving advantages of speed over the enemy.[134] He led his troops from the front, creating the plots of countless stirring tales, and a regalia sword that legendarily bore the marks of his teeth from a time he scaled an enemy stockade.[135] In the chronicles' accounts, Naresuan has a very physical presence. According to De Coutre, "He went out [virtually] naked, with just a loincloth that hid his private parts, without any other clothes."[136]

Pegu launched attacks on Ayutthaya for four successive years from 1584 to 1587 but the investments in defense and Naresuan's tactics prevailed. The struggle climaxed in 1593 with a battle at Nong Sarai that has passed into legend. According to the Thai chronicles, Naresuan and the Burmese *uparaja* fought an elephant-back duel which self-consciously marked the transition between eras. Naresuan summoned his rival to the duel saying, "In the future there won't be any more kings to fight elephant duels!" and dispatched the *uparaja* with a sabre slash after his elephant had unbalanced the opponent.[137] In the Burmese chronicles and several European accounts of the event, however, the historical transition had already happened: the *uparaja* was killed by a gunshot, either fired by Naresuan, an unidentified soldier, or a Portuguese.[138] Whatever actually

---

[131] Breazeale, "Thai maritime trade," 28; *Khamhaikan khun luang ha wat*, 14–15.
[132] RCA, 151, ll. 44–5 (BM), slightly modified according to *Phraratcha phongsawadan krung si ayutthaya chabap mo bratle*, 167.
[133] Diogo da Couto in Breazeale, "Portuguese impressions of Ayutthaya," 55.
[134] Charney, *Southeast Asian warfare*, 166–7.
[135] *Khamhaikan khun luang ha wat*, 13.
[136] Borschberg, *Memoirs and memorials*, 112.
[137] *RCA*, 131 (*BM*); *Khamhaikan khun luang ha wat*, 10–12.
[138] Nai Thien, "Intercourse between Burma and Siam," 50–1; Terwiel, "What happened at Nong Sarai?"

happened, the symbolism of the event is rich. The elephant had played a central role in this age of warfare, but their usefulness had gradually declined with the rise of gunpowder technology as elephants were often panicked by explosions.[139] Elephants remained vital for military transport and for display, but declined in importance on the field of battle. From this point forward, there is no story of an elephant duel.

Naresuan used his military advantage to reestablish control over the strategic areas for commerce. Immediately after the Nong Sarai elephant duel, he sent his generals to retake Tavoy and Tenasserim and impose a new provincial government. Two years later, the Tenasserim governor "rebelled," and Naresuan sent an army with orders to have the governor beheaded and impaled. In 1595 the Ayutthaya armies pressed northwards up the west coast of the peninsula, took Moulmein (Mawlamyine), and tried but failed to draw the local Mon lords into an alliance against Pegu. In 1599, Naresuan for the first time led an Ayutthayan army in an attack on the Burmese capital. On the outward march, his army massacred the inhabitants of Martaban, and on the return journey they repopulated the city with captives.[140] Ayutthaya again had control over the portage across the upper peninsula, lost in 1569.

Lovek

Besides reestablishing control on the neck of the peninsula, Naresuan also attempted to extend influence over the rival port center on the lower Mekong.

After 1569, the Khmer capital at Lovek took the opportunity of Ayutthaya's weakness to increase its standing as a commercial and political center by encouraging traders from the interior (Lanna, Lanxang) to reroute down the Mekong River rather than through Ayutthaya. Beginning immediately after the fall, Lovek parties raided into the Chaophraya Plain to seize people. In 1575, they sailed up the Thachin and Maeklong rivers to Suphanburi; in 1578, they besieged Phetchaburi unsuccessfully; in 1581 they took the town and "had all the inhabitants of Phetburi captured and taken away as prisoners of war"; and in 1584, they were stopped at the edge of the Isan Plateau (Chaibadan).[141]

In 1587, the Ayutthayan armies marched into the Khmer country but the expedition failed because scorched-earth tactics resulted in a lack of food.[142] In the following year, Naresuan recruited a much larger force

---

[139] Charney, *Southeast Asian warfare*, 160–1.
[140] *RCA*, 133, 134, 136–7, 155–8, 160–2, 165–8, 173.
[141] *RCA*, 84 (*PC*).
[142] *RCA*, 139–40 (*BM*).

which converged on Lovek by land, river, and sea. This attack destroyed Lovek's pretensions to supplant Ayutthaya as a commercial and political center, though the exact details are unclear. According to the Van Vliet chronicle, Naresuan enthroned the Khmer king's son and hauled the king himself away to Ayutthaya, but later allowed him to return. According to the later Ayutthayan chronicles, Naresuan had the Khmer king ritually killed to fulfil a vow to "wash his feet" in the king's blood, but this story is an invention.[143] In 1602, Naresuan installed a captive Khmer prince on the throne, and sent armies to defend him against revolt two years later. As a result of these messy exchanges, Lovek had effectively become a dependency of Ayutthaya.

Finale

Naresuan succeeded as king on his father's death in 1590. According to the Van Vliet chronicle, he spent only two years of his reign at his capital (though this is somewhat exaggerated) because of a vow to remain away until he had taken the Burmese capital. From the mid-1590s, he criss-crossed the region constantly, fighting campaigns in Lovek, Lanxang, Burma, Lanna, and the Mon country, but these expeditions were increasingly marked by famine, disease, and failure because of the strength of town defenses, the use of scorched-earth tactics, and possibly a phase of low rainfall.[144]

Naresuan invaded Burma and laid siege to Toungoo in 1599, but supply lines were stretched: "They ran out of food and lost their strength … and they died from starvation in great numbers." Rice was expensive, and the rains started. Troops deserted the siege and faded into the countryside in search of food. Naresuan retreated, "plundering over a wide area throughout the country and carrying away many treasures and prisoners."[145] According to Pimenta, when Naresuan then besieged Pegu, the Burmese king slaughtered 7,000 Siamese in the city, presumably captives from earlier campaigns, in order to make more food available for others.[146] This siege also failed.

On the return from this invasion, Naresuan's brother Ekathotsarot detoured to Lanna where the local city lords initially rushed to offer him fealty, horses, elephants, and people. As at Toungoo and Pegu, the presence of the invading army soon caused problems. Food was scarce,

---

[143] *RCA*, 142–54 (*BM*); *Van Vliet's Siam*, 232.
[144] Lieberman, *Strange parallels*, vol. 1, 276; Lieberman and Buckley, "Impact of climate on Southeast Asia."
[145] *RCA*, 168, ll. 21–3 (*LP*); 178 (BM); *Van Vliet's Siam*, 231.
[146] Pimenta, "Indian observations," 214.

prices soared, an epidemic broke out, the army began to break apart, and the Lanna lords pleaded with the Ayutthayan prince to go elsewhere.[147]

In 1605, when Burma sent an army to reestablish control in Lanna and the Shan states, Naresuan set out north again, but died on the march. According to legend, Naresuan commanded his brother and successor, Ekathotsarot, to complete the campaign so that Naresuan could enter Toungoo as a corpse strapped to the head of an elephant.[148] Instead, Ekathotsarot marched back to Ayutthaya. Although he had been Naresuan's constant companion on campaign, after succeeding to the throne he appears not to have led out another army.

The cross-range invasions and sieges which had been roughly biennial between the 1550s and 1605 now came to an abrupt end. There followed a fifty-year peace, and 150 years in which warfare was for the most part limited to minor skirmishing over the strategic areas for commerce, especially the upper peninsula.[149] The Burmese took control of Martaban in 1613,[150] occupied Tavoy and Tenasserim briefly in 1613/4, and then captured Tavoy more decisively in 1622, resulting in a division of control over the west-coast ports – Tenasserim and southwards under Ayutthaya; Tavoy and northwards under Burma. This arrangement lasted until the mid-eighteenth century. The Burmese recaptured Chiang Mai in 1613, and held off several Ayutthayan attempts to reassert control in the 1660s. A new Khmer king (Chai Chettha) in 1618 revoked suzerainty to Ayutthaya, and the army sent to re-enforce control in 1621/2 failed badly.[151] For the most part, these were small engagements with armies of limited size which ended with famines, epidemics, and signs of popular discontent.[152] War no longer worked.

Conclusion

Between roughly 1400 and 1600, there was a rise in warring across Mainland Southeast Asia as ambitious rulers competed to control the resources that were the building blocks of power – people to man armies, skilled craftsmen to embellish royal capitals, Palladian images and elephants, and access to trade for stocking royal treasuries and acquiring weapons.

[147] *RCA*, 182–6 (*BM*).
[148] *Van Vliet's Siam*, 232–3; *RCA*, 194–5 (*BM*).
[149] According to Neijenrode ("Account and description," 13–14), a combined force of 200,000 from Ava and Lanxang threatened Ayutthaya in 1615, but the incident is not reported elsewhere.
[150] Breazeale, "Whirligig of diplomacy," 60–1.
[151] *Van Vliet's Siam*, 236.
[152] Dhiravat, "Political history of Siam," 307–8, 333.

As a result of Ming maritime policy and advances in shipping technology, trade in the southern seas had increased in scale and value. Besides being a source of royal revenues, maritime trade gave access to gunpowder technology and mercenary soldiers. By this logic, coastal polities rose to dominance over inland states across the region. By the later fifteenth century, the choke-points of maritime trade – the Melaka straits and the portage route across the upper peninsula – had become the foci of political rivalry that now spanned across the separate river basins.

Over the course of these two centuries, war became the root of greater social regimentation. The system of registering people so their services could be demanded for fighting and other uses had been around in the region for a long time, but was systematized and rigorously applied in this era. The ethos of this society is reflected in the glorification of war in *Yuan phai*, the gory climax of *Lilit phra lo*, the battle stories in the chronicles, the scale of the annual military parade described in the Palace Law, and De Coutre's description of the tigers tethered to Naresuan's throne.

Two events, whether truth or myth, are symbolic markers of the end of this era: the elephant duel at Nong Sarai in 1593, which may have been decided by a bullet, and which marked the end of the elephant's prominence in warfare; and Ekathotsarot's decision not to enter Toungoo with his brother's corpse strapped to the head of an elephant, reneging on an oath, a vital bond of the personal politics of this era, and rejecting a gory gesture that fitted perfectly with the ethos of *Yuan phai*. After coming to such a climax over the past two decades, the warring now stopped almost dead.

Guns were now so easily available that advantages were even. Better defensive techniques – masonry walls, scorched-earth tactics, harassing raids – had neutralized the offensive advantages of cannon and massive armies. Rising casualty rates had reduced the attraction of engaging in warfare as a means to pursue wealth and social advancement. In echoes of the Mon revolt at Pegu, the Burmese kings faced repeated revolts by war prisoners, including by the Siamese prisoners at Pegu. Nandabayin (1581–99) could raise armies only a third the size of his father, Bayin-naung, because many people had entered the monkhood or fled to the forests. A German observer commented, "He had indeed much artillery, but no men to handle it."[153]

Although Naresuan is now revered as the great hero figure of Thai history, this is a recent appraisal. The Thai chronicles portray him as ruthless in victory; in 1593, his troops "slashed and killed Burmese and Mon all along the way to Kancanaburi. Corpses were scattered about and those from Taphang Tru alone numbered somewhat over twenty thousand."[154]

[153] Sebastian Münster in Trakulhun, "Suspicious friends," 188.
[154] *RCA*, 131, ll. 31–3 (*BM*).

The usually phlegmatic Luang Prasoet chronicle records in 1594, "At that time the King was enraged with the Mons and had about one hundred and fifty Mons taken and burned to death."[155] Europeans of the time called him the "Black Prince." A Portuguese account written in 1603 claimed that he killed twenty Portuguese by frying them in coconut oil.[156] De Coutre left a similar story, though written long after the event.[157] Portuguese friars in the 1590s reported that he was "much feared but at the same time loved."[158] The Van Vliet chronicle, compiled from "learned monks" and Ayutthaya nobles thirty-five years after Naresuan's death, reflects a revulsion against this age of warfare:

His reign was the most militant and severe of any which was ever known in Siam. Many stories and living eye-witnesses report that in the twenty years of his rule he killed and had killed by law more than 80,000 people, excluding those who were victims of war. Whether on an elephant, on horseback, in a perahu [boat], or even on his throne in a meeting with his mandarins, he was never without a weapon. He always had a quiver resting on his lap and a bow in hand. When he saw someone who did the least thing which did not please him, he shot an arrow at the offender and asked that person to bring the arrow to him. He often had pieces of flesh sliced off from those (even among mandarins) who committed the smallest mistakes and had them eat their flesh before his very eyes. He made others eat their own feces.[159]

There was no eulogy of Naresuan written in his era, unlike Trailokanat before him, and Prasat Thong and Narai after him. In the Luang Prasoet chronicle, compiled in the late sixteenth century, Naresuan is not portrayed in heroic terms. In the *Testimony* documents from the late eighteenth century (see pp. 285–6), his warring is described but not celebrated.[160]

The contest between Ayutthaya and Burma had resulted in a division of spheres of influence. To the north, Burma had taken control of Lanna, and extended its influence across to Lanxang. To the south, Ayutthaya controlled the portage across the upper peninsula, and extended its influence eastward along the coast to the Khmer capital of Lovek. For the next 150 years, this division remained stable with almost no warring between Ayutthaya and Burma. The decline in violence paved the way for an age of peace, commerce, and prosperity.

---

[155] *RCA*, 142 (*LP*).
[156] Pedro Sevil de Guarga in Smith, *Creolization and diaspora*, 67.
[157] Borschberg, *Memoirs and memorials*, 139–45.
[158] Ribanedeira, *Historia del archipelago*, vol. 1, 163, 424.
[159] *Van Vliet's Siam*, 229.
[160] Tun Aung Chain, *Chronicle of Ayutthaya*, 38–43.

4   Peace and Commerce

Anthony Reid proposed that Southeast Asia experienced an "age of commerce" from 1450 to 1680, begun by integration of the region into the global trading system, and ended by a global downturn coupled with the advent of formal colonialism.[1] Victor Lieberman argued that Reid's timing was determined by the spice trade and hence suited Island Southeast Asia but not the mainland where the spice trade was unimportant.[2] Geoff Wade proposed a longer-term trend of regional expansion, beginning in the tenth century and driven primarily from southern China, demoting the European spice trade to a minor theme.[3]

In Siam, geopolitics also affected the timing of commercial growth. Through the sixteenth century, the mainland's integration into global trade was disrupted by inter-basin warfare. After conflict subsided around 1600, Ayutthaya became one of the great entrepots of Asia outside the control of Europeans. Resources were switched from warfare to trade. By the 1630s in the interior, "most of these city walls have entirely decayed … so that in the whole kingdom there is hardly to be found a single well walled city or a good fort."[4] The society began to produce a wider range of goods for export – through agriculture, manufacture, mining, and gathering. The kings took a dominant role in overseas trade, and commercial wealth transformed the monarchy. For the nobility, warrior skills diminished in importance compared to official patronage and access to commerce. Noble families sought ways to accumulate wealth and pass it down to successors, and kings tried to prevent them. The transitions from one reign to the next became occasions when social tensions and political competition exploded into violence. In the last of these contests in the seventeenth century, the mob made its entrance onto the Siamese political stage.

[1] Reid, *Southeast Asia in the age of commerce*, esp. vol. 2, chs. 1 and 5.
[2] Lieberman, *Strange parallels*, vol. 1, 18–21.
[3] Wade, "Early age of commerce."
[4] *Van Vliet's Siam*, 109.

The history thickens in the seventeenth century as the sources include contemporary observations by outsiders, including European visitors conscious of a duty to add to the stock of knowledge about the world, and the resident Dutch merchants who kept daybooks, mined by today's scholars, especially Dhiravat and Bhawan.

Entrepot between East and West

During the warring of the later sixteenth century, Ayutthaya lost its prominent role in the trade of the South China Seas, but with Naresuan's reestablishment of control over the portage route in the 1590s, and the abrupt decline of warring after 1605, an era of commerce began. In the first few years after his accession in 1605, King Ekathotsarot made contact with the Portuguese, the English, and the Dutch. By the early 1610s, Japanese, Chinese, and Indian Muslims were trading at Ayutthaya.[5]

As in the past, the trade to China was of major importance to Siam. The Ming ban on private trade in China had been lifted in 1567. By the 1600s Ayutthaya had regained a role in the exchange between China and Mainland Southeast Asia, but no longer dominated as before.[6] New ports on the Vietnamese coastline competed to deliver forest goods to China by a shorter route. Traders from the interior complained about the terms offered by the Ayutthaya port and took their business down other routes to the sea.[7]

The Manchu-Qing takeover of China in 1644 initially disrupted commerce. The emperor banned all overseas travel and trade as part of its strategy against Ming-loyalist rebels. When it lifted the ban for non-Chinese traders in 1652, Siamese ships were the first to be admitted at Guangzhou (Canton) and subsequently other ports. Initially only tributary trading missions were allowed under strict conditions. Siam was limited to a three-ship mission every three years with a cap of one hundred on the size of each ship's crew and no private trading on the side. Narai sent five missions between 1652 and 1688. With the connivance of local authorities, the emperor's restrictions were soon eased or circumvented. Allowance was made for "ballast," in fact filled with private trade goods of around 300 to 350 tons per ship. Supplementary ships were allowed. While the tribute mission made the eight-month overland trip between Guangzhou and Beijing, the little fleet returned to Siam for "conditioning" the ships, and came back to Guangzhou stacked with more cargo.[8]

---

[5] Farrington and Dhiravat, *English factory in Siam*, 73; Smith, *Dutch in seventeenth-century Thailand*, 85.
[6] Reid, "Documenting the rise and fall," 8–9.
[7] *Van Vliet's Siam*, 126–8.
[8] Sarasin, *Tribute and profit*, 31–41.

From Songtham (1610/11–28) onwards, the kings also conducted private trade, owning junks but employing Chinese as captains and agents. According to Van Vliet, "some of them [Chinese] have been appointed to high positions and offices and others are considered the best factors, traders and sailors."[9] A report of 1678 stated that all the king's shipping and trading was managed by Chinese.[10] By the late 1680s, private trade also flourished and "ships from the Great Qing – from Guangdong, Zhangzhou and Xiamen – as many as 14 or 15 ships, visited Siam."[11]

In this era, two new factors transformed Ayutthaya's commerce. First, the arrival of the Dutch, French, and British with better ocean-going ships increased the flow of trade between Asia and Europe. Siam produced little that the European markets wanted except pepper, but Siam became important in the "country trade," the traffic around Asian ports by which the Europeans acquired the capital to invest in home-bound cargoes. The Dutch established a factory in Ayutthaya from 1608 and inserted themselves into the eastbound trade in order to earn Japanese silver. Later in the seventeenth century, British and French traders settled at Mergui as part of the country trade around the Indian Ocean.

Second, and more importantly, Ayutthaya became a great entrepot between east and west. To the east lay the great market and production center of China, a more open, stable and prosperous Japan under the Tokugawa shogunate, and Spanish Manila. To the west lay the three flourishing Islamic empires of Ottoman Turkey, Safavid Persia, and Mughal India. Ayutthaya became a mart for the exchange of high-value goods between these rich places to east and west.

Many Asian traders used Ayutthaya as an entrepot. "Malays in small Prowes" brought forest goods from the archipelago for onward transmission to China, and carried camphor, pepper, and bird's nests from Ayutthaya to coastal ports. Fragrant wood came from Cochinchina for re-export to Japan. Cloth from Surat and southern India was bought and sold in Ayutthaya before being sent onward to Japan, China, and Manila.[12] Spanish wine and contraband American silver came from Manila to Ayutthaya for distribution through Asia. Van Neijenrode noted the constant arrivals "from places like Patani, Johore, Jambi, Malacca, Cochinchina, Champa, Cambodia, Borneo and Japan, places where they have much shipping to and fro, especially to China."[13]

---

[9] *Van Vliet's Siam*, 139.
[10] Anderson, *English intercourse with Siam*, 426.
[11] Ishii, *Junk trade*, 41, 53.
[12] Anderson, *English intercourse with Siam*, 425.
[13] Reid, "Documenting the rise and fall," 8; Breazeale, "Thai maritime trade," 16–22; Neijenrode, "Account and description," 27–8; Smith, "Princes, nobles and traders."

Ayutthaya might seem an unlikely site for an entrepot. The portage across the peninsula was difficult because of "numerous tigers' assaults … the unbearable heat of the day and the icy cold of the night";[14] but these perils were preferred, particularly by Asian traders, to the dangers of dealing with the Dutch and the pirates in the Straits of Melaka, particularly for goods of high value such as ceramics and metals. Ayutthaya was not on the coast but up a river. The distance was shortened in the sixteenth century by cutting two three-kilometer canals at river meanders, and further shortened by two five-kilometer canals dug in 1607–08 and 1635–36.[15] Ships still had to negotiate a sandbar at the estuary and spend several days working their way upriver,[16] but the inconvenience was outweighed by the security. Coastal ports were vulnerable to pirate raids. Ports on the peninsula such as Pattani and Songkhla were sacked several times. The river also acted as protection against European aggression. European ships came to dominate the Asian oceans, but they were vulnerable in rivers because of their deep draft, limited ability to maneuver, and dependence on fickle winds.[17] A Spanish ship which attempted some aggression along the Chaophraya in 1624 was quickly overwhelmed, with 150 Spaniards killed and 200 more imprisoned.[18]

Being an entrepot at the crossroads of multiple trading networks had profound effects on Ayutthaya's society and politics. The city became extraordinarily cosmopolitan. Commerce was inseparable from politics. Foreign trading groups became involved in the affairs of the court and nobility. At the start of this age of commerce, the two important groups were the Japanese and the "Moors," meaning primarily Persians.

The Japanese

Trade with Japan had begun in the late sixteenth century but is largely invisible in its early years. The first trace is a Japanese junk carrying arms bound for Siam that took refuge from a storm at Manila in 1589. In 1592, a Japanese permit was issued for a junk to trade with Siam, Ligor, and Pattani. After the establishment of the shogunate at the turn of the seventeenth century, both the shoguns and the western *daimyo* were interested in developing maritime trade.[19] The shogun, Tokugawa Ieyasu, sought

---

14   Polenghi, "Giovanni Filippo de Marini," 52.
15   Takaya, *Agricultural development*, 184–6.
16   Gisbert Heeck took a week, see *Traveler in Siam*, 37–53.
17   Charney, *Southeast Asian warfare*, 128–9.
18   Smith, *Dutch in seventeenth-century Thailand*, 18–19.
19   Iwao, "Japanese foreign trade in the 16th and 17th centuries," 1–8.

trading relations with Pattani, but switched his attention to Ayutthaya after Japanese traders were badly treated there. Ieyasu's main objective was to acquire "the splendid saltpeter produced in your country."[20] Of the two ingredients of gunpowder, Siam had a lot of saltpeter but little sulfur, and Japan vice versa. Since the 1540s, Wang Zhi, the most famous of the "pirates" defying the Ming trading ban, had carried Siamese saltpeter to Japan and Japanese sulfur to Siam in large quantities. In the 1600s, the shogunate sent missions to Siam almost annually with generous presents, and Ieyasu made very clear that guns and saltpeter were "what I desire more than gold brocade."[21] The Siamese side was equally enthusiastic and sent missions to Japan in 1616, 1621, 1623, 1626, and 1629. Under the shogunate's system of licensing junks, fifty-six vermilion seals were issued for junks trading to Siam between 1604 and 1635, a fifth of the total. Besides saltpeter, the main exports from Siam to Japan were deer hides and rayskins, used in military dress and equipment, while imports included copper and silver.[22]

Japanese were among the soldiers of fortune who arrived in Ayutthaya in the sixteenth century. A unit of 500 Japanese was part of Naresuan's forces in 1592/3.[23] The numbers of Japanese in Siam were swelled in the 1590s by people fleeing the wars that preceded the establishment of the shogunate, or fleeing the persecution of Christians which began in 1597. A Japanese village may have existed to the southeast of Ayutthaya by 1579, and certainly did by 1617. In a confused incident in 1612, a group of some 300 Japanese soldiers attacked the palace in Ayutthaya and seized the recently installed King Songtham on behalf of a pretender to the throne, but were overwhelmed and "departed with a great treasur, using muche violence att theyre departure."[24] The group also threatened Bangkok, and took control of Phetchaburi for a time. Possibly these were soldiers of fortune, unemployed after the abrupt ending of the age of warfare.

In 1612, Yamada Nagamasa arrived in Siam. He was a man of common origins who had served as a palanquin-bearer for a *daimyo* lord before setting off to make his fortune. Around 1620, when he was

---

[20] A missive from an aide to Ieyasu dated October 10, 1608, quoted in Iwamoto and Bytheway, "Japan's official relations with Shamuro," 90.

[21] Sun, "Saltpetre trade," 142, 148; Iwamoto and Bytheway, "Japan's official relations with Shamuro," 90.

[22] Nidhi, "Ayudhya and the Japanese," 86; Iwamoto and Bytheway, "Japan's official relations with Shamuro," 102–4; Iwamoto, "Yamada Nagamasa"; Reid, "Documenting the rise and fall," 9.

[23] *RCA*, 128, ll. 34–6 (*BM*).

[24] Floris, *His voyage to the East Indies*, 56–8; Nidhi, "Ayudhya and the Japanese," 92; *RCA*, 208–9 (*BM*); Van Neijenrode's account in Giles, "A critical analysis," 180–1.

thirty years old, he became head of the Japanese village in Ayutthaya. Soon after, without any standing, he inserted himself in the diplomatic negotiations between the shogunate and Siam. By the mid-1620s, he had been ennobled as Okya Senaphimuk, head of the Japanese community in Ayutthaya. Over 1628–29, he played a major role in the drawn-out succession dispute which installed an ambitious noble as King Prasat Thong (see below), but he thereby became too powerful. He was either appointed as governor of Ligor, or fled there from Ayutthaya in fear of his life, and died either by the sword or poison in Ligor, after which his son and followers took refuge in Cambodia.

The incident disrupted relations with Japan, but only briefly. The shogunate refused to recognize Prasat Thong on grounds that he was a usurper, and official trading missions ceased. Between 1633 and 1639, Japan withdrew into *sakoku* isolation: Japanese inside or outside the country were prohibited from engaging in maritime trade, and the issue of vermilion seals lapsed. However, this allowed the Dutch and Chinese, and the Siamese king to take over the shipping on this valuable route. Some 130 vessels sailed from Ayutthaya to Nagasaki between 1647 and 1700. The Siamese king's ships reappeared at Nagasaki in 1661, and took a large share of the trade for the rest of the century. Chinese junks traded regularly between Siam and Nagasaki, often carrying royal cargoes.[25] At Ayutthaya, the Japanese were rapidly rehabilitated. The settlement numbered some 300 to 400 in 1637, and by 1638 a Japanese held the post of Okphra Chula heading the department of eastern trade. From the 1640s to the 1670s, Kimura Hansaemon was one of the biggest traders operating from Ayutthaya, including a major role in the tin trade.[26] Japanese troops continued to figure in the few military expeditions of the era, and in the succession wars. A Japanese, who held the noble title of Okya and was reportedly son of a former Okya, commanded an army sent to Pattani in 1691.[27] The number resident in the Japanese settlement rose to between 1,000 and 1,500 in the later seventeenth century.[28]

Yamada was the first foreigner to occupy high office and play a prominent role in Ayutthaya's politics. His example set a pattern, because the kings found such figures useful. The prominent foreigners through the mid-seventeenth century were Moors.

[25] Dhiravat, "Political history of Siam," 192; Nagazumi, "Ayutthaya and Japan," 102; Iwao, "Reopening"; Ishii, *Junk trade*.
[26] Schouten, "True description," 133; Nagazumi, "Ayutthaya and Japan," 101–2.
[27] Ishii, *Junk trade*, 59.
[28] Nidhi, "Ayudhya and the Japanese," 88–91; Nagazumi, "Ayutthaya and Japan," 100–1.

The Moors

Moors had been present since early Ayutthaya. In 1403, a Muslim from the "western ocean" joined a tribute mission from Ayutthaya to China.[29] According to a Timurid chronicler, the Persian Gulf port of Hormuz traded with Ayutthaya in the 1440s.[30] Over the sixteenth century, Persian traders spread across from the Persian Gulf to many port cities in India, the peninsula, and the archipelago.[31] Pires reported a large community of Moors resident at Ayutthaya in the early sixteenth century. In the early 1600s, two Persian brothers, who arrived in Ayutthaya via India, helped to reorganize the Phrakhlang ministry, presumably to administer the increased westward trade since the recovery of control over the portage route. Possibly from this time, the ministry was split into two parts, administering the eastern and western arms of trade.[32] One of the brothers, Sheikh Ahmed Qomi, remained in Ayutthaya and became involved with the court. In 1612, he probably served in the king's personal guard which suppressed the fracas by Japanese mercenaries. In 1629 he may have helped Prasat Thong come to the throne. He became head of the right division administering the westward trade, then Phrakhlang, and then head of Mahatthai. His son was given the title Chaophraya Aphai Raja, was allowed to present a daughter as a consort of Prasat Thong, and later also became head of Mahatthai.[33]

Ayutthaya's westward trade developed as the seventeenth century progressed. The exports from Siam included hides, forest goods, elephants, tin, copper from Japan, and metals and manufactures from China. Imports included large amounts of cloth and ornaments from India, plus goods for re-export to China. South Indian weaving centers produced textiles designed for the Ayutthayan market. From a base in the textile trade, Tamil Muslim merchants known as Chulia established settlements in ports all down the west coast of the peninsula, dominated the management of the portage route for a time, became the major traders in tin, and set up as shopkeepers in Ayutthaya. Persians, who had become well-established in Masulipatam, the main port of the Golconda kingdom, dominated the trade from there to Mergui. In 1621, Van Neijenrode listed sixty varieties of Indian cloth suitable for import to Siam and

---

[29] Wade, *Southeast Asia* online no. 5. The Chinese recorded his name as Ha-zhi, presumably Haji.
[30] "Narrative of the voyage of Abd-er-Razzak," 5–7.
[31] Andaya, "Ayutthaya and the Persian and Indian Muslim connection," 121–4.
[32] Breazeale, "Thai maritime trade."
[33] "Prawat kan sueb sai khong wong chek amat"; Julispong, *Khunnang krom tha khwa*, 139–44.

Cambodia, each in quantities ranging from a hundred to a thousand pieces, estimated the import would yield a profit rate of 50 to 60 percent, and insisted "one cannot possibly bring in too much."[34]

Across Asia in this era, prominent Persians acted not only as traders but as administrators, envoys, and political agents. The second of the two brothers who arrived in Ayutthaya at the start of the century returned home, but his son Aqa Muhammed Astarabadi arrived back in Ayutthaya in the 1640s, quickly mastered the language, and became an associate of the future King Narai. Although Persians numbered only around a hundred in Ayutthaya at the time, Aqa Muhammed organized them and other mainly Muslim groups in the succession battle that placed Narai on the throne in 1656. Afterwards Aqa Muhammed created a new 500-strong palace guard for Narai, mostly Muslims from India. He was rewarded with the noble title of Okphra Sinaowarat, and was given Narai's permission to marry his cousin, the sister of Chaophraya Aphai Raja.[35]

Under Narai, the Persians prospered. The son of Chaophraya Aphai Raja succeeded his father to the post of head of Mahatthai. Abdur Razzaq Gilani, born in Ayutthaya from Caspian heritage, emerged as the leader of the Persian community, held the title of Okya Phichit, and effectively served as Phrakhlang, though he may have occupied only a deputy post. In 1663, probably as the result of a commercial dispute with the Dutch, he was upbraided for "vile" behavior, jailed, then exiled, and his considerable wealth was confiscated by the crown.[36] Aqa Muhammed Astarabadi took his place, and did become Phrakhlang at some point in the 1660s. From this position he acquired a dominating role in the westward trade as a financier of cargoes rather than a shipper.

From the 1660s, Narai used the Persians and Chinese as a counterweight to the monopolistic ambitions of the Dutch. Aqa Muhammed Astarabadi owned junks and financed voyages to Macao and Japan, often working in partnership with Narai to evade restrictions imposed on this trade by the Dutch and the Japanese. He also gained a monopoly to collect eaglewood from Cambodia. By the 1670s, he had inserted Persians as governors at all the towns along the portage route – Mergui, Tenasserim, Pran, Kui, and Phetchaburi – while a Turk was governor at Bangkok. In 1676, he installed two Persian associates in charge of Ujung Salang (modern Phuket) and Bangkhli, two emerging centers of tin production, but they were killed soon after. Narai's factories in Macao and Bengal

---

[34] Neijenrode, "Account and description," 27, 38–48.
[35] Aubin, "Les Persans au Siam"; Andaya, "Ayutthaya and the Persian and Indian Muslim connection."
[36] Dhiravat, "Political history of Siam," 298–9; Dhiravat, *Siamese court life*, 181; Muhammad Rabi, *Ship of Sulaiman*, 94–8.

were also managed by Persians selected by Aqa Muhammed. When an embassy arrived from Safavid Persia in 1685, they were first welcomed at Mergui by a Persian governor, and then entertained at Bangkok by a Turkish governor and "several members of the Iranian community in Siam." The embassy scribe mentioned another Persian who "had little good fortune" at home but "came to Siam and was made governor and chief over this whole forest region" on the peninsula's western coast. Two years later the French envoy Ceberet met a Turk who was successively governor of Bangkok and Phetchaburi.[37]

In 1665, Narai sent an embassy to Golconda, and appointed a consular agent at the Golconda port of Masulipatam. In 1668 and 1682, he sent embassies to Persia, though the first was waylaid. At the height of Aqa Muhammed Astarabadi's influence in the 1660s and 1670s, the Ayutthaya court was flooded with Persian influences. Narai wore a robe and slippers in Safavid style and these garments became fashionable for the nobility. Narai's palace at Lopburi was built by Persian architects or engineers, evident from the pointed arches on doors and windows, the use of water for cooling, narrow entrances and staircases for security, and other details found in Isfahan and elsewhere. The pointed arch, borrowed from the Muslim Deccani kingdoms of central India, was used extensively in doors and windows at Lopburi, and more generally in *wat* architecture from this era on (Figure 4.1).[38] Narai's new audience hall at the Ayutthaya palace, the Banyong Rattanat, was probably influenced by contemporary palaces at Isfahan.[39] A Persian was among Narai's doctors.[40] *Wat* murals, manuscripts, and scripture cabinets were adorned with adaptations of the Persian tree-of-life motif, complete with flora and fauna unknown in Siam. Decorative motifs found in carving, painting, and textiles may have been developed from Persian forms. Several Persian words entered into Thai, and several dishes into royal cuisine. Sheep were raised to supply both the Persian community and the royal table. A Persian-style garden was created at Lopburi, and a "Grape Garden" appeared in the southwest corner of the Ayutthaya palace, perhaps planted with Shiraz vines. The Persians occupied some of the most splendid houses in the city, distinguished by their brick construction, two storeys, and bath houses. The French embassy to Ayutthaya in

---

[37] Muhammad Rabi, *Ship of Sulaiman*, 46, 50–1; Aubin, "Les Persans au Siam"; Andaya, "Ayutthaya and the Persian and Indian Muslim connection"; Gilbert White's 1678 report on trade in Andersen, *English intercourse with Siam*, 421–8; Jacq-Hergoualc'h, *Etude historique et critique*, 144.

[38] Julispong, "Khwam samphan."

[39] The building itself was in Siamese style, but was surrounded by water, gardens, and pavilions.

[40] Muhammad Rabi, *Ship of Sulaiman*, 140.

Figure 4.1. Islamic-style pointed arches and encircling pond at the Envoys' House in Lopburi (photograph courtesy of Julispong Chularatana)

1685 was lodged in one "which belonged to a great Mandarin, a Persian by Nation"[41] (Figure 4.1). Persian became the language of diplomatic discourse, used even in the English East India Company's missives to Ayutthaya. The scribe of the Safavid embassy wrote, "From the beginning of this king's reign up until just recently, all important business and matters of state were in the hands of the Iranians. They were the source of the king's power."[42]

After "30 yeares together that hee was of this Kings Cabinet Council,"[43] Aqa Muhammed Astarabadi fell from favor in the mid-1670s. The ostensible cause was "corruption" though most likely he had simply become too powerful, like Yamada and Abdur Razzack earlier. He was executed in 1678/9 by having his lips sewn up. Two of his sons were also executed after being implicated in a plot against Narai. Yet the lineage remained important. Two sons were ennobled, and one later became head of the right division of the Phrakhlang. Other Persian lineages also retained some status.

Because Ayutthaya was now more than ever a state mounted on commerce, trade and politics were inseparable. The Japanese and Persians became part of the system. They traded in partnership with the king and nobles, learned the language, took noble titles, and kept private armies that guarded their goods and participated in the succession disputes. As most were male, several married locally and merged gradually into the demographic background. Over time they added words, foods, dress, and aesthetic values to the local culture.

The Dutch

The Dutch arrived in 1604.[44] They had larger and faster ships, and a readiness to use force. They rapidly replaced the Portuguese and local traders in the archipelago, and seized Melaka in 1641. Like the Portuguese earlier, the Dutch could find no prospect in Siam for exchange with Europe, but saw opportunities for country trade. They identified the export of hides to Japan as the most promising enterprise, and signed the first treaty in 1617. Profits did not come easily. Japanese traders resident in Ayutthaya selected, cured, and packed hides specially for the Japanese market, and left the Dutch with the low-margin business. The Dutch tried to overcome such difficulty by demanding a monopoly. The kings

---

[41] Tachard, *Voyage to Siam*, 148.
[42] Muhammad Rabi, *Ship of Sulaiman*, 58.
[43] Gilbert White in Anderson, *English intercourse with Siam*, 425.
[44] This section is based on: Dhiravat, "Political history of Siam"; Smith, *Dutch in seventeenth-century Thailand*; Bhawan, *Dutch East India Company merchants*.

knew the power of monopoly and were reluctant to grant such power to others. The Dutch bargained by offering their naval and military strength to the king for expeditions against Cambodia, Pattani, and truculent port-polities on the peninsula (see below). In return for these services, Ayutthaya granted the Dutch a monopoly on hides in 1634 and again in 1647–52, but each time the grant was revoked after a short time. Later, the Dutch turned their attention to tin, and again asked for monopolies. In the 1670s, Ayutthaya conceded monopolies at Ujung Salang and Ligor, but the Dutch reaped little benefit. As Ujung Salang was scarcely under Ayutthaya's control and highly lawless, the Dutch soon gave up trying to operate under such conditions. At Ligor they found that the Phrakhlang who had allotted them the monopoly was their biggest covert competitor.

In 1663–64, the Dutch blockaded the Chaophraya River to protest against the influence that Persians wielded within the Phrakhlang ministry, and extracted new types of concession for raising the blockade. Besides the tin concessions in the south, they demanded immunity from local judicial process (extraterritoriality), and they tried to exclude Siamese royal ships from the Japan route by outlawing the use of Chinese captains, without success.

Unlike the Portuguese, Japanese, or "Moors," the Dutch were not individual traders but a company. They were more circumspect about local liaisons, almost never settled down, and refused to take up posts in the Ayutthayan bureaucracy. They could not be controlled through the devices of patronage and punishment employed with the Moors and Japanese. Although they initially agreed to bargain their naval power for trading privileges, from 1650 they resolved to steer clear of political involvements. Despite their prominence in trade, they had little impact on the society or culture.

"This City Is Excellent. It Has Everything."

In 1621, the Dutch merchant Van Neijenrode reported that the city of Ayutthaya surpassed "any place in the Indies (except for China) in terms of populace, elephants, gold, gemstones, shipping, commerce, trade and fertility."[45]

With its new eastward and westward links, Ayutthaya's trade not only increased but changed in character. Forest goods collected from the interior were still important, but Siam began to export a larger range and volume of locally produced goods. Rice was exported to the peninsula and

---

[45] Neijenrode, "Account and description," 8, quoted in Bhawan, *Dutch East India Company merchants*, 55.

the archipelago in years of abundant harvests. Sugar from cane "planted on hillsides"[46] was sent to Japan later in the century. Siamese timber was prized for shipbuilding and both Mergui and the lower Chaophraya sprouted boatyards. The tin deposits on the western and eastern sides of the mid-peninsula were mined for export to Japan, India, and the Persian Gulf. Skins of rays, deer, and other animals were sent to Japan and India to be made into apparel, armor, and decorations. The export of deerskins in particular averaged around 150,000 pieces a year and often much higher. One consignment in 1629 contained 500,000 hides and fifty-seven tons of sappanwood.[47] Ceramics were exported, though probably in smaller quantities than before. The kilns at Sukhothai and Sawankhalok may have ceased production in the turmoil of the 1580s, but jars fired in Singburi kilns were valued in Japan and China for storage of water and wine. In the 1660s, royal ships carried export cargoes of coarse pottery which may have been made in Siamese kilns.[48]

These rising exports stimulated the internal economy. While the entrepot trade was concentrated at Ayutthaya, these export trades were often routed through other ports and involved many local communities – Mons specializing in timber and rice; Portuguese mestizos in hides and sundries; Lao in gold and forest products; Malays trading down the peninsula; Indians importing cloth and gems.[49] Inland trade increased and the usage of money spread. Coinage was still rare and simple in the mid-sixteenth century, but by the late seventeenth a silver currency with four grades of coins was in general use, a mint was established within the Ayutthaya palace, and silver was imported from Japan and Manila to increase the supply. Cowrie shells, used for small denominations, were imported from the Maldives, Moluccas, and Manila under a royal monopoly, but also smuggled.[50]

Ayutthaya city prospered and expanded. The earliest plans and views done by Dutch company draftsmen in the mid-seventeenth century show a lattice of canals had been cut across the island to serve as both water supply and transport. The encircling river was crowded with boats. Around the port at the south-east corner, a jumble of houses spilled out over the water. Behind the port was a dense market area (Figure 4.2). Two

[46] Ishii, *Junk trade*, 56. This one Japanese shipper reported carrying sixty tons of sugar to Japan each year.
[47] Schouten quoted in Nagazumi, "Ayutthaya and Japan," 96.
[48] Brown, *Ming gap*, 66; Ho, "Export phases for Menam Basin ceramics," 106–9; Volker, *Porcelain and the Dutch East India Company*, 180, 191, 207–8; Piriya, "Pathakatha phi-set," 189–90.
[49] Smith, "Princes, nobles and traders," 9–10.
[50] Ronachai, *Evolution of Thai money*, section C; Gervaise, *Natural and political history*, 101–2; *Studies of old Siamese coins*.

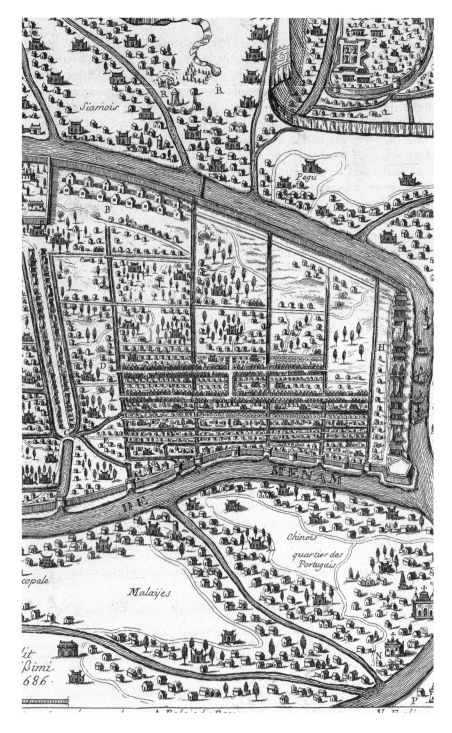

Figure 4.2. The crowded market area in the southeast of Ayutthaya on the Courtaulin map, 1686 (courtesy of the Siam Society)

streets led first west then north towards the center of the island, lined by over a hundred brick houses "belonging to the Chinese, Hindostanians and Moors."[51] In this market area, according to Heeck in 1655, there was "a wide long street with shops on both sides where daily you could find almost anything for sale, up to and including objects made of silver and gold."[52] Around the island center was the largest and densest settlement, mainly of Siamese "artisans":

> It has numerous wide streets with shops on both sides, and spacious squares for the markets. The markets are held every day, morning and evening, and are abundantly supplied with fish, eggs, fruit and vegetables, and an infinite quantity of other things ... The throng of people there is so great that it is sometimes very difficult to make one's way through.[53]

Starting in the sixteenth century, the city had spread outwards across the moat in all directions.[54] European maps show separate areas designated for the "camps" of the resident Chinese, Mons, Cochinchinese, Japanese, Malays, Macassars, Dutch, and French. Jacques de Bourges, who visited in 1669, wrote, "There are few cities in the whole of the East where one can see so many different nationalities as in Siam, and more than twenty different languages are spoken there."[55] Proverbially the city was said to accommodate "forty different nations."[56] This commercial activity was not confined to Ayutthaya. Schouten noted, "The divers Towns of this Countrey have their several Trafficks and Commerce."[57] Even a provincial center like Phitsanulok had its community of exotic traders, mainly Malays.[58]

All the European observers were struck by the sheer abundance of produce. Van Vliet concluded that "Siam is a country that has more than most other countries of everything that the human being needs."[59] La Loubère added that with rice and fish so cheap, and arrack available at two sous for a Parisian pint,

> it is no wonder if the Siameses are not in any great care about their Subsistence, and if in the Evening there is heard nothing but Singing in their Houses.[60]

This appreciation of the city was not confined to visitors. Probably in the 1680s, a court poet began *Kamsuan samut*, the "Ocean lament,"

---

[51] Kaempfer, *Description of the Kingdom of Siam*, 44.
[52] Heeck, *Traveler in Siam*, 59.
[53] Gervaise, *Natural and political history*, 33.
[54] *Van Vliet's Siam*, 110.
[55] Smithies, "Jacques de Bourges," 27.
[56] La Loubère, *New historical relation*, 10–11.
[57] Schouten, "True description," 108.
[58] La Loubère, *New historical relation*, 4; Choisy, *Journal of a voyage*, 233.
[59] *Van Vliet's Siam*, 107.
[60] La Loubère, *New historical relation*, 35.

not with the conventional eulogy of the king, but with a hymn to the city:

> This city is excellent. It has everything.
> It deserves more praise than heavens high, made and beautified by
>   Brahma.
> A city of delights. A royal city with the nine gem attributes.
> The world's finest, built by Lord Rama himself.
>
> The fame of Ayutthaya rings down from sky to earth.
> Just scan your eyes across the world – it is the single celestial flower.
> Thousands and millions have found no single, tiny blemish.
> The Three Gems illuminate the world and all the heavens.[61]

Ayutthaya and the Peninsula

Ayutthaya's influence down the peninsula had shrunk over the fifteenth and sixteenth centuries as Malays in-migrated from the archipelago, Islam became established, and traders, clerics, and adventurers arrived from the Islamic world. With its attentions focused elsewhere, Ayutthaya made no attempt to resist this trend. There is no record of an Ayutthaya expedition south in the sixteenth century.

According to Portuguese accounts from the mid-sixteenth century, several peninsular ports were dependencies of Siam (see above, p. 88), but these were alliances of mutual convenience, modeled on the Chinese tribute system under which local rulers sent tribute to gain access to trade and perhaps some extra legitimacy. Ayutthaya may have claimed some kind of overlordship, but the local rulers considered themselves independent and often faced tribute demands from other suzerains. Pires made the best attempt at describing the situation; the listed places down the peninsula were

all ports belonging to lords of the land of Siam, and some of these are kings. They all have junks; these do not belong to the king of Siam, but to the merchants and the lords of the places ... other ports all have lords like kings ... every one of these is a chief port and they have a great deal of trade, and many of them rebel against Siam.[62]

In the 1560s, Mudhaffar Syah rose to rule in Pattani after a period of fierce local conflict. He traveled to Ayutthaya to formally submit to the king, and was rewarded with gifts which confirmed and glamorized his rule – regalia, a marriage alliance (which he refused), and 160 war

[61] Winai, *Kamsuan samut*, 39–46.
[62] Pires, *Suma Oriental*, 105–6, 110.

prisoners from Lanxang and Pegu.[63] Ayutthaya gained the benefit of listing such places as dependencies, and occasionally demanded that they
send tribute, usually in the symbolic form of *bunga mas,* model trees
fashioned from silver and gold. The Kedah ruler probably reflected his
colleagues when he insisted that these gifts were no more than marks of
friendship, submitted to maintain good trading relations.[64] Many ports
also sent tribute to other overlords in parallel, particularly to the Malay
sultanate at Johore. Ayutthaya had difficulty gaining any more substantial
benefit than symbolic tribute. When Ayutthaya called on Pattani for help
against Pegu in the 1560s, Mudhaffar Syah duly arrived with a force of
300 men, but proceeded to attempt a coup.[65] When the Dutch, Japanese,
and British traders visited Pattani and Ligor, the local rulers concluded
trading agreements without any reference to Ayutthaya.[66]

The tribute system was originally a loose association between unequal
trading partners, but over the seventeenth century Ayutthaya attempted
to impose stronger control. The increase of population on the peninsula
changed its importance for Ayutthaya. Besides the in-migration of Malays,
many Chinese settled in the ports. According to legend, a Fukienese fleeing for his life with 2,000 followers captured Pattani and married the
Malay ruler's daughter.[67] After the Manchu invasion of China in the
mid-seventeenth century, many opponents of the Manchus fled to ports
all around Southeast Asia. These new settlers brought expertise – Malays
in pepper cultivation and Chinese in tin mining. The best tin deposits were along the west coast where the mountains fall steeply into the
sea. The deposits were under-exploited because there was little land for
growing rice to feed a workforce. By the early seventeenth century, with
the rise of trading all around the Bay of Bengal, these areas could import
rice from Siam, Burma, and India's eastern coast. Phuket (Ujung Salang,
Jonsalem, Junkceylon), which had been a near-deserted, jungle-covered
island, became a tin-mining center, settled by Malays and Chinese, and
soon visited by Portuguese, Dutch, Arab, Malay, Indian, and Ayutthayan
merchants.[68] For the trading state of Ayutthaya, the value of the port
polities of the middle peninsula was no longer merely as symbolic dependencies but as sources of profit. That prompted Ayutthaya to become
more assertive.

[63] Teeuw and Wyatt, *Hikayat Patani,* vol. 2, 154–7; *Van Vliet's Siam,* 128–9.
[64] Andaya and Andaya, *History of Malaysia,* 69.
[65] *RCA,* 49 (*LP*); Teeuw and Wyatt, *Hikayat Patani,* vol. 2, 157–61.
[66] Floris, *His voyage to the East Indies in the Globe,* ch. 4; Farrington and Dhiravat, *English factory in Siam,* 128–45; Dhiravat, "Towards a history of seventeenth-century Phuket"; Nidhi, "Nakhon si thammarat."
[67] Skinner, *Chinese society in Thailand,* 4–5, 7.
[68] Dhiravat, "Towards a history of seventeenth-century Phuket"; Nidhi, "Jak rat chai khop."

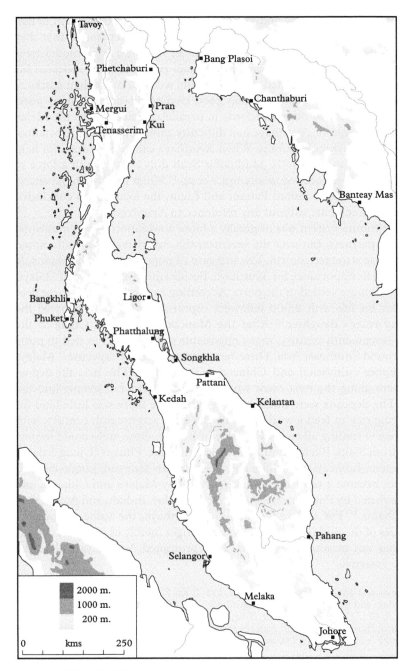

Map 4.1. The peninsula

In 1628, the ruler of Ligor was summoned to Ayutthaya and dismissed for some wrongdoing, and the Japanese Yamada Nagamasa was possibly dispatched to Ligor in his place. This may have been the first attempt by Ayutthaya to impose an appointee on Ligor (or any other peninsula port). At the outset, it failed. Yamada was killed and the other Japanese put to flight. What happened next is unknown, but most likely the local rulers remained in place while giving Ayutthaya a dominant influence in Ligor commerce. When the Dutch later tried to trade in tin at Ligor, they found that their competitors were Narai, his Phrakhlang, and the local ruler. Ligor also became Ayutthaya's intermediary for imposing its influence over the tin-mining areas on the west coast.[69]

From this period onwards, any defiance of Ayutthaya by a southern port is portrayed in the chronicles as a "revolt," as if they had been in dependent status earlier, but this vocabulary is part of Ayutthaya's increased aggression.

On the east coast, the most important port after Ligor was Pattani. For a century from the 1570s, the port was ruled by a lineage of Muslim merchant queens. As was common in such port cities, their claim to rule was based on the fact they were the wealthiest merchants. One queen proved her claim to succeed by piling up all her property for public view, a process that took three days.[70] The Pattani queens welcomed European traders, lent them money at usurious rates, bought their languishing stocks of cloth for a pittance, gouged them with port taxes, and entertained them with dances and song.[71] Most foreign traders soon abandoned Pattani, however, because the harbor was a muddy estuary and the town vulnerable to pirate attacks.

Pattani balanced Ayutthaya to the north against the Muslim rulers to the south. Raja Ungu, the reigning queen in the 1620s, had been married to the ruler of Pahang and gave her daughter to marry the ruler of Johore. In 1624, she reportedly rejected the grant of an Ayutthaya title, perhaps because it would complicate her relations to the south. In 1629, the Dutch in Ayutthaya were told she had revolted on grounds that Prasat Thong was "an usurper of the Crownland, a rascal, murderer, and traitor." Ayutthaya dispatched a large force, which besieged Pattani and destroyed outlying settlements, but failed to make Pattani submit. The Pattani chronicle mocks the Ayutthaya forces for not knowing how to sail and for failing to supply their troops, who withdrew because "they suffered from starvation." However, Raja Ungu's daughter and

[69] Dhiravat, "Political history of Siam," 314–15; Dhiravat, "Towards a history of seventeenth-century Phuket," 102.
[70] Teeuw and Wyatt, *Hikayat Patani*, vol. 2, 185.
[71] Farrington and Dhiravat, *English factory in Siam*, 113, 117, 135–6.

successor formally submitted to Ayutthaya, and dutifully visited the capital in 1641.[72]

In the 1680s, Ayutthaya attempted to appoint a governor of Pattani, but his arrival "created uproar among the people" and he was forced to withdraw. Perhaps as a result, after the succession at Ayutthaya in 1688, it was again alleged that Pattani rebelled, and another army was sent "consisting of one hundred large and small military vessels with about fifty thousand men on board." The Pattani queen evacuated the town and hid in the mountains. Before long, "most of the [Ayutthaya] soldiers succumbed to the conditions [of poor food and water] and many died." In 1693, after the Siamese sent reinforcements, the Pattani queen came down from the hills and agreed to send tribute again.[73]

The other major port on the east coast was Songkhla (Singora). Here too in the mid-1630s, Ayutthaya accused the Malay ruler of revolt and sent an army which razed the port to the ground. The town was rebuilt by an adventurer from Java who declared himself a sultan. Ayutthaya again interpreted this as "revolt" and sent four military expeditions over 1646 to 1653, with the largest amounting to 25,000 men supplemented by troops and supplies from Ligor, but these forces failed to subdue the town.[74] In 1676, after the old ruler had died, his eldest son hastened to Ayutthaya to gain Narai's endorsement because his brothers had challenged for the succession. Narai showed his pleasure by granting him the title of "Oya Sultan" and showering him with presents.[75]

On the west coast, where many of the settlements were newer, rougher, and more remote, imposing Ayutthaya's influence was even more difficult. The ruler of Kedah repeatedly rejected summons to appear at Ayutthaya by feigning illness, prompting Narai to send him a gold plate showing his image along with optimistic instructions on how it should be revered.[76] Ayutthaya gave the Dutch a monopoly on Phuket tin, but they withdrew after their factory was burnt to the ground in 1658. When they tried again in 1670, armed with a new license from Narai, a Dutch ship was burnt and another ship's crew was massacred. The Dutch believed the local elite was behind all these events, and effectively abandoned Phuket in 1675. Ten years later, the French were offered a "monopoly of the commerce of tin" in Phuket but were soon aware that this grant was useless.[77]

---

[72] Teeuw and Wyatt, *Hikayat Patani*, vol. 1, 17–18; vol. 2, 178–80, 182–3.
[73] Teeuw and Wyatt, *Hikayat Patani*, vol. 2, 206–7; Ishii, *Junk trade*, 59, 63–4, 66, 72–4, 120–2.
[74] Dhiravat, "Political history of Siam," 178; Dhiravat, *Court, company and campong*, 16–17.
[75] Bhawan, *Dutch East India Company merchants*, 131.
[76] Andaya and Andaya, *History of Malaysia*, 69.
[77] Munro-Hay, *Nakhon Sri Thammarat*, 157–9.

In sum, the rising population and productive capacity down the peninsula drew Ayutthaya's gaze back to the south in the seventeenth century. By accusing the rulers of the peninsula port-polities of "revolt," Ayutthaya laid claim to overlordship down to Pattani and Phuket, and occasionally further to Kedah and Kelantan. The military expeditions to enforce these textual claims were some of the largest in this era, but Ayutthaya's military might was over-stretched at this distance. Attempts to subcontract the task of imposing control to the Japanese and Europeans also came to little. With some difficulty, Ayutthaya was able to enforce its claim to tributary overlordship, but was thwarted in attempts to appoint administrators.

Royal Wealth and Power

The shift from war to trade transformed the Ayutthayan monarchy. After Naresuan's death, the king almost never led an army to war.[78] Kings became the chief merchants in the maritime trading economy, and the crown became spectacularly wealthy. Successive kings attempted to create new foundations for a king who was no longer the chief warrior. Songtham lavished money on religious construction, and new forms of ritual. Prasat Thong shrouded the monarchy in mystification and claimed an Angkorian heritage. Narai sought association with the glittering courts in the outside world, first with Safavid Persia and then with Bourbon France.

Royal Income

At the start of the century, Ekathotsarot raised revenues by taxing the nobles, and forcing them to contribute to his building projects, for which he was reckoned "more covetous than any of his predecessors." Commerce was a safer source of royal income. By the 1630s, royal junks were trading to India and to China. "When all the boats return," reported Van Vliet, "the yearly profits are immense."[79] By 1684, the king's trading in one year was estimated as five or six junks to China, two or three to Japan, between one and three to Tonkin, maybe one to Macao, one to Surat and others to Cambodia, Timor, Cochinchina, Borneo, and upriver to Lanxang. Of the 234 voyages recorded as departing Ayutthaya between 1629 and 1694, 153 belonged to the kings and royal kin.[80] In addition, Prasat Thong greatly expanded the range of articles covered

---

[78] Narai went north during campaigns against Chiang Mai in 1660 and 1661–62, but not as the army commander; *RCA*, 251–3, 295–300 (*BM*).

[79] *Van Vliet's Siam*, 121, 234.

[80] Smith, "Princes, nobles and traders," 11.

by royal monopolies. Foreign merchants were forced to buy their main export goods (sappanwood, tin, lead, and saltpeter) from the royal warehouses, which could extract a heavy margin – buying saltpeter locally for five ticals a picul, and selling it on at eight to seventeen.[81]

The kings also invested in internal trade. In the 1630s, "the inland trade produces a large sum of money and many trading stations have been established in the various provinces."[82] Narai imported textiles and "not contented with selling by Whole-sale, he has some Shops in the Baazars or markets, to sell by Re-tail [and] sends them into his Magazines of the Provinces."[83] Narai also controlled the internal trade in betel leaf and areca nut, universally chewed as a mild stimulant.[84] The crown exacted death duties from noble families, and special contributions for financing construction projects and events. La Loubère concluded, "the present King of Siam has augmented his Revenues a Million."[85] Van Neijenrode estimated in more detail:

In sum, the means and income of the King of Siam … come to the amount of 20,000 catty Siamese silver annually, which, as I saw it reckoned, comes to about twenty-five tonnes of gold average over the years, of which he pays out yearly no more than fifteen tonnes … such that, in Siam an enormous treasure has been gathered and stored in the treasure houses.[86]

The main royal treasury was sited immediately behind the hall used for audience and residence in the palace, and some European visitors were invited to visit. Count Forbin, who was impressed by nothing else in Siam, waxed lyrical about "this heap of gold, silver and precious stones of immense value" which constituted "all the riches of the royal treasure, which are truly worthy of a great king, and enough to make one in love with his court."[87] Gervaise recorded that the king had "eight or ten warehouses … that are of unimaginable wealth," piled "to the roof" with jewels, metals, exotic goods, and "great lumps of gold-dust."[88] The Jesuit Tachard gulped on seeing the interior of the royal Wat Phra Si Sanphet where "there is nothing to be seen but Gold … it must needs touch one to the quick to see one single Idol richer than all the Tabernacles of the Churches of Europe."[89]

[81] Anderson, *English intercourse with Siam*, 253; Sun, "Saltpetre trade," 161–3.
[82] *Van Vliet's Siam*, 121.
[83] La Loubère, *New historical relation*, 94.
[84] Choisy, *Journal of a voyage*, 186.
[85] La Loubère, *New historical relation*, 95.
[86] Neijenrode, "Account and description," 15–16. A catty here was 1.3 English pounds or 20 tael.
[87] Smithies, *Siamese memoirs of Count Claude de Forbin*, 60.
[88] Gervaise, *Natural and political history*, 183–4.
[89] Tachard, *Voyage to Siam*, 180–1.

The palace housed several other storehouses for valuable goods including European articles imported from Dutch Batavia, porcelain from China, silks from Japan, and other textiles from India. A list of gifts sent from Ayutthaya to French royalty in the 1680s reads like the inventory of a museum of Asian luxuries: Japanese furniture, silverware, pottery, and weaponry; Chinese cabinets, silks, and porcelain reckoned "the best and most curious of all the Indies"; Persian and Indian carpets; and countless figurines, powder boxes, flasks, and curiosities.[90]

King and Buddhism

As kings ceased to be generals, they sought ways to adapt the institutions of kingship to new circumstances. Through the sixteenth century, however, these efforts were not consistent. Each reign followed its own path.

At first, the kings sought to restore and expand the royal patronage of Buddhism. From the early fifteenth century onwards, almost every king had undertaken construction of a major temple at the start of a reign, plus other religious benefactions. In the age of warfare, this activity diminished. From the Phitsanulok takeover in 1569 to Naresuan's death in 1605, the chronicles record no major religious building, repair, or ceremony except perhaps a stupa or massive Buddha image made around 1600 to commemorate victory over Burma.[91]

After 1605, the kings revived their attention to Buddhism. Ekathotsarot built "a holy and excellent chief temple" for the forest-dwelling sect, endowed it richly, produced a version of the Tipitaka, and had five Buddha images cast, occasioning "a seven day celebration, with staged amusements."[92] Yet, the Van Vliet chronicle, which probably drew from contemporary chronicles compiled in *wat* rather than palace, judged that Ekathotsarot "was not devout, only slightly fond of the monks." His successor, who had spent time in the monkhood before ascending the throne, was judged by the same source quite differently:

He was not warlike, but very studious, devout, fought continually against idolatry, improved the religion and laws of the land, and shared many good things with the poor and the monks. He built and repaired more temples, pyramids and living quarters for the monks than any of his predecessors ... His Majesty was considered so holy that Siamese claimed that he had no enemies in the world.[93]

---

[90] Smithies, *Aspects of the embassy*, 137–49; Woodward, "Seventeenth-century Chinese porcelain," 30, 37 fn. 30.

[91] Sujit, *Jedi yutthahatthi*; Tun Aung Chain, *Chronicle of Ayutthaya*, 41; *Khamhaikan khun luang ha wat*, 13.

[92] *RCA*, 199–200, 206.

[93] *Van Vliet's Siam*, 233, 235.

At the end of his reign he composed a "royal edition" of the Great Jataka (Phra Vessantara) and a "complete edition" of the Tipitaka.[94] Though his regnal name was probably Intharacha, he appears in the chronicles as Songtham, upholder of the *dhamma*, a name perhaps conferred because of his exertions on behalf of Buddhism.

Two innovations suggest Songtham also reshaped the relationship between monarch and religion. During his reign, a hunter discovered a footprint of the Buddha on a hill around 45 kilometers northeast of the capital. The king built an elaborate complex around the site, known as Phra Phutthabat (Phra Buddhapada), which became a place of royal pilgrimage, visited annually in an elaborate procession. Such footprints are evidence that the Buddha visited this place in the far past. The attention given to the footprint dramatized the king's role as protector of the religion. In the chronicles, the discovery of the footprint is the high point of Songtham's reign, and a pilgrimage there by his successor, Prasat Thong, is described in great detail.[95]

In the annual cycle of royal ceremonial in the Palace Law, the only Buddhist ceremony is Visakha Puja.[96] During Songtham's reign, Schouten for the first time mentions the royal *kathin*, a traditional merit-making ceremony of presenting robes to monks at the end of the Buddhist rains-retreat. The royal version may have existed earlier but not been recorded.[97] While Visakha Puja is a celebration of the historical Buddha, the *kathin* ceremony portrays the king as both patron and disciple of the monkhood, involved in an act of giving, a key duty of a *bodhisatta*, a Buddha-to-be. By Prasat Thong's reign, the *kathin* ceremonies had also become massive displays of royal power. The procession to Wat Mahathat included the royal family, the major ministers, a hundred elephants, and in total "about six to seven thousand persons" according to Van Vliet, or fifteen to sixteen thousand according to Schouten. During visits to other *wat* by water, "The total number of boats amounts to 350 to 400, and 20,000 to 25,000 persons take part in this procession."[98] Watching the water procession during the Narai reign, the Jesuit Father Tachard thought there were "about twenty thousand Balons [boats], above two hundred thousand souls," while his French colleagues raised the estimate to six hundred thousand.[99]

[94] *RCA*, 210, ll. 24–7 (*BM*).
[95] *RCA*, 209–10 (*BM*), 217–20 (*BM*); Ishii, "Religious patterns and economic change," 188.
[96] Baker and Pasuk, *Palace Law of Ayutthaya*, 69, 111, 116–30.
[97] Portuguese friars in Ayutthaya in the 1590s described Naresuan going in a water procession that may have been a *kathin*; see Ribanedeira, *Historia del archipelago*, vol. 1, 424.
[98] *Van Vliet's Siam*, 117–20; Schouten, "True description," 128–9.
[99] Tachard, *Voyage to Siam*, 128–9.

Songtham had begun to emphasize the king's role as a *bodhisatta* accumulating merit by good works, and as a patron of the monkhood. His efforts, however, were not sustained by successors who took different paths.

Hiding the Royal Body

Prasat Thong set out to mystify the monarchy. Central to this process was the hiding of the king's body. In the sixteenth century, there were some restrictions on viewing the king at ceremonial occasions, but these were compromised by the visibility of the king as a military leader. By the 1630s, Schouten noted that the king "seldom shews himself to the People, and very sparingly to the Grandees and Officers of the Kingdom."[100] At royal audience, blasts of music warned nobles that the king was about to appear so that they could bend forward and keep their eyes fixed to the ground.[101] When the king visited *wat* in the city, people were expected to line the route, but still to abase themselves and look away. Pellet archers targeted the eyes of offenders. During the massive *kathin* processions, "all the windows and doors of the Houses were shut, and the Port holes of the Ships too," and "No body is seen in his way or sight; but upon their knees, with folded hands, and bowed heads and bodies."[102] Van Neijenrode recorded, "I have seen some put to death, whoever did not salute the King timely, sufficiently or properly."[103]

Until the early seventeenth century, the palace was only partially walled and the Palace Law had clauses forbidding trespass by foreigners stumbling in unawares and by lovers using the gardens for trysts.[104] Beginning in 1632, Prasat Thong roughly doubled the area of the palace and enclosed it for the first time with an encircling wall, penetrated by "only one street and two little pathways."[105] La Loubère stated, "The Gates of the Palace are always shut."[106] This was not true, as people entered the northeastern corner where ministers and officials carried out the work of government, but the palace was designed to give an impression of being closed. The perimeter wall had over twenty gates, mostly named in Pali-Sanskrit, sacred languages incomprehensible for most people. Several

---

[100] Schouten, "True description," 97–8.
[101] La Loubère, *New historical relation*, 109. Van Vliet stated that Naresuan "was the first to make the mandarins come creeping before the king and lie continually with their faces downward"; see *Van Vliet's Siam*, 229.
[102] Tachard, *Voyage to Siam*, 190; Schouten, "True description," 98.
[103] Neijenrode, "Account and description," 12.
[104] Baker and Pasuk, *Palace Law of Ayutthaya*, 84–6 (clauses 17, 21).
[105] *Van Vliet's Siam*, 110.
[106] La Loubère, *New historical relation*, 96.

gates were assigned to specific uses involving only royalty – for attending cremations, for removing corpses, for ritual bathing in the river, for processions. At the few gates where others were admitted, visitors had to leave their weapons, have their breath sniffed for liquor, and remove their shoes "though it is so dirty, that people sometimes step in the mud up to the calf of their Legs, if they do not keep an exact balance in walking over the small planks, that are laid for them." While nobles paraded elsewhere with great retinues, "even an ordinary Mandarin dare not enter but attended only with one servant."[107] The palace gates were part of a drama of concealment.

The concealment extended to the king's name, which was not disclosed until after his death. Europeans were told this was "for fear lest any Enchantment should be made on his Name."[108] The royal women were even more definitely part of this concealment. About the chief queen, La Loubère reported,

none but her Women and Eunuchs do see her. She is conceal'd from all the rest of the People; and when she goes out either on an Elephant, or in a Balon, it is in a Chair made up with Curtains, which permit her to see what she pleases, and do prevent her being seen. And Respect commands, that if they cannot avoid her, they should turn their back to her, by prostrating themselves when she passes along.

Queen Yothathep was prominent through three reigns and constantly discussed by the European residents, but "no Man ever saw her neither publicly nor privately."[109]

From the Prasat Thong reign, those queens assigned titles that gave high royal status to their sons were limited to close relatives. Prasat Thong married the elder daughter of King Songtham, and gave his own daughter in marriage to his brother. Narai married a paternal half-sister, while his own sister married a paternal half-brother.[110] These alliances concentrated the legitimacy available from both male and female descendants of former kings.

Khmer Revivalism

Prasat Thong set out to revive the traditions of early Ayutthaya and its links back to the glory of Angkor. He may have claimed Khmer descent. Siamese envoys sent to Portugal in 1684 were briefed to inform questioners

---

[107] Kaempfer, *Description of the Kingdom of Siam*, 44–5.
[108] La Loubère, *New historical relation*, 101.
[109] Tachard, *Voyage to Siam*, 274; Bhawan, "Kromluang Yothathep."
[110] Kemp, *Aspects of Siamese kingship*, 25–6.

that his son, Narai, was descended from the kings of Angkor.[111] Prasat Thong may have stemmed from the Lopburi family, but more likely, he was an inventor of tradition. Although he is known to history as Prasat Thong (golden tower), probably because of his repair and gilding of Wat Mahathat, his regnal name may have been Ramathibodi, echoing the name of the city founder.[112] Van Vliet reported that he "renewed the great feast days that had been introduced by the fortune-fated King Phrachao Ramathibodi," meaning the founder-king U Thong, and that many people said "His Majesty is like the first founder of the Siamese kingdom in so many ways."[113] Prasat Thong's revision of the calendar (see below) may have been the revival of a Khmer version.[114] He named a new building inside the palace as Si Yasodara Mahaphiman, using an old name for Angkor.[115] His modification of the palace gave Ayutthaya a groundplan that echoed Angkor Thom – divided into quadrants by two main roads, with the palace in the northwest quadrant.[116]

According to the later chronicles, Prasat Thong "sent artisans to copy and bring back plans of the Holy Imperial Metropolis [*nakhon luang*, Angkor] and of the palaces of the Capital of the Kamphucha Country," and used the plans to design a palace on the route to the footprint, naming the palace after Angkor.[117] In addition, Wat Chai Watthanaram, a temple he built on the site of his mother's home in the revived tradition of building a major temple at the start of a reign, had many elements possibly inspired by Angkor, including the square plan, shape of the main tower, and bas reliefs in galleries all around.[118] Prasat Thong seems to have made a special identification of himself with this temple in a manner similar to later Angkor kings (perhaps continued by his successors, as foreign maps call it the "King's pagoda" into the eighteenth century). He cast many crowned Buddha images with regal bearing and elaborate decoration which alluded to the similarity between monarch and Buddha, and placed eight of them in the towers around the central *prang*. His

---

[111] Smithies and Dhiravat, "Instructions given to the Siamese envoys," 127; La Loubère, *New historical relation*, 102.

[112] *Khamhaikan khun luang ha wat*, 24; another story states that he discovered a miniature golden tower in an anthill through a childhood dream.

[113] *Van Vliet's Siam*, 242–4.

[114] Vickery, "Composition and transmission," 152.

[115] *RCA*, 216, ll. 25–8 (*BM*); the Cushman translation obscures the name.

[116] Noticed by Nopanant Tapananon.

[117] *RCA*, 216, ll. 3–9 (*BM*). The remains are still known by the Thai name for Angkor, Nakhon Luang. As Piriya notes (*Sinlapa sukhothai lae ayutthaya*, 192–7), the building resembles a Rajasthan wind-palace more than anything at Angkor.

[118] He may have used a faulty plan of Angkor made by a Japanese pilgrim, but this is unlikely. McGill, "Art and architecture," 128–32; Fouser, *Lord of the golden tower*, 31.

concealment and mystification of the royal body may have been based on a conception of the grandeur and remoteness of the Angkor kings.

Prasat Thong favored the court Brahmans and Brahman ritual. The chronicle contains an elaborate account of his anointment as king in which the court Brahmans administer the rite with no one else present. After the king had built the Si Yasodara Mahaphiman, the "holy teachers, domestic chaplains, astrologers, elders and preceptors" berated him for not honoring Indra in the palace's name and hinted that the consequences could be grave. He accordingly renamed it the "palace of Indra the emperor."[119] In the mid-1630s, the king became concerned about the astrological significance of the approach, in April 1639, of year 1000 in the Chula Sakkarat calendar. To avert catastrophe, he decided to rebase the calendar in a magnificent ceremony staged in an elaborate reconstruction of the Three Worlds geography, with the court Brahmans, dressed up as the Hindu gods, acting as the main officiants. Shortly after, he held the "One Hundred Great Donations," a massive act of charity in which the Brahmans were the primary recipients.[120] According to the chronicle, he named his son Narai because at his birth "holy relatives and kinsmen at first glance thought he was endowed with four arms" like Vishnu.[121]

The prominent role of the court Brahmans is evident in the *phitsadan* chronicle itself. Beginning late in the Naresuan reign, and intensifying under Ekathotsarot, the style becomes more florid and the titles of kings and other royalty become more elaborate. Under Songtham, the chronicle returns to a simpler style and shorter length, hinting that the Brahmans may have lost this task under this assiduously Buddhist king. Under Prasat Thong, they returned with a vengeance. Kings are prefixed with elaborate titles, such as Somdet Boromma Bophit Phraphutthajaoyuhua, which Cushman translated as "the Supreme-Paramount-Refuge-Paramount-Reverence-and-Holy-Buddhist-Lord-Omnipotent," rather than the simpler Phrajao favored earlier. Over half the content of the chronicles is taken up with activities in which the Brahmans are involved, including not only royal ceremonies but the chief astrologer's ability to predict a bolt of lightning that burnt the main audience hall to the ground.[122]

This Brahmanical trend continued into Narai's reign. Phra Maharatchakhru, head of the Brahman department, composed a eulogy of Prasat Thong that focuses on the attempt to change the calendar

[119] *RCA*, 216 (*BM*); Dhiravat, "Political history of Siam," 198–9; "Khamchan sansoen phrakiat somdet phraphutthajao luang prasat thong," 30–2.
[120] *RCA*, 222–5 (*BM*).
[121] *RCA*, 217 (*BM*).
[122] *RCA*, 219, 226–7 (*BM*).

and makes no mention of any royal patronage of Buddhism.[123] Prasat Thong's funeral and Narai's coronation were elaborate Brahmanical affairs. Narai's coronation title included the entire Brahmanical pantheon, occupying twelve lines in the printed versions of the chronicle. Narai had five images of Shiva and one of Brahma cast. He performed a "Holy Royal Ceremony of the Five Rites" which included a procession to the jail where the king "had robbers executed."[124] Late in the reign, a Brahman official composed a poetic eulogy of the king. The conventional opening pays homage to the Hindu trinity, and the finale extends the list to around fifteen Hindu gods and goddesses, with no mention of the Buddha or the Three Jewels.[125]

Gervaise wrote, "There has never been any court in the world more ritualistic than the court of the king of Siam. There are ceremonies for walking, for speaking, for drinking, for eating, even for cooking."[126]

Hunts, Contests, Poems, Histories

The seventeenth-century court gave itself up to the kind of pursuits favored by a warrior caste which no longer spends so much time on the battlefield. Elephant hunting became a recreation practiced far beyond the military demand. Ekathotsarot "found great pleasure in going on the hunt, going horseback riding, fighting on elephants."[127] Narai moved his court to Lopburi for much of the year in part because he could hunt there almost every day. His expeditions lasted several days and captured around 300 elephants every year. At Ayutthaya, besides several "white" and otherwise auspicious elephants kept inside the palace, there was another 400 to 500 stabled in the city. While elephants were exported as articles of trade,[128] their main use was for procession and display. In the northeastern corner of the city was an enclosure where the king presided over representations of the hunt staged for foreign visitors. The court also hunted deer, wild buffalo, and crocodiles, and staged tiger-baiting, cockfights, elephant fights, elephant-and-tiger fights, and other contests.

The navy was also reoriented to display. The first description of a royal barge procession appears in the chronicles in the Ekathotsarot reign involving not only a dozen named royal barges, but others for "the various *thao*

---

[123] "Khamchan sansoen phrakiat somdet phraphutthajao luang prasat thong," 35–49.
[124] *RCA*, 232–4, 244–5 (*BM*).
[125] Winai and Trongjai, *Moradok khwam songjam haeng nopphaburi*, 61–140, esp. 62, 123–40.
[126] Gervaise, *Natural and political history*, 187.
[127] *Van Vliet's Siam*, 208.
[128] Dhiravat, "Catching and selling Siamese elephants."

phraya [lords], tributary kings, ministers, statesmen, chiefs, and nobles," followed by boats for various units of soldiers, guards, craftsmen, and civilians.[129] The parade was a prelude to Atsawayut, an annual ceremony for good fortune featuring a boat race. The elaborate barge procession was later adapted for the *kathin* ceremonies, and for impressing foreign envoys on their arrival in the capital. These processions and hunts required the mobilization of people on a large scale. Gervaise reckoned that 30,000 were required for Narai's elephant hunts, lasting several days.[130]

These hunts and displays kept the machinery of mobilization in good trim. They recalled in dramatic form the military vigor of the court in the Naresuan era. Most of all, they signaled the unique power of the king, who alone could stage such spectacles. After seeing the court and its public display, the republican Dutchman Schouten found "this reverence better becoming a celestial Deity, than an earthly Majesty." By contrast, the royalist Frenchman found it rather wonderful; Forbin thought there were "few sights in the world finer than when the King of Siam goes abroad in public," and Gervaise concluded, "In the Indies there is no state that is more monarchical than Siam."[131]

Peace made space also for gentler pursuits. Ekathotsarot had theatres built for dance. The funeral for Prasat Thong was celebrated with "musical instruments, conch-shell trumpets, gongs, drums, masques, shadow plays and classical theatre dancing." At great ceremonial events, people were treated to performances of Chinese comedy, Lao puppets, Siamese tumblers, *khon* masked drama, *lakhon* drama, epic recitations, and *rabam* figure dancing.[132] The variety was a side-benefit of the entrepot's cosmopolitanism.

In the court, Narai patronized poets and dabbled himself. In contrast to the martial themes of the military era, this court poetry dealt with peaceful pursuits. While *Yuan phai* had highlighted Trailokanat's army, the eulogy of Narai describes his Lopburi palace, highlighting the piped water system:

> There is water, clear and fresh,
> Flowing from the interior hills and valleys
> Rushing down through pipes and tubes
> To swirl up in the heart of the palace ...
> Through a lion's mouth
> Into the crystal bathing pond for the king's ablutions.[133]

---

[129] *RCA*, 204 (*BM*).

[130] Gervaise, *Natural and political history*, 177; see also Tachard, *Voyage to Siam*, 233–4.

[131] Schouten, "True description," 98; Smithies, *Siamese memoirs of Count Claude de Forbin*, 77; Gervaise, *Natural and political history*, 53.

[132] *RCA*, 204, 233–4 (*BM*); La Loubère, *New historical relation*, 47–8.

[133] "Eulogy of King Narai," stanzas 22–3, translated by Dhiravat na Pombejra, in Winai and Trongjai, *Moradok khwam songjam haeng nopphaburi*, 84–5.

While *Yuan phai* climaxed in a victory on the battlefield, the eulogy of Narai climaxes with an elephant hunt.[134] Similarly the eulogy of King Prasat Thong, written in the Narai reign, recounts the king's efforts in religious construction, his attempt to change the calendar, and his patronage of elaborate ceremonies and festivities.[135]

Verse was written in complex meters to show off skill and erudition. Poems did not tell stories or debate ideas but expressed emotions, particularly erotic experience and appreciation of nature. These were combined in *nirat* ("parting"), a genre in which the poet embarks on a journey through space or time, lamenting separation from his beloved. In perhaps the earliest example, *Nirat hariphunchai*, adapted from a Lanna original in the early seventeenth century, the poet travels to visit a relic, observing people and places which trigger thoughts of his beloved.

> The river is too dry for boats.
> Carts and crowds of people wade across.
> Drivers shake and snap the reins.
> When a cart falls, they rush as fast as darting fish to push the rear.
>
> O trees, go back to give news to my beloved.
> Yellow leaves fall, leaving branches almost bare.
> Not seeing you, my heart has slipped from my breast.
> Seeing withered leaves makes my heart wither too.[136]

The melodic sound of the verse was considered at least as important as the meaning. Poets exploited the potential for rhyme, alliteration, assonance, and onomatopoeia in a monosyllabic, tonal language. A court astrologer composed a treatise on prosody, *Chindamani*, which set out the rules of metrical composition, and advised poets to learn many languages – Pali, Khmer, Mon, Sinhalese, Burmese, and northern Thai – to master the vocabulary to express emotion within the constraints of meter. *Chindamani* also set out rules for spelling and pronunciation, necessary because of the large influx of loan words into the language in the cosmopolitan environment.[137]

Among the written products of this era were histories. The first which has survived was compiled by Van Vliet in 1640. He set out to reconstruct the history of Ayutthaya by consulting "learned monks" who preserved oral tradition as well as "the old Siamese histories," unidentified written

[134] Winai and Trongjai, *Moradok khwam songjam haeng nopphaburi*, 61–140, esp. 79–87, 109–26.

[135] "Khamchan sansoen phrakiat somdet phraphutthajao luang prasat thong."

[136] Stanzas 50–1, Prasert, *Khlong nirat hariphunchai*, 8–10, 52–4; Manas, "Emergence and development," esp. 141, 150.

[137] "Chindamani," 475; Davisakd, "Pursuit of Java," 97.

documents.[138] The account proceeds reign by reign, detailing the succession, main events, and king's death, very similar to the style of the *tamnan* and chronicles written in the *wat*, which may have been Van Vliet's main source. Little space is allotted to accounts of war. Each king is *judged* as either good or bad, using three main criteria: a good king has to be a powerful warrior to protect the religion and people; has to patronize the monkhood; and must rule by upholding the law and exercising compassion. Ramesuan (1388–95) attracted a good judgment: "He was merciful, full of pity ... brave in the handling of weapons ... gave many alms to the ecclesiastics and to the poor, building and repairing many temples and monasteries." By contrast, Intharacha from the late fifteenth century was pronounced "no warrior and not studious ... lustful" with the result that "his reign was not prosperous but a troubled one."[139]

The second history was compiled in 1681 under Narai and is now known as the Luang Prasoet chronicle after an official who discovered the manuscript in the early twentieth century. It is the only lengthy history written in Thai to have survived from the Ayutthaya period.[140] It traces the story from the founding of Ayutthaya through to 1605, with an approach markedly different from the Van Vliet chronicle. La Loubère mentions that Narai took a great interest in the "Art of Ruling" and "design'd principally to study it from the History of the King,"[141] perhaps a reference to this chronicle. In the early part, the entries for each reign are brief and descriptive, covering the manner of succession, the major events of the reign, the king's death, and wonderful events with astrological significance – earthquakes, eclipses, strange sightings. From the sixteenth century, the narrative become slightly fuller, still devoting most of its attention to warfare, but also mentioning epidemics, inflation, royal patronage of religion, elephant hunts, building city walls, great fires, and revolts. There is no trace of judgment. This chronicle tells a story which invests the city and its royalty with continuity through time.

Nobility and Monarchy

As a result of the transition from an age of warfare to the rising prosperity of an age of commerce, there were major changes in the nature of the nobility and its relationship to the crown.

---

[138] See Wyatt's introduction in *Van Vliet's Siam*, 186–93; and Vickery, "Review article: Jeremias van Vliet."

[139] *Van Vliet's Siam*, 205, 208.

[140] The "2/k.125 fragment," renamed as the Wachirayan Chronicle, shows that events were recorded at the time, possibly serving as input to the later *phitsadan* chronicles; see Vickery, "2/k.125 fragment" and Winai, "Phraratchaphongsawadan krung si ayutthaya chabap ho phra samut wachirayan."

[141] La Loubère, *New historical relation*, 100; Hodges, "Time in transition."

Decline of Provincial Lords

The rulers of provincial cities within Siam ceased to be little kings. Ayutthaya had appointed governors of the cities in the lower Chaophraya Plain at an earlier date, but now the powerful lords of the Northern Cities and some from the upper peninsula were dislodged in favor of Ayutthaya appointees. Possibly the opportunity arose because many were killed, deposed, or put to flight in the warring of the late sixteenth century. In the 1580s, Naresuan swept people down from the Northern Cities to defend Ayutthaya, then returned the people to these cities, and appointed their governors in the following decade.[142] With the death of Naresuan's father, the Sukhothai-Phitsanulok royal title of Maha Thammaracha disappeared, as did the royal titles from other Northern Cities. The governors now had the title of Okya. As seen in the account of Persian influence above, governors in the ports and towns along key trade routes were appointed from the capital under the influence of the Phrakhlang.

Under Prasat Thong, "the Governors of the principal provinces ... are usually required to remain in Iudia [Ayutthaya], where the King can keep an eye on them."[143] Narai continued the practice, making many appointments acting rather than permanent.[144] By the 1680s, La Loubère reported that "The Kings of Siam have ruin'd and destroyed the most potent Tchaou-Meuang [*jao mueang*, city lords], as much as they could, and have substituted in their place some Triennial Governors by Commission." Ayutthaya had also imposed an administrative system, modeled on Ayutthaya's practice and designed with overlapping jurisdictions to dissipate authority.[145] In the main provincial cities Ayutthaya appointed a *yokkrabat*, an official who served as the king's direct representative and as "a strict Spy upon the Governor."[146] The *yokkrabat* gradually took over judicial duties, acting in the king's name, and had power to try the provincial governor. At Phitsanulok, where the king had ordered officials to try the governor for malpractice, "He was convicted within an hour, and the death sentence they passed on him was carried out in their presence."[147] The extension of central power was probably less decisive and less universal than the European observers thought, but marked the start of a trend that continued into the following century.

[142] *RCA*, 133 (*BM*).
[143] *Van Vliet's Siam*, 318.
[144] *RCA*, 234–43 (*BM*); Nidhi, *Kanmueang thai samai phra narai*, 29–31.
[145] Suphawat, "Phra aiyakan kao"; possibly this system is described in the Law of revolt and warfare, clause 7, *Kotmai tra sam duang*, vol. 4, 127–8.
[146] La Loubère, *New historical relation*, 83–5.
[147] Gervaise, *Natural and political history*, 58.

The Service Nobility in the Capital

The service nobility had developed as the society prospered and the scope of government expanded. In the civil and military lists probably compiled in the seventeenth century, there were almost 3,000 people in the capital with official posts and *sakdina* of 400 or more. All were male except for a few women who administered the inner palace. Those at the peak of the pyramid of rank numbered a little over 200.[148]

Prowess in war ceased to be such a factor in determining wealth and status throughout society, but especially within the nobility. Patronage was now everything. Only established nobles were in a position to present their sons to be royal pages which was the training ground for high office. Their subsequent rise depended on ability and personal favor. Established officials could also offer their daughters as royal consorts with a chance to rise within the hierarchy of the inner palace and promote the fortunes of their kin through the politics of the backstairs. The fact that Sheikh Ahmed Qomi's descendants filled senior posts in the Phrakhlang ministry and other choice offices for generation after generation down to the fall of Ayutthaya suggests how well these systems were working.

Nobles were not paid and were expected to remunerate themselves through the powers of their office. All the ministries had their own law-courts which were a source of revenue through fines and fees. Nobles could also tap the prospering economy through the people under their command. As warring eased, the systems for marshaling manpower were not relaxed. High officials acquired an entourage of people including *phrai* and slaves inherited, bought, or granted by the king (see Chapter 5). As war diminished and commerce grew, the nobility became conspicuously richer.[149] A law on inheritance was introduced and amended twice in the early seventeenth century, hinting at a growing need to manage disputes over wealth. Clauses in the law mention "rich householders (*setthi karuehabodi*), with or without official rank."[150]

The Phrakhlang grew to be the most important ministry; foreigners regularly mistook its head for a "prime minister." Nobles in the ministry lent money to maritime traders, financed cargoes, and occasionally became ship-owners. Of the 234 voyages recorded as departing Ayutthaya between 1629 and 1694, fifty-two were mounted by nobles.[151] The Phrakhlang officials also earned income from other merchants. In

[148] *Kotmai tra sam duang*, vol. 1, 219–328; Terwiel, *Thailand's political history*, 41.
[149] Manop, *Khun nang ayutthaya*, ch. 4, esp. 209–11.
[150] *Kotmai tra sam duang*, vol. 3, 21–58.
[151] Smith, "Princes, nobles and traders," 11.

the daybook kept during a crisis for the Dutch company during 1636, Van Vliet describes repeatedly calling on officials in the Phrakhlang with gifts of gold, rich cloth, and other valuables.[152] In the 1640s, one of the richest and most powerful figures was Okya Sombatthiban, a senior official in the western department who became Phrakhlang in 1654/5. Officers of the Dutch company visited him in the evening "on a daily basis" to seek information and privileges, and rewarded him handsomely with gifts.[153] His wife traded in partnership with Soet, a low-born Mon woman who had become a bridge across the cultural gap between the court and the Dutch. While having access to a queen and the Okya Phrakhlang, Soet slept with a series of top officials of the Dutch company. With these contacts she was able to broker deals, garner profitable supply contracts, and share some of the proceeds with Okya Sombatthiban.[154]

The kings preferred a foreigner as Phrakhlang for several reasons: foreigners had the commercial expertise and overseas contacts; they had no *phrai* of their own; they depended totally on their royal patron; and they were easy to dislodge when they became too powerful. For similar reasons, the kings also increasingly relied on foreigners for their personal protection. Narai's guard in the 1680s included "two Companies of thirty Moors each ... a Company of Chinese Tartars armed with Bows and Arrows," horsemen from Lanxang, and some fifty Rajputs "who boast themselves to be of the Royal blood."[155]

The nobles in other ministries were increasingly overshadowed by those in Phrakhlang, and may have constituted a lobby for military adventurism designed to improve their status. In the early 1660s, there were at least three northward military expeditions which are aberrations in this generally peaceable era. The Dutch were told that Narai was being pushed into these campaigns by "young counsellors."[156] The Ayutthaya chronicles hail the first expedition in 1660 as a success, but the Chiang Mai chronicle declares it a complete failure. Two further expeditions followed, with an attempted attack on Ava, but both seem to have petered out. An Ayutthaya garrison left at Chiang Mai was driven away by 1663.[157]

From the 1630s, kings attempted to constrain the growing administrative and commercial power of the senior nobles in the capital. Prasat Thong "was the first who made the mandarins so slavish that they come

[152] *Van Vliet's Siam*, 45–88.
[153] Bhawan, *Dutch East India Company merchants*, 121.
[154] Dhiravat, "VOC employees and their relationships with Mon and Siamese women."
[155] La Loubère, *New historical relation*, 97–8; Tachard, *Voyage to Siam*, 166.
[156] Dhiravat, "Political history of Siam," 290–1.
[157] Tun Aung Chain, *Chronicle of Ayutthaya*, 55–68; *RCA*, 250–68 (*BM*); Wyatt and Aroonrut, *Chiang Mai chronicle*, 127.

to court every single day but are not permitted to speak with one another except in a public meeting place." The senior nobles' wives were expected to spend at least half the week at court.[158] Prasat Thong also "changes the highest offices so frequently that none of the Mandarins are fully able to establish themselves in their posts."[159] A council of nobles had been formed earlier, possibly to manage affairs while Naresuan was constantly absent, but Prasat Thong by-passed this council and Narai ignored it completely. When senior posts fell vacant, Narai often left them unfilled, installed junior officials in an acting capacity, or appointed one man to occupy two positions (one central, one provincial).[160]

After the succession battle that made him king, Narai refused to move from the front palace to the main palace, presumably for fear of factions, plots, and vengeful sentiments among the palace household. After two months, he faced a revolt by a group of senior nobles including Kalahom, the lords of Sukhothai and Phichit, several deputies and department heads of military and guard units, and at least 5,000 men. He carried out a massive purge, and did not refill several posts. He developed a second capital at Lopburi, initially just as a retreat convenient for hunting, but also as a place where he was "not obliged to be shut up" as in Ayutthaya,[161] and could separate the traditional nobles from their retinues. By the early 1670s he spent four to five months a year there, extended to eight to nine months by the early 1680s, when the court moved to Ayutthaya only for a short season of religious festivals during the Buddhist rains-retreat.[162]

In this age of growing commerce, limiting the officials' *material* power became even more critical. Death duties had existed since the fifteenth century. The kings claimed a portion of a high noble's estate on grounds that such nobles controlled some government property.[163] In the 1620s and 1630s a noble's estate was trisected, with one part for the heirs, one for the king, and one for the *sangha* or charity, but often the king took two-thirds or "declares himself to be the universal heir of the assets they left behind."[164] Prasat Thong would seize the widow and other family members, and interrogate them, sometimes with torture. In his reign, "One mandarin will often spy on another in order to discover whether anything

[158] *Van Vliet's Siam*, 243; Bhawan, *Dutch East India Company merchants*, 94–5.
[159] *Van Vliet's Siam*, 318.
[160] Schouten, "True description," 125–6; Nidhi, *Kanmueang thai samai phra narai*, 30–4.
[161] Tachard, *Voyage to Siam*, 191.
[162] Nidhi, *Kanmueang thai samai phra narai*, 37–8.
[163] Breazeale, "Whirligig of diplomacy," 63–4.
[164] *Van Vliet's Siam*, 164–5; Van Vliet quoted in Bhawan, *Dutch East India Company merchants*, 95; Neijenrode, "Account and description," 15.

is being concealed."[165] Narai dispensed with the three-way division in favor of total discretion, seizing anything between all or none of the estate.[166]

Many individual nobles lost both life and property in the succession disputes and subsequent purges which punctuated the century (see below). In the succession battle which brought Prasat Thong to power in 1629, the Kalahom, a former Phrakhlang, and the governor of Tenasserim were "cut in pieces" and the bodies displayed in public. Their property – which in the Kalahom's case included 2,000 slaves and 200 elephants – was distributed to other nobles. Several lesser nobles were beaten or thrown into prison and "their houses and goods were given over to pillage."[167] At a later stage of the crisis the Okya of Kamphaeng Phet was executed, his body displayed in public, and his property, slaves, and women distributed, while the Okya of Phitsanulok, formerly the Phrakhlang, was executed and "His house was pillaged and his slaves, horses and elephants were confiscated."[168] Van Vliet summed up: "in a short period of time, great changes occurred in the Siamese kingdom because many great Lords fell from their powerful positions into slavery, while others were raised from humble positions to occupy the highest offices." Certain nobles had been targeted because of "their prominence and wealth."[169]

The succession of Narai in 1656 involved four rounds of conflict. After the first round, the Chakri was trampled to death by an elephant, while the Phrakhlang was executed along with two of his sons, and his property plundered. At the second stage two months later, the Chakri's replacement was executed. And at the fourth stage after another three months, several of the most senior figures were executed along with their wives.[170]

Besides these general purges, individual nobles were brought down from time to time. In the 1630s, Prasat Thong had two senior ministers (Maha Upparat and Yommarat) disgraced. Their slaves were redistributed and their property looted. In 1636, Okya Phitsanulok was executed, his property confiscated, his wife made a slave, and his son demoted from the nobility, while Okya Chakri was condemned to death for treason, but escaped by surviving an ordeal by fire. Shortly after, one Phrakhlang was sentenced to death and only narrowly reprieved, while another was chained up with corpses.[171]

---

[165] *Van Vliet's Siam*, 243.
[166] Gervaise, *Natural and political history*, 96.
[167] *Van Vliet's Siam*, 262.
[168] *Van Vliet's Siam*, 316; see also 290, 309.
[169] *Van Vliet's Siam*, 287; Bhawan, *Dutch East India Company merchants*, 97.
[170] Dhiravat, "Political history of Siam," 259, 265, 271–2.
[171] Dhiravat, "Political history of Siam," 186–8; Bhawan, *Dutch East India Company merchants*, 107–8.

In 1644, an Okya in charge of the royal elephants was arrested and his house given over to plunder.[172] The Okya Sombatthiban, the richest noble trader of the 1640s and 1650s, was arraigned for a naval failure in 1654, exposed under the sun in chains for four days, reinstated, dismissed on allegations by foreigners, rearrested in the wake of the Narai succession crisis, submitted to ordeal by fire, and hung outside his house which was opened for public plunder.[173] In 1660/1, the Chakri, one of Narai's closest supporters, fell from favor through machinations of a queen.[174] In 1683 Kosa Lek, the Phrakhlang and most prominent general in the 1670s, was found guilty of accepting bribes to avoid corvée work, flogged so severely that he was "rendered prostrate," and died soon after.[175] His estate, including 8,000 slaves, was seized by the king, leaving his family with nothing. Shortly after, Narai "had two prominent mandarins executed in a very cruel manner ... which has instilled no little fear in everyone, above all the grandees."[176] Forbin recorded that 300 nobles were killed in the mid-1680s to protect Phaulkon.[177]

These events had a pattern. The victims were rich and powerful. The accusations against them – usually of spectacular bribe-taking – emphasized the danger of becoming too wealthy. The offender was executed, often along with his heirs, in a cruel and public manner to emphasize the lesson. Slaves were distributed, while other types of property were opened up for looting, so accumulated wealth was dissipated. La Loubère believed that some families were able to maintain their offices over a long period and "do become more illustrious and more powerful; but they are rare." In earlier reigns, "the Court was formerly very magnificent" and attended by many fine nobles but since Prasat Thong had "cut off almost all the most considerable, and consequently the most formidable Siameses," the luster had quite disappeared.[178]

These conditions shaped the pattern of elite consumption. European observers related that ordinary homes were virtually bereft of any possessions, and even the mansions of the great nobles were surprisingly sparse.[179] After visiting the household of Kosa Pan, the most brilliant noble of the period and then at the summit of his career, Kaempfer noted

---

172 Dhiravat, "Life, work and gossip."
173 Dhiravat, *Court, company and campong*, 1–10; Heeck, *Traveler in Siam*, 47.
174 Dhiravat, "Political history of Siam," 290.
175 Hutchinson, *1688 Revolution in Siam*, 14–15.
176 Dhiravat, "Political history of Siam," 356 quoting de Bèze, and 343 quoting a VOC officer; Bhawan, *East India Company merchants*, 120.
177 Smithies, *Siamese memoirs of Count Claude de Forbin*, 66.
178 La Loubère, *New historical relation*, 42, 78.
179 *Van Vliet's Siam*, 162 on houses; La Loubère, *New historical relation*, 29–30, 34; Kaempfer, *Description of the Kingdom of Siam*, 26, 44; Gervaise, *Natural and political history*, 97–9.

that the courtyard was "dirty and nasty," the reception hall was "full of Dust and Cobwebs," and there was little decoration or furniture. Yet Kaempfer also recorded that Kosa Pan, like other senior officials, was always accompanied in public by crowds of retainers, that his compound included "a large Elephant," that he was in the process of cremating his mother in a fashion "pompous and magnificent beyond expression," and that he had built an impressive *wat*.[180]

Van Neijenrode noticed that the well-off invested heavily in their personal appearance. After washing, "they anoint themselves with all sorts of sweet-smelling herbs ... with very costly ointments containing sandalwood, *calambac*, *ambergris*, mixed in rosewater, musk and more of such, yielding very pleasant fragrances." Men sported "gold rings on nearly all the fingers of both hands," while women fixed their hair

with a golden needle about one-and-one-half fingers long and thick as a swan's pinion. They have large holes in their ears, through which they insert their major ornament, gold bars about as long as a finger, round as the hole they have in their earlobes, artistically shaped and set with gems such as diamonds, pearls, rubies and emeralds; and their hands are ornamented with costly rings, of both gemstones and fine gold, and gold bracelets encircle their arms.[181]

Nobles and their wives also wore gorgeous cloth, often in distinctive designs presented by the king or reserved for those of status. Much of this cloth was produced in India using Siamese designs.[182] Nobles also spent on fine porcelain from China. Over a thousand tons of pottery have been recovered from the riverbeds around Ayutthaya, including many shards of fine blue-and-white ware. As with cloth, demand from Siam was significant enough for Chinese kilns to produce articles specifically for this market.[183] Wealth was spent on sumptuary display which signaled status in this life, and on the acquisition of merit for the future.

Noble families sought ways to preserve wealth across generations. They liked to accumulate gems, especially diamonds, because they were easy to conceal.[184] Land was only slightly popular as a store of wealth because land was readily available and not covered by any legal protection. There was no development of banking. Hence, the principal strategies for conserving wealth had to be political – making the right friends, remaining in royal favor, and backing the right side at royal succession.

[180] Kaempfer, *Description of the Kingdom of Siam*, 21–9.
[181] Neijenrode, "Account and description," 20–1.
[182] Guy, *Woven cargoes*, 130–4.
[183] Natthapatra, *Khrueang thuai jin*, 220–1; Woodward, "Seventeenth-century Chinese porcelain," 27–9.
[184] La Loubère, *New historical relation*, 52–3.

Wars of Succession

With the monarchy elevated and remote, and with worldly success dependent on royal favor, the selection of the monarch became the focal point of political conflict. In 1605, Ekathotsarot succeeded his brother Naresuan with no apparent difficulty. The two had fought alongside one another, and Naresuan had no son to complicate the succession. But thereafter, the method of royal succession at Ayutthaya throughout the seventeenth century was battle.

European visitors struggled to discern any rules for succession. Schouten and Van Vliet argued that the younger brother of a deceased king had precedence.[185] Given that many kings died before their sons had matured, succession by a younger brother was practical, but there is no evidence that this practicality was enshrined in a rule. In effect, the succession was an "elimination process."[186] Kings tried to control the process by nominating their favorite as *uparaja*, but often without success. These contests were not solely affairs of the royal clan. Groupings of nobles, foreign merchants, and foreign mercenaries lined up behind the rival candidates in hope of future gain. The succession disputes were part of the competition for personal advancement and access to commercial opportunities.

In 1610, intrigues began while Ekathotsarot was still alive. According to the chronicles, his eldest son and *uparaja* committed suicide when discovered plotting rebellion. According to European accounts, the king's death was engineered by a powerful noble who had the support of 180 Japanese guards, and who installed a half-blind second son as a pawn. Within months, a third son seized the throne, and executed both his brother and the ambitious noble. The Japanese then seized the palace, while another prince fled to Lanxang and returned with an army as far as Lopburi, but the third son overcame these threats and survived to reign as King Songtham.[187]

The next transition, in 1628–29, was similar but bloodier. In an attempt to rebuild the royal line, Songtham had taken several wives and sired nine sons, but all were still young. The contest began as a classic struggle between a brother and son of the late king, again with other ambitious nobles and Japanese guards involved. A first cousin of Songtham grabbed

---

[185] *Van Vliet's Siam*, 256–7.

[186] Dhiravat, "Political history of Siam," 273.

[187] Floris, *His voyage to the East Indes*, 55–7; Dhiravat, "Political history of Siam," 121–3; Neijinrode in Giles, "A critical analysis," 180–1. King Mongkut related that Ekathotsarot was deposed "on account of mental derangement," after which "Phra Siri Sin Wimontham was called by the nobles from the priesthood to the throne ... he was not of the Royal Family." See Bowring, *Kingdom and people of Siam*, vol. 2, 343.

the post of Kalahom and orchestrated the succession of the late king's fifteen-year-old son with the help of the powerful Japanese merchant, Yamada, and the Japanese guards. Songtham's younger brother, Sisin, resorted to Phetchaburi and raised a force of 20,000, but lost the ensuing pitched battle, and was executed along with many noble supporters. A few months later, the Kalahom carried out a coup against his protégé, mounted an attack on the palace, and killed the king, his mother, and many nobles who had failed to support him. He installed another of Songtham's sons as king, and proceeded to eliminate his own erstwhile allies and potential rivals by engineering the Okya Kamphaeng Phet's execution for treason, and by sending Yamada to Ligor. After a third coup, the Kalahom assumed the throne, and executed the young boy-king soon after.[188]

This Kalahom, who reigned as Prasat Thong, belonged to the royal clan but not the direct line. He reputedly wanted to marry Songtham's queen, but she refused to accept her son's murderer. He then took between one and eight of Songtham's daughters (depending on source) as consorts. Those who refused were reportedly killed. Five years later he executed five of Songtham's remaining sons and another of Songtham's consorts.[189] In 1642, another son of Songtham attacked the palace with 200 followers, held it for one night, and was killed in a counter-attack. Several of Songtham's remaining kin were killed in the following purge, and several noble supporters fled to Burma. Another son of Songtham along with other relatives may have been executed in 1644 when another "conspiracy" was discovered, but they possibly survived after the king's own mother intervened on their behalf.[190] In 1650, when the king suspected a plot was afoot to usurp him, a Dutch visitor reported (probably with great exaggeration) that 2,900 people died in the ensuing purge, including "many rare Personages."[191]

The succession in 1656 also began as a contest between the late king's son and brother. Prasat Thong formally nominated his son, Chai. The day after the king's death, his brother, Sutham Racha, attacked the palace in alliance with another son, Narai. Sutham Racha executed Chai and was anointed as king. Two and a half months later, Narai stormed the palace with cannons and elephants, battered down the gates, and fought a night-long battle in which thousands died, according to the Dutch. Sutham Racha was executed and Narai anointed as king. Three

[188] *Van Vliet's Siam*, 255–322; Dhiravat, "Political history of Siam," 132–52.
[189] Dhiravat, "Political history of Siam," 175.
[190] Dhiravat, "Political history of Siam," 216–19; Dhiravat, "Thasai prince's rebellion of 1642"; Dhiravat, "Life, work and gossip."
[191] Struys, "*Perillous and most unhappy voyages*," 200–2; *RCA*, 220, locates this purge earlier.

months later, two of Narai's half-brothers prepared their bid, but were caught and executed, along with many noble supporters.[192]

After each of these succession battles, the new king had to cope with aftershocks of dissident tributaries, rebellious cities, and palace plots. But once these were weathered, the remainder of the reign was calmer. The fourth in this series of succession battles, in 1688, was more complex, and had more lasting consequences.

1688

Until the late 1670s, Europeans other than the Dutch had little role in the cosmopolitan society of the Siamese court. Some Portuguese served as soldiers, but most had faded into the local population and fallen on hard times. The titular head of the community in the 1680s was seventy years old and in "severe poverty."[193] A Portuguese embassy sent in 1684 to promote trade failed in part because this man was arrested on account of his general incompetence.[194] Narai employed several adventurous Europeans who had technical talents. An early Jesuit visitor was recruited to design fortifications. A Frenchman and an Italian built houses and waterworks at Lopburi.[195] A French doctor, Daniel Brochebourde, was sent from Batavia in 1672 to attend on Narai. A Dutch pyrotechnicist was employed to supervise the preparation of ammunition.[196] The Dutch acceded to some of Narai's many requests for craftsmen such as goldsmiths, enamellers, and stone-cutters, but not always with great success. One Dutch enameller drank himself to death on arrack and another was dismissed as incompetent.[197]

An English East India Company ship first visited in 1612, and an agency was briefly established in 1612–23, but the company could see no value in Siam, while the officers it placed in Ayutthaya were "drunk every day."[198] Only in the last quarter of the century did the British and French begin to expand their "country trade" around the Bay of Bengal, including the Ayutthayan ports on the western coast of the peninsula, especially Mergui. As they displaced the Moors in the trading arena, they also started to displace them in the Ayutthaya bureaucracy.

[192] Nidhi, *Kanmueang thai samai phra narai*, 25–7; Dhiravat, "Political history of Siam," 275–7; Bhawan, *Dutch East India Company merchants*, 115.
[193] Smith, *Creolization and diaspora*, 110.
[194] Seabra, *Embassy of Pero Vaz de Siqueira*, 187–8, 212–17.
[195] Gervaise, *Natural and political history*, 36.
[196] Bhawan, *Dutch East India Company merchants*, 142.
[197] Dhiravat, *Siamese court life*, 189–90.
[198] Hutchinson, *English adventurers in Siam*, 32; Bassett, "English relations with Siam"; "Introduction" in Farrington and Dhiravat, *English factory in Siam*, 1–22.

In the mid-1680s, there were French governors at Phuket, Mergui, and Bangkok. The court was happy to discover that these new Europeans, unlike the Dutch, were prepared to merge into the Ayutthayan system. The French carried consignments for the king and nobles on the Bay of Bengal routes. The British adventurers were even more tractable. In 1665, and again in 1675, they established a factory at Ayutthaya without their company's knowledge, used it as a cover for their own private trade, gladly accepted employment in the Siamese bureaucracy, and left the company with the problem of closing down the factory and sorting out its complex debts.[199]

Phaulkon, France, and the Missionaries

Among these European adventurers who arrived in Siam in the late 1670s was Constantine Phaulkon, a Greek who had spent much of his life employed on British ships. When Ayutthaya discovered that the East India Company was probably gun-running to Pattani and other truculent ports, the Company deputed this smart Greek to charm the Ayutthayan officials. Phaulkon so ingratiated himself with the Phrakhlang that he was taken into service and was soon lording it over his old employer. He rapidly learnt Thai, and exploited his role as go-between to become the most powerful figure in the European trading community. He was offered (but refused) the post of Phrakhlang twice in 1684–85, becoming the head of Mahatthai instead. Like the Persians before him, he began placing his colleagues in strategic posts, including two English adventurers, Richard Burnaby and Samuel White, to govern Mergui, whence they ran privateering expeditions and amassed a considerable fortune. By 1687, there were fifty Englishmen employed by Phaulkon in the service of the king – far more than ever worked for the English East India Company in Siam – and over 200 Europeans in total. During 1686–87, White and his associates utilized the name of King Narai to declare war against their commercial rivals and rob Muslim and Peguan cargo ships in the Bay of Bengal.[200]

As Europeans replaced Persians in employment at court, the source of cultural influence changed in parallel. According to La Loubère, Narai was "curious to the highest degree."[201] He seems to have sensed

---

[199] Farrington and Dhiravat, *English factory in Siam*, 11–16; Bassett, "English relations with Siam."

[200] Julispong, *Khunnang krom tha khwa*, 225–30; Collis, *Siamese White*, and Collis' main source, Francis Davenport's report in Farrington and Dhiravat, *English factory in Siam*, 1186–256, and subsequent documents.

[201] La Loubère, *New historical relation*, 52.

the importance of the scientific advances in late Renaissance Europe, especially in geography, mathematics, and astronomy. Earlier he had bombarded the Dutch with requests for scientific equipment, especially clocks, astronomical models, globes, and telescopes. He was fascinated by the scholarly Jesuits who arrived in Ayutthaya in 1685 on their way to China, and possibly requested the larger group of fourteen Jesuits sent by Louis XIV with the French diplomatic mission in 1687. He built astronomical observatories in Ayutthaya and Lopburi, where he viewed a lunar eclipse in the company of the Jesuits in 1688.[202] In the latter few years of the reign, Europe (and especially France) replaced Persia as the source of cultural influence on the court. Narai wore French clothing on the hunt. Phaulkon's Japanese-Christian wife is credited with introducing Portuguese desserts into Siamese cuisine. However, this influence was much more limited than that of Persia, because the time was limited and the ending went badly.

Like Yamada Nagamasa and Aqa Muhammed Astarabadi earlier, Phaulkon enjoyed a brief brilliance and then a crashing fall. The drama was enhanced because the fall became entwined with another classic succession battle and with French missionary ambitions.

The first French missionaries had arrived in 1662, and in the early 1670s they interested Narai in diplomatic relations with Paris.[203] In 1680, Narai dispatched a first embassy to France at roughly the same time he sent another to Persia. After the envoys to France were lost at sea, Narai sent another, non-ambassadorial, mission which excited the French enough to send an embassy. This arrived in 1685, the same year as a return diplomatic mission from Safavid Persia. By this time, Phaulkon was at his zenith, and he orchestrated the ambassadorial visits. The French asked for trade privileges but, as usual, were fobbed off with invitations to establish factories in parts of the peninsula which Ayutthaya barely controlled. Phaulkon's priority was to secure a detachment of French troops to serve as his private army in the forthcoming succession battle. He suggested the French should send troops along with

sixty or seventy men of good character ... I will obtain for them the most important positions in Siam, such as governorships of provinces, cities and fortresses, or the control of forces on land and sea. I will introduce them into the palace and into State affairs, not excepting even the royal household.[204]

---

[202] Hodges, "Time in transition."
[203] Launay, *Histoire de la mission*, 12–21.
[204] Hutchinson, *Adventurers in Siam*, 112, quoting Phaulkon's secret letter to Tachard, December 1685.

The French delegation included a clerical element which had conceived the idea that Narai might convert to Christianity, bringing his countrymen with him. The Persian delegation had exactly the same notion of a conversion to Islam. Both had probably been misled by the Siamese king's readiness to grant freedom for proselytism, and even to sponsor religious buildings and festivals of non-Buddhist communities. For Ayutthaya, this was just part of being a successful entrepot.[205] The zealots of both Catholicism and Islam misread it as an invitation.

The French clerics, who initially saw Buddhism as "idolatry," gradually came to respect its sophistication but also grew frustrated at their inability to interest the Siamese in the promise of salvation by a providential god. Louis Laneau, who was bishop of the French mission from 1674, wrote and distributed books in Thai in which he "refuted and destroyed the religion of the Siamese, step by step."[206] In their memoirs, some visitors to Siam recorded laughing openly at the "follies" they found in Buddhist temples. Both French and Persian envoys left written accounts brimming with arrogant superiority and ignorance of the religion they wished to supplant.[207] To increase his chances of securing a detachment of French troops, Phaulkon intimated to the French that the Christians had some chance of success in converting Narai. Siamese ambassadors traveled back with the French party, enjoyed a great social success in Paris, and returned in 1687 with the French troops and yet more French clerics, just in time for the succession battle. Persuaded by their own claims of superiority, the French had decided to demand control of Bangkok and Mergui. The French memoirs show they had little idea how much the trade of these places mattered to the king and nobility and hence how aggressive this demand seemed. Rumors that the British were planning to seize Mergui provoked a massacre of the Europeans there in July 1687.[208]

Many of the 600 troops brought from France had died on the journey, and several more were sick to incapacitation. Only 450 remained fit, and after some had been distributed to garrison Mergui and other tasks, the remaining 200 were not powerful enough to influence events, and spent the crisis bottled up in the fort of Bangkok. Some became separated from the garrison and lived by begging and theft. The palace guard at Ayutthaya had to be strengthened "to prevent the French from

---

[205] Daniel Brochebourde, who was doctor and friend to Narai, told the Dutch that Narai was "poking fun at all the priests." Quoted in Bhawan, *Dutch East India Company merchants*, 145.

[206] Launay, *Histoire de la mission*, 95–6.

[207] See Muhammad Rabi, *Ship of Sulaiman*, and the memoirs by Choisy, Chaumont, and Tachard.

[208] Collis, *Siamese White*, ch. 38.

looting."[209] According to Dutch observers, local women were "publicly caught, abused, and raped on the street" by these soldiers.[210] The French troop commander, General Desfarges was surprised when "the market women took fright at the sight of him and ran away as though from an enemy."[211]

This appearance of foreign soldiers, commanded by foreign officers and outside the traditional systems of supervision, had a powerful effect on local sensibilities. Perhaps from this time stems a striking image in *wat* murals – Europeans as soldiers, especially among the demon troops who threaten the Buddha as he meditates to achieve enlightenment (Figure 4.3).[212] Although other foreigners appear in these scenes, the frock-coated Europeans are the most common and most prominent. In murals painted at Wat Ko Kaeo Suttharam, Phetchaburi, in 1743, the Buddha's great enemy, Devadatta, is portrayed as a westerner, perhaps a Jesuit.

European mentality had changed over the seventeenth century. The creation of colonial empires had begun. Beliefs in European superiority had developed. The combination of uncontrolled soldiery, clumsy diplomacy, and missionary attempts at conversion provoked a rise of anti-European feeling in a society marked for its cosmopolitan character and its tolerance. This added an emotive element to a succession dispute which focused the social forces and divisions of this age of commerce.

Narai, Nobility, and Sangha

Within the nobility, especially among the traditional nobles in Mahatthai and Kalahom, there was a growing discontent over the decline in their own importance, the concentration of wealth in Phrakhlang, and the king's reliance on foreigners as trading partners and personal guards. Constantine Phaulkon became a lightning rod for this resentment. By the mid-1680s, Phaulkon had exploited the patronage of Narai to gain an overwhelming share of foreign commerce. According to a French trader, "He does more business than all the Merchants put together; he has two audience a day with the King."[213] According to Père de Bèze, "Some outcry went up in consequence from individuals who now found

---

[209] Hutchinson, *Adventurers in Siam*, 166, quoting the Abbé de Lionne.
[210] Bhawan, *Dutch East India Company merchants*, 129, quoting Keijts, the VOC head in Ayutthaya in November 1687.
[211] Hutchinson, *Adventurers in Siam*, 166, quoting the Abbé de Lionne.
[212] European-looking foreigners also appear in murals being drowned after shipwreck in the Mahajanaka Jataka, and holding up the sky as *withayathon*, hermit-like creatures famed for mischief.
[213] Hutchinson, *Adventurers in Siam*, 69–70, quoting André Boureau-Deslandes.

Figure 4.3. European figures in the demon army threatening the Buddha as he meditates to achieve enlightenment; at Wat Khongkharam (courtesy of Viriyah Business Co. Ltd.)

themselves excluded from the profit they reaped before."[214] Even such a figure as Kosa Pan, who had a large stake in the Phrakhlang monopolies, who had led the embassy to Paris, and who had overseen the rise of Phaulkon, opposed the emerging alignment between Narai, Phaulkon, and the French.

Narai had created resentment within the *sangha*. He had continued Prasat Thong's trend of enlarging the role of the court Brahmans. At the start of his reign, he broke the tradition of building a major *wat* and built the resplendent Banyong Rattanat palace instead. After the early years of his reign he does not seem to have cast any Buddha images or commissioned any religious construction.[215] By abandoning the capital for much of the year, he forsook the role of the patron-king, regularly visiting the major *wat*. In 1676, he abolished the annual ceremony for chasing away the waters at the end of the monsoon after an unseasonal storm caused the waters to rise immediately after the rite. He reduced the annual number of appearances at *kathin* processions and other displays from five or six to two. Only rarely did he consult the heads of the *sangha* "whose credit in other matters he depresses as much as he can."[216] According to Gervaise and the French missionaries, some monks plotted to assassinate Narai when he entered a *wat* without his armed escort, but were discovered and "all put to the sword by the soldiers of the guard."[217] In 1674 and again in the mid-1680s, the king ordered that monks be examined to weed out *phrai* fleeing the corvée. The second of these campaigns "reduc'd several Thousands to the Secular condition, because they had not been found learned enough." Some forest monks refused to cooperate, but "thousands of men still wearing monk's robes could be seen working on the land, carrying bricks, and suffering punishment." Rumors about French plans to convert the king further unsettled the *sangha*. In October 1685, Narai brushed aside the French envoys' call for him to consider adopting Christianity, but a fear of "religion in danger" spread among monks and followers.[218]

The *Testimony*, depositions taken from prisoners swept away to Burma in 1767, contains the Siamese nobility's view of the history of this era. Their account praises Narai's military abilities, but damns him in other

---

[214] Hutchinson, *1688 revolution in Siam*, 19.
[215] Piriya ("Revised dating of Ayudhya architecture," part 2) believes he made major modifications to Wat Phra Ram and Wat Chaophraya Thai.
[216] La Loubère, *New historical relation*, 43, 48, 103; Dhiravat, "Political history of Siam," 325; Kemp, *Aspects of Siamese kingship*, 20–1.
[217] Gervaise, *Natural and political history*, 161–2.
[218] Gervaise, *Natural and political history*, 130; La Loubère, *New historical relation*, 115; Nidhi, *Kanmueang thai samai phra narai*, 57–8.

ways such as by claiming he forced his consorts to have abortions. The account also conspicuously omits any mention of Narai's foreign contacts and the *éclat* he strove to create.[219]

Phra Phetracha, Monks, and the Mob

From 1683 Narai sickened, and another succession battle approached. Narai had no son. Following the purges of recent reigns, his only close male kin were two half-brothers. One of these, Aphaithot, was deformed or "paralytic" and "subject to passionate outburst of temper and much addicted to strong drink."[220] The other, Noi, was reputedly caught with one of the king's consorts in 1683 and flogged so badly that he either lost the power of speech or pretended to.[221] Narai had adopted Pi, the son of a courtier, and was expected by some at court to nominate him as heir.

In the mid-1680s, the plots started. A refugee Macassar prince resident in Ayutthaya planned to seize the palace and control the succession. The plot was discovered but two months were required to quell the fierce Macassar fighters. Factions in court were suspected to lie behind the failed coup.[222] A noble usurper and plots involving the foreign troops at Ayutthaya were standard components of Ayutthaya succession struggles. Two new elements, presaging the future, were the monkhood and the mob.

In the latter part of Narai's reign the economy had been strained, first by the wars of the 1660s and early 1670s, and then by the extension of royal taxes and monopolies. The mid-1660s saw a series of local famines and epidemics, and the years from 1680 to 1700 were a phase of low average rainfall.[223] In 1681–82, a smallpox epidemic ravaged Ayutthaya and Lopburi. In 1685, a French missionary reported that "trade has been disrupted to the point where the Chinese and Moors had to depart, leaving only those who have no ready capital for trade."[224] Narai's decision to intervene in a succession battle in Cambodia resulted in renewed mobilizations in 1684–85, and a bloody defeat of the Siamese army.[225] In 1685, in a recurring pattern in such times of stress, a dumb simpleton was heralded as a *phumibun* (man of merit) who "would one day become

[219] *Khamhaikan khun luang ha wat*, 28–49; Tun Aung Chain, *Chronicle of Ayutthaya*, 49–68.
[220] Père de Bèze quoted in Dhiravat, "Political history of Siam," 345.
[221] According to de Bèze, the consort was fed to tigers. See Hutchinson, *1688 Revolution in Siam*, 56; Le Blanc, *History of Siam in 1688*, 18–19.
[222] Dhiravat, "Political history of Siam," 406–9.
[223] Lieberman and Buckley, "Impact of climate on Southeast Asia," 1057–9.
[224] Nidhi, *Kanmueang thai samai phra narai*, 68.
[225] Gervaise, *Natural and political history*, 173–4.

a God," and "People flocked to him from all Parts, to adore him," until the court put a stop to it.[226]

A leader emerged in the traditional nobility. Phra Phetracha came from an established noble family. His mother had been Narai's wet nurse, while his sister and another close relative were royal consorts. He had been a prominent soldier, especially in the Chiang Mai expeditions, a confidant of the king, and now held the post of keeper of the royal elephants.[227] Narai appointed him as regent during his final sickness.[228] La Loubère noted in 1685, "The people ... think him invulnerable, because he expressed a great deal of Courage in some fight against the Peguins."[229] He had twice spent time in the monkhood and was admired within the nobility and *sangha* for his religious devotion.[230] When the contingent of French troops was about to enter Siam in 1687, Phetracha raised the specter of colonial aggression while addressing the King's council:

In a speech of ninety minutes duration he enlarged upon the fate of each Eastern Prince in turn who had admitted European troops into his land – first the Portuguese and later the Dutch – only to be despoiled and reduced to the level of slaves.[231]

Phetracha had the personality and disposition to be a popular leader. In the words of a Jesuit observer, he "obtained much credit among the people for his popular manners," and "assumed with everyone very popular and winning manners."[232] He was close to the *sangharaja* (*sankharat*, monastic head) of Lopburi, and he cultivated the simmering resentment in the monkhood. According to de Bèze, "Pitracha was inciting unrest in the Provinces. His agents were local Talapoins [monks]," who spread dissidence to provincial towns, including a "rumour ... that the King was about to become a Christian and raze every *wat* to the ground." The royal astrologers issued a public prediction that "the French will be expelled from the land with much loss of life among themselves and their supporters." In 1685, a monk foretold that Narai would die because of his enmity to Buddhism. In early 1686, a notice posted on a tree in front of the Lopburi palace warned of "the dangers that threatened the Buddhist

[226] La Loubère, *New historical relation*, 136–7.
[227] Dhiravat, "Political history of Siam," 417, 425.
[228] *RCA*, 309 (*PC*).
[229] La Loubère, *New historical relation*, 89.
[230] Smithies, *Three military accounts*, 22–3, from Desfarges; Le Blanc, *History of Siam in 1688*, 20.
[231] De Bèze quoted in Hutchinson, *1688 revolution in Siam*, 68.
[232] Le Blanc, *History of Siam in 1688*, 20–1.

faith, and invited all men to open their eyes to a matter which concerned the public weal."[233]

By early 1688, as Narai's health worsened, the monks in Lopburi called on people to take up arms. According to a French observer,

the whole country was arming. The road from Lop'buri to Ayudhya was thronged with armed men, and even boatmen and the very dregs of the populace carried weapons. This state of things could only occur in time of great stress and revolution.[234]

A trip along this road persuaded the French garrison commander to keep his troops in Bangkok.

The father of Pi, Narai's favorite and suspected heir, mobilized 14,000 men in anticipation of the coming battle, but Phetracha had at least 30,000, including the Persian palace guards. In April 1688, when Narai tried to rein him in, Phetracha called out the mob in Lopburi: "Some had their axes for cutting wood, others had bamboos with iron tips or burnt ends, and the mandarins came with their sabres and shields."[235] According to the Jesuit eye-witness, "the townsmen followed the Sancras [sangharaja]; a few Talapons [monks] ccompanied him, and the group was born aloft, shoulder-high, at the head of the procession to the Palace," which they captured with Narai inside.[236] Another mob attacked and plundered the houses of Pi and his father.[237] A small French contingent that tried to intervene was "overpowered and ill-treated by a large mob."[238] Phetracha executed Pi, then Phaulkon, and then Narai's two half-brothers. By the time Narai died on July 11, Phetracha faced no rival claimants. He declared himself king and descended to Ayutthaya.

There was no general reaction against foreigners and no lapse into isolation. The English freebooters had already slunk away. The French ambassadors and Jesuits had returned to Paris at the start of the year. The French garrison was winkled out of Bangkok after a bad-tempered siege. The Dutch, however, rushed to greet Phra Phetracha while he was still on his way from Lopburi to Ayutthaya, and soon after signed a new treaty to extend their trading privileges. Persians remained prominent at court. Qing China's reopening to trade in 1684 made up for any shortfall elsewhere. Even the French missionaries were allowed to resume their

[233] Hutchinson, *1688 revolution in Siam*, 68, 72, 77; Nidhi, *Kanmueang thai samai phra narai*, 73–5; Dhiravat, "Political history of Siam," 409–10.
[234] Hutchinson, *Adventurers in Siam*, 166, quoting the Abbé de Lionne.
[235] Le Blanc, *History of Siam in 1688*, 50.
[236] Hutchinson, *1688 revolution in Siam*, 88.
[237] Nidhi, *Kanmueang thai samai phra narai*, 58.
[238] Hutchinson, *Adventurers in Siam*, 173.

activities after a short spell in jail. Useful Europeans like the medical Brochebourde family lived on in Ayutthaya for three generations.[239]

Phetracha had been part of the royal circle but probably had no trace of royal blood. He rectified this by drawing on the female line, taking both the sister and daughter of Narai as queens. For Sorasak, his son, lieutenant in the succession battle, and successor as king, the chronicles manufactured a royal lineage – as a son that Narai had sired in a bucolic liaison and entrusted to Phetracha as foster-parent.[240]

At base, 1688 was another of the century's succession crises, but with an important difference – not the involvement of Phaulkon which was little different from that of Yamada in 1628–29 or the Persians in 1656, nor the involvement of French troops who were effectively sidelined, but the division within the nobility, the role of the *sangha*, and the involvement of the mob. As in previous succession disputes, once the result was clear, the excitement quickly subsided – in Nidhi's graphic words, "the gates of the palace in Ayutthaya closed up the ruler inside and kept the people outside, as it had been for centuries."[241] But in the longer term, the consequences were more profound.

Conclusion

When warfare in Mainland Southeast Asia subsided around 1600, Ayutthaya began to benefit from the global integration of Anthony Reid's "age of commerce," but in a particular form. Ayutthaya had almost no direct participation in exchange between Europe and Asia. It added some manufactures and crop products to its roster of exports, but its main role was as an entrepot between Asian empires to east and to west. It cultivated this role by controlling the portage across the upper peninsula, and by providing a port and exchange which was free of both pirates and European domination. Japanese, Persians, Chinese, and Indians became prominent in the commerce and politics of Ayutthaya. The Europeans – first the Dutch, later and more ephemerally some French and English – visited this entrepot as part of their "country trade" around the Asian seas.

As a city, Ayutthaya prospered spectacularly in this role. European visitors again saw it as one of the great port cities of Asia. Ayutthaya also became more of a capital of Siam, partly because other cities in the Chaophraya Plain could see more benefit in being subordinate, partly because the warring of the late sixteenth century had destroyed the little

---

[239] Dhiravat, "Ayutthaya at the end of the seventeenth century"; Launay, *Histoire de la mission*, 87–8.
[240] *RCA*, 300–1 (*BM*).
[241] Nidhi, *Kanmueang thai samai phra narai*, 81.

kings, especially in the Northern Cities. As the population of the peninsula increased, and hence also its economic potential, Ayutthaya gradually extended its power southwards.

The monarchy was strikingly successful in taking a large share in
the growing prosperity – by imposing monopolies, by owning junks, by
entering into joint ventures with traders from east and west, and by seizing wealth from the nobility. The palace treasury drew gasps even from
Europeans grown blasé about the fabled wonders of the orient. With this
wealth, the kings were able to hire people from all over Asia and Europe
as their soldiers, guards, shippers, commercial agents, craftsmen, suppliers, and administrators. By deft diplomacy, the kings were able to draw
on the military and naval power of the Europeans to assist their political
expansion on the peninsula.[242] In part by relying on foreigners, the kings
were able to reduce the status and pretensions of the traditional nobles,
who had lost their primary function as warriors, and limit the emergence
of wealthy families who shared in the profits of commerce. The kings
also seem to have constrained the potential power of the *sangha*, partly
by lavish patronage, and partly by some administrative control. This was
a merchant absolutism of a form specific to an entrepot in an era of great
mobility for people of entrepreneurial and administrative talent.

As a consequence of this concentration of power and wealth in the
monarchy, the succession became the focus of all political competition,
resulting in a series of bloody battles which culled many in the royal lines
and top nobility. From Songtham onwards, kings seemed aware of a need
to create new foundations for the monarchy, but there was no consistency in their choices. Songtham began to craft a model for a "Buddhist
king" through public display of devotion and meritorious works. Prasat
Thong shrouded the monarchy in mystery and appealed to the historical
memory of Angkor and the city's founder. Narai acted as a modernizer
for his time – building splendid palaces with foreign touches; showing
his far-flung links by welcoming foreign embassies with enormous pomp;
adopting culture from Persia and Europe; and associating himself with
technology and innovation such as clocks and astronomy. He may have
impressed the outside world more than his own subjects.

The events of 1688 have often been seen as a crisis over Siam's relations with the outside world. But the France–Siam connection was probably more important in the French imagination than the Siamese. Every
major surviving French participant went home and wrote a book about

[242] This began in the 1610s when Songtham tried to use Portuguese military power to
consolidate Ayutthaya's hold on the upper west coast of the peninsula; see Breazeale,
"Whirligig of diplomacy," 60–1, 89–90.

it. But 1688 was fourth in the century's series of succession battles, and the role of the Europeans was similar to that of Japanese and Persians in earlier rounds. The political involvement of the French in Siam lasted less than a decade, and had no lasting impact on the culture, language, dress, architecture, or cuisine.[243] The new element in 1688 was the people of Ayutthaya and Lopburi, egged on by monks to take up weapons to show their discontent. Behind these events lay divisions within the nobility, popular discontents, and the social importance of Buddhism. These stresses, created in the age of commerce, would result in more turbulence over future decades.

[243] Jacq-Hergoualc'h, *L'Europe et le Siam*.

5   An Urban and Commercial Society

Early Siam is usually imagined as a peasant society, as found in most parts of the early modern world. This chapter presents an alternative view of Siam in the mid-Ayutthaya era as a mainly urban and commercial society.

In the history of early Ayutthaya, the ordinary people are invisible. The sources, both local and external, focus on wealth and power. From the seventeenth century, however, there are accounts by observers intent on explaining Siam to the outside world. Of course, their accounts are strained through a cultural filter, yet taken along with some indigenous literature, they enable construction of a much fuller picture of the society than is possible for earlier years.

This chapter looks at how many people there were in Siam, where they lived, how they made a living, how they related together in sexual and familial relations, how their labor was utilized, how they worshipped, and how they communicated together and thought of themselves.

A Sparse Population

In his account of Siam from his visit in 1687–88, La Loubère made an estimate of the population:

The Siamese do therefore keep an exact account of the Men, Women and Children; and in this vast extent of Land, according to their own Confession, they reckon'd up the last time but Nineteen Hundred Thousand Souls. From which I question not that some retrenchment is to be made for Vanity and Lyes, but on the other hand, thereunto must be added the Fugitives, which do seek a Sanctuary in the Woods against the Government.[1]

The area is not stated, but he probably means the Chaophraya Plain, as the estimate is based on the recruitment rolls. Some scholars have surmised that this figure of 1.9 million included only the able-bodied men recorded in the registers, and that the total would be more than double. However, La Loubère specified "Men, Women, and Children,"

[1] La Loubère, *New historical relation*, 11.

and the figure is consistent with later estimates. A French missionary estimated 3 million in 1718. Crawfurd proposed a figure of 2.8 million in the 1820s, Bowring estimated around 2 million in 1855, and Prince Dilok Nabarath reckoned 3 million in the 1900s.[2] Seen in the perspective of these figures, La Loubère's figure is credible. Many foreign visitors noted the emptiness. Schouten found much of the country "mountainous, woody and moorish." Gervaise recorded that

> The forests of this kingdom are so enormous that they cover over half of its area and so dense that it is almost impossible to cross them ... there are fearful deserts and vast wildernesses where one only finds wretched little huts, often as much as 7 or 8 leagues distant from one another.

La Loubère found the territory "almost wholly incultivated and cover'd with woods." According to the scribe of the Persian embassy, "From Mergui all the way to Shahr Nāv [Ayutthaya] there were no settlements, villages or buildings to speak of."[3]

The density of population in Mainland Southeast Asia as a whole was far lower than that of contemporary India, China, and Java. Estimating the difference is difficult because all the figures are uncertain, but the gap is dramatic, perhaps in the range of five to ten times.[4] Why should this have been?

The high availability of food and the relative strength of women in society (see below) mean there is little reason for low fertility due to poor nutrition. The fact that many women worked may have resulted in some restriction on child-bearing – prophylactics and abortion methods are found in traditional medicine. However, a high death rate rather than a low birth rate is the more likely cause of low population. This can be derived from the subsequent history. Siam's population grew only slowly through the nineteenth century, and then accelerated in two steps – first in the early twentieth century after measures to control epidemics, particularly of smallpox and cholera, and second after World War Two with campaigns to control malaria and other fevers. As a result, the population increased roughly ten times over one century. Infectious and epidemic diseases had kept the population low.

Early legendary histories are full of epidemics. In a legend of Chiang Saen, perhaps from the eleventh century, the whole city is wiped out

---

[2] Bowring estimated 4.5 to 5 million for the total country, which would give around 2 million in the Chaophraya Plain. Bowring, *Kingdom and people of Siam*, vol. 1, 81; *Dilok*, Siam's *rural economy*, ch. 3; Forest, *Missionaires français*, 117–18; see also Terwiel, *Through travellers' eyes*.

[3] Schouten, "True description," 95; Gervaise, *Natural and political history*, 23, 45; La Loubère, *New historical relation*, 11; Muhammad Rabi, *Ship of Sulaiman*, 47.

[4] Reid, "Low population growth and its causes."

except for a single woman.[5] In the chronicle of Nakhon Si Thammarat, the city is abandoned due to epidemics on six occasions.[6] In a tale from early Lamphun, the whole population decamps to the Mon country after "an epidemic of cholera raged for six years."[7] In one of the foundation stories of Ayutthaya, U Thong flees from the Khmer capital after an epidemic, and in another he migrates from Kamphaeng Phet for the same reason.[8]

La Loubère noted, "there are some contagious diseases, but the real Plague of this Country is the Small Pox. It oftentimes makes dreadful ravage."[9] Smallpox and several other infectious diseases spread across the world through trading links in the early first millennium. The chronicles and astrological records contain several mentions: in 1533, the king died of the disease; in the 1560s in Phitsanulok, "everyone came down with smallpox and many died"; in the 1570s, Naresuan was stricken while on campaign in Lanxang; an epidemic broke out in Chiang Mai in the 1590s; outbreaks are recorded at Ayutthaya in 1454/5, 1563/4, 1621/2, and 1622/3; and French missionaries reckoned a smallpox epidemic killed 40,000 people in 1695–96. However, the Thai term used for smallpox, *(khai) thoraphit*, meaning "severe poison (fever)," may have covered several diseases.[10] Some of these outbreaks may have been cholera, which is passed through contaminated water. There were repeated epidemics in India since the sixteenth century, and close trading contacts with Siam over that period.

Besides the diseases transmitted among humans, tropical and semi-tropical forests harbor many diseases which prey on animal populations and may be transmitted to humans, particularly via insects. As Philip Stott noted, in traditional Thai thinking there was "a contrast between Tai 'civilized' space and Nature beyond normal social control."[11] The *mueang* (town) was civilized and safe, whereas *pa* (forest) was wild and dangerous, in part because of deadly diseases including malaria and typhoid. In 1881, when Carl Bock proposed a trip into the Phetchaburi hills, he was told by his Thai companion that "the jungle was danger-ous, and, if four of us went, two would be sure to die on the road of fever."[12] Another of Ayutthaya's foundation myths hints at the association

[5] Notton, *Annales du Siam*, vol. 1, 198.
[6] Wyatt, *Crystal sands*, 72, 76–7, 84–5, 88, 98, 124.
[7] Ratanapanna Thera, *Sheaf of garlands*, 104; Swearer and Sommai, *Legend of Queen Cama*, 105–6.
[8] Terwiel, "Asiatic cholera in Siam"; *RCA*, 9–10 (*BM*). Terwiel wonders if this epidemic might be the "black death."
[9] La Loubère, *New historical relation*, 39.
[10] *RCA*, 20, 44, 78, 184; Terwiel, "Asiatic cholera in Siam," 146; Forest, *Missionaires français*, 116–17.
[11] Stott, "Mu'ang and pa," 146.
[12] Bock, *Temples and elephants*, 87.

between such fevers and stagnant water: U Thong comes upon a stinking marsh and gets rid of its resident dragon, after which the city flourishes.[13] La Loubère noted that fevers were common at Ayutthaya, with varying degrees of severity:

The *Siameses* are sometimes attackt with burning Fevers, in which the transport to the Brain is easily formed, with defluxions on the Stomach. Moreover, Inflammations are rare, and the ordinary continual Fever kills none, no more than in the other places of the Torrid Zone.[14]

Modern epidemiology shows that human populations can develop immunities and convert diseases from epidemic and disastrous to endemic and manageable, but it requires a certain size of community and a long time. Fenner estimated that an interactive population of one to two hundred thousand people is needed to make smallpox endemic.[15] Perhaps the population density in Siam was too low to make this process effective. For some strains of malaria, survivors acquire resistance that is passed on in the genes. Archeological research has shown that some communities living in the Chaophraya Plain had developed such resistance in prehistoric times.[16] Forest-living communities had probably acquired such immunity, but in urban populations the resistance would have been weaker.

The contrast in population densities between Southeast Asia and neighboring regions may stem from their differing histories of forest clearance. In India and China, the clearances began in the early first millennium CE. In the initial phase, deaths from forest infections would have been high, but over generations the acquired immunity or resistance spread through the population. The clearances created tracts of open plain where a majority of people lived at some distance from the forests. In Siam there was no similar history. The population was concentrated in strips along the rivers. The forest was not far away.

Two other factors are migration and warfare. Population movement brings together people with different immunities. In southern Africa, Bantu peoples had been involved in forest clearance for centuries and had acquired immunity to the strains of malaria carried by the anopheles mosquito which flourishes in newly cleared land. When the Bantu moved into new areas and began clearing forest, the impact on the earlier residents who had not acquired the immunity was often disastrous.[17] Perhaps

---

[13] *Van Vliet's Siam*, 104–5, 200–1.
[14] La Loubère, *New historical relation*, 38.
[15] Fenner, "Smallpox in Southeast Asia."
[16] Webb, "Malaria and the peopling of early tropical Africa"; Carter and Mendis, "Evolutionary and historical aspects"; Higham and Rachanie, *Prehistoric Thailand*, 53, 77.
[17] Webb, "Malaria and the peopling of early tropical Africa"; Carter and Mendis, "Evolutionary and historical aspects."

there has been a similar pattern in Siam. Over the centuries, there has been a constant trickle of new peoples into the Chaophraya Plain.

Wars bring increased incidence of disease for many reasons: mixing of peoples with different epidemiological backgrounds, movement into areas where people are not acclimatized, stress and trauma, insanitary conditions, and the collapse of rules of social behavior. In European wars of the nineteenth century, 2.5 soldiers died from disease for every one that died in battle. In the British armies during the Napoleonic Wars, the ratio was seven to one (not including civilian deaths). The main diseases responsible were cholera, dysentery, plague, smallpox, influenza, and malaria.[18] The warring in Southeast Asia in the fifteenth and sixteenth centuries probably increased the death rate. The armies were often large. They marched long distances over thickly forested watersheds into unfamiliar areas. War prisoners were hauled away to new locations in large numbers. Soldiers living off the land and looting at will added to the devastation. Casualty rates among soldiers could amount to "more than half their Armie," and wars often led to famine and epidemics. Three of the kings who led armies across the Tenasserim Range died from disease on campaign (see p. 103). For ordinary soldiers, the risk would have been higher.

The population of Siam may have fallen over the sixteenth century, and especially over its second half, when the warring was intense. In 1594, De Coutre visited Suphanburi, which had been in the path of armies marching between Ayutthaya and Pegu. He described this major city as "very large and in ruins," populated only by war elephants and their mahouts, and overrun by "tigers, of which there were so many in the area that we were not safe from them even sleeping in our perahus [boats]."[19] A few decades later, Van Vliet reckoned that "owing to former wars large tracts along the frontiers have grown wild," and Schouten noted that "the borders of these kingdoms [Ayutthaya and Pegu] are quite ruined and unpeopled."[20] The population may then have increased from 1600 onwards, when the intensity of warfare dropped, and suffered another decline in the renewed warring from the 1760s to 1800s.

Agriculture and Food

Most studies assume that early modern Siam was an agrarian society in which the majority of people lived in villages and engaged in the production of food. Yet this agrarian society is hard to find in the sources. The

---

[18] Smallman-Raynor and Cliff, *War epidemics*, esp. 4–5, 32–8.
[19] Borschberg, *Memoirs and memorials*, 121–2.
[20] *Van Vliet's Siam*, 126; Schouten, "True description," 102.

Ayutthaya chronicles mention rice fields or peasants only a handful of times. The laws collected in the Three Seals Code pay scant attention to land, livestock, or irrigation. Peasants and villages are almost wholly absent from literary works. The portrayals of everyday life in the *wat* murals in late Ayutthaya have no trace of a peasant, a plow, or a paddy field. Foreign visitors penned many descriptions of urban Siam but left no portrait of a Siamese village.[21]

In the temperate zones of the world in the pre-modern era, most of the population had to work in agriculture in order to generate a surplus to feed a minority in the towns. In Britain in 1500, the ratio of rural to urban population was around three to one. In the tropical and subtropical zone, plentiful water and higher temperatures greatly facilitated the production of food, especially grains, with a much lower labor input.

Gervaise wrote, "The country is very fertile and, without needing great labor for its cultivation, anything that one may plant flourishes."[22] The scribe of the 1685 Persian mission to Siam described rice cultivation around Ayutthaya as follows:

When the time is right for planting, they plough the land in a careless manner and scatter seed all over the surface of the soil. Then they depart and wait for nature to provide them with results. The monsoon arrives just after their ploughing and the fields become saturated with water. Every day the water mounts up until it finally covers all the land. Under water the seeds turn into green plants and raise their heads up through the earth. They actually spring to the height of five or six cubits. When the plants reach maturity, the farmers return in their boats and gather the harvest.[23]

La Loubère sketched the same process: "They till them and sowe them, when the Rains have sufficiently softened them, and they gather their harvest when the waters are retired."[24] Land was prepared with a simple wooden plough or by trampling with buffaloes. Seed was sown broadcast. Nutrients were supplied by monsoon rains and river silt. Monsoonal flooding dealt with weeds. In some places, the water height was controlled by bunding the fields,[25] but around Ayutthaya the "floating rice" simply grew upwards as the floodwaters rose. The only period of more intense labor input came at the time of harvest, threshing, and storage. The yield per unit of area was low and unreliable but the yield per unit of labor was high. After describing these techniques used in Siam,

---

[21] For a more detailed discussion, see Baker and Pasuk, "Early modern Siam."

[22] Gervaise, *Natural and political history*, 19.

[23] Muhammad Rabi, *Ship of Sulaiman*, 153–4.

[24] La Loubère, *New historical relation*, 19.

[25] Heeck, *Traveler in Siam*, 51.

a Japanese junk captain noted in 1690, "Because cultivation is such an easy task there the price of rice is far cheaper than in other countries."[26]

Other sources of carbohydrate were freely available. Bananas grew everywhere. Edible roots such as sweet potatoes, taro, and yams were found in forests. Lotus seeds and various nuts grew in waterways and ponds. Gervaise noted that "No commodity anywhere in the country is cheaper than brown sugar," made from the juice of a palm tree.[27]

Proteins and vegetables were found by everyday hunting and gathering. Gervaise commented that that "the river abounds in fish," and "without stirring out of doors, anyone can catch more fish in an hour than he can eat in several days."[28] The Abbé de Choisy put it more sensually, "there are so many [fish] in the river that when bathing they come and rub against your legs."[29] Fish, prawns, and shellfish were mainly caught by labor-economical forms of trapping.[30] The scribe of the Persian embassy noted, "In Siam the region around the city and even the very edges of the city itself provide much game."[31] Other protein came from lizards, frogs, snakes, and insects, also collected or trapped, and larger animals such as wild boar and deer, hunted in nearby forests. Fruit and vegetables were not cultivated commercially until the early nineteenth century, instead people kept small kitchen gardens, and collected fruits, roots, leaves, shoots, and cress that grew wild in hedgerows, paddy field banks, ponds, and rivers. European visitors marveled at the easy availability of food. Heeck, visiting in 1655, was struck by the "superabundance."[32] Van Neijenrode, writing in 1621 after five years in Siam, also used the term "superabundance" and noted "even in lean years people can look after themselves very comfortably."[33] Alexander Hamilton in 1719 called Siam "as fruitful as any spot of ground in the world."[34] Frederike described how a Southeast Asian army could live off the land:

I have seene with my proper eyes, that those people and souldiers have eaten all sort of Wilde beastes, that are on the earth ... yea, I have seen them eate Scorpions and Serpents, also they feede of all kinde of hearbes and grasse. So that if such a great armie want not Water and salt, they will maintain themselves a long time in a bush with rootes, flowers, and leaves of trees.[35]

---

[26] Ishii, *Junk trade*, 56.
[27] Gervaise, *Natural and political history*, 20.
[28] Gervaise, *Natural and political history*, 8, 12.
[29] Choisy, *Journal of a voyage*, 170.
[30] Chatthip, *Thai village economy in the past*, 19.
[31] Muhammad Rabi, *Ship of Sulaiman*, 72–3.
[32] Heeck, *Traveler in Siam*, 57.
[33] Neijenrode, "Account and description," 8.
[34] Hamilton, *New account of the East Indies*, 445.
[35] Charney, *Southeast Asian warfare*, 194.

Unlike the temperate zones, where crop production and care of live-stock required a year-round commitment of labor, enough food could be produced in Siam by a small daily measure of hunting and gathering and a few days a year for rice farming. People did not have to live in settle-ments dedicated to agriculture, but could live in towns and travel out to paddy fields nearby. The areas immediately adjacent to cities were known as *thung*, meaning a (rice-growing) plain. The chronicles refer to "the *thung* of the walled city of Nakhon Ratchasima" or "the *thung* of Kamphaeng Phet,"[36] meaning the fields adjacent to that city that supplied its staple.

People commuted between city and *thung*. During an attack on Ayutthaya in the 1580s, the besiegers "planned the campaign as a lengthy undertaking and would maintain positions to prevent the inhabitants of the Royal Metropolis *from being able to issue forth to work the paddy fields*."[37] Similarly, in 1766 "The inhabitants [of Ayutthaya] went out to gather the rice, but were surprised by the Burmese, who led them captive to their camp."[38] Early in the reign of King Borommakot,

At the season for threshing rice, however, His Majesty went to thresh at the Sweetmeat Plain crown fields. Then He took the rice and placed it in small ox carts and He had all His Holy Royal Sons, His Holy Royal Daughters, His maids in waiting and His ladies pull them to the interior of the Palace Enclosure.[39]

These "crown fields" (*na luang*) were situated on the *thung hantra* rice plain to the northeast of the city. Great noble households probably had similar holdings to feed their many dependents. Gervaise mentioned that one segment of their slaves "works in the country cultivating the land." Ordinary folk had smallholdings. Van Neijenrode noted in 1621, "every-one, whatever his status, cultivates land of his own (especially rice and paddy) and engages in fishing."[40]

Enough rice to supply the population of Ayutthaya could be grown in a circle of around 10 kilometers' radius.[41] This rice-growing tract was not circular, but stretched along the rivers and canals which extended from Ayutthaya in all directions. Heeck and Le Blanc noted the paddy fields along the river just south of Ayutthaya.[42] Tachard recorded "vast plains reaching out of sight covered with rice"[43] along the river from Ayutthaya

[36] *RCA*, 96, ll. 15–16 (*PC*), 104–5 (*BM*).
[37] *RCA*, 104, ll. 18–19 (*PC*) (Emphasis added). See also harvesting before the Burmese attack of 1587, *RCA*, 115, ll. 21–4 (*BM*).
[38] Turpin, *History of the Kingdom of Siam*, 105.
[39] *RCA*, 423–4 (*BM*).
[40] Gervaise, *Natural and political history*, 97; Neijenrode, "Account and description," 10.
[41] For the basis of this calculation, see Baker and Pasuk, "Early modern Siam."
[42] Heeck, *Traveler in Siam*, 50–1; Le Blanc, *History of Siam in 1688*, 8.
[43] Tachard, *Voyage to Siam*, 193.

to Lopburi, and De Choisy repeatedly mentioned the "broad landscapes of rice" close to the city.[44]

Some rice was grown outside the floodplain, using methods of transplantation and water control, and was brought to the capital by boat. This type of rice was more expensive but stored better and thus was favored for provisioning junks.[45] From the 1620s, the Dutch carried rice to Batavia in years of shortage there, and later also to Melaka and Formosa, but only in modest amounts.[46] In the eighteenth century, rather more was exported to southern China (see Chapter 6). Probably the export grain came from these inland areas because of its storage quality. Enough rice to feed the city could be grown on areas reachable by boat in a few hours.

The Ayutthaya laws stated that all land belonged to the king and its sale was forbidden, but other clauses show that land was sold and mortgaged. Officials were ordered to intervene in disputes over occupancy, and to reassign rice land that had been abandoned.[47] These clauses were designed to manage disputes. The laws did not address the management of land in general. Some taxes were collected from agricultural products, but the amounts were small compared to the returns from the taxes and monopolies on trade. There was no section of the bureaucracy devoted to land revenue. Gervaise noted, "rice, like corn in France, is tax-free."[48]

In sum, because of the relative ease in growing or finding food, there was no need for a majority of the population to be dedicated to food production, as was the case in the temperate areas of the world. Because of the low population density, enough space for growing the city's rice supply was available close at hand. Many practiced agriculture as a part-time activity by commuting from an urban residence. Of course, some people did live in villages but these were clustered around the urban centers, especially along the nearby rivers. The fear of wild animals, forest disease, and people-raiding also encouraged people to cluster in larger settlements. The landscape has to be imagined, not as today's stipple of villages, but as urban centers, each with a penumbra of rice plains, separated by areas of forest and wilderness. This was primarily an urban society.

---

[44] Choisy, *Journal of a voyage*, 152, 172.

[45] La Loubère, *New historical relation*, 19; Gervaise, *Natural and political history*, 19–20; Baker, "Markets and production," 40–2.

[46] As a proportion of estimated rice consumption by Ayutthaya city, exports to Batavia averaged 3.3 percent over 1624–26, 1.9 percent over 1642–52, and 0.4 percent over 1664–94. Outside these years, little or no rice was exported. Calculations from data in Smith, *Dutch in seventeenth-century Thailand*, 53–67, 82.

[47] See Miscellaneous laws 43, 52, 54, 61, 62, 63, *Kotmai tra sam duang*, vol. 3, 110, 114–17, 120; Tomosugi, *Structural analysis*, 108–14.

[48] Gervaise, *Natural and political history*, 100.

An Urban Society

Anthony Reid estimated the population of seventeenth-century Ayutthaya city in the range of 150,000 to 200,000,[49] but his figure may be slightly low. In 1617, the East India Company board believed the city was "as great a city as London." In 1685, Véret, the manager of the French company in Ayutthaya, thought it was "a bigger city than Paris," and a Dutchman estimated the population as half a million.[50]

Reid may underestimate the area of the city by using seventeenth-century European maps, which showed suburbs around the southern and eastern sides, but had little detail on areas to the north or west.[51] The twenty ferries across the moat from the suburbs were distributed rather evenly around the island (see Map 5.2), suggesting the population was rather evenly distributed too.[52] Van Vliet noted, "All round the town and on the other side of the river there are many villages, residences, houses of farmers, temples, monasteries, and pyramids, and the population here is just as thick as in the town itself."[53] Judging from the location of old *wat*, the occupied area off the island was at least twice that on the island, giving a total city area of 20–25 square kilometers as against Reid's estimate of 15 square kilometers.

Reid's estimate also ignores the population living on the water. Because the area flooded every year, many people chose to live on boats. Schouten reported that the rivers were "full of small boats aboard on which whole families lived, ate, and slept quite comfortably on carpets and mattresses."[54] While walking around Ayutthaya in 1690, Kaempfer drew sketches of these houseboats (Figure 5.1), made maps showing them moored in several parallel lines along the rivers around the city, and reported that each housed not one family but "two, three, or more Families each."[55] Besides these boats there were houses placed on rafts "made of very big bamboo canes that are strongly tied together. [They] resemble floating islets."[56]

---

[49] Reid, *Southeast Asia in the age of commerce, vol. 2*, 69–73. For comparison, London was an estimated 350,000 in 1650, Paris 420,000 in 1634, Venice 150,000 in 1630, and Osaka 220,000 in 1650.

[50] Anderson, *English intercourse with Siam*, 69; Choisy, *Journal of a voyage*, 148; De Voogd quoted in Sternstein, "'Krung kao'," 98, n. 60.

[51] Reid cited Sternstein "'Krung kao'," which reproduced the maps from La Loubère and Choisy.

[52] Baker, "Final part of the *Description of Ayutthaya*," 186, 189–92.

[53] *Van Vliet's Siam*, 110.

[54] Quoted in Smith, *Creolization and diaspora*, 106; see also Gervaise, *Natural and political history*, 98.

[55] Michel and Terwiel, *Kaempfer Werke IV*, 42, 503–7, 520, 524; Kaempfer, *Description of the Kingdom of Siam*, 49.

[56] Marini quoted in Smith, *Creolization and diaspora*, 99.

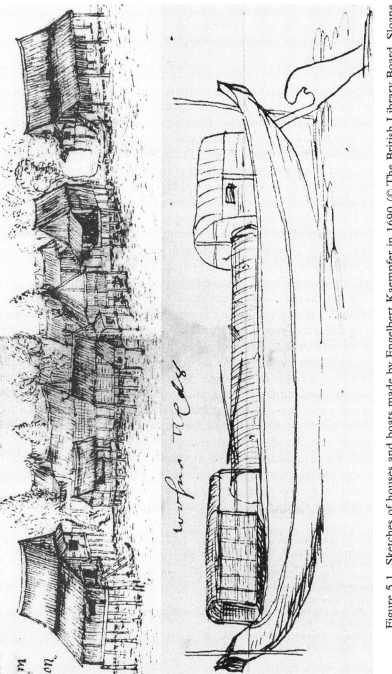

Figure 5.1. Sketches of houses and boats made by Engelbert Kaempfer in 1690 (© The British Library Board, Sloane 3060 f.433r and f.438r)

Arriving at any reliable estimate of Ayutthaya's population is impossible, but a minimum of 250,000, based on an average density of 10,000 per square kilometer on land plus 50,000 people resident on the water, seems reasonable.

On other urban centers of Siam there are no eye-witness accounts of any detail, but there are three sources which identify the major towns: places that appear in the chronicles with the prefix *mueang*; towns of first, second, and third class, meaning administrative centers, in the provincial list in the Three Seals Code;[57] and major places identified in the accounts and maps composed by foreign visitors.[58] These three sources largely coincide, giving a total of around seventy places plotted on Map 5.1.

A handful of these towns were sizeable. Phitsanulok had been a capital in its own right until the mid-sixteenth century, and was still the "second city of the kingdom," according to Gervaise, and "a city of great commerce, fortified with fourteen Bastions," according to La Loubère. In 1644, Prasat Thong was building a palace in Phitsanulok for his son to reside in an echo of the old pattern of twin capitals.[59] Gervaise called Kamphaeng Phet "an ancient city and of great importance in the Indies. It is almost as large as the capital and has an equally numerous population."[60] Kamphaeng Phet is one of few old city sites that have not been hidden or destroyed by modern urbanization. Its walled city was much smaller than Ayutthaya, but there are ruins scattered over an area of 20 square kilometers to the north, and another 5 square kilometers across the river to the south. Si Satchanalai, another old city site that has not been hidden by modernization, has ruins scattered over an area around half the size of Kamphaeng Phet. Phitsanulok's past has been more heavily obliterated, but the extant monuments are spread on both banks of a five kilometer stretch of the Nan River.[61]

Mergui was an important port, situated on "a great and populous Island."[62] Along with the inland town of Tenasserim, also a "considerable place,"[63] it dominated the portage route across the upper peninsula. Khorat was a garrison town and another assembly center for forest goods. Lopburi was a

[57] *Kotmai tra sam duang*, vol. 1, 318–27.
[58] Smithies, "Seventeenth century Siam," with the addition of data from Heeck, *Ship of Sulaiman*, Valentyn, and De Coutre.
[59] Gervaise, *Natural and political history*, 33–4; La Loubère, *New historical relation*, 4; Dhiravat, "Life, work and gossip."
[60] Gervaise, *Natural and political history*, 33–4.
[61] The estimates in this paragraph come from walking around these places and peering at Google Earth.
[62] La Loubère, *New historical relation*, 4.
[63] Collis, *Siamese White*, 42.

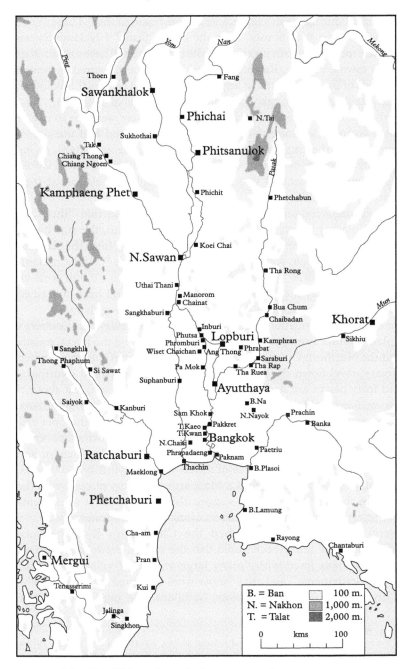

Map 5.1. Urban places in the seventeenth century

second capital during Narai's reign, and Choisy reported that "The suburbs cover half a league with houses, as in the city of Siam."[64] Nakhon Sawan stood at the most important junction on the river system. These and another three old towns, Phichai, Ratchaburi, and Phetchaburi, figured in several visitors' lists of the ten or so most important provincial centers.[65] Sukhothai, Tak, Chanthaburi, and Bangkok also appeared in some of these lists.

On the above admittedly sketchy information, there were ten to twelve principal towns. Assuming that the largest were around half the size of the capital, and the smallest had a population of at least 20,000, giving an estimated average of 50,000 each, the capital and these towns would have accounted for around two-fifths of La Loubère's estimated total population of 1.9 million.

Other towns were much smaller. Gervaise reported that "there are only nine [places] which can justifiably be called cities, the rest being, strictly speaking, only small towns and villages, lacking both the size and amenities to make them comparable to towns in France."[66] If the remaining sixty "major towns" ranged in size from 5,000 to 10,000 with an average of 7,500 each, then the towns and cities would have contained around 1.2 million or around three-fifths of the total population.

The rest of the population was strung along the waterways. La Loubère's map plots another twenty-six unnamed places, all along the rivers, mostly around the Northern Cities. In the *Tale of Khun Chang Khun Phaen*, when characters travel down the river from the Northern Cities to Ayutthaya, around forty places are named which are not in the accounting above.[67] The poem *Nirat nakhon sawan*, relating a journey upriver from Ayutthaya in 1656, records many of the same places. Between them, the poet saw only "the lush greenery of the great forests / plants intertwined covering the ground / ... dead quiet save for the cries of animals."[68] Valentyn and La Mare each mapped the course of the river from Ayutthaya to the sea, with Valentyn showing eight and La Mare around twenty places not in the accounting above. These sources suggest there were smaller settlements sited at intervals of 10 to 20 kilometers along the major waterways.

Several foreign visitors described the Chaophraya River between Ayutthaya and the sea. Heeck noted that the stretch between Ayutthaya and Bangkok was lined with "many large and small villages, hamlets, and other settlements" and that "most were occupied by farmers who made their living with horses, cows, buffaloes, and pigs ... [and] also

---

[64] Choisy, *Journal of a voyage*, 191.
[65] See for example, Gervaise, *Natural and political history*, 33–41; *Van Vliet's Siam*, 108–9; La Loubère, *New historical relation*, 4–5; Schouten, "True description," 124.
[66] Gervaise, *Natural and political history*, 31.
[67] See maps in Baker and Pasuk, *Tale of Khun Chang Khun Phaen*, 848, 850, 852.
[68] "Nirat nakhon sawan," 784–95, quote on 791.

keep many chickens and ducks." On the approach to Ayutthaya, "the city houses crowded along the banks, particularly on the right-hand side, which was so lively with people that it was as if one had entered a suburb [in the Netherlands]." These villagers had occupations other than agriculture, with each settlement having its own specialization:

we saw that in some of them there lived none but various types of potters, and in others only cutters of firewood ... In some villages there lived only boat-builders, and in some only carpenters or those who had tree nurseries ... We also passed a village where only coffins were made.[69]

Even here, low down the settlement hierarchy, food production was not the sole activity, and perhaps not the major one either. These were not the semi-subsistent rice-growing villages of a peasant society, but riverside ribbon rurbanism.

Urban Society at Work

If most people lived in cities and towns, what did they do there? Van Vliet observed that "the people earn their living by trade, court services, navigating with junks, barges and prauws, fishery and industries, and handicrafts by making of ingeniously worked golden and silver objects."[70] Gervaise noted more concisely, "the majority of the population is engaged in trade," and praised the quality of construction work, decorative arts, textile making, carpentry, brocading, goldsmithing, and medicine.[71] La Loubère wrote, "The most general Professions at Siam are Fishing for the common people, and Merchandize for those that have wherewith to follow it."[72] The longest list of occupations, compiled by Van Neijenrode, included

house carpenters and shipwrights, sculptors, gold and silversmiths, masons, goldbeaters, stonecutters, painters, tinkers, weavers, plumbers, coppersmiths, turners, brickmakers and potters, lumber and timber sawyers, chest and cabinet makers, minters, and thousands of pedlars of cloth and other goods ... surgeons and thousands of doctors, scribes and jurists of a kind, sellers of sweets, foods and clothing ... fishermen and tillers of land ... masses of labourers and common slaves ... no lack of scribes, attorneys or lawyers.[73]

In the *Description of Ayutthaya* (see p. 286), Ayutthaya appears as a thriving commercial and industrial city. The document lists thirty-eight fresh markets and forty specialized markets on the island, another thirty markets

---

[69] Heeck, *Traveler in Siam*, 44–5, 53.
[70] *Van Vliet's Siam*, 168.
[71] Gervaise, *Natural and political history*, 87, 91–3, 98.
[72] La Loubère, *New historical relation*, 71.
[73] Neijenrode, "Account and description," 9–11.

in the outskirts, and thirty-eight production centers in the outskirts.[74] These lists show the commerce and production of a city with several functions.

First, as a port. There are separate settlements specializing in making fishnets, lead weights, and other gear for fishing, ribs and other timbers for boat building, oil for caulking, and anchor ropes. Potteries make various storage jars which are bought by long-distance traders for storing ship-born export goods. Other settlements make barrels and chests which may in part have been sold to traders.

Second, as a capital. There is a workshop for making elephant howdahs (the conveyance of kings and nobles), several boatyards for building royal barges and war craft, workshops making *sa* (mulberry) paper and accordion books needed for administration, markets selling books and white-clay (*dinso*) powder used for writing, a quarter specializing in the sale of musical instruments, probably used in court entertainment, and another making and selling fireworks for cremations and public celebrations.

Third, as a religious center. One locality makes incense sticks along with other aromatics and cosmetics; three others make coffins and other articles for cremations; one makes Buddha images, while another produces gold and silver leaf to affix to images as an act of worship. Two settlements catch fish and birds sold for people to release for making merit at festival times. Four markets specialize in monks' robes and other monastic requirements; another sells small votive images; and two localities prepare betelnut and other items for ordinations and other ceremonies.

Finally, the city is a center of population creating demand for a wide range of everyday goods. Several places sell house components including timber posts; beams and joists; wall panels of wood, woven bamboo, or woven leaves; tiles of various designs; and nails and other metal fixings. Many more make and sell everyday household articles such as: rattan or wooden furniture; trays, tables, and salvers; knives, axes, and other metal implements; earthenware pots and jars; metal and brass bowls and other receptacles; mattresses and other bedding, children's toys, cradles, woven mats, basketware containers, teeth polishers, and flints and torches for lighting. There are four settlements of weavers, and many markets selling thread, parts for spinning wheels, and parts for looms, suggesting a sector of household textile production. Several localities specialize in processing food: milling rice, making sweets, pressing oil, distilling liquor, slaughtering pigs, and making noodles.

The neighborhoods within cities are often named after prominent buildings, historical events, or old villages. In Ayutthaya, however, most of the neighborhoods were named after the products that were made or sold there, reflecting pride in the city's production and commerce (Map 5.2).

---

[74] Baker, "Markets and production." The list of production centers on the island seems to be lost.

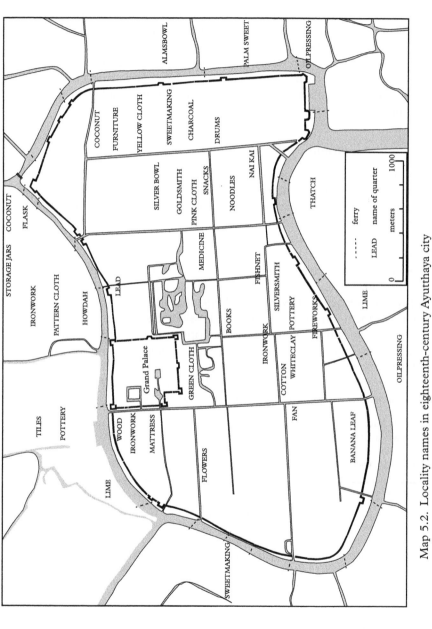

Map 5.2. Locality names in eighteenth-century Ayutthaya city

From other towns, there is almost no description. De Choisy reported a list of the products from Phitsanulok which suggests something of its commercial activity: "elephants teeth, rice, saltpeter, rhinoceros horns, skins of wild animals like buffaloes, deer, tigers, etc., and the red gum from which Spanish wax is made, sugar-canes, onions, tobacco, wax, honey, links made of pitch and oil, wood for building ships, cotton, sappan wood, etc."[75] As in other societies, the secondary urban centers probably mirrored the activities of the capital with minor adjustments and a diminished scale.

Servitude

In most agrarian societies, states depend on land revenue. At Ayutthaya, land taxation was insignificant. Instead the state raised revenues by ways appropriate to an urban society, including profits and taxes on commerce, and levies on people's labor.

By the early sixteenth century, adult males were registered to facilitate military recruitment on a model found in other Tai states and probably originating in China (see pp. 31, 73, 100). In the era of intense warring in the late sixteenth century, this system was tightened and extended. The *Testimony* reported of Naresuan, "Organizing the men in his service, he formed them into service groups."[76] Possibly this was an extension of the system into something like mass conscription in the core Ayutthaya kingdom. Naresuan recruited armies from all around the lower Chaophraya Plain.

With the decline in warfare after 1600, this conscription system was not abandoned but converted into general servitude:

He [Ekathotsarot] demanded that all subject lands and cities under the Siamese crown list their slaves. After that he had the people counted in all of these places … His Majesty also divided all those born and settled in his country (even thought they were not slaves) under heads (called *nai* in Siamese) like district masters. The result of this was great subjection, because no one since has been free of servitude and has always been under the obedience of his *nai*.[77]

By the 1630s, according to Van Vliet,

in the whole country the common class of people, who are not slaves, are divided under quartermasters. The latter have control over 1,000, 500, 400, 300, 200, or 100 men … if His Majesty needs people, these quartermasters are requested to provide the required number.

[75] Choisy, *Journal of a voyage*, 233.
[76] Tun Aung Chain, *Chronicle of Ayutthaya*, 42; *Khamhaikan khun luang ha wat*, 14.
[77] *Van Vliet's Siam*, 234.

With this system, the king could raise an army of sixty to eighty thousand men in a few days, and 300,000 at the maximum, and each year a levy of ten to thirty thousand was raised for practice.[78] Fifty years later, La Loubère reported that all males were registered at age sixteen, and people were considered so important that "they count them every year."[79] More likely, the censuses were less frequent. One was ordered in 1644 after a military failure.[80] At the capital, there was a registration hall inside the southeast corner of the palace compound under the command of the chief registrar, Phra Satsadi. "'Tis an Office," reported La Loubère, "very subject to Corruption, by reason that every particular person endeavours to get himself omitted out of the Rolls for money." Children were entered on the rolls at four years of age. In the new system of administration in the provincial towns, there was an official to keep the rolls.[81] At some point, a law was introduced requiring anyone wishing to have access to the law courts to be registered as a *phrai*.[82]

Those on the conscription rolls were divided into two groups, each required to work for the king on alternate months. These *phrai luang* were assigned to work under various ministries. Possibly as war diminished and commerce expanded, labor was transferred accordingly. In the seventeenth century there were many royal construction projects such as Prasat Thong's massive expansion of the palace complex, Narai's new second capital at Lopburi, many new *wat*, and roads and bridges in the capital. Gervaise noted that one segment of the royal *phrai* were "those in public service, such as the earth-carriers, brickmakers, woodcutters and miners."[83] The king also used these labor resources to man ships, port facilities, and warehouses, and allowed some people to commute their forced labor into the collection of forest goods for export.[84]

Some *phrai* came under the control of great nobles, and were also bound to work for six months, though how this transfer happened is unknown. Probably *phrai* assigned to ministries were appropriated by the nobles in charge, but others may have placed themselves under the protection of a noble. In *The tale of Khun Chang Khun Phaen* (described below), one major theme is the search for protection against risks, dangers, and uncertainty. People look for someone they can depend on (*thi phueng*), and who will feed or support them (*liang*). When the father of a main character dies, his

---

[78] *Van Vliet's Siam*, 149, 122.
[79] La Loubère, *New historical relation*, 11.
[80] Dhiravat, "Political history of Siam," 230.
[81] La Loubère, *New historical relation*, 84–5.
[82] Law on acceptance of cases, clause 10, *Kotmai tra sam duang*, vol. 2, 32.
[83] Gervaise, *Natural and political history*, 98–9.
[84] La Loubère, *New historical relation*, 94.

servants lament "We have lost our protector," and fear harassment by local officials. When news arrives that the hero has died on a military campaign, his mother-in-law's first thought is "Who'll protect us?"[85] A good patron is someone with enough influence to provide protection against other people and other authorities. The father of the hero, Khun Phaen, is an effective patron in the provincial town of Suphanburi because he has an official post as a soldier and recognition from the king, so local officials "shook their heads [and] knew never to cross him." After the father is killed, his servants lament that, "nobody dared bully us, because everyone feared Khun Krai. But now they'll all come and push us around."[86]

Gradually these non-royal *phrai* were recognized in the law, initially under several names that were eventually consolidated as *phrai som*. As with royal *phrai*, they were used to build residences and religious buildings, to serve as personal retainers, and staff trading enterprises.[87]

Many people had a legal status as *that* (Pali: dāsa) which the Europeans translated as "slaves." These included war captives, whose numbers must have increased in the sixteenth century, and others who became slaves through debt – they had borrowed money placing themselves (or their wives and children) as collateral, and then failed to repay, or they had failed to pay fines levied as punishment for crime.

According to the law, masters had absolute power over their slaves other than the right to take their lives. The status was hereditary, though children of union between a freeman and a slave woman were divided between the two statuses, and debt slaves could redeem themselves.[88] None of the European observers describe a slave market, but they mention transactions, particularly the sale of slaves after a master died. People were seen as commodities. When asked to comment on portraits of European people, Ayutthayan nobles responded by estimating the money value of the people portrayed.[89]

Many slaves were personal retainers. They worked in the household, tilled the noble's land, accompanied their master in public as a demonstration of status, and were remunerated in both kind (paddy and clothing) and cash. Others worked for a living in the urban economy, and either paid a daily or monthly release fee to their master or were required to hand over half of their annual earnings. Van Vliet concluded, "most

[85] Baker and Pasuk, *Tale of Khun Chang Khun Phaen*, 28, 207.
[86] Baker and Pasuk, *Tale of Khun Chang Khun Phaen*, 8, 35.
[87] Gervaise, *Natural and political history*, 98–9; Busakorn, "Ban Phlu Luang dynasty," 74–7, 294–5.
[88] Law on slavery, *Kotmai tra sam duang*, vol. 2, 285–343.
[89] La Loubère, *New historical relation*, 28.

of the mandarins have no other profits than from their own slaves."[90] La Loubère gave a similar picture:

They employ their Slaves in cultivating their Lands and Gardens, and in some domestic Service; or rather they permit them to work to gain their livelihood, under a Tribute which they receive from four to eight *Ticals* a Year, that is to say, from seven Livres ten sols, to fifteen Livres.[91]

Rather than land-lords, these nobles were man-lords.

Some people sold themselves into slavery as a strategy to escape the forced labor of a *phrai* and at the same time raise capital for engaging in the commercial economy. La Loubère commented, "Liberty is oftentimes more burdensome than servitude," and quoted a local proverb that the Siamese found liberty so "abject" that they would sell it to eat a durian, but the scribe of the 1685 Persian embassy was more accurate: "This is the way the Siamese accumulate capital to enter business and carry on trade."[92]

By the mid-seventeenth century, so much manpower was committed to the commercial economy that diverting some to military recruitment resulted in disruption of trade. In the 1660s, when large armies were raised to attack Lanna, the impact on the export of products such as skins was immediate as the recruits included the men who collected and transported these goods. The effect was also felt in the rice economy, where the subtraction of people resulted in three consecutive years of bad harvest, and an outbreak of "fevers." Probably as a result, the military target in the 1670s shifted to raids into Lanxang to capture people.[93] In 1674, the king passed a law that attempted to regain control over *phrai* alienated to nobles – the beginning of a struggle to control labor that is a theme of the later decades of the Ayutthaya era (see Chapter 6).

Family, Gender, and Sexuality

The roles and relations of men and women in Ayutthaya society, especially below the ranks of the nobility, had some special features. In most of the sources, these relations are invisible, but there is one exception. *The tale of Khun Chang Khun Phaen* is the only literary work of the era

---

[90] *Van Vliet's Siam*, 148–9.
[91] La Loubère, *New historical relation*, 77; see also Gervaise, *Natural and political history*, 88.
[92] La Loubère, *New historical relation*, 77, 107; Muhammad Rabi, *Ship of Sulaiman*, 132.
[93] Dhiravat, "Political history of Siam," 287, 307, 311, 332–3.

that aims to present a realistic picture of the society.[94] Drawing on a single source is obviously not ideal, but the source is substantial – 14,000 lines – and is not the product of a single imagination; it evolved from an oral tradition in which, through interactions between performers and audiences over many decades, a work comes to reflect the values of its society. The tale offers two different views of the family, one among commoners, and the other among the nobility.

Commoners: Female Families and Loose Males

The first part of the tale is set in the society of a provincial town with the focus on three families that range from rich gentry to struggling commoner. Strikingly, the family is mainly an association of women. The tale opens with a celebration of the heroism of childbirth in which women are center stage as mothers, female relatives, and midwives, while men are incidental. In all three families, the father dies early and the children are raised by a single mother. Later in the tale, the children's children are again raised by a single woman. When the principal characters visit a hill village and find only women there, nobody thinks this is strange, and nobody asks where the men have gone. Women are not only progenitors and care-givers, but also managers of the family property and providers of the family income. One leading female character manages a cotton plantation and another runs a shop. In the background, the majority of the people working either in manual jobs or trading activities are women.

In the 1420s, Ma Huan observed that "all affairs are managed by their wives." From then until the mid-nineteenth century, visitors to Siam regularly reported much the same thing. In the 1630s, Van Vliet wrote "the women, (who are well built and pretty), do most work in the fields. These women also row the boats on the river and besides many other things."[95] In the 1680s, La Loubère observed, "The women plough the Land, they sell and buy in the Cities."[96] The scribe of the Persian embassy in 1685 noted,

It is common for women to engage in buying and selling in the markets and even to undertake physical labour … Thus you can see the women paddling to

---

[94] Written versions of the tale date to the nineteenth century but were based on older originals. The analysis here relies heavily on older texts. See the Afterword in Baker and Pasuk, *Tale of Khun Chang Khun Phaen*, esp. 882–902; and Baker and Pasuk, "Gender, sexuality and family in old Siam," for a fuller statement of the argument in this section.

[95] *Van Vliet's Siam*, 162.

[96] La Loubère, *New historical relation*, 50.

the surrounding villages where they successfully earn their daily bread with no assistance from the men.[97]

In the early eighteenth century, Alexander Hamilton recorded: "The Women in Siam are the only Merchants in buying Goods, and some of them trade very considerably. The Husbands in general are maintained by the Industry of their Wives."[98]

In *Khun Chang Khun Phaen*, adult men are not tightly attached to the family. Young males leave home to seek education and experience, while adult males roam around as monks, soldiers, traders, and bandits. The hero, Khun Phaen, typifies the loose male. Two days after marriage, he goes off to war. On return, he is thrown into jail. On release a dozen years later, he goes off to war again. Only at the close of the tale, when already a grandfather, does he settle down. Women comment ruefully on the culture of the loose male: "How much does a husband love? He can just go down three steps and be gone."[99]

La Loubère noted how corvée duty isolated men from the local economy:

Whilst the Men acquit themselves of the six months work, which they every one yearly owe to the Prince, it belongs to their Wife, their Mother, or their Children to maintain them. And when they have satisfy'd the Service of their king, and they are return'd home, the generality know not unto what business to apply themselves, being little accustomed to any particular Profession ... He works not at all, when he works not for his King; he walks not abroad; he hunts not; he does nothing almost but continue sitting or lying, eating, playing, smoking and sleeping.[100]

In *Khun Chang Khun Phaen*, women are portrayed as confident of their sexuality. Aged around fifteen, the heroine Phim describes herself as "just blooming." At the start of the romance which is the core of the plot, she takes the lead, flirting with the hero and flaunting her sexuality, even though he is in the robe as a novice monk. Later in the tale, we hear the inner thoughts of a girl on the physical appearance of a boy she has just met:

He has a bright face and cheeks like nutmeg. His lips look as if painted with rouge ... His hair is cute as a lotus pod ... The black pupils of his eyes gleam like jet. A strong chest and curvy waist. Everything looks perfect. If he came to lie with me for one night, I'd gobble him up.[101]

This open sexuality is not confined to the young or to the private world. In the markets, female vendors flirt with young soldiers, sometimes

[97] Muhammad Rabi, *Ship of Sulaiman*, 139.
[98] Hamilton, *New account of the East Indes*, 457.
[99] Baker and Pasuk, *Tale of Khun Chang Khun Phaen*, 775, 1190.
[100] La Loubère, *New historical relation*, 50.
[101] Baker and Pasuk, *Tale of Khun Chang Khun Phaen*, 581–2.

baring a breast as temptation. Widows tout their experience in competition with their younger colleagues:

"You've never made love so what do you know? You young girls have got as much inner rhythm as a Lao corpse. Just because you're breathing, who's going to love you? When it comes to the tricks, watch out for us widows. A young chap like this is a pushover. Just tug his string and he'll tremble."[102]

When soldiers are leaving for war or returning, women throng the streets and riverbanks, calling out their thoughts:

"Oh sir, this young and going to war already." "So slight I can't take my eyes away." "Such a pretty body, I'd not go to sleep at all." "I'd love to go to war with you but the action would make my clothes filthy!" … "I'd like to jump up in his saddle for a ride."[103]

A midwife strips naked at the moment of delivery to distract the attention of any evil spirits that might harm the new-born.

Terwiel notes, "Women's fashion involved a generous display of bare skin."[104] Foreign visitors were sometimes surprised at the alluring way some women dressed:

Modesty is not great among the women, and their way of dressing is indecent. Their whole outfit consists of a chemise, which goes down only as far as the waistband and is entirely open in the front, leaving the whole bosom exposed. Their skirt, which is a kind of underskirt, is likewise open in the front, leaving the whole thigh in view.[105]

Because of warfare, the monkhood, corvée, and the culture of the loose male, men were in a short and unreliable supply. In commoner society, female sexuality was strong and open because it was not constrained, but also because it served a function in fulfilling the female responsibility to sustain the family. Marriage as portrayed in the tale fits this pattern. The marriage between the hero and heroine is dramatized as a sale of the man into the family of the woman. The hero's mother offers her son, using a traditional form of words: "As we're poor and short of cash, I've come to sell you young Kaeo so you may use his services … Think of him like a pair of leather shoes." After a negotiation, the heroine's family agree to pay a certain price, including providing the house extension for the new couple. After a ceremony, the male is delivered into the house of the female's family.

---

[102] Baker and Pasuk, *Tale of Khun Chang Khun Phaen*, 617.
[103] Baker and Pasuk, *Tale of Khun Chang Khun Phaen*, 569–70.
[104] Terwiel, "Body and sexuality," 44.
[105] Breazeale, "Memoirs of Pierre Poivre," 192, at Mergui in 1745.

Nobles: Male Dominance and Female Submission

The second half of the tale is located in the capital among the society of the nobility. The hero's family has been wafted up the social scale by appointments to noble rank as reward for success in war. The portrayal of gender and sexuality is very different – a more familiar picture of patriarchy, privileged male sexuality, and constraints on women.

The noble family revolves around the male head who provides protection to wife, children, and servants. A good husband shelters his wife like the spreading branches of a *bodhi* tree, and a good father shelters his children from all dangers, even the menace of sun, wind, and insects. According to Ayutthaya law, a man had absolute rights of ownership over wife and children, including rights to sell or mortgage them. Adultery was analogous to theft.[106]

Men monopolize the active roles as courtiers, soldiers, judges, and officials. Women are advised how to serve their husbands unconditionally, in terms similar to those found in etiquette manuals in late Ayutthaya:

As for a good wife, the text lays down four qualities: One, looking after her husband with kindness; two, sharing hardship and happiness equally; three, paying respect and obeisance to her husband; and four, giving her body willingly for his use.[107]

Woman's other role is as prizes, awarded to men for success in war and other services to the king.

In noble society, male sexuality is highly privileged. Multiple wives and liaisons are not merely accepted but expected, with kings serving as the model. All the main noble characters have multiple wives. When told he is about to gift a woman to a noble who already has a wife, the king responds, "However many wives he has is fitting. If he had ten, it would be even better."[108] By contrast, female sexuality is severely constrained. Women are expected to be immaculate, passive, and submissive. The heroine, who is fought over by two men, suffers nothing more than pangs of conscience in the first part of the tale, but in noble society, she is pilloried for having two husbands and eventually is executed. The latter part of the tale portrays unrestrained female sexuality as a source of social chaos, rather in the same way that the chronicles present the story of Si Sudachan (see pp. 75–6).

Marriage in this noble social context is a transfer of ownership of the female from the father to the husband. The event takes place in the

---

[106] Law on slavery, clause 3, *Kotmai tra sam duang*, vol. 2, 288; Law on marriage, clauses 10, 51, 68, *Kotmai tra sam duang*, vol. 2, 208, 211–12, 232–3, 242.
[107] Baker and Pasuk, *Tale of Khun Chang Khun Phaen*, 520.
[108] Baker and Pasuk, *Tale of Khun Chang Khun Phaen*, 734.

groom's family house, where the father gifts the bride to the groom. In the Ayutthaya Law on Marriage, which seems largely applicable to the nobility, woman found guilty of adultery are subject to public shaming, and the wronged husband has the right to kill both his wife and her lover.[109]

Gender in a Commercial Society

The extreme difference between these two models of gender and sexuality is testament to the steepness of the social hierarchy. The portrayal of the female family in commoner society may be rather extremely drawn in the tale. In the background, there are glimpses of commoner families where males have a greater role. Yet, the poem may still capture the essence of a society structured differently from either agrarian societies or modern urban societies. Warfare, corvée, long-distance trade, and the monkhood made men mobile and unreliable – very different from a society in which men are tied to the land. Women were the mainstays of the commoner family as progenitor, care giver, property manager, and provider. This position may have developed from the relatively strong position of women in older Tai societies where bilateral kinship gave relatively equal weight to male and female lines of descent,[110] but the role of commoner women at Ayutthaya was also shaped by the characteristics of an urban and commercial society. In agrarian societies, men are able to leverage their superior physical strength to establish a dominant role. This has been the pattern in agrarian societies all over the world, and became the case in Siam when a peasant society developed in the nineteenth century.

Buddhism and Urban Society

The form of Buddhism that spread from Sri Lanka and is now known as Theravada was distinctive in teaching and practice. The early followers had agreed on a version of Gotama Buddha's teachings and written them down; there was no splintering into sects adhering to earlier Buddhas or schisms over philosophy. The *sangha* or monkhood was made up of self-sustaining lineages of ordained monks; kings could patronize and regulate the *sangha*, but not control it. Any male could become a monk,

---

[109] Law on marriage, clauses 7–9, *Kotmai tra sam duang*, vol. 2, 206, 210–11; Old laws, clause 65, *Kotmai tra sam duang*, vol. 5, 190; New laws, clause 37, *Kotmai tra sam duang*, vol. 5, 343–5.

[110] And this in turn may have developed from proto-Tai societies in southern China; see Barlow, *Zhuang*.

for either a short period or a lifetime, and monks depended on daily patronage by the laity, creating a thick interface between society and religion. The *sangha* had not attacked older beliefs in Hindu deities, spirits in the natural world, or supernatural practices but had absorbed them. As a result, Buddhism had become deeply embedded in the everyday life of the society.

European visitors in the sixteenth and seventeenth centuries were struck by the numbers and richness of the temples, and by the numbers of monks. Schouten thought there were "more than three hundred faire Temples" and thirty thousand monks in Ayutthaya. Van Vliet raised the estimated number of temples to 400 or 450 and found them "very well built with many towers and pyramids, of which almost every one is gilded." Fifty years later, Gervaise estimated over 500 temples and 60,000 monks; the scribe of the Safavid embassy thought there were 5,000 temples; and Choisy reported that "Twenty thousand [monks] have been enumerated within the city confines, and many more in the quarters on both sides of the river, stretching two leagues above and below the city."[111]

For the nobility, building temples was a way of earning both religious merit and worldly reputation. La Loubère commented, "There hardly is a Siamese rich enough to build a temple, who does it not, and who buries not the Riches he has remaining."[112] Gervaise noted, "the great mandarins have them built in emulation of each other and spare nothing to surpass each other in the richness and magnificence of their buildings."[113]

Gervaise sought to understand Buddhism by delving into *wat* libraries and conversing with monks. He summarized the "beliefs of the Siamese" as follows:

> the attainment of divinity is nothing but the reward and the recompense of virtue ... They must first go through all manner of states of existence by a kind of circulation from one state to another ... having first come into being as an ordinary individual, they are reborn another time as a mandarin and in succeeding generations as a prince, a king, a monk, a saint and angel and finally a god ... When ... a soul has climbed step by step to the highest point of perfection ... he suddenly disappears and goes to take his place in *Nyreupan* [*nibbana*], which is a place of rest and delight set aside to be the abode of the gods.[114]

---

[111] Schouten, "True description," 97, 105; *Van Vliet's Siam*, 105, 158; Gervaise, *Natural and political history*, 33, 139; Muhammad Rabi, *Ship of Sulaiman*, 116; Choisy, *Journal of a voyage*, 171.
[112] La Loubère, *New historical relation*, 124.
[113] Gervaise, *Natural and political history*, 139.
[114] Gervaise, *Natural and political history*, 107–8.

As a consequence, "they firmly believe that happiness in the present is no more than a reward for virtue in the past" and hence merit-making was the core of religious practice: "They have continually on their lips the words *Tam boune* [*tham bun*, make merit], meaning 'Do good works.'" Merit was made by building *wat* or lesser constructions, supporting the monks through almsgiving, observing holy days, and "serving their neighbor. They help the poor, visit the sick and build houses of retreat in the country."[115] Van Vliet and Gervaise also described how birds and fish were released to make merit, and how old cattle were cared for in the *wat*.

Mendicant Portuguese friars who arrived in Ayutthaya in the late sixteenth century were impressed by the simplicity of the monks' lives, their dependence on alms, their everyday services for people including ceremonies, blessings for boats, prayers for the sick, and schooling for the young. They were also impressed by the devotion of the laity, the "many donations ... given by the rich and well-to-do" for the upkeep of *wat*, and the contributions by the poor in form of labor for "cleaning, sweeping, dusting, etc."[116] The Dutch and French observers in the seventeenth century confirmed these impressions. Heeck found the interior of a preaching hall "as beautiful and elegant a display as one is likely to find in all of papistry." He watched a monk giving a sermon to a congregation loaded down with offerings, and found the reverence "very devout."[117] Van Neijenrode noted that the monks "are much respected and valued, and, even though they are innumerable, many thousands of them, are held in high esteem." He observed how the monks were supported by alms from

the humble and the great alike ... since the nation greatly honours its priests of scholars and students and obeys them respectfully, hence surpassing some of our nation ... I myself saw and heard a highly placed priest reckon that for gods, shrines, etc. within the jurisdiction of Siam annually more than two tonnes of gold is the amount offered by the community and used to advantage at the behest of the priesthood.[118]

Tachard noted the simplicity of the monastic code, the close contact between the monks and the people who gave alms on a daily basis, the special respect for monks who adopted strictly ascetical practice, and the way crowds of people listened to monk's sermons "with much reverence and attention." He chanced on the funeral of a famous monk which

[115] Gervaise, *Natural and political history*, 108.
[116] Paschal, "Buddhist monks and Christian friars," 13–16; Ribanedeira, *Historia del archipelago*, vol. 1, 422–38.
[117] Heeck, *Traveler in Siam*, 62–4.
[118] Neijenrode, "Account and description," 16–17, 24.

was as elaborate as a noble funeral and attracted "an infinite number of People."[119]

In these descriptions, Buddhism is deeply embedded in everyday life. Monks chant at the *wat* every morning. Many people attend ceremonies on two holy days in each month. "Several times in the year ... there are extraordinary and large festivals, which are celebrated very solemnly by a great many people."[120] At the new-year festival of Songkran, which extends over two weeks, "Preaching goes on from morning till night. As soon as one monk leaves the pulpit another takes his place, and for each sermon there is a fresh audience of quite extraordinary size." At this festival, devotees bring special gifts and offerings to the monks, and at some major *wat*, people "flock to see boat races and running races, bull-fights and a hundred different games invented to amuse the populace." At a second major festival towards the end of the year, lanterns are lit on poles both at the *wat* and at houses through a whole month.[121] More festivities were offered at the ordination of monks and the funerals of important people, which were celebrated "with indescribable profusion and magnificence." At the funeral of a queen, "monks came from all over the country to pay their last respects," while at that of the Phrakhlang, "The water of the river could not be seen for the vast multitude of *balons* [small boats] which covered it." Theatrical shows were performed all day long for several days, and fireworks were displayed.[122]

The *wat* served as school and dispensary. According to Gervaise, each *wat* had a "learned monk" who taught the novices "to read and write Thai, the history and customs of the country, and Pali script and grammar."[123] La Loubère added pupils were "taught principally to Read, to Write and to cast Accompt; by reason that nothing is more necessary to Merchants and that all the Siamese do exercise Traffic."[124] For sickness, the monks dispensed potions and charms. Monks also helped to manage the spirits controlling natural forces through the use of verbal formulas (*mantra*) and graphical devices (*yantra*) incorporating various symbols of power. Adept monks dispensed these devices to cure the sick, to provide protection against all kinds of danger, and for good fortune.[125] In *Khun Chang Khun Phaen*, the hero is educated in these devices by two abbots.

---

[119] Tachard, *Voyage to Siam*, 191–2, 306.
[120] *Van Vliet's Siam*, 159.
[121] Gervaise, *Natural and political history*, 112.
[122] Gervaise, *Natural and political history*, 144–5; La Loubère, *New historical relation*, 123–4.
[123] Gervaise, *Natural and political history*, 130.
[124] La Loubère, *New historical relation*, 59.
[125] Gervaise, *Natural and political history*, 130–1.

Van Vliet observed that "In case of sickness they have strange feasts with many ceremonies, gambling, drinking, dancing, jumping," featuring old ladies who cavort remarkably despite being "bent and stiff" – similar to modern accounts of spirit possession.[126]

Beliefs in supernaturalism were common. According to La Loubère, people believed that the Buddha, through ascetic practice, acquired supernatural powers including immense strength, perfect knowledge, and the ability to transform his body and travel through time.[127] Gervaise noted that a few monks who dedicate themselves to "meditation on celestial things and the mysteries of religion" are the "most highly esteemed and richest. They never leave the pulpit without being showered with presents."[128]

The monkhood was divided into town-dwelling and forest-dwelling chapters, with the latter focusing more on ascetic practice. According to Gervaise and La Loubère, there were four *sangharaja* (*sankarat*, monastic heads) appointed by the king who each oversaw a separate division of the *sangha* from four major temples. Van Vliet claimed the *sangharaja* were very powerful, but La Loubère believed that their role was largely ceremonial, and that they had no authority over the abbot of each *wat* who was elected by the community of monks, usually choosing the most senior or most learned.[129]

These accounts show Buddhism providing not only a focus of worship but also schooling, health care, advice and assistance on the mysteries of life, management of death, festivities, and entertainment. Popular practice emphasizing the law of *kamma* and the importance of merit-making existed side by side with beliefs in supernaturalism and spirit power. The organization of the monkhood was rather localized. Reid and Lieberman have argued that across the region in this era there was a shift towards religious orthodoxy and standardization driven by wider use of texts and tighter administration.[130] In Siam, this trend is hard to see. The resurgence of Lankan Buddhism in the thirteenth and fourteenth centuries established the role of the Theravada monk embedded in the local community, but did not usher in any widespread usage of the texts now considered "canonical" which, Nidhi argues, were not widely used prior to the Bangkok era.[131] The popular beliefs summarized by Gervaise seem

---

[126] *Van Vliet's Siam*, 161.
[127] La Loubère, *New historical relation*, 137.
[128] Gervaise, *Natural and political history*, 131.
[129] *Van Vliet's Siam*, 155, 158; Gervaise, *Natural and political history*, 121–3; La Loubère, *New historical relation*, 114, 118.
[130] Reid, *Southeast Asia in the age of commerce*, vol. 2, ch. 3; Lieberman, *Strange parallels*, vol. 1, 258–63, 313–23.
[131] Nidhi, *Pen and sail*, 263–4, 267–9.

based mainly on the *jataka* tales. Theravada Buddhism accommodated itself to popular local beliefs, particularly concerning spirits and super-naturalism. Pressure for reform and regimentation of the *sangha* built in the last century of Ayutthaya (see Chapter 6), but had no effect until the Bangkok era.

Languages and Identity

"There is no city in the East where is seen more different nations than in the capital city of Siam, and where so many different tongues are spoken."[132] This judgment by the Chevalier de Chaumont, French ambassador to the court of King Narai in 1685, was echoed by many other visitors in this era. This extraordinary variety was a result of the gradual accretion of peoples in a port-city over three centuries, but certainly intensified over the seventeenth. This variety affected the Thai language, and the relationship between language, community, and identity.

Cosmopolitan Ayutthaya

A Chinese community had been present since the earliest records of Ayutthaya (see Chapter 2). Portuguese first arrived as soldiers of for-tune in the early sixteenth century, and their numbers swelled when the Portuguese community was expelled from Macassar in 1668. Over the years, the Portuguese intermarried with other Christians, particularly those from Japan and southern India. By the seventeenth century, the mestizo community numbered around five to six thousand, occupied in petty trading and service.[133] Japanese had arrived as soldiers, trad-ers, and Christian refugees in the sixteenth century. More Japanese Christians came in the early seventeenth century after facing fam-ine or other troubles in China and Cochinchina, while several dispos-sessed samurai (*ronin*) "went to settle in Siam in great numbers" after the battles of the early Tokugawa period.[134] A community of "Moors," meaning "Turks, Persians, Golcondans, and those of Bengal,"[135] had been present since the heyday of mercenaries in the early sixteenth cen-tury, and still supplied soldiers and guards throughout the seventeenth, while others worked as sailors, sugar palm growers, weavers, binders,

---

[132] Smithies, *Aspects of the embassy*, 104.
[133] Smith, *Creolization and diaspora*, 44–64, 93–128.
[134] Gunzo Uchida in Smith, *Creolization and diaspora*, 117.
[135] Chaumont in Smithies, *Aspects of the embassy*, 84.

and dyers.[136] Persian trader-officials flocked to the city in the early Narai reign, and though the numbers dropped after the fall of Aqa Muhammed Astarabadi in the mid-1670s, some three to four thousand remained a decade later.[137] Many Indian Brahmans had settled in Ayutthaya, working as priests and traders. In addition, there were many smaller groups including some Spanish, also descended from mercenaries, some fifteen or sixteen families of Armenians, mostly serving as "horsemen of the king's guard," and a few French including missionaries and "a certain Thomas the Frenchman, a free burgher who ... makes his living by tapping beer, arrack, and punch for the sailors and others," and probably ran a brothel on the side.[138]

A large number of people heralded from elsewhere in Southeast Asia. They had arrived as traders, as mercenaries, as slaves seized on military expeditions, and as refugees. Chaumont noticed, "The Malays are in fairly great numbers, who are most of them slaves." Probably they had been seized in the campaigns against Pattani and other peninsular ports. Chaumont also saw "Makassars, and several of the people of the isle of Java,"[139] who had come as mercenaries or coastal traders. The largest group was probably Mon, including old communities long resident in the Chaophraya Plain but also migrants who first arrived in significant numbers after the slave revolt at Pegu in 1564 (see p. 105), and came in successive waves following Burmese invasions of the Mon country. By the early seventeenth century, a French Jesuit estimated there were 100,000 Mons in Siam, while Chaumont claimed "The Peguans are as numerous in the country as the original Siamese." Some had settled along the Chaophraya River between Ayutthaya and Bangkok where they were "subsisting by growing rice and plantations, raising animals, and engaging in other farming activities." Mon communities around Lopburi, Khorat, Kanchanaburi, and along the Maeklong River may also date from this era.[140] Chaumont also counted a hundred families of Cochinchinese and a few Tonkinese, and stated that Laotians were a "fourth part of the Kingdom of Siam," particularly "towards the north," possibly referring to people from Lanna and Lanxang.[141] Gervaise reckoned that "over a third" of the population of the kingdom consisted of "foreigners," especially "descendants of people from Laos and Pegu

---

[136] Smith, *Creolization and diaspora*, 86.
[137] La Loubère, *New historical relation*, 112.
[138] Chaumont in Smithies, *Aspects of the embassy*, 84; Heeck, *Traveler in Siam*, 57.
[139] Smithies, *Aspects of the embassy*, 84.
[140] Smithies, *Aspects of the embassy*, 84; Heeck, *Traveler in Siam*, 50; Van Roy, "Safe haven," 154–9; Halliday, "Immigration of the Mons," 11–13.
[141] Smithies, *Aspects of the embassy*, 84–5.

whom the Siamese took as prisoners of war."[142] Groups of Khmer had also settled.[143]

Chaumont counted twenty different communities in Ayutthaya. The major ones were settled in specific areas, known as "camps," often bounded by canals, and placed under a head responsible for the community's conduct. These provisions were intended to minimize the contact and potential for friction, but in their everyday life as soldiers, officials, and traders, people needed to communicate with one another, creating a need for lingua franca.

Languages and Identity at an Entrepot

From the late fifteenth century onwards, most surviving literary works from Siam are in the Thai language. So too is the Luang Prasoet chronicle from the late seventeenth century, and the law codes that accumulated through this era. Thai was clearly the language of government. However, Thai was not the only language. Many religious texts were written in Pali using a Khmer script. Translation was extemporized during sermons by monks reading a Pali excerpt and then expounding in Thai. Monks compiled Pali–Thai notebooks to facilitate this translation. In the *wat*, monks used an argot of verbs and nouns derived from Pali, Sanskrit, and Khmer for everday actions and things. Pali was also used in the diplomatic correspondence between Siam and Lanka.[144]

Such a cosmopolitan place needed lingua franca. Ayutthaya had at least three, introduced from the trading world of the region. The first was Malay, which was "the most valuable lingua franca" around Southeast Asia prior to the sixteenth century,[145] and continued to be used in Siam's dealings with India and other places to the south and west. The Portuguese officer sent to open relations between Melaka and Siam in 1511 was possibly selected because he spoke Malay. A letter sent from the Portuguese governor of Melaka to Naresuan in 1595 was in Malay. Phaulkon made his first mark in Siam as a translator using Malay. King Borommakot sent Malay translators to accompany his mission to revive Buddhism in Sri Lanka in 1753.[146]

---

[142] Gervaise, *Natural and political history*, 45.
[143] *RCA*, 248, 401.
[144] Gervaise, *Natural and political history*, 111, 130; McDaniel, *Gathering leaves and lifting words*, esp. ch. 5; Nidhi, *Pen and sail*, 202–6; *Jotmaihet rawang ratchathut langka lae sayam*, 71–131.
[145] Reid, *Charting the shape*, 159.
[146] Cruysse, *Siam and the West*, 5, 24–5; Davisakd, "Pursuit of Java," 84–90; Hutchinson, *Adventurers in Siam*, 58.

Persian became another lingua franca in the region in the sixteenth century with the appearance of prominent Persian trader-officials in many ports. The third and most important language of regional communication from the early sixteenth century was Portuguese. Alexander Hamilton noted,

along the Sea-coasts, the *Portuguese* have left a Vestige of their Language, tho' much corrupted, yet it is the Language that most *Europeans* learn first, to qualify them for a general Converse with one another, as well as with the different inhabitants of *India*.[147]

As the Portuguese role in trade and soldiery diminished, several Portuguese mestizos at Ayutthaya continued to earn their living as translators and interpreters.[148] When the French embassy appeared at the court of King Narai in 1685, its official missive was translated from French to Portuguese and then from Portuguese to Thai. The Franco-Siamese Treaty of 1687 was drafted in Thai, French, and Portuguese.[149] When the Dutch head of state sent a missive to King Songtham in 1628, "In accordance with the usual procedure, the letter was translated from Dutch into Portuguese, from Portuguese into Malay and from Malay into Siamese."[150]

How languages of inter-communication were used in everyday life in Ayutthaya is more difficult to determine. The Dutch had interpreters for dealing with the court, but also used informal intermediaries who were skilled in several languages. During a crisis between the Dutch company and the court in 1636–37, these intermediaries included a Portuguese mestizo, a Mon, a Javanese, and a Chinese.[151] The Portuguese was "one of the Berckelang's people," that is, in the service of the Phrakhlang minister. The Javanese was a wealthy merchant in the service of the Kalahom. The Chinese was probably an interpreter in Phrakhlang. The Mon was Soet, a low-born woman who acted as an all-purpose liaison between the Dutch and the court (see p. 153). Phaulkon's career at court began in this world of multilingual translation when he quickly added Portuguese and Thai to his knowledge of English and Malay.

In such a cosmopolitan city, many people would have been knowledgeable in two or more languages, at least for matters that affected their business and everyday life. Davisakd Puaksom notes that in the Thai translations of the Panji-Inao tales that appeared in the eighteenth

---

[147] Hamilton, *New account of the East Indies*, 8–9.
[148] Smith, *Creolization and diaspora*, 208.
[149] Smithies, "Portuguese as a language of communication," 271.
[150] Brummelhuis, *Merchant, courtier and diplomat*, 18.
[151] See "Diary of the picnic incident (1636–37)" in *Van Vliet's Siam*, 35–88.

century, many words and passages were left in Javanese and Malay, suggesting the translators knew the audience could understand them.[152] Similarly, in *Khun Chang Khun Phaen*, Chinese, Mon, Burmese, and Vietnamese characters occasionally speak in their own languages, with no translation provided.

In this multilingual environment, the Thai language changed a great deal. New ways of constructing a sentence were developed. New forms of orthography were devised for such purposes as verse and official documents. A much larger vocabulary appeared, with infusions of words from Portuguese, Malay, Tamil, Japanese, Khmer, Chinese, and Mon. Many words and constructions were also lost along the way. Pronunciation changed with a switch from three tones to five tones – a change which affected other tonal languages in eastern Asia, and which had knock-on effects on spelling and prosody.[153] These changes were so great that scholars today have difficulty in understanding older literary works.[154]

In such an entrepot, where translation, interpretation, and multilingual conversations were part of everyday life, the relation of language and identity differed greatly from the situation today, after language has become tightly linked to notions of origin, ethnicity, and nation. In the vocabulary of the time, peoples were referred to as peoples of different languages (*phasa*) or different countries (*prathet*). They were defined by where they came from and what they spoke, not by membership in an imagined community bound by blood.

A ruler qualified as a *cakkavattin* emperor by lording over many peoples. In earlier centuries, as reflected in such works as *Yuan phai*, the great king acquired this glory through conquest. In 1684, the Phrakhlang told a Portuguese embassy that Narai was "a Lord with absolute dominion over eleven Kingdoms," and hence "was indeed worthy of the title of Emperor … the Emperor of China had less reasons to be called Emperor than he did."[155] Increasingly in later Ayutthaya, eulogies stressed the number of lords and people "who came to shelter under the king's protection," implying they came voluntarily to enjoy the benefits of rule by a good Buddhist monarch.[156] There was no stress on Siam being uniquely Thai. In the Luang Prasoet chronicle, the word "Thai" does not appear. In the early parts of the *phitsadan* chronicles, "Thai" is a synonym for "Ayutthayan," applied to the king, army, soldiers, ambassadors, capital,

---

[152] Davisakd, "Pursuit of Java," 97, 102–7.
[153] Gedney, "Siamese verse forms in historical perspective," 502–3.
[154] See Baker and Pasuk, *Yuan phai*, 6–10.
[155] Seabra, *Embassy of Pero Vaz de Siqueira*, 319.
[156] See the eulogy of Narai in Winai and Trongjai, *Moradok khwam songjam haeng nopphaburi*, 67–75.

and dependent towns. In cases such as the army and soldiers, these were often not "Thai" in the modern sense of nationality.

On popular attitudes about identity, there is little evidence, but one suggestive hint. At funerals, troops of monks sometimes entertained the mourners with "twelve-language chanting," meaning they performed songs and sketches posing as different peoples using clothing, props, and snatches of language. In the portrayal of this practice in *Khun Chang Khun Phaen*, the monks perform as Mon, Indian, Lao, Khmer, Vietnamese, Chinese, and Farang but also as Thai.[157] This was not an opportunity to make fun of foreigners – an act of exclusion, exploiting difference for entertainment – but an act of inclusion, celebrating variety.

Over the seventeenth century, Asian attitudes were affected by the European's growing assumption of superiority and appetite for territory. A decree issued in 1663 offers a glimpse of the court's emerging definition of sociopolitical difference.

Nowadays many Khaek, Farang, English, Khula, and Malayu from various countries are coming to shelter under the king's protection. In future, Thai, Mon and Lao must not covertly have carnal relations with Khaek, Farang, English, Khula, and Malayu who uphold wrong-thinking, so that people do not go to ruin but follow right-thinking and are not mixed together ... Overseers will bring those who have carnal relations with wrong-thinkers to be punished with death.[158]

This concern was new. As most traders or mercenaries settling at Ayutthaya had been male, many had liaisons with local women. Early Chinese records boasted how much Thai women liked Chinese men, perhaps a misreading of Thai female sexuality.[159] European and Asian traders contracted "temporary marriages" with financial settlements.[160] This practice had excited no interest from the court except in cases of Dutchmen who wished to take their local wives and children along when they were posted elsewhere. The court objected strongly, perhaps because the removal of wives and children subtracted from manpower resources and offended against the principle that people should flow *towards* the benevolent king.

In this 1663 decree, the distinction between "self" and "other" is based on religion. The terms for right and wrong thinking use Pali words found in Buddhist texts. The phrase here translated as "carnal relations" is also Pali-based (methunaṃ dhamma). The "other" is composed of three

---

[157] Baker and Pasuk, *Tale of Khun Chang Khun Phaen*, 50–4.
[158] Old decrees, clause 36, *Kotmai tra sam duang*, vol. 5, 98–9.
[159] Ma Huan, *Ying-yai Sheng-lan*, 104.
[160] Reid, *Southeast Asia in the age of commerce*, vol. 1, 154–6.

groups: Muslims and others from India and the Middle East (Khaek); Muslims and others from the peninsula and archipelago (Khula,[161] Malayu); and Christians from Europe (Farang, English).[162] The "self" includes not only Thai, but also Lao and Mon, fellow Buddhists present both in Ayutthaya and neighboring territories. Similarly, a 1730 decree against proselytization applied to Thai, Mon, and Lao.[163] These definitions omit many peoples present at Ayutthaya including Chinese, Japanese, Khmer, Burmese, Cham, and Vietnamese. Some of these are Buddhist and others are perhaps seen as not threatening to Buddhism in the same way as Muslims and Christians. They occupy a hazy middle ground.

The conception of identity in this decree is analogous to the political idea of *mandala*, a conception of space that is not defined by a sharp boundary but by relative closeness to the center, allowing both variety and variation.[164]

Conclusion

The society glimpsed in the sources for early modern Siam differs strikingly from modern Thai society but also from many societies in the early modern world. It was a predominantly urban society, meaning most people congregated in larger settlements known as towns or cities and worked at something other than the production of primary goods. This was made possible by a very low population density combined with abundance of food. The low population was largely a function of high mortality from disease, exacerbated by warfare. Settlement did not spread across the landscape but clustered in cities, towns, and adjacent strips along the waterways because of fear of the forest, fear of predators, and perhaps also some social understanding of the need for numbers to build immunities to disease. In early modern Europe, three people living and working on the land were needed to create the surplus for one living in a town, but in early modern Siam, probably only a small proportion of people were full-time farmers.

In the age of warfare, a system of registration was developed for military recruitment. As warring diminished, the system was adapted to give king and nobles control over forced labor for public and private uses. Kings used these dependents for construction and other public projects, but also for staffing royal commercial enterprises. Nobles used some as

---

[161] *Khula* or *kula* is an old word meaning a stranger, often referring to people of the archipelago.

[162] Thai of this era used lists or partial lists rather than collective nouns. Here "Khula, Malayu" and "Farang, English" each means these and similar people.

[163] Smith, *Creolization and diaspora*, 204.

[164] Wolters, *History, culture, and region*, esp. 27–31.

personal retainers and took a share from others working in the commercial economy. Both king and nobles were "man-lords."

Among the common mass, the family had a distinctive form, molded by the historical roles of warfare, commerce, and Buddhism. Young men left home early to seek education and experience, while older men were drawn away to military service, corvée duty, the monkhood, long-distance trading, and collection of forest goods. Probably men died earlier than women on average because of their exposure to risks. In this culture of the "loose male," men were intermittently and precariously attached to the family. It fell on the women not only to ensure continuity through their roles as progenitor and mother, but also to manage the property, and provide the upkeep. Foreign visitors regularly commented on the dominant role of women in the urban economy, especially in commerce. Because males were in short and unreliable supply, an open and forceful female sexuality was accepted and normal.

The culture of the nobility was modeled on the king and the concept of possession. Just as the king owned the realm and its people, each noble had property-like rights over his family and dependents. Sexual privilege was modeled on the king's possession of women in large numbers as a symbol of royal power. In this culture, the duty of the females was to serve, and female sexuality was severely constrained as a source of potential chaos.

Theravada Buddhism was deeply embedded in this urban society. Building *wat* offered kings, nobles, and merchants the opportunity both to earn merit and to display their status. The *wat* in turn provided opportunities for the mass of the people to participate in almsgiving to monks, a daily and monthly calendar of ritual, and an annual round of festivals and entertainments. The *wat* also furnished basic education, including commercial skills, some health care, along with forecasting and magic to combat the uncertainties of life. Popular Buddhist teaching, with its emphasis on the inevitable consequences of good and bad actions and the importance of merit-making, served as a moral basis for urban living. The *wat* and its teaching easily made space for older beliefs in spirits and supernatural forces. Kings acted as great patrons, but imposed only minimal administrative control. Given this freedom to be shaped by the society, Buddhism became a powerful social force with an important role in late Ayutthaya's history.

Ayutthaya's function as an entrepot created an extraordinarily diverse polyglot society. Translation, interpretation, and multilingual conversation were part of everyday life. Perceptions of ethnic identity were blurred by the everyday realities of such a cosmopolitan society and by the *cakkavattin* ideal of power over many peoples. By the late seventeenth century, proto-colonial pressure had begun to provoke new thinking about identity based primarily on religion, with a line dividing Buddhism from Islam and Christianity.

6   Ayutthaya Falling

The history of late Ayutthaya is overshadowed by the tragedy of 1767. Beginning with the *Testimony* compiled by Ayutthaya nobles after the city's fall and the chronicles written in early Bangkok, histories are focused on explaining how such a flourishing city could be wiped off the map. They describe a decline before the fall. Yet only a few years prior to the fall, some from Ayutthaya's nobility felt very happy about the way things were. Looking back to the mid-eighteenth century, Phra Phonnarat, a monk-historian of the Bangkok first reign wrote:

At that time Ayutthaya was free from all misfortunes, serene and joyful, beautiful as a heavenly city, replete with food and other necessities in abundance, and without any enemies harboring evil intent.[1]

The city and much of its hinterland was prospering, largely on the stimulus of trade with China. A larger swathe of the society participated in this prosperity. Prior to the 1760s, no enemies threatened, and few resources, including human lives, were wasted on war.

The society was in the throes of three major changes. The old systems of forced labor were gradually decaying in the face of a growing commercial economy, creating frictions such as crime and revolt. The nobility was becoming richer, more secure, and more assertive. The monarchy was increasingly out-of-step with this changing society, as evident from the portrayal of kings in writings of the era. These changes prompted moves to transform institutions of the state to manage the conflicts of a more complex society.

In response came two trends: an expansion in the usage of law to make society more peaceful, and an enlarged role for Buddhism as a moral basis for social order and responsible kingship. Siam was imagined as a Buddhist society and as a center of the Buddhist world. King

---

[1] Referring to the Borommakot reign; see *Wannakam samai rattanakosin lem 3: Sangkhittiyawong*, 235.

Borommakot (1733–58) began to remake the monarchy in line with these aspirations.

Descriptions by foreign visitors are sparse in this period, and the chronicles, written to damn the Ban Phlu Luang dynasty, have to be used with care, but there are many other sources including literary works, law codes, religious texts, the oral history found in the *Testimony* documents, the detailed portrayal of the city in the *Description of Ayutthaya*, visual expressions in murals and manuscripts, and outstanding works by Thai historians including Busakorn, Sarasin, Nidhi, Sunait, Saichol, and Bhawan.

Trade and China

The crisis of 1688 removed the French and British from the scene, making room for a return of the "Moors," and an expansion of influence by the Chinese at Ayutthaya.

The British withdrew from Siam, saying in 1691, "Syam never did nor never will bring the [English East India] Company two-pence advantage, but many thousands of pounds loss." The Dutch remained, but their archipelago trade was booming, while Siam was scarcely profitable. They closed their factories at Ligor and Songkhla in 1706, and maintained only a small presence at Ayutthaya, mainly to secure rice exports to Batavia, finally abandoning the Dutch lodge in November 1765 as the Burmese armies approached.[2] But the departure of the Europeans represented no retreat to "isolation" and caused no sustained reduction in trade.

The battles of 1688 had a dramatic effect on the court elite. According to Dutch observers, forty-eight nobles were executed in the first purge, and more in later rounds. According to Dhiravat, the victims came from "the most ancient and distinguished families in the kingdom," with the result that "a generation of *khun nang* was almost wiped out."[3] As a consequence, opportunities for foreigners remained. The "Moors" returned in strength. In 1719, the post of Okya Sinaowarat was held by a man who "was a *Persian* by birth, but had come to Siam with his father when very young, and had remained about 40 Years at *Siam*"[4] An Indian became *shahbandar* (harbormaster), another became keeper of the elephants, and a Pathan became royal favorite in the palace guard. The Persian family descended from Sheikh Ahmed Qomi, which had provided three heads

---

[2] Dhiravat, "Ayutthaya at the end of the seventeenth century," 265–9; Bhawan, *Dutch East India Company merchants*, chs. 6–7.
[3] Dhiravat, "Princes, pretenders," 111.
[4] Hamilton, *New account of the East Indies*, 459.

of Mahatthai under Prasat Thong and Narai, again occupied that post by the reign of Thaisa (1709–33).[5]

Amongst the foreigners at court, the Chinese soon became the most important. This was partly a function of more Chinese settlement. In the tumultuous transition from the Ming to Qing era in China over the 1640s to 1680s, many Chinese fled overseas, including members of the educated mandarin elite. Narai's chief doctors were Chinese. In 1678, a leading trading official in Ayutthaya was a Chinese "of great quality." In 1690, a "learned" Chinese held the post of Okya Yommarat, minister of the city in charge of justice – the first report of a Chinese as a minister other than Phrakhlang. Chinese also became tax farmers, especially for gambling taxes.[6] Around 1700, Phetracha appointed a Chinese as Okya Sombatthiban who functioned as the Phrakhlang. This man was executed for choosing the wrong side in the succession battle of 1703, but was replaced by another Chinese.[7] From this point, Chinese influence became dominant, reaching a peak under yet another Chinese Phrakhlang who held the post throughout the Thaisa reign. A French missionary noted in 1714,

this mandarin, knowing the ways of the court, has taken all possible measures to strengthen his position, and render himself formidable to his enemies. He has found the means of introducing into the Palace Chinese women and girls to be near the queen and princesses continually. He has put Chinese into the most prominent posts, above all those which have some connection to trade, so that at present it is the Chinese who do all the trading in this kingdom.[8]

Two years later, a Dutchman reported that the Chinese "have in their control the best and most prominent positions at the court as well as in the provinces."[9] Their influence spread down to Nakhon Si Thammarat where they pried the tin trade away from the Dutch and became virtual "owners" of the place, causing the Dutch to close their factories temporarily.[10] The king's trust in his Chinese Phrakhlang was so great that he appointed him to lead a military expedition against Cambodia even though he was, according to Alexander Hamilton, "altogether unacquainted with War."[11] In 1730 Chinese authorities noted that the

---

[5] Gervaise, *Natural and political history*, 24, 39; Dhiravat, "Ayutthaya at the end of the seventeenth century," 258; Wyatt, "Family politics in seventeenth- and eighteenth-century Siam," 104–6.

[6] Anderson, *English intercourse with Siam*, 426; Kaempfer, *Description of the Kingdom of Siam*, 38; Sarasin, *Tribute and profit*, 204.

[7] Dhiravat, "Princes, pretenders," 113.

[8] Vicar Apostolic Mgr. De Cicé in Dhiravat, "Princes, pretenders," 124.

[9] Imel Christaen Cok in Dhiravat, "Princes, pretenders," 117.

[10] Dhiravat, "Princes, pretenders," 116–17, 122.

[11] Hamilton, *New account of the East Indies*, 458.

Siamese "employ Chinese as officials, as administrators, and as finance and tax comptrollers."[12]

In 1733, the Phrakhlang took the wrong side in the succession battle, fled to the monkhood, but was dragged out and executed. As replacement, King Borommakot appointed a close supporter, Chamnan Borirak, from a Brahman family. A year later some Chinese took part in a failed attempt to seize the palace and install an alternative king. Either ten or forty were executed and others flogged. Chinese resentment at the fall of the Phrakhlang may have been a factor, yet the revolt was a typical aftershock of succession battles and the 300 rebels included other dissidents, while some prominent Chinese helped in the suppression. The king sent a missive to the Chinese emperor to explain the incident which brought no repercussions from the imperial court. The Chinese remained powerful within the Phrakhlang ministry. Chamnan Borirak married his daughter to a Chinese who succeeded him in the post after his death in 1753.[13]

The Chinese ascendancy in the Ayutthaya court in the early eighteenth century developed in parallel with the importance of China in Ayutthaya's overseas trade.

Rice Trade to China

Early Qing restrictions on private trade eased in the late seventeenth century. The authorities in the southern Chinese ports quietly encouraged private trade, as well as petitioning the emperor to relax restrictions. In 1684, the emperor lifted the ban on private trade, though supposedly only for licensed merchants at certain ports. Immediately many junks from Siam appeared in the southern Chinese ports, including lots of small peddling traders. In the 1710s, the Chinese authorities detected that a thousand ships were sailing out every year, but only half that number returning – in effect an illegal export of Chinese-built junks. They again banned private trade, forbade expatriate Chinese to return as traders, and made the sale of Chinese ships a capital offence, but the southern port authorities protested vigorously, ensuring the ban was short-lived. In 1740, trade was restricted after a Dutch massacre of Chinese in Batavia, but again the hiatus was brief.[14]

One reason for the easing of trade restrictions was a desperate shortage of rice in southeastern China. The population surged from the late

---

[12] Skinner, *Chinese society in Thailand*, 19.
[13] *RCA*, 426–7 (*BM*); Busakorn, "Ban Phlu Luang dynasty," 88; Sng and Pimpraphai, *History of the Thai-Chinese*, 51–2; Dhiravat, "Princes, pretenders," 124–5.
[14] Sarasin, *Tribute and profit*, 42–56, 69–70, 88.

seventeenth century. Rice-growing land was limited in extent and poor in quality, while transport from rice-surplus areas on the middle Yangzi was difficult. Local famines became common. The first imports of rice were allowed from Luzon in the 1710s. In 1722, when southern China suffered a general shortage, Siam sent a tribute mission carrying a letter pointing out that Siam's supplies of rice were cheap and plentiful. The Chinese requested imports. In response, Siam asked for freedom of private trade outside the tributary structure, and the emperor promptly conceded. According to Sarasin, "Siamese merchant vessels commenced trading to China in sizable numbers."[15]

The incentives were gradually increased. Tax exemption on rice was initially granted as a special case and then made general policy. Other goods carried on the same ships were still taxable, but from 1743 full exemption was granted to ships carrying 10,000 piculs of rice and partial exemption for those with smaller cargoes. The captains and senior crew of the ships became eligible for the "presents" (usually bolts of silk) given to official staff of tribute missions. In 1724, the emperor exempted ninety-six Chinese merchants manning a junk from Siam from the usual ban on expatriate Chinese traders "to demonstrate our magnanimity."[16] Subsequently all Chinese manning the rice ships were exempted on grounds that they had been long resident in Siam. By the 1750s, under the system of mandarin rewards, Chinese merchants were awarded titles and medals depending on the amount of Siamese rice they imported. The tribute missions also benefited. From 1700 to 1766, there were twelve full tribute missions and another four supplementary missions. Besides exploiting the usual loopholes for private trade, these missions gained tax exemption for their "ballast cargoes" and won permission to export restricted items including copper, silver, saltpeter, iron, and horses.[17] Data on the rice exports are fragmentary, but Sarasin estimates that from the 1720s to 1760s the volume may have averaged 100,000 piculs (over 6,000 tons) a year, and possibly higher.[18] In addition, Ayutthaya exported rice to ports around the gulf where the population was swollen by new Chinese settlement.

The outflow of people from China following the rise of the Qing affected not only Ayutthaya but ports all around the gulf and down the peninsula. Many Ming rebels initially congregated in Formosa (Taiwan),

---

[15] Sarasin, *Tribute and profit*, 83.
[16] Skinner, *Chinese society in Thailand*, 17–8; Sarasin, *Tribute and profit*, 81–90; Cushman, *Fields from the sea*, 128.
[17] Sarasin, *Tribute and profit*, 77, 135–40.
[18] Sarasin, *Tribute and profit*, 88. This *average* figure is roughly four times the *highest* annual export reported in the seventeenth century. See p. 181.

but when Qing armies crushed this Cheng kingdom in 1683, refugees spread further afield. One group with seventy war junks and 3,000 armed men arrived on the Vietnamese coast in 1682–83 and was sent to colonize areas in the Mekong delta. Another Cantonese, Mac Cuu, migrated to Cambodia in 1671, entered the service of the Khmer ruler, and was sent south to the port of Banteay Mas (Ha Tien), where he opened gambling dens to service the large community of Chinese, Vietnamese, Khmer, and Malay merchants. Over the next decades, Mac Cuu developed a mini-state around Banteay Mas, which coexisted with the Khmer administrative structure, but also minted coins, raised its own army, and patronized Chinese literati to the extent that "the entire lifestyle of the court seems to have been the same as that of a court in China."[19]

Pattani and Ligor received a new influx of Chinese. Wu Jang, a Hokkienese who arrived in Songkhla and began as a tobacco planter, was established enough by the 1760s to bid for the birds' nest concession and subsequently became governor. Other Chinese emigrants settled in ports around the gulf. Bang Plasoi (near Chonburi) became a major Teochiu settlement. Chanthaburi was occupied by Teochiu, Cochinchinese, and Khmer traders who rivaled the Cantonese at nearby Banteay Mas.[20]

Economic Expansion and Chinese Settlement

Although Ayutthaya's commerce may have suffered from the disruption of 1688, the lull was short-lived. In the transition to the eighteenth century, two trends begun in the later seventeenth became more marked. First, there were more opportunities for non-royals to trade. Officials of the Phrakhlang financed cargoes sent in the "ballast" of tribute missions. A Dutch observer reported in 1733 that over a thousand "native" craft traded each year between Ayutthaya and Cambodia, Cochinchina, Tonkin, and ports down the peninsula to Johore and Melaka.[21] Second, more of the export goods were articles made or grown in Siam. Because supplies of durable ironwood were plentiful and cheap, both junks made on the Chaophraya and the timber itself were exported to China.[22]

The city's population may have increased over its last century. The "French Engineer's Map" drawn in 1687 shows a large area in the southwest of the city as "Quartier Champêtre" (rustic area), which Kaempfer described as "thinly inhabited ... by reason of the morassy ground."[23]

---

[19] Sakurai and Kitagawa, "Ha Tien," 159–60; Chen, "Mac Thien Tu."
[20] Adisorn, "Chantaburi."
[21] Wybrand Blom reported in Dhiravat, "Princes, pretenders," 119.
[22] Cushman, *Fields from the sea*, 49–50; Sarasin, *Tribute and profit*, 93.
[23] Kaempfer, *Description of the Kingdom of Siam*, 42–3.

In later maps and descriptions, some of these areas are crisscrossed by canals, suggesting a drainage scheme, and populated by temples and markets, suggesting settlements. Residential boats on the waterways around the city greatly increased in number. Seventeenth-century visitors had mentioned some, but the pre-fall description estimated that "the number of rafts used as both dwellings and shops is about twenty thousand – certainly no fewer," stretching all around the south side of the city and 2 to 3 kilometers southward down the river towards Bangkok.[24]

Part of this population increase came from an influx of Chinese. Around 1700, the Chinese community in Ayutthaya numbered over 3,000. In the 1720s, an English observer called the Chinese residents "very numerous." In the 1730s, a French missionary estimated there were 20,000 Chinese in Siam. The readiness of the Chinese emperor to accept that the Chinese manning junks "have lived in Siam for a long time and also have their families there" was not only good economic diplomacy but true in many cases. Ong Laihu, who outfitted ships for King Borommakot, was a son of Ong Heng-Chuan, who had performed the same service for King Thaisa.[25]

By the final years of Ayutthaya, the Chinese had a large presence in the city. The largest market, in the southeast behind the main port, was named Nai Kai, a Chinese term meaning "inner (city) road,"[26] its main street was called Chinese Street, and the nearby gate was called Chinese Gate. The market stretched over half a kilometer selling "all kinds of goods from China, including food and fruit." A second market, also called Chinese Market, lay just south of the palace. A third major Chinese settlement was found at Chinese Village on the opposite bank of the river to the southwest. Here too there were "many Chinese shops in brick buildings, selling more Chinese goods than Thai goods." In addition, "actress-prostitutes have established four halls behind the market where they provide men with sex for hire."[27]

Chinese produced and sold various goods. Four settlements off the island made liquor. Two also raised pigs and one made noodles. On the island, close to the main Chinese market, there were Chinese settlements making sweets, noodles, barrels, water jars, rattan furniture, and metal goods. In another locality to the northeast, Chinese made and sold rattan furniture. In front of Wat Mahathat, Chinese ran a flea market for secondhand goods. Among the landmarks of the city were three Chinese

---

[24] Baker, "Markets and production," 58.
[25] Sarasin, *Tribute and profit*, 46, 153–5; Dhiravat, "Princes, pretenders," 122.
[26] In a Fujianese dialect, see Sng and Pimpraphai, *History of the Thai-Chinese*, 426–7, fn. 112.
[27] Baker, "Markets and production," 43, 63.

shrines, two temples, the house of Jaosua Chi (the name suggesting a big Chinese merchant), and a nearby market with "a long row of sixteen two-storey brick houses with shops in the lower storey and living quarters above," suggesting Chinese-style shophouses.[28] The goods carried from China to Siam in the early eighteenth century included metals, cane sugar, tools, copper basins and pails, crockery, silks, sweetmeats, dried fruits, dyes, gums, and thread – mostly consumer goods,[29] suggesting that the city was not only growing but prospering.

The city had become perhaps even more cosmopolitan. The *Description of Ayutthaya* details many trading communities besides the Chinese: Lao who hawk live birds; Mons who manufacture brass and other metal wares; Chams who weave cloth and high-quality mats; Pattani Khaek who weave silk and cotton cloth; Moken sea gypsies who sell fish; Indians who sell cloth, incense, jewelry, and cosmetics; and trading settlements of people from Java, the Malay Peninsula, and Vietnam.[30] Envoys from Sri Lanka who visited Ayutthaya in 1750 saw traders from "Pattáni, Moors, Wadiga, Mukkara, men of Delhi, Malacca, and Java, Kávisi, Chinese, Parangis, Hollanders, Sannásis, Yógís, English, French, Castilians, Danes, men from Surat, Ava, and Pegu, representing every race." They also marveled at the goods available along the street leading up to the palace:

it was one unbroken stretch of gold-worked cloths of five colours, trays and boxes of silver and gold, ornaments of copper, bronze, brass, and zinc, red and white sandalwood, embroidered quilts and curtains, all kinds of medical stores, rice, cocoanuts, plantains, mandarin oranges, oranges, sweet-meats, all manner of flowers, all manner of eatables and drinkables, with sweets and meats; the shops were adorned with gilding, and the street a blaze of splendour.[31]

In the *Testimony*, there is an estimate of the "taxes collected at Ayutthaya, excluding *suai* and silver" (see Table 6.1). The taxes fall into four main parts: customs levies on internal and external trade; liquor and gambling taxes; commutation dues for avoiding *phrai* service; and tax farms on various products. The range of revenue sources, and the distribution, is similar to the situation known in greater detail from a century later in the Bangkok era before the Bowring Treaty of 1855.[32] This is one of several indicators that Ayutthaya in the mid-eighteenth century had achieved a situation in terms of trade, taxation, Chinese immigration,

---

[28] Baker, "Markets and production."
[29] Sarasin, *Tribute and profit*, 51.
[30] Baker, "Markets and production," 50–2, 59–66.
[31] Pieris, *Religious intercourse between Ceylon and Siam*, 14, 16.
[32] See Hong, *Thailand in the nineteenth century*, ch. 4.

Table 6.1. *Estimate of taxes in late Ayutthaya*

Tax	Chang
internal customs	800
external customs ("junk entry")	3,000
liquor tax	2,500
gambling tax	2,500
tree tax	200
market dues	300
commutation fees	500
garden tax	3,000
betel tax	500
ceramics tax	500
land tax	n.a.
gold *suai*	n.a.
Total	13,800

Source: *Khamhaikan chao krung kao*, 260–1.

literary production, and religious practice that was recovered in Bangkok almost a century later.

Labor, Disorder, and Revolt

As the economy grew and diversified, the demand for labor rose, and hence also competition over the control of labor. The *phrai* system under which the king and nobles had access to supplies of unfree labor was pulled apart, but gradually and incompletely. With this major change, old forms of authority came under challenge.

Decline of Forced Labor

Increased trading opportunities and labor demand induced *phrai* to free themselves to participate in the commercial economy. There were several ways to do this. Since the seventeenth century, *phrai* had sold or mortgaged themselves or their dependents (wives and children) into slavery as a way to free themselves of corvée obligations and to raise some capital at the same time. As Lingat notes, the legal principles and the documentation in the law on slavery were the same as in the law on debt.[33] Like debtors, those sold into slavery required guarantors, their contracts were recorded in documents called *krommathan*, and they could redeem

[33] Lingat, "Les origines du prêt à intérêt au Siam."

themselves by paying off the sale or mortgage price. Around the turn of the eighteenth century, a new section was added to the law on slavery, probably because the practice of self-selling had increased. The additional clauses dealt particularly with cases where slaves had run away from their master and then sold or mortgaged themselves to a *nai ngoen*, literally a "money master," often in a new town or city. In these new provisions, slaves were granted rights to own and inherit property, to enter into contracts, and to have access to the courts – all rights important for those participating in trade.

Another route to freedom was through the monkhood. The numbers of men who took the robe but then engaged in work and trading in defiance of the disciplinary code provoked one monk to a diatribe:

Some are ordained but live at home, working and doing business, trading in rice and garden land ... weaving basketware, day labor, craftwork ... making sugar, farming paddy or upland crops ... doctors of massage or medicine, astrologers ... trade to the south or the north ... cutting timber, making boats ... liquor, tobacco, and opium.[34]

In the 1680s, French visitors reported that the king "had just reduc'd several Thousands to the Secular condition" after imposing an examination on all in the monkhood.[35] A 1748 law tried to stop monks who disrobed escaping *phrai* status by bribing the labor registrars.[36]

At some point a provision was introduced to allow royal *phrai* to evade their corvée obligation by paying for the cost of a hired replacement, but the rate was kept high to prevent over-use. Another way to avoid corvée was to fetch forest goods in demand for the export trade and thus become reassigned as *phrai suai*. This obligation could also be commuted into a payment, far lower than that required for a royal *phrai*. As a result, a 1748 law reported that "royal *phrai* are draining away."[37]

The rising export of rice to China prompted the clearance of forest for paddy land in the Chaophraya Plain. Most likely, the exported rice was grown not on the floodplain around Ayutthaya but outside the flooding area, where transplanting and water control produced a grain that stored better. An area to the east of the city became a center for milling rice brought by boat from these tracts.[38] In 1748 government noticed that land clearance had become significant, and alerted officials to monitor the process, issue deeds to facilitate collection of taxes, and

[34] *Pradontham*, quoted in Saichol, *Phutthasasana*, 49–50.
[35] La Loubère, *New historical relation*, 115; Gervaise, *Natural and political history*, 130.
[36] Old royal decrees 48, *Kotmai tra sam duang*, vol. 5, 144.
[37] Old royal decrees 48, *Kotmai tra sam duang*, vol. 5, 139.
[38] Baker, "Markets and production," 57.

fine farmers that failed to declare new land. The government's growing concern over "runaway *phrai*" from the late seventeenth century
onwards was partly caused by movement to these new agrarian tracts.
In 1690, officials were commanded to arrest runaways. In 1727, the
king ordered all officials to round up "*phrai* who have avoided registration, *phrai* who have run away from their master, gone to another city,
or hidden in the forest."[39] In 1742, the king sent officials to chase down
"commoners who do not have a principal master and have escaped to
live in the provincial municipalities in great numbers." The areas cited
were Suphanburi, Nakhon Chaisi, and along the Chaophraya River
from Singburi to Nakhon Sawan, all prime areas for growing paddy.
Sinhalese monks who visited this tract in 1750 saw, "The grain was in
every stage: the young shoot, the ripening ear, the flower, the tender
corns, and some already mown." Officials managed to round up "many
tens of thousands" from this tract, suggesting the scale of the migration
to this emerging land frontier.[40]

As the pool of coerced labor shrank, competition to control it increased.
From the early Ban Phlu Luang era, the kings gave certain royal sons and
other important relatives a *krom*, meaning a department, but in effect an
allocation of people which provided both income and status. At first, this
practice was limited to a handful of major sons, but then became more
widespread as the size of the royal clan expanded and its internal politics became more complex. This required many royal *phrai* and resulted
in shortages elsewhere. By 1727, the court had to use wage labor for
some public works, such as building residences for provincial governors.
At Queen Yothathep's funeral early in 1735, there was difficulty finding
enough *phrai* for the procession.[41]

Great families hoarded people under their protection. When royal
phrai were allotted to a government department, noble officials drafted
them under their own command, and used them for private purposes.
Some put their *phrai* or slaves to work in the commercial economy and
extracted a share of their earning. Under the law, this was a legitimate
use of a slave, but nobles used *phrai* in the same way through intimida-
tion. In two places in the *Tale of Khun Chang Khun Phaen*, the king criti-
cizes his high nobles:

"You're only good at cheating your own men for corrupt gain, and using fancy
words to get blood out of a crab."

---

[39] Old royal decrees 23 and 44, *Kotmai tra sam duang*, vol. 5, 40–1, 120–1; Division of
people, *Kotmai tra sam duang*, vol. 2, 1–7.
[40] Pieris, *Religious intercourse between Ceylon and Siam*, 34; *RCA*, 436 (*RA*).
[41] Busakorn, "Ban Phlu Luang dynasty," 167–71, 312; Old royal decrees 23, *Kotmai tra
sam duang*, vol. 5, 38.

"You're all chatter and no substance. You're good only at cheating your own men out of money by using your clever tongues ... Your property and rank are a burden on the realm."[42]

The kings attempted to counter the nobles' competition for control over labor through legislation. The additions to the slavery law dealt with theft of slaves, including cases in which the thief took "a whole chain of slaves," hinting at the scale of such theft. Another law on kidnapping, possibly from the same time, seems designed to combat organized trafficking of runaway slaves.[43] The "Law on division of people" of 1690 set out to register all men outside the nobility, including children from age nine, with all details inscribed on a *tabian hang wao*, a "kite-tail record," compiled by a *munnai* or overseer and lodged with the Registration Department. The system was elaborated further in 1726 by requiring each household to keep its details on a *sammano khrua*, a household record, and deputing officials to monitor changes such as people moving house or entering the monkhood.[44] Laws introduced in 1748 imposed harsh penalties for stealing *phrai* by falsifying the registration detail, and required officials to question *phrai* who had fled to the forest to uncover who had oppressed them and how.[45] A 1756 law declared that "the king has great compassion towards all the peoples within the territory," and urged people to send petitions for the redress of any trouble or exploitation.[46] Around 1746, Borommakot had two senior nobles flogged for over-working *phrai* engaged to bring a white elephant to the capital, and a royal decree asked: "Is this the way to help support and sustain the imperial subjects so they can live in happiness?"[47]

The repetitive nature of the legislation designed to enhance the pool of royal *phrai* and reduce the nobles' exploitation of labor suggests the kings were fighting a losing battle.

Bandits, Crime, Corruption

The disintegration of controls over people lay behind several forms of disorder including banditry, crime, corruption, and revolt.

According to a law of 1743, banditry had spread "because the authorities have been lax, have employed criminals to till lands and keep livestock,

---

[42] Baker and Pasuk, *Tale of Khun Chang Khun Phaen*, 418, 544.
[43] Slavery law, clause 62, and Law on kidnapping, *Kotmai tra sam duang*, vol. 2, 1–20, 324.
[44] Law on division of persons, *Kotmai tra sam duang*, vol. 2, 1–26; Old royal decrees 14, *Kotmai tra sam duang*, vol. 5, 1–6.
[45] Old royal decrees 23, 42, 48, 49 in *Kotmai tra sam duang*, vol. 5, 37–43, 115–18, 137–46.
[46] Old royal decrees 42, *Kotmai tra sam duang*, vol. 5, 115.
[47] *RCA*, 444 (*BM*).

have allowed some bandits to escape, and have taken bribes to let them go."[48] As a result of increasing trade, highway robbery in particular was on the rise. Some overseers were running robber gangs. Some provincial governors accepted bribes to look the other way.[49] A bad agricultural season in the early 1750s promoted an outbreak of banditry in Sawankhalok, where several gangs were armed with guns. The central authorities lashed the local officials for not doing their duty and for taking bribes. They sent out orders to organize regular patrols, compile registers (complete with sketches) of guns and of property vulnerable to stealing such as livestock, keep records of people moving from place to place, and offer bounties for arrests. New laws laid down harsh punishments for robbers including cutting off their ears and hands, or tattooing their faces and chests, so that "everyone can recognize them." After a robber gang escaped jail in Ang Thong, the governor and his officials were punished by seizing their property, wives, children, and slaves.[50] A law of 1748 lamented, "people in bands beat, abuse, and kill one another a great deal ... causing chaos in the realm."[51]

Through the early eighteenth century, the court issued a series of laws about people using power to make money and money to gain power – signs of new wealth disrupting an old social order. According to these laws, officials of royal kin who visited provincial cities tended "to bully and oppress people, seizing property, gold and silver, and causing distress and hardship to the people." Tax collectors embezzled a portion of their collections and made up the difference by squeezing the poor. Provincial governors were prone to "seizing women as their wives or servants." Overseers extorted food and clothing from royal *phrai* under their charge, and accepted bribes for allowing able-bodied men to escape corvée. Merchants paid bribes to get licenses to set up illegal gambling dens and to collect unauthorized taxes. Judges extorted excessive judicial fees and accepted bribes to influence their verdicts.[52] People outside the nobility were able to gain power by buying positions:

There are [people in official posts] who have paid bribes to officials to dismiss good men and appoint them in their place. They then oppress, bully, and cheat their *phrai* and other people to make money to recoup the bribe ... with no worry or shame over sin ... If someone of no lineage, of low birth, someone's slave or servant, makes money at gambling, redeems himself, bribes his way to become a

[48] Old royal decrees 11, *Kotmai tra sam duang*, vol. 4, 125–6.
[49] Saichol, *Phutthasasana*, 39
[50] Old royal decrees 3, 11, 12, *Kotmai tra sam duang*, vol. 4, 295–6, 329–30, 335–48.
[51] Old royal decrees 49, *Kotmai tra sam duang*, vol. 5, 146.
[52] Old royal decrees 39, 42, 48, 50, 53, *Kotmai tra sam duang*, vol. 5, 107–8, 115, 141–2, 162–3, 170.

royal page ... and gets to see the splendor of the king's palace and hear the king's voice, he gets carried away by the thought that he can become powerful ... claims he has access to the royal audience, and oppresses the people.[53]

In a moral tract from this era, the author railed against social decay:

Some have gone off to become bandits. Many villagers and cityfolk have been ruined and scattered to the winds ... There is nobody to rely on. Those who rely on people of rank are even more likely to drown ... There is nobody with compassion for the people ... Those who know only trading ... fight for what they can get like crows and vultures ... These villains steal taxes and dues at will, with no fear of the law.[54]

Revolt

The years after 1688 saw revolts in larger numbers and of a new type. Disturbances had occurred after previous dynastic upheavals, but the post-1688 outbreaks displayed levels of popular involvement which went beyond elite conflicts over the throne. These were the aftershocks of the final years of Narai, when ordinary people had been organized, often by religious leaders, to protect Buddhism against foreign influence.[55]

Soon after his accession, Phetracha faced revolts in Khorat and Nakhon Si Thammarat where the governors challenged his legitimacy by refusing the summons to Ayutthaya to drink the water of allegiance. The Khorat governor was supported in rebellion by a local monk. These revolts were especially significant because the two cities were first-class towns and the acknowledged sub-headquarters of their regions. The Nakhon governor was a local lord, possibly a Malay, but the Khorat governor was a senior Ayutthaya noble, who had held the title of Phraya Yommarat during Narai's reign.[56]

The revolts were difficult to suppress. Ayutthaya initially sent ten thousand troops and considerable artillery to Khorat, but the town held out for three years. When the military supply lines failed, "Those who slipped away and fled from the brigades of that army were numerous." Phetracha recalled the commanding officers to Ayutthaya and had them flogged, "paraded in disgrace on land and by boat for three days," stripped of their property, and "put to death in great numbers."[57] Only after another army was sent, and bombs dropped on Khorat from kites, did the town

[53] Old royal decrees 50, *Kotmai tra sam duang*, vol. 5, 148–51.
[54] *Pradontham*, quoted in Saichol, *Phutthasasana*, 40–1.
[55] Nidhi, *Kanmueang thai samai phra narai*, 86.
[56] *RCA*, 320 (*PC*).
[57] *RCA*, 345 (*BM*).

submit, but the governor and his close followers escaped and joined the revolt in the south. Suppression required another large army with a hundred boats, and took a further three years. The Khorat governor was killed but the Nakhon governor again escaped with help from a fellow Malay in the Ayutthaya forces.[58]

Another revolt, which broke out in 1689 and was probably the largest uprising in the Ayutthaya era, mixed the anti-dynastic theme with undercurrents of popular discontent. According to the Dutch, Thammathian was a former retainer of Narai's brother Aphaithot who had become a monk, been arrested for a crime in Tenasserim, and imprisoned in Ayutthaya.[59] According to the chronicles, he was impersonating his former master, claiming to be "the eldest of the late King's brothers ... and consequently ... the next Heir to the Crown."[60] After 1688, he escaped to the east, studied magic, and began a revolt by disguising himself as the dead prince, and appearing on a bull elephant, abetted by a "rascally Kula, a slave, as his mahout." On his advance towards Lopburi, he "swept up those groups of men and women who were working in the paddy fields and brought them along in great numbers." They armed themselves with "spears and swords, rods and sharpened bamboo sticks, and rice shoulder poles and scythes." Kaempfer reckoned this "undisciplined rabble" numbered 10,000.[61]

Led by a flag-carrier "riding a carabao," Thammathian's men almost captured the king's son Sorasak and then besieged the capital. One chronicle reports that Phetracha brought Naresuan's sword out of the collection of sacred regalia, and had cannon fired from the walls, killing Thammathian as he was crossing into the city. According to the Dutch, the fighting in the city lasted three days, most of the city population fled, and the rebel leader was captured in the jungle after his forces were defeated. A visiting Japanese sea captain recorded that the government mobilized 40,000 troops. "Those routed and fleeing away into the jungle were so numerous," according to the chronicles, that large areas of Lopburi, Saraburi, and Nakhon Nayok were "utterly abandoned." Three hundred rebels were captured, and mostly flogged and then executed or enslaved. Kaempfer reported that Thammathian was "expos'd for a publick spectacle for some days; afterwards his belly was cut open he being alive, and his Intestines given to the Dogs to tear and devour."[62]

---

[58] *RCA*, 348–55 (*BM*); Forest, *Missionaires français*, 107–8.
[59] Bhawan, *Dutch East India Company merchants*, 161–4.
[60] Kaempfer, *Description of the Kingdom of Siam*, 37.
[61] *RCA*, 322 (PC), 341 (*BM*); Kaempfer, *Description of the Kingdom of Siam*, 37.
[62] Bhawan, *Dutch East India Company merchants*, 161–4; Ishii, *Junk trade*, 48; *RCA*, 344 (*BM*); Kaempfer, *Description of the Kingdom of Siam*, 37; Turpin, *History of the Kingdom of Siam*, 74.

Shortly after, another revolt broke out in Khorat. The leader, Bun Khwang, was described as a "nobleman possessing expertise" who began with just twenty-eight supporters. As in the case of Thammathian, he was rumored to be either a relative or former retainer of Narai. He took the town because the governor and other officials were "in fearful awe of the wretch because of the primacy of the excellence of his expertise." He held out for a year, left at the head of an army of 4,000 men and eighty-four elephants, and "swept up people in great numbers" on his way to Lopburi. Ayutthaya prepared an army of 5,000 which quickly suppressed the rising. In reprisals at Khorat, according to the Dutch, "innocent peasants" and "local traders" were tortured and killed, and their corpses displayed on the walls around the city.[63]

The Dutch believed this revolt was another aftershock of the succession dispute in 1688. They reported that Narai's daughter Yothathep and several nobles, including Kosa Pan, had stirred up the revolt in an attempt to overthrow Phetracha. Whether true or not, Phetracha took the opportunity for a purge which killed at least forty-eight nobles including several of ministerial rank, some Malays, and two heads of the Japanese community. Kosa Pan died from illness, possibly induced by some punishment, possibly from suicide.[64]

In 1691, Pattani also defied Phetracha by pointedly not sending tribute, and the Dutch reported that both Kedah and Phatthalung followed suit.[65] An expedition was dispatched to bring Pattani to heel, with some difficulty (see p. 138). What happened in Kedah and Phatthalung is unknown. In 1712, Pattani once more refused to send tribute. Over 1712–13, a rebel force attacked Tenasserim and Mergui. Yet again, the rumors claimed the leader was either a monk expert in magic or a surviving relative of Narai. The rebels plundered the towns but were eventually defeated. In 1717–18, the governor of Phetchaburi was in revolt, though no details are known. In 1734, as described above, a group of Chinese and others tried to capture the palace. In 1746, on a visit to Lopburi, King Borommakot was confronted by a revolt led by "one Khmer named the Eminent Som." Three hundred troops were sent to suppress it. In the 1760s there were two outbreaks among Mon communities which had recently migrated to settle in the same region.[66]

[63] *RCA*, 358–61 (*BM*); Busakorn, "Ban Phlu Luang dynasty," 45; Bhawan, *Dutch East India Company merchants*, 172.

[64] Dhiravat, "Princes, pretenders," 110–11; Bhawan, *Dutch East India Company merchants*, 170–1.

[65] Bhawan, *Dutch East India Company merchants*, 168.

[66] Bhawan, *Dutch East India Company merchants*, 181; Dhiravat, "Princes, pretenders," 115; *RCA*, 443 (*RA*), 488 (*BM*); Nidhi, *Kanmueang thai samai phrajao krung thonburi*, 10.

The accounts of these revolts are filtered through the perceptions of Dutch traders and Japanese sea captains, or the prejudices of later chroniclers. There are no reports of what the leaders promised to their followers and only limited indications of who the followers were, so interpretation is difficult. Never before had Ayutthaya faced such prolonged resistance from two of its cardinal outposts, Khorat and Nakhon Si Thammarat. In no earlier revolt, had a "rabble" come close to capturing a royal son or engaging the king's troops in a three-day battle for the palace. Perhaps the mobilization of people and monks in the crisis of 1688 had a lasting effect. Certainly the area towards Lopburi, stirred up in 1688, figured in several of these incidents. Two other features recurred. First, leaders were claimed or rumored to be related to Narai. Second, the leaders were often monks with a reputation for magic or supernatural ability. This combination of royal associations, religion, and magic perhaps promised something powerful enough to challenge a reigning king.

Power and Lore

Beliefs in supernatural power were widespread. People of special ability were believed able to control the spirits or to manipulate forces in the natural world through spoken formulas, special substances, and graphic devices. In Siam this tradition went under many names including *wicha* (Pali: *vijja*), meaning learning or knowledge, similar to the past meaning of the old English word "lore." Skill in lore came with ascetic practice, and lore was closely associated with the ascetic tradition in Buddhism. Lore played a part in everyday popular ceremonial to bring good fortune and protection from dangers. In official culture, it featured mainly in warfare. A fragmentary version of the *Manual of victorious warfare* dating to the eighteenth century is specially focused on omens for predicting the result of battles and ceremonies to achieve victory.[67] In the chronicles' account of his visit to France in 1686–87, Kosa Pan demonstrates the invulnerability of Thai soldiers by allowing 500 French troops to fire volleys at seventeen Thai men without causing them any harm.[68]

In late Ayutthaya, kings were often credited with supernatural powers. A 1734 inscription at Pa Mok praises King Thaisa for "residing in the Ten Virtues of Kingship and having sacred and supernatural powers."[69] In the oral history of Siam that appears in the *Testimony*, supernatural

---

[67] Saichol, *Phutthasasana*, 56–7, from Damrong's preface to the manual.
[68] *RCA*, 273–4 (*BM*).
[69] Saichol, *Phutthasasana*, 56

events are prominent. Narai is given his name as a youth because he was seen to have four arms, like Vishnu, when he climbed onto the palace roof to extinguish a fire caused by lightning. He shows off his "meritorious power" by riding an untamed wild elephant, subduing an elephant in musth, and controlling the level of the water in the river.[70] A prominent monk has the ability to "bore through the earth, fly through the sky, and walk on water." Sorasak had

miraculous ability and supernatural power, and expertise in lore; at night he made himself invisible and went around listening to the people's troubles. He could shoot birds at night and crocodiles hidden underwater ... He was invulnerable ... He appointed an adept in lore as a page in close attendance ... His powers of lore surpass anything in history.

Borommakot's mission to Lanka (see below) miraculously survives a storm at sea. Monks make rain to avert a drought. When lightning fells a fig tree beside the palace on the eve of Ekkathat's ascent of the throne, the omen is read as good and the tree made into a throne.[71]

Such supernatural power was threatening to authority because authority had no monopoly on its use. Most rebels of this era claimed some expertise in lore. Not by chance, lore and revolt are a prominent theme in *The tale of Khun Chang Khun Phaen*, which first developed in an oral tradition of recitation for local entertainment, possibly beginning in the seventeenth century, and became so popular it was elaborated to epic length. The plot is a classic love triangle in which an ordinary man is pitted against wealth and power. Khun Phaen, who is poor after his military father is executed for a mistake in the king's service, contests for the lovely Wanthong against Khun Chang who is the richest man in their provincial town. When Khun Chang uses his money and his court connections to pry Wanthong away, Phaen turns to the lore he has acquired in training to become a soldier. He acquires a magic horse, an enchanted sword, and a personal spirit. He uses verbal formulas to make himself invisible, to immobilize his enemies, to induce love in others (including the king), and to conjure up warriors from bundles of grass. The king declares Phaen is in revolt, and throws him in jail. Although Phaen shows he can free himself from jail, defeat royal troops, and charm the king himself, he accepts his fate. In the dramatic finale, the king has Wanthong executed to remove the source of Phaen's unruliness. The tale mocks

---

[70] *Khamhaikan chao krung kao*, 101; *Khamhaikan khun luang ha wat*, 29; Tun Aung Chain, *Chronicle of Ayutthaya*, 50.

[71] *Khamhaikan chao krung kao*, 101, 120–1, 134–5, 139, 145–7, 149; *Khamhaikan khun luang ha wat*, 30, 51–2, 69–70, 73–4; Tun Aung Chain, *Chronicle of Ayutthaya*, 50, 68, 70–2, 86, 91–2, 94.

the *sakdina* order throughout. The king is a figure of fun who issues sentences of execution at the slightest provocation. The nobles are spineless. Only Khun Phaen can defend Ayutthaya against its enemies with the help of a handful of fellow jailbirds who are skilled in lore.

Khun Phaen offers a model of power that contrasts with the traditional theories of kingship. His power is based on his personal talent and his education in lore rather than on his lineage or his rank and position in the *sakdina* hierarchy. The knowledge of lore is passed down from father to son and from monk to pupil, rather than through institutions of the court. Phaen is a classic outsider, with many analogies to the old legends of Robin Hood. Possibly this rebellious theme, as well as the tragic romance at the core of the plot, contributed to the story's popularity as local entertainment in the late Ayutthaya era, and also prompted the court to take ownership of the tale in order to domesticate it.[72]

Nobility Rising

In the eighteenth century, the nobility became richer and more assertive. Several factors contributed. The economy prospered, especially through the growing trade with China. The relaxation of royal monopolies allowed others to share in the prosperity. In the disintegration of the old systems of forced labor, nobles increased the numbers of people under their control and used them to swell both their income and their status. Noble families at the capital benefited from increasing central control over the provinces. More governors were appointed from among the Ayutthayan nobility, both in Siam proper and areas down the peninsula. A decree of 1740 laid down that senior officials including city governors had to come from an established noble lineage.[73] Ayutthaya nobles were also sent to provincial centers as *yokkrabat*, officials who originally worked as the king's envoy and spy in the locality, but were gradually transformed into a chief magistrate as well. These posts could be lucrative. Magistrates who wielded the increasingly important power of the law were able to extract high fees and outright bribes, prompting legislation to control these abuses. Sometime around the early eighteenth century, the provincial towns in the north were placed under Mahatthai, and those to the south under Kalahom, and a little later, these arrangements were adjusted to include Phrakhlang. In effect, these ministries

---

[72] "Afterword" in Baker and Pasuk, *Tale of Khun Chang Khun Phaen*; Baker and Pasuk, "Revolt of Khun Phaen."

[73] Nidhi, "Nakhon si thammarat nai ratcha-anajak ayutthaya"; Nidhi, *Kanmueang thai samai phrajao krung thonburi*, 51–2, fn. 2; Old royal decrees, 20, 23, 32, 50, 51, *Kotmai tra sam duang*, vol. 5, 28–30, 37–43, 84–7, 147–67.

became territorial sub-states, increasing the patronage in the hands of their senior officials.

As a result, the great noble households prospered, and were better able to accumulate wealth across generations. A prominent example is the Siriwatthana family which traced back to a Brahman at the court of Prasat Thong during the period of Khmer revivalism. His son held one of the main "Brahman" posts under Narai, and his two grandsons both rose to Chaophraya rank with one holding the prestigious post of governor of Phitsanulok. One son in the next generation played a key role in the succession struggle of 1733, after which Borommakot rewarded him with the title of Chaophraya Chamnan Borirak and appointment as Phrakhlang. He held the post for two decades and was succeeded by his son-in-law, while his two sons headed Mahatthai in succession over the years 1742–58.[74]

The lineage of the Persian Sheikh Ahmed Qomi (see p. 125) had a similar trajectory. The sons, grandsons, and great grandsons of the founder held posts in Mahatthai and Phrakhlang throughout the seventeenth century. During the Borommakot reign, a member of the lineage, who held the title of Phraya Phetphichai in the royal guard, was encouraged by the king to adopt Buddhism. He was promptly rewarded with the higher rank of Chaophraya, and given control over the Cham and Japanese units in officialdom. His daughter was married to the Kalahom. His son succeeded to his noble title and functions. This convert branch of the family, which became known as the Bunnag, expanded its influence in the nobility in the last decades of Ayutthaya and beyond.[75]

Such resplendent families were very few. Wyatt identified only four – the Persian Bunnag, Chinese Ong, Brahman Siriwatthana, and Mon-Thai lineage of Kosa Pan. Another sign of the resilience of this emerging elite was that Kosa Pan's descendants survived his humiliation and death in 1699, and within a few years became prominent in Mahatthai.

These same themes of growing prosperity and greater continuity were replicated at less elevated levels of the official and trading elite. The Amatayakul family stemmed from a middle-ranked official in Phrakhlang during the Borommakot reign, whose son rose to head the right division of the ministry and married into another prominent family. Some of these rising stars were Chinese such as the future King Taksin, whose father arrived in the early eighteenth century. Taksin's early career has been obscured by retrospective attempts to accord him the upbringing

---

[74] Wyatt, "Family politics in seventeenth- and eighteenth-century Siam," 104–6; Wyatt, "Family politics in nineteenth-century Siam," 115.
[75] Julispong, *Khunnang krom tha khwa*, 246–51.

and connections of a member of the Thai elite (see Chapter 7), but Nidhi suspects he was a cart-trader operating along the Ping River from Ayutthaya to Lanna who gained appointment as governor of Tak through patronage or bribery. When Taksin began his political ascent after 1767, his early followers were similarly adventurous mid-level noble-officials, with many from Chinese or other non-Thai backgrounds.[76]

Particularly in the higher rungs of this emerging nobility, there were signs of an emerging class. Families intermarried across linguistic boundaries, suggesting they consciously belonged to a new aristocracy rather than to distinct communities. The Brahman Siriwatthana family intermarried with the Chinese family of Ong Heng Chuan, and with the Mon-Thai family of Kosa Pan.[77] These families adopted practices formerly associated exclusively with the monarchy. Chamnan Borirak was given a glorious funeral with his corpse place in the "holy royal gift of a funeral urn ... wearing the paraphernalia of a *chada* crown ... having [his remains] referred to as a Holy Corpse and ... having a *meru* tower built" – the first such funeral for a noble mentioned in the chronicles.[78] Noble families laid on expansive celebrations at their children's tonsure ceremonies, a lifecycle rite long celebrated by royalty. Big families also arranged great feasts complete with entertainments and fireworks. Performance of drama by an all-female troupe with plots based on the *Ramakian* and other classics remained a preserve of the court (*lakhon nai*, inner drama), but nobles sponsored all-male troupes playing plots that came from *jataka* stories and folk tales (*lakhon nok*, outer drama).[79] Reports by Dutch residents in the early eighteenth century show "a picture of officials who were confident in displaying their wealth and status as well as enjoying a certain degree of freedom of action."[80]

The prosperity of the nobility is evident from the variety of luxury goods in the capital's markets. Jewelry vendors sold "*talap* caselets, ornaments of silver and black nielloware, wrist and ankle bangles, lotus hairpins, *krajap-ping* [an ornament for infants], chili ornaments, *khunphet* linga, gold chains and breastchains." Betelnut containers, which had once been insignia of rank conferred by the king, had become an everyday luxury and mark of status, available in the marketplace. The well-off and status-conscious consumer could choose among

[76] Nidhi, *Kanmueang thai samai phrajao krung thonburi*, 90–132.
[77] Wyatt, "Family politics in seventeenth- and eighteenth-century Siam," 103–6; Wyatt, "Family politics in nineteenth-century Siam," 115.
[78] *RCA*, 452 (*BM*).
[79] Mattani, *Dance, drama, and theatre*, 45–6.
[80] Bhawan, *Dutch East India Company merchants*, 192.

betel bags in wool and silk; betel bags in patterned cloth used on royal service, only by men, for keeping betel to eat; wool pouches for betelnut embroidered in gold and embellished with glass; ordinary betel pouches; pouches for tobacco embroidered in gold embellished with glass; ordinary tobacco pouches; and pan leaf holders in various colors.[81]

One evidence of elite prosperity comes from the distinctive five-colored Chinese ceramic ware known as Benjarong, which may have first appeared in the 1720s, following the gift of multicolor ceramics, fashionable in China at the time, as official presents to the Ayutthaya court. Large quantities of Benjarong pieces and shards have been found in the ruins of the palace and elsewhere in Ayutthaya. Many are in shapes specific to Siamese tableware with Thai motifs, showing that these pieces were produced in China on commissions from Siam. Three production centers in southern China which had developed the technology for producing ceramics to order from Batavia were the probable source. As Pimpraphai concludes, "the volume of Benjarong imports in the Thaisa and Borommakot reigns shows the wealth of Ayutthaya and the proficiency of the Chinese trading community."[82]

The *Testimony* compiled by the nobles hauled away to Ava in 1767 offers the nobility's view on the history of this era. In the *Testimony*'s account of the royal succession in 1688, Phetracha becomes king "because all the officials were united in the wish for him to rule." At the accession of Thaisa in 1709, the *Testimony* states that "all the officials invited the late king's son to become king," and repeats this formula at the accession of Borommakot and Ekkathat.[83] In the many accounts of these successions in other sources, the nobles have no role, but in their own retrospective account, nobles now made kings.

A Society Looking at Itself

The social changes in late Ayutthaya were reflected in artistic expression, particularly in literature, drama, and painting.

Dramas of Change

The court poetry of the Narai era focused on the expression of emotions, using complex meters and a command of vocabulary from many languages. Court formalities were obligatory, including invocations of

---

[81] Baker, "Markets and production," 61–2.
[82] Pimpraphai, "Kan kha khrueang krabueang," 157.
[83] *Khamhaikan khun luang ha wat*, 62–3; *Khamhaikan chao krung kao*, 122, 129, 133, 149; Tun Aung Chain, *Chronicle of Ayutthaya*, 68–9.

the king and gods. Over the next century these constraints lifted. A small but important reading public emerged, which overflowed the boundaries of the court. Conventions relaxed, plots became important, and realism intruded.

A transitional work between these eras is *Kamsuan samut,* "Ocean lament," probably dating to the 1680s. In the style of a *nirat,* the poet flees from Ayutthaya by ship, lamenting his love left behind, but the work strays from old conventions. The opening of the poem does not praise the king in the conventional way, but celebrates the city of Ayutthaya. The poet describes local people along the route in a realistic way, including drunken soldiers throwing up. The poem is legendarily attributed to a court poet named Si Prat who was expelled from Narai's court for an affair with a consort, and banished to Nakhon Si Thammarat, where he repeated the crime with the minor wife of the governor, who had him executed; the king then pined to hear Si Prat's poetry again, and had the governor executed with the same sword.[84] This Si Prat story might itself be an invention of court gossip.[85] Both the poem and the romantic story of Si Prat are examples of a heightened realism and sensuality.

Prince Thammathibet, one of Borommakot's sons, also wrote *nirat,* perhaps of even greater erotic intensity, and he too was executed for translating art into life among the ladies of the court (see below). Thammathibet wrote a cycle of poem using the rhythms chanted by oarsmen in royal water processions. By abandoning the complexities of court verse, these verses achieved an affecting realism:

> Now I've enjoyed you, I enquire, yet you murmur no sound.
> Are you shy of me? I beg you, tell the truth.
> Dazzled by your beauty, I clasp, kiss, stroke your neck and chin,
> pluck your thin breastcloth, ply you with pleasing caresses.
> Seeing a figure so loveable, a face so alluring,
> a slender waist so elegant, a spirit so appealing to a man,
> anyone seeing such a gift for the eye, forgets all their sorrows,
> desires a maiden's perfect body, cannot forego love for a minute.[86]

Also probably in the early eighteenth century, court poets plucked *The tale of Khun Chang Khun Phaen* from the oral tradition of popular entertainment and began to write it down and adapt it to court tastes. The plot is set into a panorama of the society ranging from the court to the jail, with the social contrasts in full view. The setting rambles all around the Ayutthayan territory with the same fascination to capture space as shown by the *nirat.*

[84] *Khamhaikan chao krung kao,* 127–9.
[85] Winai, *Kamsuan samut,* 21–7.
[86] "He bot sangwat," song on lovemaking, in Thammathibet, *Kap he ruea.*

A new demand for stories with a plot resulted in imports from over-seas, including the *Anirut* tales from India, the Panji stories from Java, the Arabian *Thousand-and-one nights,* the *Duodecagon* from Persia, and a vampire tale from Sanskrit (*Vetala pancha-vinshati*). Some had been known in Siam for a long time but were now recast to suit a new audi-ence. The *Anirut* tales, for instance, had probably arrived from Cambodia and circulated in Sanskrit in early Ayutthaya, but were now adapted into an immense epic with greater focus on the love story and the addition of Thai spirit beliefs.[87] The Javanese Panji tales, known under the title *Inao,* were mined for episodes that combined eroticism and adventure. Several tales were adapted to dance and drama performances which became popular in Narai's court and flourished under Borommakot. Earlier court performances tended to select episodes which glorified princely success or romantic escapades,[88] but now extracts were chosen from the *Inao* story to show what befell a prince who acted badly.[89] In the Thai version of the Ramayana (*Ramakian*), the heroic spotlight is focused less on Rama, the royal, and much more on Hanuman, the clever courtier, the *khun nang.*

While the court and popular traditions were separate, through this era they increasingly borrowed from each other. The forum for this interchange was often the *wat,* which was open to all social levels, and which was often the staging place for dramas and recitations.[90] The kings sponsored festivals associated with important events. Phetracha staged a three-day celebration on the completion of a temple built to honor his birthplace. Borommakot "held festivals to celebrate for three days" at three new monasteries, and transformed the court's annual pilgrimage to the Buddha's Footprint in Saraburi into a public festi-val, with music performances, *khon* mask-plays, *lakhon* dramas, shadow puppet shows, *mongkhrum* drum performances, *rabeng* dances, Mon dances, tightrope walking, jumping through flaming hoops, sword dances, wrestling, and "daring acrobatics." The event, described in the poem *Bunnowat khamchan,* lasted seven days, punctuated by occasions for the king to scatter alms of gold, "when all the people came, every single one, to receive the royal alms, clapping their hands in joy, and fighting among themselves."[91]

Several literary works used a new metrical form, *klon,* which developed in this era from rhythms used in the tradition of counterpoint singing

---

[87] Cholada, "Thai tale of Aniruddha."
[88] Mattani, *Dance, drama, and theatre,* 45–6.
[89] Davisakd, "Pursuit of Java," ch. 2.
[90] Nidhi, *Pen and sail,* 16–21.
[91] *RCA,* 348, 424, 435 (*BM*); *Bunnowat khamchan,* 26–9.

found in popular entertainment. The simplicity and flexibility of *klon* made it both easier to compose and better suited to telling stories than older, more formalized meters which excelled at expressing emotions. Before long, *klon* was used for poems, dramas, histories, and even medical treatises.[92]

The alternative drama tradition outside the court (*lakhon nok*) sometimes took plots from the so-called *Fifty Jatakas*, a collection of tales which have the distinctive format of a *jataka* but are not found in the original Pali collection of *jataka*. Many originated as folktales, which were adapted into stories of the Buddha's past lives. Two of the most popular, adapted to *lakhon nok* and other forms, were *Suthon–Manora* (Sudhana-Manohara) and *Rothasen* (Rathasena). Manora is a *kinnari*, a human–bird hybrid found in the Himavanta Forest in the Three Worlds cosmology. After she is captured and presented to Prince Suthon, their great love sparks jealousies, forcing Manora to flee back to the Himavanta Forest to escape death. Suthon's pursuit, crossing the boundary between the human and mythical worlds and overcoming countless obstacles, is a classic quest story. In *Rothasen*, twelve royal consorts are blinded and consigned to a cave through the machinations of an evil queen. A *bodhisatta* born to the youngest consort first acts as their provider and then leaves on a quest to recover their eyes and return their sight. These stories have strong hero figures who overcome obstacles through their own strength and goodness, with occasional assists from the god Indra. The adaptations display the new interest in realism. In a dance-drama version of the Suthon–Manora tale, mother and daughter hold a fierce argument, complete with intimate cursing – something unknown in the more formal original.[93]

The *Fifty Jatakas* present a commentary on kingship. In the set-up portion of these tales, the *bodhisatta* is often born in a city where the king is either weakly prey to the machinations of an evil queen, prince, or Brahman, or is actively malevolent, launching wars for pride, handing down harsh punishments without a thought, and coveting the wives and property of ordinary people. In the finale, the *bodhisatta* often becomes the king and rules in an exemplary way – observing the precepts, giving alms, performing good deeds, teaching his subjects to follow his example, and ruling with justice and compassion. The tales offer a clear view of bad kings and good kings.[94]

---

[92] Nidhi, *Pen and sail*, 9–11, 26–9.
[93] Davisakd, "Pursuit of Java," 158–60.
[94] *Panyat chadok*; Fickle, "Historical and structural study of the Paññāsa Jātaka"; Niyada, *Panyat chadok*.

Tales and Reflections in Wat Murals

Themes found in literature also appeared in the painting of *wat* murals, particularly the use of stories and the celebration of real life.

The early history of painting murals in Thai *wat* is little known. Illustrations of the *jataka* and Buddhist scenes were painted in *wat* at Sukhothai and early Ayutthaya but were hidden away as part of the intrinsic sacredness of the site.[95] In *wat* architecture up to the sixteenth century, windows were too few and too small to admit enough light for murals to have any didactic purpose. European accounts suggest murals were still rare in the seventeenth century. Van Vliet, Heeck, Tachard, Kaempfer, and Chaumont left detailed descriptions of *wat* that they visited without mentioning any sign of a mural.[96] Heeck noted that "The ceilings, walls, pillars, and beams were all painted with artful foliage and gilded right up to the very top" and Van Vliet recorded that many buildings "inside and outside are beautifully gilded and painted," but neither mentioned any pictorial illustration.[97] On painting in general, Chaumont recorded "they are ignorant in the use of it," Gervaise concluded "they are not good painters," and La Loubère omitted painting from his detailed list of arts and crafts.[98]

Gervaise and La Loubère have left the only record, from the 1680s. Speaking of "six or seven old ones [temples], on which the kings of Siam have spent immense sums," Gervaise noted:

The walls and the pillars are very neatly painted in red and yellow with quite well drawn scenes taken from their legends or showing the joys of paradise and torments of hell or depicting the monks who have rescued from the latter those people from whom they have received most charity.[99]

La Loubère recorded, "In one of their Temples I saw a very pleasant Picture in *Fresco*, the Colours of which were very lively."[100] These accounts suggest that murals were rare in the late seventeenth century, confined to a few royal temples, and that the subjects may not have included the storytelling of the Buddha's life which would have fascinated observers like Gervaise and La Loubère.

---

[95] Most famously at Wat Si Chum in Sukhothai (Skilling, *Past lives of the Buddha*), but also in the crypts of Wat Ratchaburana, Wat Mahathat, and Wat Phra Si Sanphet in Ayutthaya.

[96] Heeck, *Traveler in Siam*, 61–6; Tachard, *Voyage to Siam*, 180–4; Kaempfer, *Description of the Kingdom of Siam*, 47–9, 54–62; *Van Vliet's Siam*, 155–88.

[97] Heeck, *Traveler in Siam*, 63; *Van Vliet's Siam*, 157.

[98] Smithies, *Aspects of the embassy*, 86; Gervaise, *Natural and political history*, 93.

[99] Gervaise, *Natural and political history*, 139–40.

[100] La Loubère, *New historical relation*, 70.

The earliest surviving examples of *wat* murals date to the late seventeenth or early eighteenth century. They were executed in a limited palette (black, red, brown, ochre) with two main themes: the Buddhas of the past, arrayed in lines in the pose of meditation; or the convocation of the deities in which various gods, deities, and mythological beings are seated in lines, bodies turned towards the main Buddha image in worship. These scenes were painted in the hall used for ordination and were perhaps, like the hidden *jatakas*, part of the heightened sacredness of this building.

Change came probably from the late seventeenth century. Buildings were constructed or renovated with larger windows, often using arch construction learnt from Persian architects.[101] New materials expanded the palette, particularly with blues and greens. Most importantly, murals now appeared in preaching halls, more public than the ordination halls, and they told stories with a didactic purpose taken from the ten last *jatakas* and episodes from the life of the Buddha.

The ten last *jataka* tales relate how the Buddha, in his last ten incarnations as a *bodhisatta*, acquired the ten perfections that prepared him to gain enlightenment in his subsequent incarnation as the Buddha. The last and Great Jataka or *Mahachat* illustrates the perfection of giving through the story of Phra Vessantara (Wetsandon). This story had long enjoyed prominence in Siamese Buddhism. Kings had commissioned recensions of the manuscript. Listening to a chant of the full tale in Pali was believed to confer great merit. Sometime in late Ayutthaya, a new version was composed wholly in contemporary Thai, and sometime in the mid- to late-seventeenth century murals of the story began to appear in *wat* preaching halls.[102] Some *wat* were painted with all ten *jatakas*, and a few portrayed the non-canonical *Fifty Jataka*, especially the Suthon–Manora story.

Murals on the life of the Buddha also appeared from the early eighteenth century. At Wat Ko Kaeo Suttharam in Phetchaburi, murals painted in 1734 show the Seven Great Stations, recording the activities of the Buddha in the seven weeks after enlightenment, and the Eight Great Sites, recording key events of the Buddha's life.[103] At Wat Chaiyathit in Thonburi murals were painted on the Buddha's early life beginning from the marriage of his parents, his birth, early life in the palace, and departure to become an ascetic. At Wat Khongkharam in Ratchaburi, there is a

[101] Julispong, "Khwam samphan."
[102] Nidhi, *Pen and sail*, 199–226; Santi, *Temples of gold*, 27; Jory, *Thailand's theory of monarchy*, ch. 3.
[103] Siriphot, "Naeo khit nai kan ok baep jittrakam fa phanang ubosot."

similar sequence with details such as hairstyle, architecture, and painting technique that attest to an eighteenth-century origin.

By the fall of Ayutthaya, a conventional layout of *wat* murals had emerged and persisted in the Bangkok era. Scenes from the ten *jatakas* or the life of the Buddha were painted in the spaces between the windows that were now found along the side walls. The convocation of the deities was consigned to the space above these windows. Behind the Buddha image were representations of the Three Worlds cosmology, and opposite was Buddha overcoming Mara to achieve enlightenment. The *wat* had become a visual classroom.

The older mural subjects, especially the convocation of the deities, emphasized devotion. The stories of the Buddha's life and past lives offered models of living in this world, and dramatization of moral lessons. Besides this didactic purpose, the storytelling of the *jatakas* and the Buddha's biography gave the artists the opportunity to place events into a contemporary landscape – to celebrate life around them. Most strikingly, these murals celebrated the city itself, analogous to the portrayal of Ayutthaya at the opening of the "Ocean lament." At Wat Chaiyathit, scenes from the Buddha's early life were crowned with a splendid, distinctly Siamese roofscape of *wat* and palaces, flashing with gold, and bounded by walls, gates, forts, pavilions, bastions, and the occasional intimate glimpse of an ordinary wooden house with a caged mynah bird hung on the verandah. At Wat Pradu Songtham in Ayutthaya and at Wat Ko Kaeo Suttharam in Phetchaburi, the scene of the Buddha's cremation was embellished with vignettes of the entertainments at cremations and other great celebrations: crowds watch a folk version of the *khon* mask-play, a dance performance, a *like* drama, a *ngiu* Chinese opera, a boxing match, acrobats, and firework displays.

Artists took the opportunity to fill the margins of these scenes with glimpses of everyday urban life (Figure 6.1). Kids play games and chase chickens. Vendors carry goods. Criminals hobble along in a yoke. Outside the wedding ceremony of the Buddha's parents, cooks sit and chat around a pot. On the river, a boat vendor negotiates a sale of liquor, while a man practices his fiddle on the bank. Men hollow out dugout boats, climb sugar palms, watch a busker with a monkey, and sit around in a drinking circle. Women pound rice and carry goods to market on shoulder poles. The faithful give alms to monks. Teenagers brawl in the street. Mahouts slouch on their elephants' necks, passing the time of day while waiting to be summoned to work. The cast of characters includes Thai, pigtailed Chinese, bearded Moors, head-shaven Japanese, and overdressed westerners. Episodes of the Buddha's life are watched by crowds showing great variety of dress, hairstyle, facial type, and skin color. The overall

Figure 6.1. Street scene depicted in murals of the Vidhura Jataka at Wat Chong Nongsi, Bangkok (courtesy of Viriyah Business Co. Ltd.)

impression is of a varied and busy society – all sorts of people doing all sorts of things.[104]

In many of these marginal scenes, there is an erotic or bawdy element. On the fringes of a *jataka* tale, soldiers are abducting several beautiful and bare-breasted ladies from the side door of a palace. On the street, a young lad prepares to lasso the exposed testicles of a man pounding rice (Figure 6.1). Two palace ladies fondle each other's breasts. Four intertwined legs are glimpsed through a window, and the neighbors crowd around to look and listen. As a group of peddlers passes through a wilderness, a man drags a startled woman away behind some rocks. Two monkeys copulate in a tree. Similar vignettes remained part of mural painting until the intrusion of Victorian prudishness in the late nineteenth century. They appear only centimeters away from an episode in the life of the Buddha, rather like the opening stanzas of the "Ocean lament" where the poet praises Ayutthaya as both the site of splendid temples and a great place for flirting in the evening.[105] Perhaps these scenes were intended to dramatize the bestiality of humankind compared to the serenity of the Buddha and the gods.[106] But perhaps the artists were simply striving to capture the energy and intimacy of the city.

A society was looking at itself, and sharing the view.

The Ban Phlu Luang Dynasty

The dynasty begun by Phetracha in 1688 was retrospectively called the Ban Phlu Luang dynasty after Phetracha's birthplace in Suphanburi. The royal chronicles of this period, written and rewritten in the Thonburi and early Bangkok eras, lampoon the Ban Phlu Luang kings (except Borommakot) in order to blame them for the tragedy of 1767. In these chronicles, the kings and their sons go on fishing expeditions, ravage under-age girls, box at village fairs, commit diplomatic *faux pas*, and fight viciously among themselves. Yet this dynasty lasted longer than any other during the Ayutthaya era.[107]

Perhaps because of the rising trend of revolt, the Ban Phlu Luang kings visited upcountry centers more than their predecessors, especially to dispense religious patronage. The pilgrimage to the Buddha's Footprint in Saraburi had by now become an annual fixture and an

---

[104] Muang Boran has published illustrated books of most of the *wat* with important surviving Ayutthaya-era murals. See also Ringis, *Thai temples*, Santi, *Temples of gold*, and Jaiser, *Thai mural painting*.
[105] Winai, *Kamsuan samut*, 46–50.
[106] Wray et al., *Ten lives of the Buddha*, 135.
[107] A fact pointed out by Nidhi, *Kanmueang thai samai phrajao krung thonburi*, 11.

ever more splendid event. In 1737, the king's party was comprised of "120 large rowing vessels of various makes, the smallest one manned by forty oarsmen," and the expedition took seventeen days.[108] Phetracha visited Phitsanulok where he founded an ordination hall, pavilion, and stupa. Sorasak visited Phetchaburi. Thaisa had the reclining Buddha at Pa Mok moved so it would not collapse into the river, and Borommakot returned there in a grand pilgrimage. Borommakot also went on a tour to the famous Jinaraja and Jinasi Buddha images in Phitsanulok, taking in other significant religious sites along the way, and had Buddhas cast at both Phitsanulok and Nakhon Si Thammarat. Sorasak and Thaisa also ordered a great deal of canal-building – both to speed the route from Ayutthaya to the sea, and to facilitate east-west travel – and personally visited the sites to oversee construction.[109]

The violence of the 1688 succession and its aftershocks seems to have eroded some of the protective gloss surrounding the monarchy. Public airing of sexual scandals within the palace was a regular feature of the age. In 1697, rumor reported that a daughter of Prince Sorasak was sneaking out of the palace to sleep with servants and actors. The "Si Prat" scandal described above is dated to same era, as are stories of Phetracha beating up Queen Yothathep.[110] In 1755, the Kalahom got among the palace women and was "flogged up to seven hundred strokes until he died in neck fetters"[111] Shortly after, the royal heir, Prince Thammathibet, confessed under torture that he had relations with four of his father's consorts, and these ladies implicated him in a coup plot to assassinate his father and many others. Thammathibet, the four ladies, and others involved all died as a result of flogging.[112] Soon after, two brothers of one of Ekkathat's queens were found to have interfered with "a great number of the ladies of the Interior." Both were flogged. The elder brother died and the king "had his corpse taken to be impaled to advertise his wickedness at the Gate of Victory."[113] Perhaps such events had always been part of palace life, but now they found their way into the city's gossip, picked up by the resident Dutch, and eventually written into the chronicles and the memoirs of the nobles. A decree of 1740 lamented, "In the past, royal matters were talked about only by lords and nobles, but today they are talked about improperly on every road and street."[114]

[108] Raben and Dhiravat, *In the King's trail*, quote on 11.
[109] *RCA*, 376, 392, 394, 405, 407–10, 424–5, 434; *Khamhaikan chao krung kao*, 143.
[110] *Khamhaikan chao krung kao*, 127–8; Bhawan, *Dutch East India Company merchants*, 172, 174.
[111] *RCA*, 456.
[112] Bhawan, *Dutch East India Company merchants*, 201–2.
[113] *RCA*, 480.
[114] Old royal decrees 50, *Kotmai tra sam duang*, vol. 5, 151.

Succession

The succession was marked by conflict of increasing intensity. Phetracha drew on the female line to increase his legitimacy by marrying both Narai's sister and daughter under some duress, and fathering children on both, thereby embedding a source of conflict within the royal lineage. Similar to other new dynasts, the early Ban Phlu Luang kings fathered many children to increase the presence of the lineage, thereby increasing the potential for competition. In an attempt to bring order, the kings created a more elaborate internal hierarchy with gradations of rank signified by newly created titles and types of regalia, but this did little to limit competition.[115]

More than in earlier times, the kings seem to have been (rightly) fearful of impatient sons, and tried to manage the problem by balancing factions within the royal kin. According to rumor, Phetracha believed his elder son Sorasak had been involved in several coup plots, and accordingly conferred troops and honors on his minor son Phra Khwan, fathered on Narai's daughter, Yothathep. As Phetracha sickened in 1703, Sorasak occupied the palace with 3,000 troops and had himself crowned once his father had died. Yothathep plotted to have Sorasak assassinated, without success. Sorasak removed her royal title and properties and threw her out of the palace. Sorasak may have conciliated Khwan by promising to abdicate once Khwan came of age, but then had him executed, and the body displayed to discourage impersonators fomenting revolts in his name. Before long, Sorasak suspected two of his own sons of plotting a coup, had them imprisoned and whipped, and would have executed them if Narai's daughter had not intervened. Like Phetracha he improved his legitimacy by marrying a lady of Narai's lineage, but then suspected her of conspiracy, and had her executed along with her father.[116]

In 1709, Sorasak was succeeded by Thaisa, his first son who had married his own half-sister. This was the only non-violent succession between Ekathotsarot's accession in 1605 and the fall of Ayutthaya. Shortly after, Thaisa eliminated Dam, the only remaining son of Phetracha.

Thaisa ruled for twenty-four years, allowing time for several sons to grow up to fighting age.[117] When the king sickened in 1732, at least three factions prepared for the contest. The king's younger brother and *uparaja*, Phon, had aspirations to succeed. On his deathbed, however,

---

[115] Busakorn, "Ban Phlu Luang dynasty," 157–9, 167, 197.

[116] Bhawan, *Dutch East India Company merchants*, 174–6; Dhiravat, "Princes, pretenders," 113; *RCA*, 387–91.

[117] The *Testimony* names ten or twelve children, see Tun Aung Chain, *Chronicle of Ayutthaya*, 76; *Khamhaikan chao krung kao*, 129.

Thaisa nominated his second son, Aphai. Phon fled into the monkhood, while his followers built stockades in the center of the city and released prisoners to swell their own ranks. According to Turpin's melodramatic account, one side amassed 40,000 troops. When Thaisa died, the two sides fought with cannons for three days. Aphai and another brother lost and fled into the forest, but were captured and executed. A fourth prince was also killed. The Phrakhlang and Chakri, who had backed Aphai, took refuge in a *wat* but were hauled out by some Muslim Malays. According to the Dutch, the victor wanted the Phrakhlang "killed in a cruel manner." Phon emerged from the monkhood and was crowned as the king known usually as Borommakot. He did not occupy the Ayutthaya palace at first because "he did not trust the palace staff." In this contest, Turpin noted that "more perished by the sword of the executioner than on the battlefield."[118]

The impact on the high levels of the nobility was close to that of 1688. At least three ministers – Phrakhlang, Chakri, and Yommarat – were killed along with many *khun nang* of the second level. A year later some survivors joined the "Chinese" revolt (see p. 214) which resulted in another purge. When Borommakot fell ill in the following year, one son immediately tried to kill his brother and, failing, fled into the monkhood. The king "feared going outside the palace ... and had to hurry back within an hour at the most."[119]

Borommakot reigned for twenty-five years and fathered around eighty children.[120] In the *Testimony* account of his reign, the major princes, their marriage links, and their factional alignments are described like a great family drama that the nobles are watching on a stage. By the time his sons had grown to adulthood and Borommakot had entered old age, the plots had become labyrinthine. Prince Thammathibet, the king's designated heir, was brought down by sexual scandals in 1757 (see above) either because he was plotting to oust his father, or because his siblings framed him on this charge to undermine his chance to succeed. In replacement of Thammathibet, the king nominated a second son Uthumphon as heir, prompting his elder brother Ekkathat to enter the monkhood. On his deathbed Borommakot confirmed his choice and swore four other sons to agree. Once the king died, however, Ekkathat left the monkhood and the brothers fought for three days behind the closed palace gates. The *sangha* leaders negotiated a truce, but the brothers went straight back to amassing troops. Ekkathat

[118] *RCA*, 413 (*BM*); Turpin, *History of the Kingdom of Siam*, 77–9; Dhiravat, "Princes, pretenders," 121; Bhawan, *Dutch East India Company merchants*, 182–4; "Phra krasae phrabatsomdet phraphutthajao luang," 105.

[119] "Phra krasae phrabatsomdet phraphutthajao luang," 105–6.

[120] Estimates vary, see Wood, *History of Siam*, 233; *Khamhaikan chao krung kao*, 108.

had three of his siblings arrested. In the chronicles' dramatic account, one announced: "Why be afraid of dying? It is natural for those born into this Grand Family of the White Umbrella. Just how many people get to die better?"[121] The three were tortured and executed. Uthumphon ascended the throne but after ten days, a visit to the Buddha's Footprint, and some religious endowments, he abdicated in favor of Ekkathat and took the robe. A year later, a revolt to restore Uthumphon failed. According to the Dutch, after several high nobles were purged, four or five pages associated with Ekkathat were "elevated from the lowest background to the highest ranks," and acted as "extortionists" on traders.[122]

Looking back, a rueful memoir recorded the desecration of the nobility:

Officialdom had dwindled away because of killings over several reigns. In the Songtham reign, the old nobles of Prince Si Saowaphak were killed. In the Prasat Thong reign, the nobles of his elder brother were killed, but rather few. In the Narai reign, the nobles of Chaofa Chai and Phra Si Suthammaracha were almost all killed, changing the whole team. In the Phra Phetracha reign, Narai's nobles were killed, bit by bit, almost all of them … In the Sua [Sorasak] reign, many were killed for supporting Phra Khwan … In the Thaisa reign luckily few were killed but only because King Sua reigned for a short time and had not yet filled every post. In the Borommakot reign, almost all the palace staff died except for the *samuha nayok* alone … Think. In ninety years, there have been seven killings, almost one every thirteen years. And those who survived became royal *phrai* cutting grass for elephants. Seven times in ninety years, nobles became *phrai* and *phrai* became nobles.[123]

Law and Buddhism

In the last century of Ayutthaya, there was an expansion in the use of law, and attempts to give Buddhism a more active role in society. Both trends can be seen as responses to the growing complexity and disorder of society.

Expansion of Law

Siam had a tradition of royal law-making stretching back at least to the fifteenth century. Individual laws began life as specific court judgments

---

[121] *RCA*, 465 (*RA*), translation slightly edited for clarity.
[122] *RCA*, 463–7 (*BM, RA*), 470–1 (*RA*); Busakorn, "Ban Phlu Luang dynasty," 110; *Khamhaikan chao krung kao*, 148–9; Bhawan, *Dutch East India Company merchants*, 202–5; Masuda, "Fall of Ayutthaya," 84.
[123] "Phra krasae phrabatsomdet phraphutthajao luang," 106. The calculation of "ninety years" is wrong as there were 123 years between the accessions of Songtham and Borommakot.

or royal proclamations, and were later edited and sorted into codes on a wide variety of "causes of disputes among people," including the management of *phrai* and slaves, inheritance, marital relations, contracts, debt, and robbery. By late Ayutthaya, the king's role as judge had been delegated to a complex structure of courts under different departments, with the king serving as the final court of appeal. Judicial procedure was regulated by detailed codes on witnessing and other aspects of court practice.[124]

The scope and usage of this legal system increased from the early seventeenth century, and especially after 1688. In 1685, La Loubère was told the laws were kept in three volumes, one of which contained new decrees introduced since the reign of Prasat Thong.[125] In 1805, the surviving law texts from the Ayutthaya era were assembled in a collection known as the Three Seals Code, which ran to forty-one volumes. Although this cannot be directly compared to La Loubère's sketchy report of three volumes, legislation greatly increased in late Ayutthaya, including a set of "Thirty-six laws," dated between 1640 and 1756, another sixty-two "Old royal decrees," most of which date to the first half of the eighteenth century, and additions to other codes.[126]

The additional legislation covered a wide range of subjects, but five stand out. First, many concerned the administration of control over people. They overhauled the systems of registering people, attempted to stop certain transfers of ownership, and laid down rules about the assignment of *phrai* children. Second, many concerned robbery. They introduced local patrols, made neighbors responsible for watch and ward, penalized officials for lax policing, specified punishments for fencing stolen property, and allowed officials to seize the families of robbers who absconded. Third, they strengthened Ayutthaya's control over the provinces. Several laws prescribed working procedures between the capital and its provincial appointees, including the role of the *yokkrabat*, the use of sealed documents for communication, and the referral of important court cases and appeals to the capital. Fourth, they attempted to control corruption and abuse of power by officials. They set out schedules of fees for judging cases, imposed punishments on legal officers who abused their position, required written receipts for tax payments, banned monks from interfering in government business, and outlawed buying of government posts. A decree of 1731 restated that all officials must twice a year swear an oath of loyalty and honest service before a Buddha image, and made

[124] Ishii, "Thai Thammasat"; Baker and Pasuk, *Palace Law of Ayutthaya*, 9–12.
[125] La Loubère, *New historical relation*, 81–8.
[126] *Kotmai tra sam duang*, vol. 4, 229–57, 293–354; vol. 5, 1–192.

anyone evading this oath guilty of revolt. Another decree of 1740 set out four qualities for a government official: "he must come from a lineage of officials; be aged thirty-eight or above; be expert on official duties; and be wise in dealing with issues relating to other countries, and acting properly according to the principles of worldly government."[127]

Finally, there were many amendments and extensions to the rules on judicial procedure, clarifying the ambit of particular courts, preventing excess delay, providing for appeals, and ensuring fair judgment. The preambles of several laws insisted that people use the courts rather than resorting to other methods for settling disputes. This legislation attempted to increase the scope, efficiency, and usage of the law.

Buddhism for Society

The last century of the Ayutthaya period saw an expansion in the social role of Theravada Buddhism. Although this expansion was supported and extended by certain kings, it was probably associated with the growing assertiveness of the nobility.

Noble patronage of the religion increased with growing wealth from the seventeenth century. By the mid-eighteenth century, the city was flooded with new *wat*, mostly built by the nobility. Alexander Hamilton, who visited in 1719, estimated there were 50,000 monks around Ayutthaya, and "Temples and Priests are more numerous here, in Proportion to the laity, than in any Country I ever saw out of the Dominions of *Portugal*."[128] Along with this patronage, there were movements to adjust doctrine and practice so that Buddhism played a larger role in creating order and discipline in society, in defining the duties of kings, and in giving Siam a position in the world.

As Saichol has shown, Buddhist beliefs and practices in late Ayutthaya were rather varied.[129] Popular teaching focused on the law of *kamma*, the impact of good and bad deeds in past lives on the current existence, and of good and bad deeds in the present on future lives. Various kinds of merit-making designed to influence the balance of *kamma* played a large role in worshipful practice. Popular teaching relied heavily on *jataka* stories which dramatized the practical benefits of right conduct and merit-making activities, including such benefits as long life, good health, wealth, and physical beauty. Beliefs in supernaturalism were widespread. In a popular didactic story, a monk, Phra Malai, travels to the hells and

---

[127] Old decrees 50 and 58, *Kotmai tra sam duang*, vol. 5, 149, 180–2.
[128] Hamilton, *New account of the East Indes*, 446, 465.
[129] Saichol, *Phutthasasana*, ch. 1.

heavens, where he sees the results of good and bad conduct, and dis-
cusses the causes with Indra and Phra Metteyya, the future Buddha.[130]

In opposition to this emphasis on *kamma* and supernaturalism,
there was also an interest in a rational and this-worldly approach to
Buddhism. From the late Narai era, Gervaise recorded that there
was a view, held by the "king and some of his courtiers who are more
enlightened than the rest," that the Buddha was an ordinary mortal
who "left behind for them a number of excellent maxims and good
examples."[131] A surviving text records King Phetracha posing questions about Buddhism to Phra Phuthakosajan, head of a division of the
monkhood, then resident at Wat Phutthaisawan in Ayutthaya. In his
replies, the learned monk stressed that suffering and impermanence
were the constants of this-worldly existence. Individuals had to overcome this condition by "wisdom," and by learning how to free themselves of anger, greed, illusion, and other failings, perhaps by practicing
vipassana, insight meditation, through which the individual can escape
the cycle of rebirth and "achieve full *nibbana* in the present existence."
Phra Phuthakosajan glossed *nibbana* as "a state of purity of insight and
intuition" with "suppression of all cravings that induce unhappiness."
He stressed that this could be achieved solely through the mind, and
argued that the geography of the Three Worlds was simply a metaphor
for mental states.[132]

Another document circulating in the same era was *Pradon tham*, meaning "old teachings." Organized as short essays in simple Thai for reading
or embroidering as sermons, *Pradon tham* lacked the intellectual rigor
of Phra Phuthakosajan's responses to the king but had a similar message. The author criticized people who "attribute every misfortune to
kamma made in the past without paying any attention to the good and
bad they do in this life." He set out a moral path for those in different
sections of society. Monks must uphold the precepts. Laypersons should
honor their parents and teachers. Judges must be fair. Traders should
not cheat. Rather similar to Phra Phutthakosajan, the author explained
simply, "*Nibbana* is just happiness."[133]

Some time in this era, the *Questions of Milinda* was translated into Thai.
This Pali text, which had accumulated in India since the early centuries
CE, had long been popular throughout the Buddhist world because it
explains in simple terms the basics of Buddhism from concepts such as
mindfulness through to formulas such as the Five Aggregates. Along the

---

[130] Brereton, *Thai tellings of Phra Malai*.
[131] Gervaise, *Natural and political history*, 110.
[132] "Phraratchaputcha khong somdet phra phetracha"; Saichol, *Phutthasasana*, 52–3.
[133] *Pradon tham*; see also Saichol, *Phutthasasana*, 54–5, 59.

way, the text also gives instruction in how to live a good life according to Buddhist principles.[134]

In *Pen and sail*, Nidhi argued that a rationalist and philosophical approach to Buddhism developed in the early Bangkok era in the context of an emerging "bourgeois society."[135] Saichol has shown that this development began a century earlier in a similar context of an expanding commercial economy.

Prophecy, History, and Maps

For the nobility, which was becoming stronger and more assertive, Buddhism offered a means for reforming the monarchy to reduce the risks of political conflict. *Phleng yao payakon*, "Ode of prophecy," is a poem often attributed to King Narai, but more likely a product of noble thinking, as a variant version appears in the *Testimony* composed by the nobles taken away to Burma.[136] The poem begins by portraying Ayutthaya as a perfect city, prosperous and universally admired, similar to the portrayal in the "Ocean lament." But then, in the *Testimony* version, "because the people and kings did not follow the *dhamma*, many amazing happenings arose." The social order is upended. Natural laws no longer function. Social bonds dissolve. Religion disappears and evil flourishes until "Ayutthaya, the city as happy and prosperous as heaven, reaches the end of its days."

In a longer version, disaster does not arise because of "people and kings" but specifically "because the kings did not uphold the Ten Virtues of Kingship." This version ends,

> Though *now* Ayutthaya in bliss can claim
> To shame all heaven's joys a myriad-fold,
> Yet here – behold! – are whores and sin foretold.
> Alas! Alas! Count the days 'til it shall come to pass![137]

The Ten Virtues of Kingship is an old moral code found throughout Buddhist Southeast Asia. The ten virtues are munificence, moral living, sacrifice, honesty, gentleness, self-restraint or austerity, non-hatred, non-violence or not causing harm, patience or tolerance, and

---

[134] Saichol, *Phutthasasana*, 54.
[135] Nidhi, *Pen and sail*, 110–16, 131–43, 278–82.
[136] Tun Aung Chain, *Chronicle of Ayutthaya*, 72–3; *Khamhaikan khun luang ha wat*, 71–3. The poem does not appear in *Khamhaikan chao krung kao*.
[137] Translation by Richard Cushman in Wyatt, "Translating Thai poetry," 5–11. The *Testimony* version is found in *Khamhaikan khun luang ha wat*, 71–3, and with significant differences in English translation in Tun Aung Chain, *Chronicle of Ayutthaya*, 72–3.

non-oppressiveness.[138] This code is cited many times in this era. Both inside and outside the court, the episodes of the *Ramakian* chosen as plots for drama portrayed Rama as the ideal king following the Ten Virtues.[139] Another code, the Four Principles of Harmony (*sangahavatthu*), found in many popular *jataka* tales, urged the king to win the hearts of his subjects by promoting agriculture, employing good officials, spending revenues on public projects, and being courteous in his speech and demeanor. The prominence of these codes at this era reflects attempts by the newly assertive nobility to transform kingship.

The account of Siamese history in the *Testimony* has the same moral standpoint. The early part follows the royal chronicles, but the later part from Narai onwards is different, probably the nobles' own account of the era. The telling resembles the chronicles composed in *wat* rather than palace, recording the "works of merit" of each king, including his construction and repair of *wat*, and passing judgment on the reign. This approach is similar to the Van Vliet chronicle a century earlier, with one striking difference: in the Van Vliet chronicle kings were judged positively for being strong military leaders, but here they are judged negatively. Sorasak gains approval. He built one new *wat*, repaired three, and cast a Buddha image. "He had no wish to make war against other kingdoms as it would create trouble for the populace. He devoted himself to good works." By contrast, Thaisa repaired only a single *wat* and a sleeping Buddha image, and embroiled the country in wars. The *Testimony* offers him no praise.[140] This historical account often invokes the Ten Virtues as its moral standard. The judgment on Sorasak concludes, "He practiced the Ten Virtues of Kingship. He worked for the people's happiness."

Borommakot conformed to the nobles' prescription for a good king. He had spent a long period in the monkhood before ascending the throne and he fulfilled the traditional role of generous patron. He rebuilt Wat Ratchaburana, repaired and reshaped Wat Phraram, restored Wat Mahathat, extended Wat Phu Khao Thong, constructed six other *wat*, and carried out a major restoration at the Buddha's Footprint in Saraburi.[141] In the nobles' model, a good king had to create the conditions in which his subjects could earn merit and progress towards enlightenment. In this respect, according to the *Testimony*, Borommakot

---

[138] According to legend, a royal minister who had become an ascetic found the code inscribed on a hillside; see Ishii, *Sangha, state, and society*, 44–5.

[139] Mattani, *Dance, drama, and theatre*, 46.

[140] *Khamhaikan chao krung kao*, 126–7, 130; Tun Aung Chain, *Chronicle of Ayutthaya*, 74, 76.

[141] Piriya, "Revised dating of Ayudhya architecture," parts 1 and 2; *Khamhaikan chao krung kao*, 142.

excelled. He carried out Buddhist ceremonies fastidiously, encouraged others in the elite to undertake charitable works, forced male members of the royal family to spend time in the monkhood as a condition of gaining an official appointment, and forbade animal slaughter in an area around the capital. The *Testimony* quietly omits the violence of the succession dispute that brought Borommakot to power and the violence wrought on members of his own family. It gives him the regnal name of Maha Thammaracha, the great king of *dhamma*, the old title of the kings of Sukhothai. It summarizes his reign through the image of a good king found in the *jataka* tales:

He was devoted to the virtue of the Triple Gem. He gave alms to a hundred monks each day without fail. He cared for the happiness of the kingdom's people with the kindness of a father to his children. He made war on no country, but forged alliances of friendship with many. The country was happily free of war and crime to the point people did not need to surround their houses with walls.[142]

In the *jataka* tales, such a king is a *bodhisatta* who is showered with praise by the gods and who on death is reborn in Indra's Tavatimsa Heaven. Accordingly in the *Testimony* account of Borommakot,

When he was about to die, many omens appeared. A meteor fell in the center of the capital. A comet appeared. The sky was red like flame. Stars in the sky emitted smoke. The light of the sun dimmed. The moon became red like fire. There was silence inside and outside the city. Many great events were omens that a person of merit (*phumibun*) was passing away.[143]

In 1750 Sri Lanka sent a deputation of monks to Ayutthaya to request help in reviving the Lankan *sangha*. As Lanka had been an important origin of Siam's Buddhist tradition, this request was flattering. Borommakot hand-picked the three senior monks who traveled to Lanka to instruct and ordain a new core of "purified" Lankan monks. A second Lankan monastic mission arrived in 1757. Borommakot also sent monks to Ava as a form of religious diplomacy.[144] Siam could now aspire to be a center of the Buddhist world.

This aspiration was expressed in the genre known as *samutphap traiphum*, illustrated manuscripts of the Three Worlds, which appeared in late Ayutthaya. These accordion books bring together the three most prominent elements of popular religious teaching in this era: the

---

[142] *Khamhaikan chao krung kao*, 146; Tun Aung Chain, *Chronicle of Ayutthaya*, 91.

[143] *Khamhaikan chao krung kao*, 146–7; *Khamhaikan khun luang ha wat*, 119; Tun Aung Chain, *Chronicle of Ayutthaya*, 92. Note this quote conflates elements from the different versions of this document.

[144] *Khamhaikan chao krung kao*, 138–56; Pieris, *Religious intercourse between Ceylon and Siam*.

Figure 6.2. Map in the Illustrated Manuscript of the Three Worlds (Thonburi era, Berlin mss), depicting Ayutthaya in the world of Buddhism (© bpk Museum für Asiatische Kunst, SMB, Iris Papadopoulos)

cosmology of the Three Worlds, the life of the Buddha, and the ten great *jataka* tales. At the end are maps on which five rivers originate in a representation of northern India in the Buddha's lifetime, and then snake eastward, becoming the rivers of Mainland Southeast Asia. Along these waterways are shown towns in Siam and neighboring territories along with "sites of memory" of the Buddha, namely relic stupas and footprints. Ayutthaya appears prominently as an island in the river (in the half moon to the left of center on Figure 6.2). The maps continue to the Indian Ocean, and finally to Lanka in a layout dominated by the Buddha's Footprint on Mount Si Pada (Adam's Peak).[145] These maps place the homeland and the era of the Buddha adjacent in both space and time to Southeast Asia. Siam and Lanka are shown as the two centers of the Buddhist world, with Siam closest to the origin.

In sum, within the nobility, there was a movement to draw on Buddhism to reform both society and kingship. This required a more rational and this-worldly interpretation of Buddhist teaching, emphasizing moral behavior for immediate benefit rather than merit-making activities to store up karmic assets for future lives. Kings were urged to follow the model of a good king dramatized in the *jataka* tales, codified in the Ten Kingly Virtues, and expressed as the king-as-*bodhisatta*. In the nobles' history of this era, Borommakot is presented as an exemplar of this model, while other kings are condemned. The new visual decoration of *wat* and the *Traiphum* manuscripts compressed the three most powerful aspects of popular Buddhist teaching – the life of the Buddha, the *jataka* tales, and the cosmology of the Three Worlds – into a single coordinated message, linked with an aspiration for Siam to be the center of the Buddhist world.

In the *Testimony*'s account of the Burmese attack in 1760, the nobles encourage the king to send a negotiator with a proposition suffused with Buddhist humanism:

It will be like when elephants fight. The plants and grass on the ground get crushed. In the same way, the ordinary people and soldiers get crushed to death in war. Burma and Thai have fought many times by now. Many soldiers have died. Even if one side gains victory, it will not be sufficient for the loss. So ask your lord to ally the two countries as a single golden land. Both peoples will escape from dangers. Both kings will gain fame for their kindness in freeing their people from worry.[146]

But the harsh, this-worldly reality was that prospering Ayutthaya was a more attractive prize than ever before.

---

[145] *Samutphap traiphum chabap krung si ayutthaya*; Wright, *Phaen thi phaen thang.*
[146] *Khamhaikan chao krung kao*, 157.

The Fall

The standard Thai historiography, stemming from the work of Prince Damrong, portrays the fall of Ayutthaya to the Burmese in 1767 as the culmination of a long period of unrelenting Burmese aggression. Yet the earlier conflict between the two centers was confined to the second half of the sixteenth century. In the following century and a half, Burma made only three short-term raids on the Mon country (1613, 1622, 1663), while Ayutthaya's major military activity consisted of intermittent eastward expeditions to maintain Cambodia as a tributary (1594, 1628–30, 1711).[147]

Ayutthaya felt at little risk. It had fallen only once, and then because of internal collusion. Its best defenses were the monsoon rains which flooded the surrounding countryside. From the late sixteenth century, the walls and moat were steadily improved so the city could withstand siege through one dry season. The ability to raise a large army diminished as the king's grip over *phrai* loosened, but in compensation the city bought guns in quantities which astonished the Burmese when they broke open the arsenals in 1767 and found

10,000 guns inlaid with gold and silver, as well as matchlocks and flintlocks, making a total of 2,550 guns, big and small, made of bronze and iron, including ... chariot-mounted cannon, bow-mounted cannon, elephant-mounted cannon, city-destroying cannon, enemy-repulsing cannon ... [and] four gigantic cannon [so large] the barrel could easily accommodate a man ... solid cannon balls ... canister rounds and case shot ... chain shot ... cannonade shells ... grenades fitted with fuses ... and grapeshot that scatters into a lethal wedge-shaped pattern, with stocks enough to deter a siege.[148]

Until 1760, there was no threat from outside. Neither Burma nor Siam disturbed the arrangement, prevailing since 1600, under which Burma was suzerain in the interior and Siam at the coast. After Narai's expeditions in the 1660s, no Ayutthaya army went north towards Chiang Mai. In 1717 and again in the late 1740s, Ayutthaya forces were sent east to maintain a loose suzerainty over the Khmer country in the face of Vietnamese rivalry. The armies involved were modest in size. According to the chronicles, the naval contingent, led by the Chinese Phrakhlang, was routed because, he was "timid – not brave and tough – and cowardly in warfare," but the land army won victory and forced the Khmer ruler to accept tributary status.[149] Hamilton reported, however, that the Khmer

[147] Damrong, *Our wars with the Burmese*, 180–96, 203–19, 229–33.
[148] Myint, "*Yodayar Naing Mawgun*," 78.
[149] *RCA*, 404–8.

denuded the land route of people, forcing the Siamese troops to eat their own horses and elephants, and to retreat when many fell sick.[150]

Peace was broken when a new Burmese dynasty set out to unite the Irrawaddy basin and subdue its neighbors.[151] This ambition revived the old rivalry with Siam over control of the west coast of the upper peninsula. The conflict escalated when the Burmese discovered the weakness of the Ayutthayan armies, realized that the riches of Ayutthaya could make a campaign self-financing, and determined to eliminate a rival power center which disrupted its attempts to control the Mon country.[152]

By the late 1750s, the Burmese dynast, Alaungpaya, had captured Ava, destroyed Pegu, submitted the Shan states, and invaded Manipur. His forces established themselves at Syriam, opened up trade with India, and raided down the coast to Martaban, Tavoy, and Tenasserim. A small Ayutthayan garrison was easily defeated, and the Burmese army pursued its flight across the watershed in late 1759. Ayutthaya's attempts to recruit a defense force from the provinces south-west of the capital raised only 3,000 men.[153] The Siamese fell back to defend the city against siege. The strategy worked. The walls held against the Burmese guns. Sickness thinned the Burmese troops. In May 1760 the Burmese army withdrew because Alaungpaya was sick (he expired on the march home) and the rains had begun. The Burmese hauled away only people and petty loot from the outskirts of the city.[154]

From 1762, Alaungpaya's son Hsinbyushin focused on securing control over the two strategic areas for commerce, namely the route through Lanna into China, and the neck of the peninsula. In March 1764, an army was dispatched to Lanna and Lanxang, and in 1765 another army approached the ports on the western coast of the upper peninsula. A Chinese who had taken control of Tavoy offered resistance and then fled to the protection of Ayutthaya. After a Burmese sally through the Three Pagodas Pass met very weak resistance, the Burmese ruler set his sights on Ayutthaya. Because "Yodaya had never before been utterly destroyed and crippled,"[155] he ordered the commander of the northern army, then garrisoned in Chiang Mai, to conscript local troops to increase the army to 20,000 men, while he prepared a southern army of

[150] Hamilton, *New account of the East Indes*, 458, 470.
[151] Lieberman, *Burmese administrative cycles*, ch. 5.
[152] Nidhi, *Kanmueang thai samai phrajao krung thonburi*, 13–17; Turpin, *History of the Kingdom of Siam*, 84–6.
[153] *RCA*, 477 (*RA*).
[154] Lieberman, *Burmese administrative cycles*, 268; Turpin, *History of the Kingdom of Siam*, 87.
[155] Phraison Salarak, "Intercourse between Burma and Siam, part II," 20.

the same size in Tavoy. As in the 1560s, these armies were collections of troops under local lords who expected to share in the spoils.[156] At the end of the rains in late 1765, the two armies began their advance.

They did not make straight for Ayutthaya, but subdued the major towns along the way, both to prevent them giving any help to Ayutthaya and to swell their own forces with captured elephants, horses, weapons, and men.[157] The accounts in the Burmese and Thai chronicles are hopelessly conflicting. The Thai chronicles, painting an image of Siam in disarray under the Ban Phlu Luang kings, describe the Burmese armies meeting little resistance: "No-one fought back at all. Everyone took their families and fled off into the forests."[158] By contrast, the Burmese chronicles describe their troops heroically overcoming much greater opposition.[159] Even in the Burmese account, however, only a few places resisted. The northern army had to fight at Phitsanulok, and the southern army at Phetchaburi and Kanchanaburi. Elsewhere, the towns surrendered. At Bangkok-Thonburi, the Burmese blew up the fort "without any resistance" according to the resident Dutch.[160]

After each town fell, some men were forcibly recruited by the Burmese while others volunteered in hopes of gain. The incentives were considerable. At Phetchaburi, "There was the usual looting ... the rest of the booty, including men, women, gold, silver etc., became the property of the persons who had been able to seize it."[161] By the time they reached Ayutthaya, according to a French bishop there, "it was rumoured that the Burmese armies were full of Thai who were discontented and had decided to defect from Siam to Burma."[162] According to the Burmese account, local recruits added thirteen divisions to the northern army and seven to the southern, plus horses, elephants, and weaponry; the chiefs of these Siamese recruits "were made to swear an oath of allegiance and allowed to enter royal service"; and these units were placed in the vanguard for the attack on Ayutthaya. The governor of Suphanburi was among those who fought on the Burmese side.[163]

[156] Myint, "Yodayar Naing Mawgun," 3–5, 22–3.
[157] Sunait, Songkhram khrao sia krung, 38–57.
[158] RCA, 495–7 (BM, RA); Nidhi, Kanmueang thai samai prajao krung thonburi, 30–1.
[159] Sunait, "Miyanma-sayam yut," 80; Phraison Salarak, "Intercourse between Burma and Siam, part II."
[160] Bhawan, Dutch East India Company merchants, 215.
[161] Phraison Salarak, "Intercourse between Burma and Siam, part II," 25.
[162] Nidhi, Kanmueang thai samai phrajao krung thonburi, 23, quoting Thai translations from French missionary records.
[163] Myint, Portrayal of the battle of Ayutthaya, 70, 92; RCA, 478–9 (BM); Sunait, Songkhram khrao sia krung, 43, 52; Sunait, "Miyanma-sayam yut," 81.

The northern and southern armies arrived at Ayutthaya in January–February 1766, and initially camped beyond cannon range. Ayutthaya attacked both camps without success, and thereafter relied on the monsoon floods to disperse the siege. In mid-year, the Burmese encircled the city and used guns to stop supplies entering or people leaving. At the onset of the rains, when the Siamese expected them to retreat, the Burmese set up camps at *wat* built on knolls around the city, and on a slightly elevated tract north of the city at Three Bo Trees. They planted crops, dispersed their horses and elephants to places outside the flood-plain, and waited out the rainy season. Ayutthaya started building a ring of camps outside the city to prevent the Burmese approaching the walls.

When the rains eased in late 1766, the Burmese made an outer circle of camps to prevent traffic in and out of the city, devastated the surrounding area so Ayutthaya had no food supplies, blocked the river to prevent trade, and built towers and mounds as gun emplacements. According to reports by resident Chinese, "inside the city wall of Ayutthaya the prices of daily necessaries went on rising and those who starved to death were countless. Moreover, an epidemic took lives of more than one hundred people every day."[164] Elephants starved. Some 15,000 men raised in a desperate recruitment drive turned into "the second enemy" of thieves.[165] The provincial forces drafted earlier to help the defense began to melt away. The Phitsanulok governor returned home on the excuse of his mother's funeral. Khorat, Tak, and other governors eventually followed, along with some Ayutthaya generals. The Burmese chronicle reported, "Every day, famished Siamese arrived in the Burmese camp, driven by hunger to leave the city and seek relief from suffering in the hands of their adversaries."[166] Ekkathat tried to negotiate for peace in return for accepting tributary status, but the Burmese generals replied that their king had ordered them "to destroy Ayutthaya completely and sweep all its people and property back to Burma."[167]

The Thai chronicles portray the Ayutthaya troops as weak and disorganized, yet the defense of walls and moats remained effective against the Burmese troops and guns for several months. In early 1767, the Burmese concentrated their forces to the northeast of the city and eliminated the remaining Thai camps outside the city one by one. Once they had firm control of the northeast corner, the Burmese built a

---

[164] Masuda, "Fall of Ayutthaya," 86.

[165] Bhawan, *Dutch East India Company merchants*, 214; *RCA*, 517–18 (*BM*); Turpin, *History of the Kingdom of Siam*, 108.

[166] Phraison Salarak, "Intercourse between Burma and Siam, part II," 46; confirmed by *RCA*, 517–18 (*BM*).

[167] Sunait, *Songkhram khrao sia krung*, 75, from the Konbaung Chronicle.

bamboo bridge across the river and mined the walls. The city fell on April 7, 1767.

The victorious Burmese then completed the objectives of the campaign. In the following months, they consolidated their hold on the ports on the west coast of the upper peninsula.[168] More immediately, as the Burmese chronicle recorded, "The city was then destroyed."[169]

Among the physical, human, ideological, and intellectual resources which made a city into a capital, any which could be moved were hauled away to Burma. These included "the best and the curious" from the arsenals including 500 large cannon, stocks of gold and gems found in the royal treasury, gold melted from *wat* towers and Buddha images, "700 elephants fit for a king to ride," "seven richly gilt howdahs used by His Siamese Majesty," over 800 ladies from the inner palace, several Buddha images, "boats and barges," and "royal regalia like ruby-trimmed mirrors, and rubies worth a kingdom."[170] Books were also carted away. The Burmese chronicle mentions "the Tripitaka and treatises on astrology and medicine," and a visiting Dane was told that "the chief books on medicine had been burned or taken away by the Burmese."[171] The craftsmen who had the skills to build and embellish a great city were also rounded up and removed. The Burmese chronicle lists them:

musicians and dancers, carpenters, carvers, turners, black-smiths, gold and silver smiths, copper-smiths and braziers, masons, decorators with natural and artificial flowers, painters both in ordinary colours and illuminated with gold and bright material, workers of marquetry, lapidaries, barbers, persons skilled in incantations, charms and magic; persons skilled in the cure of the diseases of elephants and ponies; breakers and trainers of ponies; weavers and workers of gold and silver thread; and persons skilled in the culinary art.[172]

According to the *Yodayar Naing Mawgun*, a Burmese martial poem penned soon after the event, "princes and princesses and their retinues, more than 2,000 in number" were hauled away to Burma along with many nobles.[173] Ordinary people were distributed as spoils "with 300 families for each commander; 50 families for each deputy commander, royal listener, and adjutant; and two families for each of the troops."[174]

---

[168] *RCA*, 523 (*BM*).
[169] Phraison Salarak, "Intercourse between Burma and Siam, part II," 54.
[170] Myint, "*Yodayar Naing Mawgun*," 18–19; Phraison Salarak, "Intercourse between Burma and Siam, part II," 51–2.
[171] Koenig, "Journal of a voyage," 154.
[172] Phraison Salarak, "Intercourse between Burma and Siam, part II," 51.
[173] Myint, "*Yodayar Naing Mawgun*," 19.
[174] Myint, "*Yodayar Naing Mawgun*," 23; Phraison Salarak, "Intercourse between Burma and Siam, part II," 53.

King Ekkathat was either shot during the final assault, or expired in the forest soon after. Uthumphon was among those taken to Ava, probably in the robe.

Any of the critical urban resources that could not be removed were destroyed. The Burmese chronicles state that the troops starting setting fires as soon as they breached the walls.[175] The *Yodayar Naing Mawgun* compared the scene to the end of a Buddhist era, when seven suns rise and incinerate the world:

the palace, buildings with tiered roofs, and even brick houses were inflamed by fire and overwhelmed with smoke. The moat and the river outside the town were clogged with corpses, and the water extremely loathsome with the color and smell of blood.[176]

The palaces and *wat* which distinguished the city as a royal and religious center were reduced to "heaps of ruins and ashes." A Dane who visited twelve years later found the place "a terrible spectacle," totally buried in undergrowth and inhabited by elephants and tigers.[177]

The historiography of 1767 has sought culprits to blame for the national calamity – dynastic decline, collapse of manpower organization, weakness of the nobility, or bad defense. What is striking about 1767 is how few seemed motivated to defend the city which some thought "deserves more praise than heavens high." Few provincial lords brought their forces to aid the defense. Many Siamese joined the Burmese forces. Among the many hauled away to Burma, there are no reports of people returning after the warring diminished, and no songs and poems of lament and loss. The Burmese chronicles relate that the Thai royalty and nobles were settled well in Ava according to their station. The best craftsmen found employment in the court. The painters, musicians, performers, and singers were so valued that styles of "Yodaya" painting, dance, and music became popular in their new home.[178]

Conclusion

There was no decline towards the fall. The withdrawal of the English and French from Siam after 1688 was no economic shock as their presence was shallow and short-lived. The end of Reid's age of commerce

---

[175] Sunait, "Miyanma-sayam yut," 82.

[176] Myint, "*Yodayar Naing Mawgun*," 18.

[177] Turpin, *History of the Kingdom of Siam*, 109; Koenig, "Journal of a voyage," 144.

[178] Phraison Salarak, "Intercourse between Burma and Siam, part II," 54 (note), 56; Beemer, "Southeast Asian slavery," 492; Beemer, "Creolization metaphors in the Southeast Asian context," 332–5.

had limited impact because Siam was always more tied to Asian trading networks than the European connection. The inflow of Chinese merchants and the outflow of rice to Chinese markets not only stimulated the domestic economy but launched a movement of peasant colonization of the Chaophraya Plain. A larger share of trade was outside the royal monopolies, and consisted of products grown or made in Siam. There were many signs of a society entering a period of fundamental structural change driven by rising prosperity: the old system of labor control crumbling; outbreaks of revolt; complaints about "crime" and "corruption" as people attempted to use new money to change old practices; an upsurge in creative expression in many forms; and an elite lament about society falling apart and the world being turned upside down.

The nobility became richer, more independent, and more assertive. A handful of big families had access to the rising commercial wealth, retained their prominence across generations, and strengthened their mutual links by marriage alliance. The nobles formed a market for luxury products such as fine cloth and ceramics, and also for new types of literature and visual expression. Most likely, this assertive nobility promoted the two major changes in government of this era, the increased use of written law and the movement to give Buddhism an enlarged role in society. Both were strategies to manage the growing trend of conflict and disorder that came with social change. Buddhism was also the medium for exerting pressure for a reform of kingship. Since 1605, only one royal succession had passed without a fight. The extent of bloodletting was not only highly damaging for the great families, but belied the aspirations to be an exemplary Buddhist society. The remote and ritualized kingship developed in the early seventeenth century was out-of-step with the growing openness and humanism seen in art and literature. The alternative model of kingship favored by the nobility was the king-as-*bodhisatta*, codified in the Ten Royal Virtues, and dramatized in the *jataka* tales where the *bodhisatta*-king is rewarded not only with rebirth in the heavens and eventual Buddhahood, but the acclaim of society in this world and this life.[179]

Yet the city fell, and was destroyed. The defeat of 1767 was primarily a failure of defense. War in the region was still an enterprise to acquire wealth, people, and scarce urban resources. The Burmese army was a cooperative enterprise between king, nobles, and common soldiers, all expectant of gain. Burmese sources stress that the campaign was designed to obliterate a rival capital. Prosperity had made Ayutthaya

---

[179] See especially the conclusion of the Vessantara Jataka in Appleton and Shaw, *Ten great birth stories*, vol. 2, 638.

more attractive as a prize. The Burmese could thus justify investment in a much larger army than seen over recent decades, and a more protracted campaign which neutralized Ayutthaya's key defensive asset – flooding by the annual monsoon.

Prosperity had also undermined Ayutthaya's military ability. Success in war was no longer the key determinant of wealth and status. Kings, nobles, commoners, and self-sold slaves pursued commerce. The martial values of early Ayutthaya had given way to interests in nature and humanism visible in literature, drama, and painting, and to concerns for peace, order, and morality underlying the nobility's version of Buddhism. The systems of forced labor on which the old strategy of defense were based had partially decayed. In compensation, Ayutthaya had invested in better walls and defensive artillery but these proved inadequate. There had been no development of diplomacy to manage relations with potentially threatening neighbors, and no advances in military organization. With the decline in warfare around the region in the sixteenth century, the demand for foreign mercenaries had collapsed. In Siam, the king's guard still included several exotic soldiers, especially from India, Japan, and the archipelago, but the numbers were limited. The navy was largely manned by Cham under a Cham noble, and many of the Mons who immigrated from the sixteenth century onwards found employment as soldiers. In Siam, there had been no development of a martial elite like the *kshatriya* or samurai, of martial groups like the Sikhs or Rajputs, or of a tradition of military service by aristocrats as in much of Europe. Possibly the kings were careful to prevent the growth of any such tradition. As a result, the army had lost the professionalism provided by soldiers of fortune, but had not developed any professionalism locally. According to Gervaise in the 1680s, there were "no more than six hundred regular soldiers, who serve voluntarily."[180]

In the traditional order, the ordinary person was attached to the polity through a chain of personal bonds that stretched through overseer and noble to the king. These bonds had decayed with the growth of commerce and political conflict, and had not been replaced by any substitute. In 1766–67, many in Siam's upcountry towns fell in with the Burmese attackers probably because they gauged this move would increase their own chances of surviving and possibly benefiting from the conflict. There was no ideology of belonging that overruled such calculations.

The fall of the city was due not so much to internal conflict or dynastic decline but to a failure to manage the social and political consequences of prosperity.

---

[180] Gervaise, *Natural and political history*, 95; La Loubère, *New historical relation*, 91; Muhammad Rabi, *Ship of Sulaiman*, 57.

7   To Bangkok

The city of Ayutthaya was abandoned. The Ban Phlu Luang dynasty vanished. A new polity was assembled by Taksin, a half-Chinese adventurer with no roots in Ayutthaya's political culture. Fifteen years after the fall, the remnants of the old elite regrouped, took power by coup, and created a new capital at Bangkok. Much changed in this transition. Even before the influence of the West was felt in the mid-nineteenth century, the society and politics of Siam had become very different from the Ayutthaya era. With renewed military vigor, Bangkok came to dominate a much larger territory than Ayutthaya ever had. The remnants of the old nobility, who were now the rulers, created a new kind of kingship. Their ambitions, visible in late Ayutthaya, to increase the political roles of law and Buddhism were now realized. The influence of Europeans, "Moors," and Japanese faded, while that of Chinese greatly increased through trading links and immigration on an unprecedented scale. The old systems of labor control crumbled away, paving the way for the emergence of a rice-growing peasantry.

This chapter draws on the chronicles of the era, but also on a rich secondary literature, including works written a generation ago by Wyatt, Reynolds, Gesick, Nidhi, and Akin, and a newer wave of Thai-language scholarship by Pramin, Saichol, and Chatri.

Taksin

There were only tree leaves, grass, creepers, roots, bark, flowers, and fruit for food. Many people were separated, and wandered about the villages ... Everybody joined together in bands, stealing paddy, rice, and salt. Some found food, but some did not, and became emaciated, just skin and bones. They huddled together in great suffering. Some people died, some survived.[1]

With no harvests for at least two years in the Ayutthaya region, food was scarce, but the devastation was localized to the city, its surrounding

---

[1] *Wannakam samai rattanakosin lem 3: Sangkhittiyawong*, 240.

area, and the army routes. People had been slipping away from Ayutthaya over the past three years. Other places had concentrated on protecting themselves rather than defending the capital. In Nidhi's judgment, "truly the Ayutthaya kingdom had fallen apart before the walls of Ayutthaya were destroyed."[2]

In the great regional centers – Phitsanulok, Nakhon Si Thammarat, Khorat – remnants of the old elite began to organize proto-states. In Phitsanulok, the old governor took over the other Northern Cities whose troops had been scattered by the Burmese. In Nakhon Si Thammarat, Palat Nu, probably an Ayutthaya appointee who had married into a rich local Chinese family, superseded the old governor who went to aid Ayutthaya and never returned. Nu installed his kin as governors of other towns including Phatthalung and Songkhla. In the east, Thep Phiphit, a member of the Ban Phlu Luang clan who had been banished to Sri Lanka after the succession battle of 1758, returned during the siege of Ayutthaya and amassed followers at Prachin. After the fall, he took command of Khorat with the help of the governor of neighboring Phimai. In all three of these regional centers, the emergent leader held some form of coronation, indicating his ambition.[3]

Elsewhere, leaders arose who depended less on traditional authority. In Fang (Uttaradit), a monk was acclaimed as a *phumibun*, a man of merit, and attracted supporters including the governors of the neighboring Lanna cities of Nan and Phrae. He established himself in a *wat* with a powerful relic, armed the monks, and sent his kin and acolytes to administer neighboring towns. In the east-coast ports, Chinese merchants collected followers and set themselves up as governors. Siam had fragmented into several units that Nidhi labelled as "congregations" (*chumnum*) or "natural governments" (*ratthaban thammachat*).[4]

Sin, the *phraya* of Tak, was one of several military commanders who quit the city at the start of 1767, around three months before its fall. His father was a gambling tax-farmer of Teochiu Chinese origin, while his mother may have been a Thai, a Mon, or a locally settled Chinese.[5] According to one account, because of miraculous signs at his birth, he was adopted by a senior official, met the future King Rama I when both

[2] Nidhi, *Kanmueang thai samai phrajao krung thonburi*, 24.
[3] Munro-Hay, *Nakhon Sri Thammarat*, 167–9; Nidhi, *Kanmueang thai samai phrajao krung thonburi*, 33–4, 59.
[4] Nidhi, *Kanmueang thai samai phrajao krung thonburi*, 41–9, 54–61, 152, 154.
[5] Chinese traders in Siam reported to Beijing: "Zheng Yong, who was from the Chenghai country of the Chaozhou prefecture in Guangdong Province got married to a Siamese native woman and Pi ya da [Phraya Tak] is their son. His real name is Zheng Xin." Masuda, "Fall of Ayutthaya," 88. On his possible Mon maternity, see Van Roy, "Prominent Mon lineages," 216.

were novice monks, entered government service as a page, and was subsequently appointed as *yokkrabat* in Tak.[6] This account may have been
constructed later to make his background slightly more worthy of a
Siamese king. According to other versions, he was a cart trader along
the Ping River route who won official favor, perhaps by bribery. Both
accounts agree that he became governor of Tak around 1759 after the
incumbent died and he secured the help of official patrons to lobby for
the post.[7] During the Burmese attack, he brought his local followers
down to aid Ayutthaya and gained a reputation for military skill. He left
Ayutthaya with some 500–1,000 followers including local officials and
lesser nobles from Tak, along with Chinese traders and minor officials
from Ayutthaya.[8] They made for the eastern coast, where Taksin won
the support of several leaders of the Chinese communities in the ports
by a mixture of negotiation and force. He established a headquarters at
Chanthaburi, and recruited followers among the Chinese, Khmer, and
Vietnamese of the coastal communities. A handful of Ayutthaya nobles
joined his cause, including a descendant of the Mon family of Kosa Pan
named Bunma, who had been a royal page before the city fell.[9]

While other emergent leaders were building power in the regions,
Taksin moved back to the center. A few months after the fall, he sailed
from Chanthaburi to the Chaophraya River with 5,000 men, established
an armed camp at Thonburi, site of a fort and Chinese trading settlement between Ayutthaya and the sea, and drove away the remaining
Burmese garrisons at Three Bo Trees to the north of Ayutthaya and at
Ratchaburi. Following these successes, he conducted some kind of ceremony in which he was seated on a throne. He also held a symbolic
cremation for Ekkathat who had died in the fall, offered protection to
remaining members of the Ban Phlu Luang clan, issued titles to his followers in the style of a ruler, called in the governors of the inner cities to
swear allegiance, and in August 1768 sent a mission to China to request
recognition as king, but the Chinese court prevaricated because there
were other claimants.[10]

The Burmese were distracted by a Chinese invasion southwards
through the Shan states. For eight years they mounted nothing more
than limited raids into the Northern Cities. Taksin used this opportunity to overwhelm the provincial centers competing for power. He

---

[6] Buntuean and Sujit, *Aphinihan banphaburut.*
[7] Nidhi, *Kanmueang thai samai phrajao krung thonburi*, 61–103; Pramin, *Phrajao tak*, 24–44.
[8] Nidhi, *Kanmueang thai samai phrajao krung thonburi*, 272–319.
[9] Nidhi, *Kanmueang thai samai phrajao krung thonburi*, 298–9.
[10] Nidhi, *Kanmueang thai samai phrajao krung thonburi*, 170, 205; Masuda, "Fall of
    Ayutthaya," 95–7.

enforced conscription, arranged food imports, imposed trade monopolies to raise revenue, and sent envoys to the Danes in India to buy weapons against barter. He moved first against the key strategic center of Phitsanulok, but was defeated. Shortly after, the Phitsanulok governor died of a coughing fit, and the Fang monk extended his influence over the area. The old nobles who had supported the governor of Phitsanulok gave this monk no support, and in 1770 Taksin took Phitsanulok easily. At Khorat, he defeated the Phimai governor, brought Thep Phiphit to Thonburi, and executed him when he attracted too many supporters. In 1769, he led an army down the peninsula which defeated Palat Nu of Nakhon Si Thammarat, hauled him away to Thonburi, and installed his own nephew instead. The final resistance came from Ha Tien (Banteay Mas) where the Cantonese merchant-ruler Mo Thien Tu (son of Mac Cuu) saw the opportunity of this disorderly period to extend his influence both westwards along the coast into Siam, and northwards into Cambodia. Mo Thien Tu made a bid to capture Taksin, sent a naval force to the Chaophraya when Taksin was in the south, and tried to foment a restorationist revolt with a Ban Phlu Luang prince who had fled to his protection. In 1771, Taksin mounted a large land and sea attack which put Mo Thien Tu to flight.[11]

All rivals had disappeared. Relations with China became warmer.[12] An epic poem composed in 1771 celebrated Taksin's success in bringing "all 104 cities of the Ayutthaya realm, from south and north" under his sway.[13] He issued a proclamation:

I swear I do not desire the kingship for worldly reasons. I desire only to allow all creatures to live in tranquility and harmony, practicing the Dhamma and seeking enlightenment. If anyone is more fitted than I to assume this royal responsibility, I will give the crown to him and seek the solitary ascetic life.[14]

Taksin's Thonburi realm in 1771 was very different from late Ayutthaya, more like a throwback almost two centuries. Taksin was a ruler on horseback, leading armies for the first time since the Naresuan era, and visible to the people in mundane activities like directing construction of fortifications, fighting fires, and planting rice. He addressed the ordinary people through proclamations using the vocabulary of *pho-luk*, father and son, and lectured his high officials like a teacher with his pupils,

[11] Nidhi, *Kanmueang thai samai phrajao krung thonburi*, 201–11; Chen, "Mac Thien Tu and Phraya Taksin"; Sakurai and Kitagawa, "Ha Tien."
[12] Masuda, "Fall of Ayutthaya," 98. The Qianlong Emperor agreed to recognize Taksin only in 1781, and the mission had not returned before Taksin was overthrown.
[13] Nai Suan, "Khlong yo phrakiat," stanza 52.
[14] Gesick, "Rise and fall of King Taksin," 97; Nidhi, *Kanmueang thai samai phrajao krung thonburi*, 246.

shedding the ritualism of Ayutthaya royal style. Also like Naresuan, he acquired a reputation for using violence, not just in battle, but to command everyday obedience. Koenig, who visited in 1779, reported: "His sons ... his nearest relatives, even his generals and ministers, he has had at some time or the other publicly punished with rotan sticks, and as the Siamese seldom wear their jackets one can see that all the grandees have had their backs torn with the rotan whips."[15]

Taksin made little attempt to endow Thonburi with the attributes of a capital in the Ayutthaya style. He gave the place no resplendent name linking it to the history of Ayutthaya. He adopted two consorts from the Ban Phlu Luang family, including a daughter of Thep Phiphit, but executed both when they were found having sexual relations with westerners, and constructed no other connection to the prior dynasty.[16] He built a residence with a Chinese look and called it a *tamnak* (residence) rather than a *wang* (palace). He concentrated construction activity on building defensive moats and walls, prominent on a map of Thonburi drawn by a Burmese spy.[17] He built no new royal *wat* but adopted a modest *wat* beside the palace site, possibly renamed at this time as Wat Jaeng, temple of the dawn, and added only a pavilion to accommodate the Emerald Buddha and Phrabang images brought from Vientiane and Luang Phrabang, respectively.[18]

The provincial administration reverted to early Ayutthaya's style of a loose association of independent city-states, ruled by local lords tied by personal ties to the king. At Nakhon Si Thammarat, Taksin soon withdrew his nephew and restored Palat Nu, who controlled the middle peninsula towns through his kin and personal connections. In the Northern Cities, he installed early followers who had distinguished themselves in warfare, and allowed many of them to develop into local dynasties.[19]

Immediately after 1767, most survivors of the old Ayutthaya nobility had fled away or joined up with pretenders from the old elite like the governor of Phitsanulok or Thep Phiphit, rather than supporting a half-Chinese adventurer. After Taksin established himself on the Chaophraya River, defeated the Burmese garrisons, eliminated his rivals, and adopted some vocabulary and practice of kingship, more nobles trickled back and offered their allegiance, but they did not return to their old duties and

[15] Koenig, "Journal of a voyage," 164. "Rotan" is rattan, cane.
[16] *Phraratcha phongsawadan chabap phraratchahatthalekha*, vol. 2, 171; Terwiel, *Thailand's political history*, 64.
[17] A copy of the map hangs in the museum at Taksin's Thonburi palace.
[18] Chatri, *Khati sanyalak*, 30–4.
[19] Nidhi, *Kanmueang thai samai phrajao krung thonburi*, 364–402; Gesick, "Kingship and political integration," 75–83.

privileges. The highest titles and the command of manpower had already been entrusted to Taksin's early personal supporters, especially those stationed in the Northern Cities. Only a handful of old nobles gained high rank, and then mostly because of their knowledge of protocol and ritual.[20]

At first, Taksin's success in driving out the Burmese and reducing hardship were enough to command respect, but as conditions improved through the 1770s, some nobles became critical of the "abnormality" of Taksin's rule. He had not recreated a proper capital. He had not restored the roles and privileges of the old nobles. In particular, he had dramatically changed the concept of a king and the king's relationship with the *sangha*.

Taksin believed that he qualified to be king because of his inherent merit, in the same way that the Fang cleric and rebels like Bun Khwang were seen by their supporters as *phumibun*, men of merit. Unlike the model of a *bodhisatta* exemplified by Borommakot, Taksin adopted the forest-monk-like route of copying the Buddha's own life practice. Already by 1771, he claimed to have special ability in meditation and bodily control. He followed the traditional royal role of religious patron – restoring damaged temples, collecting and copying texts to replace those lost in the troubles, bringing great sacred objects to embellish the capital, and commissioning a magnificent illustrated manuscript of the Three Worlds cosmology, restating that Siam was the center of the Buddhist world.[21] But he went beyond the traditional role of patron by presuming to be the teacher and effective head of the *sangha*. After defeating the Fang cleric in 1770, he personally presided over the purification of the local *sangha*, submitting some monks to trial by ordeal, and executing those who failed. He conducted a similar exercise in Thonburi, and dispatched Thonburi monks to rectify practice in other provincial areas. He summoned senior monks for discussion and lectured them like a teacher. He ordered monks to learn Pali in order to read the texts, and banned teaching using folk tales. He proclaimed a royal edict threatening to punish the guardian spirits of the city with exile if "they had no intent to help the kingdom, and consorted with evil spirits to do harm to the people, monks, and Brahmans." In 1773, he imposed a new monastic disciplinary code by royal edict, infringing on the *sangha*'s independence.[22]

In 1773, western missionaries reported that Taksin was convinced he was "no longer human." In 1779 according to Koenig, he had discovered

---

[20] Nidhi, *Kanmueang thai samai phrajao krung thonburi*, 273–4, 313–19.

[21] *Samutphap traiphum chabap krung si ayutthaya–chabap krung thonburi lem 1.*

[22] Nidhi, *Kanmueang thai samai phrajao krung thonburi*, 254–72, quote on 266; Lingat, "La double crise," 409–10; Gesick, "Rise and fall of King Taksin," 99–100.

that his body had attributes characterizing the body of the Buddha, he expected his blood to turn white, like the gods, and "with these capacities he believes he will succeed in flying."[23] He consulted senior clerics on whether a human could become a *sotapanna*, a "stream winner," who had entered the four-stage path to Buddhahood. When some denied the possibility, he had them disrobed and punished. Around 1779, he ordered monks to pay him the formal respect due to a superior or teacher, reversing the normal relations between monk and king. Five hundred monks who refused to comply were flogged, deprived of their monastic ranks, and forced into menial labor. The issue split the *sangha* and provoked plans among the old nobility to end Taksin's "abnormal" reign.

A massive Burmese attack had already begun to change the balance of power. In 1775, the Burmese general Asewunki led an army of 30,000 which devastated the Northern Cities. Although Asewunki was recalled because of internal affairs, and no follow-up attack came, the armies commanded by Taksin's closest followers were defeated and dispersed. Taksin (again in the style of Naresuan) swept the remnants down to reinforce the defenses of Thonburi. These events changed the balance of military power in Taksin's Siam. Troops were transferred from the control of Taksin's old allies in the Northern Cities, to the generals in Thonburi, especially to two brothers, Bunma and Thongduang.

Bunma had been the only member of an old Ayutthaya noble family to join Taksin in Chanthaburi. Subsequently he became Taksin's most experienced and effective general, leading armies into the Lanna, Lao, and Khmer regions. Sometime after Taksin was well-established in Thonburi, Bunma introduced his older brother, Thongduang, who had not been in central Ayutthaya service but held a post in Ratchaburi where he had married into the leading family. Thongduang replicated his brother's success as a military commander and his ascent up the ladder of promotion, becoming Chaophraya Chakri in the late 1770s.

Thongduang-Chakri emerged as leader of the *phu di kao*, the old nobles, who were increasingly unsettled by Taksin's "abnormal" practices. Rather than attempting to stem Thongduang's growing influence, Taksin accepted Thongduang's daughter as a major wife, and may have embellished Thongduang's titles after she produced a son. But he also may have had Thongduang flogged for a failure on the battlefield, as happened to many nobles, and perhaps flogged his wife for some offence also.[24] After the split within the *sangha* in 1779–80, the group around Chakri became convinced that Taksin had to be removed, and plans were laid for a coup.

---

[23] Koenig, "Journal of a voyage," 164–5.
[24] Pramin, *Chamlae phaen yuet krung thonburi*, 151.

In 1781, Bunma and Thongduang led an army to Cambodia. As the army returned towards Thonburi, Thongduang's nephew, who was governor of Khorat, quietly moved to Thonburi to prepare the coup. The situation was complicated when another group, headed by a former officer of Taksin, Phraya San, attacked Thonburi and took control within one night. Taksin offered no resistance, surrendering to the rebels with the words, "My store of merit has run out. I do not want difficulties for the *phrai*." He begged only for his life, and entered Wat Jaeng as a monk. Twenty-eight days after Phraya San's coup, Chaophraya Chakri arrived with the army, and convened a court which ruled: "The king acted improperly and unjustly, which has caused great pain for the kingdom. It is unavoidable that he be executed."[25] Around 150 other people were killed including Phraya San and several of Taksin's male relatives but some survived, including the son born to Thongduang's daughter. Messages sent to tributaries explained that "the gods destined the old king to act in contravention of ancient royal tradition, resulting in terrible death and destruction."[26]

In the crisis of the 1767 defeat, Taksin had appeared from outside the old ruling elite, and defeated more established claimants. His rule harked back to Naresuan's militant style and to the politics of personal loyalty between big and little lords, allowing little place for the *khun nang* nobles who had grown so powerful over the previous century, and offending against their conception of proper kingly conduct. Ultimately, a small network of families within the old elite engineered a coup to restore their influence. But the sack of 1767 was such a break that Siam was not so much restored as reinvented at Bangkok.

Bangkok

In April 1782, Thongduang-Chakri was anointed as king and moved the capital across the river to Bangkok. He inserted "Ayutthaya" in the name of the new capital, put "Ramathibodi," the name of the Ayutthaya founder, at the head of his own title, and delayed his full installation as king for three years until he was sure the ceremony would follow the model of Borommakot. But these concessions to tradition were limited. Bangkok was more of a new city and era than a restoration of Ayutthaya. Many of the old elite had been swept away to Burma, and been replaced by others who rose from nowhere.[27] After the warfare subsided, the

---

[25] *Phraratchaphongsawadan chabap phraratchahatthalekha*, vol. 2, 230.
[26] Nidhi, *Kanmueang thai samai phrajao krung thonburi*, 533–4, 574–6; Pramin, *Chamlae phaen yuet krung thonburi*, 137–45.
[27] See examples in Sng and Pimpraphai, *History of the Thai-Chinese*, 115–17, and Van Roy, "Prominent Mon lineages."

new capital had an imperial reach far broader than Ayutthaya had ever enjoyed. When trade revived, Bangkok was more closely linked to China than Ayutthaya had ever been. The new king was leader of a nobility that had been pressing to change kingship and the social order for the past century, and was now in a position to achieve those aims.

War and Trade

Over almost half a century of warring, Siam reverted to many practices of the earlier age of warfare. Conscription was strictly enforced. *Phrai* were tattooed to make evasion more difficult. Military leaders again won high office. Martial poetry returned to fashion.[28] With these resources, Bangkok not only drove back the Burmese, but also emboxed a new outer ring of tributary states in the south, north, and east. The chronicler of the Bangkok first reign boasted: "His [Rama I's] kingdom was far more extensive than that of the former Kings of Ayutthaya."[29] From these newly conquered regions, the Siamese armies swept up people to repopulate the Chaophraya Plain. Taksin's armies captured many thousands of Lanna Yuan, Lao Wiang, Lao Phuan, Black Tai, and Khmer. The southern expeditions brought back several thousand Malays. Possibly 30,000–40,000 Mons voluntarily migrated to Siam. In the early 1800s, the Bangkok and Lanna troops went further north to seize Khoen, Lue, and Shan. The canals, walls, palaces, and temples of the new capital were built with the labor of these war captives. A new place was built by a new population.

Only in the west, did the Siamese armies fail. Two attempts to take Tavoy and reestablish control of the portage were thwarted by the Burmese. As a result, even more than in late Ayutthaya, Bangkok's trade was focused on China. Taksin revived the junk trade, and encouraged Chinese merchants to settle. The new capital at Bangkok was on the site of an established Chinese trading community. By the time Europeans visited the new capital in the 1820s, they found the Chaophraya River at Bangkok crammed with junks, and estimated that the Chinese formed the majority of the city population, which may have reflected their prominence if not their true proportion. By the 1820s, some 7,000 more Chinese were arriving each year, and the numbers increased in later decades.

---

[28] *Talaeng phai,* "Defeat of the Mon," celebrating Naresuan's victories over Pegu, was begun in the first reign. The title and other aspects were modeled on the fifteenth-century epic, *Yuan phai.* The lionization of Naresuan began here.

[29] Flood and Flood, *Dynastic chronicle Bangkok era,* 281.

King and Nobility

The new king had no association with the Ban Phlu Luang dynasty by blood or marriage. He made no attempt to gain legitimacy by finding a marriage partner of royal descent. His regnal name, Phutthayotfa Chulalok, had no trace of Ayutthaya conventions. He became king as the acknowledged leader of the old nobility, the *phu di kao* or *khaluang doem* (former royal servants).

His family ancestry traced back to a Mon, possibly named Phraya Kiat, who came from Pegu with Naresuan in 1584, may have married a daughter of the future King Ekathotsarot,[30] and sired Kosa Pan and Kosa Lek, two of the most prominent nobles of the Narai era. The family remained powerful in the Phrakhlang ministry in the eighteenth century, and intermarried with all three of the other prominent noble families of that era (Bunnag, Ong, and Siriwatthana). As described by King Mongkut, Thongduang's father came to Ayutthaya "where he was introduced to the royal service, and became married with a beautiful daughter of a Chinese richest family at Chinese compound or situation within wall of city and in south-eastern corner of Ayudia."[31] The future king was appointed as *yokkrabat* in Ratchaburi, and married a daughter from the powerful local Bangchang lineage. His personal aide, Bunnag, who hailed from the Persian lineage descended from Sheikh Ahmed Qomi, married a younger sister of his wife. Thongduang was thus connected to all the great noble families, to the mercantile Chinese, and to the local nobility in a key city of the inner kingdom. From the mid-1770s when he and his younger brother became Taksin's leading generals, many old officials presented (*fak tua*) themselves or their sons to him as retainers, and offered their daughters as consorts. One of his sisters married into a Chinese family with Phrakhlang connections, and another married a head of the palace guard.[32] The sinews of the new Siam were this extraordinary web of kin and marital connections.

The upper nobility now realized its desire for security. A small number of families with personal connections to the king dominated the key ministries at the capital. In the provinces, many old-style local lords who had emerged during the time of troubles were able to make the governorship virtually hereditary for almost a century. In effect, these families created hereditary fiefdoms within the administration. The

---

[30] Van Roy, "Prominent Mon lineages," 217.

[31] Bowring, *Kingdom and people of Siam*, vol. 1, 65–6; Mongkut, "Phraratcha niphon."

[32] Wyatt, "Family politics in seventeenth- and eighteenth-century Siam," 102–3; Wyatt, "The 'subtle revolution' of King Rama I," 144; Nidhi, *Kanmueang thai samai phrajao krung thonburi*, 319–36.

extension of central control achieved since the seventeenth century was reversed, and the fragmentation remained until the reforms of King Chulalongkorn.

As foreign trade expanded, nobles took a larger role than ever before.[33] The contest between king and nobility over the control of *phrai* labor resumed, and once the warfare receded, the trend ran in favor of the nobility.[34] Death duties and accusations of corruption were no longer used to dissipate wealth. The great households prospered. They established grand residences, built and patronized temples, took many wives to expand their lineages, and appropriated dress and customs once reserved for royalty. The king was reduced to *primus inter pares*. The long string of bloody succession disputes tailed away. At the death of the king, the son of Taksin with his daughter was accused of revolt, and executed with some forty others, but the purge was limited to his kin or retainers, and did not spread into the nobility.[35] It was also the last such killing. Although subsequent successions were often contested and tense, senior nobles helped to negotiate the outcome without recourse to battles that scythed through their families. The nobles had created a state which allowed themselves to survive and prosper.

To aid the movement of armies during the era of renewed warfare, canals were cut across the lower Chaophraya Plain to both east and west. By the 1820s, both immigrant Chinese and refugees from *phrai* forced labor had begun to settle along these waterways. The Chinese brought expertise in cultivating vegetables to supply the city, and planting sugar, tobacco, and pepper which enjoyed good demand in the coasting trade around Southeast Asia. By the 1830s, the kings had begun to shift the tax base away from foreign trade and forest produce to these new agricultural products. Sugar mills appeared in towns on the lower reaches of the rivers. Settlement crept northwards across the plain, planting mainly paddy. By mid-century, Siam was exporting 12 million tonnes of sugar and 15 million tonnes of rice. In the next decade, rice exports quadrupled.[36] The movement of people to this agricultural frontier gradually undermined the *phrai* system, and converted Siam from the urban society of the Ayutthaya era into a classic agrarian economy and peasant society.

---

[33] Saichol, *Phutthasasana*, 93–4; Nidhi, *Pen and sail*, 57–77.

[34] Akin, *Organization of Thai society*, ch. 7.

[35] There was no attempt to eradicate Taksin's lineage, as had happened to ousted kings in the past. At least five sons remained, and had official careers. Pramin, *Kabot jaofa men*, 150–3, 160–2.

[36] Pasuk and Baker, *Thailand: economy and politics*, 15–16.

Buddhism, Law, and Kingship

In the late Ayutthaya era, there had been a movement within the nobility to give Buddhism a larger role in society. The new king in Bangkok made this a priority. Beginning in the first months of the reign, he passed ten decrees on the monkhood, effectively the first legislation on this topic. While these laws addressed problems raised by Taksin's conduct, their larger purpose was to reform the monkhood for a new social purpose. The preamble of the first law stated the king's claim to be a *bodhisatta*, working for the moral betterment of his people:

The king has resolved himself to achieve the omniscience of enlightenment. Endowed with the wisdom of great compassion he constantly keeps in mind his duty to aid all the world's living creatures.[37]

The first decree noted how few monks studied the scriptures, and how they spiced their sermons with humor, singing, poetry, the tales of Phra Malai visiting heaven and hell, and promises to meet the future Buddha, Phra Metteyya. These activities were banned, and monks were ordered to preach from the Tipitaka, and to tell the Great Jataka story of Phra Vessantara. The sixth decree on monastic discipline chastised monks for "just feeding themselves like cattle or buffalo, not improving their minds … having no fear of hell, only fear of perils in the present."[38] It forbade monks from working to make money, wandering around markets, claiming to have supernatural powers, and selling their services as masseurs, doctors, and astrologers. The last of the decrees confirmed the authority of the patriarch on matters of discipline and doctrine.[39]

So that people should not practice Buddhism ritualistically but "understand the Thai meaning of each precept," the king founded a school to re-educate monks, and had several Pali texts translated into Thai.[40] Edicts banned cock-fighting and other "sinful" pursuits because, as the law's preamble explained, "the king is intent on promoting the progress of Buddhism, both teaching and practice, for the happiness and well-being of all beings in the world."[41] Officials were ordered to live according to a moral code modeled on monastic discipline.

The project to identify Siam as the center of the Buddhist world was again taken up. The king commissioned a new version of the Three

---

[37] Sangha laws 6, *Kotmai tra sam duang*, vol. 4, 164; translation from Jory, *Thailand's theory of monarchy*, 88.
[38] Sangha laws 6, *Kotmai tra sam duang*, vol. 4, 164–9, 193–4.
[39] Wyatt, "The 'subtle revolution' of King Rama I," 146–50; Reynolds, "Buddhist monkhood," 38–42; Saichol, *Phutthasasana*, 102–7.
[40] Saichol, *Phutthasasana*, 118–27.
[41] Sangha laws, preamble, *Kotmai tra sam duang*, vol. 4, 164–5.

Worlds cosmology, known as the *Trailokwinitchai*. In its description of the geography of the human world, this text introduced the idea of the *sisa phaendin*, the Head Land, as both the place where the Buddha achieved enlightenment under the *bodhi* tree, and the place where a lotus appeared at the beginning of each era predicting the number of Buddhas by its petals. In new versions of the illustrated *Traiphum* manuscripts produced in this era, the maps which connected the sacred geography through to the real geography of Southeast Asia ended with an illustration of the Head Land. This geography was mapped onto the design of several *wat* in this era, especially Wat Phra Chetuphon (Wat Pho), where the names of Siam's cities were inscribed in a frieze around the ordination hall, replicating the geography of the Jambu Continent in the illustrated manuscripts. This design made Bangkok and Wat Pho the center of the Buddhist world.[42] The king embellished the capital with many new *wat* and had 1,248 Buddha images brought from Ayutthaya and other cities, including the Phra Si Sakyamuni from the ruins of Wat Mahathat in Sukhothai.[43] The Emerald Buddha, brought from Lanxang (Vientiane) by the future king in 1779, was installed as Palladium of the realm in a *wat* beside the palace.

In 1788, the king summoned a council to undertake a complete revision of the Tipitaka, the "Three Baskets" of the canonical Buddhist scriptures. After the work was completed in 1789, the monk-historian Phra Phonnarat compiled a "Chronicle of Buddhist Councils" (*Sangitiyavamsa*) which appended this council as ninth in the sequence of Buddhist Councils, beginning with the first after the Buddha's death. The chronicle included a summary history of Buddhism, followed by a history of Siam, listing each king of the Ayutthaya era and relating their works in support of religion, deftly merging Siam into the history of the religion.[44] In this construction, the king became part of a lineage that stretched back through the Buddha, his many previous lives as a *bodhisatta*, and many former Buddhas, to the *mahasommuta*, the "king by general consent" chosen spontaneously by the people to overcome the violence and wrongdoing that arose at the dawn of human society (see p. 108). Among his titles, the king was *mahasomuttiwong*, meaning in the lineage of this original "king by general consent." In 1797 he had the *Mahavamsa*, the Lankan chronicle which expressed this theory, translated into Thai. Phra Phonnarat's chronicle described the king and his

---

[42] Chatri, "Symbolism in the design of Wat Phra Chetuphon," 3–20.
[43] Jory, *Thailand's theory of monarchy*, ch. 3; Wyatt, "The 'subtle revolution' of King Rama I," 151–2; Woodward, *Sacred sculpture*, 157.
[44] *Wannakam samai rattanakosin lem 3: Sangkhittiyawong*; Reynolds, "Religious historical writing"; Coedès, "Une recension Pālie des annales d'Ayutha."

brother as "*bodhisattas*, future Buddhas, possessing great accumulated merit, men of great devotion and wisdom, desirous only of enlightenment."[45] In 1807, the king sponsored a public chanting of the *Mahachat*, complete with a massive display of almsgiving, associating himself with Phra Vessantara, the most prominent *bodhisatta* in Thai tradition.[46]

The king also extended the emphasis on law from late Ayutthaya. In the early years of the reign, besides the laws on the monkhood, he passed decrees on the control of people, legal procedure, behavior of officials, robbery, adultery, illegal distilling, and cock-fighting.[47] After the completion of the Tipitaka, he formed another commission to review all the law texts that had survived 1767. The preface to the resulting collection, known as the Three Seals Code, explained:

A king who rules the realm depends on the ancient laws, the codes of written law legislated by previous kings in order that judges may decide on all cases for the populace with justice ... Hence the king graciously commanded that subjects with knowledge be assigned to cleanse (*chamra*) the royal decrees and laws in the palace library ... and adjust any aberrations to accord with justice, in keeping with the king's gracious intent to be of benefit to kings who reign over the realm in future.[48]

The elite saw Buddhism and law as means to manage a new society in which market relations were replacing patronage relations, and old social institutions were in decay. The Buddhism which the elite fostered in this era stressed the potential for each individual eventually to achieve *nibbana* by living correctly and thus accumulating merit. It discouraged reliance on ritualism and opposed the belief in supernatural power which had been a theme in the many revolts since 1688, as well as being part of Taksin's "abnormality." The king was constrained to rule well, both by serving as the patron and protector of the region and monkhood, and by providing the security and opportunity for each subject to pursue the path of self-improvement. The claim to be a center of the Buddhist world was used to justify Siam's domination over its newly acquired territories.[49]

Yet the king's aristocratic approach to Buddhism ignored the reasons why supernaturalism, the tales of Phra Malai, and the promise of Phra Metteyya had such a prominence in popular Buddhism. His attempts to reform the monkhood and impose high standards of conduct had only a limited effect. Monks continued to promise protection against dangers

[45] *Wannakam samai rattanakosin lem 3: Sangkhittiyawong*, 248.
[46] Jory, *Thailand's theory of monarchy*, 81.
[47] New royal decrees, *Kotmai tra sam duang*, vol. 5, 193–372.
[48] *Kotmai tra sam duang*, vol. 1, 4–5.
[49] Gesick, "Kingship and political integration," 123.

and uncertainties, to provide entertainment at funerals, and to flaunt disciplinary rules. Texts on Phra Malai continued to be hugely popular in the early nineteenth century.[50] Cockfighting and gambling were not suppressed. Under subsequent reigns, the moral intensity relaxed, but the Buddhist underpinning of kingship and the close relationship between crown and *sangha* endured.

Conclusion

Three groups of people created the new Siam with its capital at Bangkok. First were the nobles that survived 1767, and especially the great households that clustered around the new king or came to dominate the provincial centers. They now became secure, wealthy, and powerful. They created a state in which power was fragmented among semi-independent cities and ministries, and in which law and Buddhism were deployed to manage the stresses of social change.

Second were the immigrant Chinese, whose numbers rose steadily throughout the nineteenth century. They dominated the new capital, and gradually fanned out through urban Siam, bringing new skills, technology, and entrepreneurial flair. Some gilded families worked for the court as shippers, traders, and tax-farmers, and gradually intermarried with royal and noble lineages to create a new segment of the aristocracy.

Third were the former *phrai* and slaves who came loose as the management of manpower crumbled. Prodded by export demand, they first planted sugarcane on the uplands around the Chaophraya Plain, but by mid-century had turned to the cultivation of paddy. They spread out from the cities along the rivers and newly-dug canals, gradually pushing back the line of forest, and creating a new society of agricultural villages.[51]

Amid such sweeping social changes, the old city of Ayutthaya was forgotten. The destruction continued beyond 1767. To raise revenue in the immediate aftermath, concessions were sold to allow people to search for loot in the ruins. After 1782, bricks were ferried downriver to build the new capital at Bangkok. For over a century, the physical city was neglected, and its history ignored.

In 1895, after a new elite in a new colonial era had begun to think about Siam's past, a twenty-five-year-old Mahatthai official, who had been a top student and had caught the eye of Prince Damrong, was

---

[50] Brereton, *Thai tellings of Phra Malai.*
[51] Pasuk and Baker, *Thailand: economy and politics*, ch. 1.

posted to Ayutthaya.[52] Phon Dechakupt, usually known by his later title of Phraya Boranratchathanin, recorded what he found:

The Ayutthaya palace, after the bricks from the buildings, forts, and walls had been used to build the capital of Bangkok, was abandoned and not looked after in any way. Inside the palace there were just mounds of broken bricks, and shards of plaster, overgrown with trees. Later people came to clear the trees and plant custard apple, limes, tamarind, and bael fruit, and they considered themselves owners of the plots.[53]

He began to clear the undergrowth, and identify sites mentioned in the chronicles and old maps. In 1907, he headed the organization of an event to celebrate King Chulalongkorn becoming the longest reigning king of Siam. In the ruins of the Ayutthaya palace, the king gave a speech on the importance of history, and on the formation of a new Antiquarian Society to compile a history of Siam:

I'd like to persuade all of you ... that we will collect the historical materials of the country of Siam for every city, every race, every dynasty, and every era to compile a history of Siam over the past thousand years. This history must start from the capital sometimes known as Hang Hang or Chang[54] which was the original set-tlement of the Thai race, down through Chiang Saen, Chiang Rai, Chiang Mai, Sawankhalok, Sokkhothai [Sukhothai], old Ayutthaya, new Ayutthaya, along with Lavo-Lopburi, Nakhon Chaisi, Nakhon Si Thammarat, and cities which ruled other cities such as Kamphaeng Phet, Chainat, Phitsanulok, Muang San, Suphan, Kanchanaburi, and Phetchaburi, which were important at some era in the past, and are now joined together as united Siam.

The idea is not to create a history of Siam quickly. I hope that we will help one another to collect the historical evidence and help one another to appraise the material and clarify what is not yet clear through each applying his wisdom and intelligence ... When there is enough material to print as a book then print it as a contribution to the history of Siam ... The sources should be indicated so others can see them and follow them up. If someone else reinterprets the mate-rial or has better sources, the author should not be ashamed, because he studied the material according to the knowledge and opinion of the time. If someone comes up with a better interpretation and more accurate reasoning, we should happily appreciate the major benefit of having a clearer and more reliable history of Siam.[55]

[52] Wansiri and Pridi, *Krung kao lao rueang*, 4–10.
[53] Boranratchathanin, *Athibai phaen thi*, 76, fn. 82.
[54] Unidentified.
[55] Baker, "Antiquarian Society of Siam," 97–8, translation slightly modified.

Appendix: List of Kings

This table compares the list of Ayutthayan kings in David Wyatt's *Thailand: A short history* with the details available from the Luang Prasoet Chronicle, the Van Vliet Chronicle, and *Sangkitiyavamsa*. For a discussion, see Vickery, "Review article: Jeremias van Vliet."

Wyatt	Luang Prasoet				Van Vliet		Sangkitiyavamsa	
King	dates (CE)	King	Accession (CS)	reign in years	King	reign in years	King	reign in years
Ramathibodi	1351–1369	Ramathibodi	712	20	Ramathibodi	19	Ramathibodi	19
Ramesuan	1369–1370	Ramesuan	731		Ramesuan	3	Ramesuan	3
Borommaracha I	1370–1388	Borommaracha	732	.	Khunluang Pha-ngua	18	Khun Lumphangua	18
Thong Chan	1388	Thong Lan	750	7d	Thong Chan	7d	Suwannajanthola	7d
Ramesuan (return)	1388–95	Ramesuan (return)	750		Ramesuan (return)	6	Ramesuan	9
Ramaracha	1395–1409	Phaya Ram	757		Phra Ram	3	(no name)	3
Intharacha	1409–1424	Intharacha	771		Nakhon In	20	Nakhon In	20
Borommaracha II	1424–1448	Borommaracha	786		Borommaracha thibodi	20	Boromma Racha	20
Borommatrailokanat	1463–1488	Borommatrailokanat	810		Borommatrailokanat	20	Boromma Trailokanat	20
Borommatrailokanat (Phitsanulok)	1488–1491	Borommatrailokanat (Phitsanulok)	825–850					
Borommaracha III (Ayutthaya)	1491–1529	Borommaracha III (Ayutthaya)	825–853					
Borommaracha III								
Intharacha II	1488–1491				Intharacha	37	Intharacha	37
Ramathibodi II	1491–1529	Ramathibodi	853		Ramathibodi	38	Ramathibodi	38
Borommaracha IV	1529–1533	No Phuttangkun	891		No Phuttangkun	5	Phuttangkun	5
Ratsada	1533–1534	son of above	895		Woraratsadathirat	5m	Atthathirat Kuman	5m
Chairacha	1534–1547	Chairacha	896		Chaiyaracha	13	Chaiyaracha	13
Yot Fa	1547–June 1548	Yot Fa	908		Yot Chao	3	Yotta	3
Khun Worawongsa	Jun–Jul 1548	Khun Chinnarat	910	42d	Chinnarat	40d	Chinnaracha	
Chakkraphat	1548–1569	Thianracha Maha Chakkraphat	910		Thianracha	16	Theharacha	16

Mahin	Jan–Aug 1569	Mahin	930	Mahin	7	Maha Mahin	6
Maha Thammaracha	1569–1590	Maha Thammaracha	931	Maha Thammaracha	22	Maha Thammaracha	22
Naresuan	1590–1605	Naresuan	952	Naret Rachathirat	20	Naritsaracha	19
Ekathotsarot	1608–1610/11	[Luang Prasoet chronicle ends]		Ramesuan	6	Ramesuan	7
(Si Saowaphak)	1610–1611?						
Song Tham (Intharacha)	1610/11–1628			Intharacha	19	Intharacha	19
Chettha	Dec 1628–Aug 1629			Chettharacha	8m	Chettharacha	
Athittayawong	Aug–Sep 1629			Athit Surawong	38d	Athittawong	31d
Prasat Thong	1629–1656			Si Thammarachathirat		Si Suthammaracha	18
Narai	1656–1688					Thian	1
Phra Phetracha	1688–1703					Suwanna Prasat	15
Sua (Sorasak)	1703–1709					Narai	24
Phumintharacha (Thaisa)	1709–1733					Phitcharacha	10
						Mahalona	7
						Mahajora	26
Borommakot	1733–1758					Mahakala (Rachathiracha Ramathibodi)	27
Uthumphon	1758					Uthumphon Buppha	2m
Suriyamarin (Ekkathat)	1758–1767					(no name given)	8

Based on Wyatt, *Thailand*, 312–3; Vickery, "Review article: Jeremias van Vliet," 211–3; *RCA*; *Wannakam samai rattanakosin lem 3: Sangkhittiyawong*, 217–38; Coedès, "Une recension Pālie," 31.

d = days; m = months

Ayutthaya kings in Chinese records of tribute missions

Chinese	Probable Thai	Dates of missions	Possible king in chronicles	Relationship to predecessor
Can-lie Zhao Pi-ya	Somdet Chaophraya	1371 1372	Ramesuan	
Can-lie Bao Pi-ya Si-li Duo-luo-lu	Somdet Pu Phraya Sisindara (Si Dvaravati)	1373 1374 1377 1379 1384 1393	Borommaracha I (Phangua)	Paternal uncle, succeeded because king "had become incompetent"
Zhao Lu-qun Ying-duo- luo-di-la	Chao Nakhon Intharathirat	1396 1398 1403 1404 1406 1408 1409 1410 1411 1413	Intharacha (Nakhon In)	Son. Death of father reported in 1396, but appears with kingly title only in 1403
San-lai Bo-mo-la-zhi-di-lai	Somdet Boromma Rachathirat	1416 1419 1420 1421 1422 1424 1426 1427 1428	Borommaracha II (Samphraya)	Son
Xi-li Ma-ha-lai	Si Maharat	1433 1438		No details
Gu-rong You-ti-xia	Krung Ayutthaya	1444		No details
Si-li Bo-luo-ma-na-re-zhi-la	Si Boromma Rachathirat	1446 1447		No details
Ba-luo-lan-mi-sun-la	Phra Ramesuan	1453	Trailokanat	Son
Guo-long Bo-la Lue-kun Si-li You-di	Krung Phra Nakhon Si Ayutthaya	1482		"Heir." Predecessor had "wearied of duties"
Bo Lue-kun Xi-li You-chi-ya	Phra Nakhon Si Ayutthaya	1554 1558 1559	Chakkraphat	
Hua-zhao-song	Phrachao Song [Khwae]	1573	Maha Thammaracha	

Based on Wade, *Southeast Asia in the Ming shi-lu*.

Glossary

bodhisatta	A Buddha to be.
cakkavattin	Emperor, literally "wheel roller," a righteous ruler whose chariot wheels traverse the world without obstruction, as described in the Buddhist cosmology of the Three Worlds.
Chakri	Title of the minister of Mahatthai (see below).
dhamma	Truth; morality; the teachings of the Buddha.
Farang	Term for foreigners of European origin.
Hongsawadi	Hamsawati, city of swans, old term for the Mon capital of Pegu (Bago).
jataka	Birth tale; accounts of the previous lives of the Buddha.
Kalahom	One of two major ministries overseeing the outer territories; later overseeing the south, and later the military; its minister.
kamma	Action; the consequences of past actions; the law of cause and effect; fate.
kathin	Monk's robes, and especially the practice of presenting robes to the monks during the rains-retreat.
Khaek	Thai term for foreigners of Malay, Indian, or Arabian origin.
Khun	Title for holders of low rank in the official nobility.
khun nang	A collective term for the official nobility.
Kling	A Malay term for Indian, adopted by the Dutch to refer to south India.
Lanna	A polity, centered on Chiang Mai, controlling the upper valleys of the Chaophraya River system, absorbed into Siam in the late nineteenth century.
Lanxang	A Lao polity, once with capital at Luang Prabang, which fragmented after the 1690s, with new centers at Vientiane and, later, Champasak.

Lawa	Name of a Mon-Khmer ethnic group, often used as a catch-all descriptor of non-Thai groups.
Ligor	Nakhon Si Thammarat.
Maha Upparat	In early Ayutthaya, title of the king's major son; in later Ayutthaya a minister who deputizes for the king.
Mahatthai	One of two major ministries overseeing the outer territories; later overseeing the north, and later the interior.
Metteyya, Maitreya	The future Buddha, sometimes a focus of millennarian beliefs.
Mon	A language and ethnic group, related to Khmer, now mostly found in southern Burma.
Moor	A Muslim, especially from Persia or Arabia, but also from India or the archipelago.
mueang	A city, and sometimes also the territory it commands.
munnai	Overseer; an officer in the system of *phrai* labor control.
naga	A mythical snake, modeled on a cobra.
nai	Master. Title for lower officials in early Ayutthaya.
nirat	"Parting," a genre of poems combining the account of a journey with lament for a loved one left behind.
Northern Cities	Ayutthaya's term for the cities (including Sukhothai and Phitsanulok) in the north of the Chaophraya Plain.
Okya, Okphra	The form of Ayutthayan titles used in the seventeenth century, with Okya used by ministers, generals, and city governors, and Okphra being more junior.
phrai	A commoner bound to work for the king or a noble for some months of the year; *phrai luang*, bound to the king; *phrai som*, bound to a noble.
Phrakhlang	The royal warehouse; the ministry overseeing foreign trade; its minister.
phumibun	"Man of merit," someone believed to have supernatural power.
picul	A measure of weight equivalent to around 60 kilograms.

Ramakian	"Glory of Rama," title of Thai-language tellings of the Indian epic, *Ramayana*.
sakdina	A numerical ranking system ranging from 10,000 for a high official (minister) to five for a slave.
samuha nayok	The minister heading Mahatthai or Kalahom.
sangha	The Buddhist monkhood.
sangharaja	A head of the *sangha* (*sankharat*).
sappanwood	A timber, *Caesalpinia sappan*, source of a red pigment used in dye and cosmetics.
stupa	Monument to enshrine a relic of the Buddha or ashes after cremation.
Tai	A term for the family of languages closely related to Thai.
Three Worlds	*Traiphum*, the cosmology of Theravada Buddhism.
uparaja	A deputy or second king.
wat	Buddhist temple or monastery.
Xian	Term for Ayutthaya in Chinese records; possible origin of "Siam."
yokkrabat	An official posted to a provincial city to serve as the king's representative; later assumed judicial duties.
Yommarat	Title of the minister of the city.

Titles, late Ayutthaya, in descending order

Chaophraya
Phraya, Okya
Phra, Okphra
Luang, Okluang
Muen
Phan
Khun
Nai

Notes on Some Key Sources

Many sources on Siam have problems over authenticity and accuracy. The notes below explain how we view some of the major sources.

Sukhothai Inscription 1

Piriya Krairiksh has argued that this inscription was faked in the nineteenth century. Others have suggested that it is not what it claims to be, namely a statement by King Ramaraja (Ramkhamhaeng) in 1292 CE.

The major problem with this text lies in the extravagant claims made for its significance. We believe it is a Sukhothai-era source but an unusual one. Unlike almost all other Sukhothai inscriptions, which record a certain event such as a *wat* foundation or a treaty, Inscription 1 is a description of the city, vaunting its qualities as a place to live. Possibly it was originally an oral text; it reads aloud very well, and seems designed to reach a wide audience. Its descriptions may be erroneous and inflated in parts – tendencies found among advertising copywriters of any era.

Royal Chronicles of Ayutthaya

The extant chronicles can be classified into three main traditions or clusters.

First, the Luang Prasoet Chronicle, compiled according to its preface in 1681, and named after an official who discovered the text in 1907. The early part is very similar to the records kept by the court astrologers, and that is probably its origin.[1] From the mid-fifteenth century, it becomes slightly more elaborate and expressive. Its dating is generally considered to be accurate, as several dates match with other sources (especially the Chinese records). The content of this chronicle is very limited, and sometimes the wording is obscure, but scholars believe that it is generally accurate.

[1] *Jotmaihet hon*; Hodges, "Time in transition," 33–5.

284

Second, the *phitsadan* or "elaborate" chronicles, which exist in several versions, all compiled in the Thonburi and early Bangkok eras. For the latter part of these works, from the Narai reign onwards and especially through the Ban Phlu Luang era, the accounts in the different versions vary considerably, as they have been written with a political agenda.[2] For the earlier part, the different versions vary only in minor details. They all appear to draw on the same source texts. Moreover, in this early part, the account varies from reign to reign both in the scope of its content and in the style of writing. This suggests that these accounts were originally compiled in the respective reigns, or at their close, and have never been rewritten to impose any consistency. The dating has been corrupted by later copyists, but events can usually be re-dated from the Luang Prasoet chronicle or other sources.

Third, the *wat* tradition, of which there are two examples. The *Sangitiyavamsa* or chronicle of Buddhist councils was compiled in 1789 by the scholar-monk Phra Phonnarat.[3] Section 7, headed "The ten dynasties [of Ayutthaya]," has a short account of each reign. The names of kings and their dates differ slightly from the Luang Prasoet or "elaborate" chronicles.

In the 1530s, the Dutchman Jeremias Van Vliet compiled "The short history of the kings of Siam," for which he drew on "old Siamese histories" and the testimony of "learned monks" and others.[4] The names and dates of kings in Van Vliet's work match almost exactly with those in the *Sangitiyavamsa*. There are also some other similarities in the two accounts. Vickery has argued that Van Vliet drew on a tradition of recording history in the *wat*, as did the *Sangitiyavamsa*.[5] As a result, the "Van Vliet Chronicle" is accorded more credibility than might be given to a work by an outsider. A distinguishing characteristic of these two works is that they pass judgment on each king.

Testimony

After 1767, Ayutthaya nobles swept away to Burma were debriefed on the history, geography, government, and other details of the Ayutthaya kingdom. It is believed that the interviewers were Mons, because they knew Thai, and that the material was first recorded in Mon and then translated into Burmese. From the late nineteenth century, three versions of this material

[2] See Nidhi, "History of Bangkok in the chronicles of Ayutthaya" in *Pen and sail*, 289–341.
[3] *Wannakam samai rattanakosin lem 3: Sangkhittiyawong*; Coedès, "Une recension Pālie des annales d'Ayuthya."
[4] *Van Vliet's Siam*, 179–244.
[5] Vickery, "Review article: Jeremias van Vliet."

found their way back to Siam and were translated into Thai. One of these texts was labelled as the "Testimony of the king who sought a *wat*," implying that it came from the former King Uthumphon, but this is unlikely.

Four versions of this text now exist, one in Burmese, translated to English, and three in Thai (two of which are very similar). All four are problematic. Searches in Burma have failed to find an original Mon manuscript. The extant Burmese document is a later copy, and has some material inserted which does not appear in the Thai versions. The two differing Thai versions possibly come from the Mon and Burmese original respectively. Comparison with the Burmese document shows that the Thai translators "improved" the document by adding extra material.[6]

Here these documents are collectively referred to as the *Testimony*. Their account of Ayutthaya's early history is problematic, but their account from the late seventeenth century onwards is treated as an oral history from the viewpoint of the Ayutthaya nobility.

Simon de la Loubère and Nicolas Gervaise

It is likely that both these authors, who were only in Siam for relatively short periods in the 1680s, drew on the knowledge of Bishop Louis Laneau, who had been in Siam since 1664. Gervaise's *The natural and political history of the Kingdom of Siam*, may be based wholly or largely on a draft by Laneau, while La Loubère possibly drew on Laneau's notes for much of the detail in his *A new historical relation of the Kingdom of Siam*.

Description of Ayutthaya

This detailed verbal description of the city was probably compiled in early Bangkok from memory, though incorporating some material from older documents. Two versions exist, probably an original and another with some additions and editing. This second version was inscribed in the same manuscript as a version of the *Testimony*, and later printed in this combination also, giving rise to an impression that the *Description* was part of the debriefing in Burma, but this is not so.[7]

Laws

In 1805, all surviving law texts were compiled into a collection known as the Three Seals Code. This collection is a potentially very useful source,

---

[6] Baker, "Note on the *Testimonies*"; *Khamhaikan chao krung kao*; *Khamhaikan khun luang ha wat*; Tun Aung Chain, *Chronicle of Ayutthaya*.
[7] Baker, "Note on the *Testimonies*."

but it has problems over dating. As Michael Vickery has shown, many of the dates in the prefaces of individual laws are clearly wrong, and the titles of kings in these prefaces are not precise enough to indicate a specific reign, though they may indicate a general period.[8] Dating is difficult also because law-making was cumulative. Clauses originated as court judgments or royal decrees and were subsequently added to the thematic laws. Only in a few cases are these additions dated.[9] Analysis of the language used might help in dating the laws, but so far this has not been attempted.

Parts of some laws can be dated by context and subject. This is true of the Palace Law, which we use to analyze kingship in early Ayutthaya. But we have been wary of using other laws which have not been subject to scrutiny. From the later seventeenth century, new laws are dated, and these are a very important source for this latter period.

Literary Works and Murals

Dating of old Thai literary works is vexed, as there was no tradition of single authorship and preservation of originals. Old texts could be revised and extended by subsequent authors.

The tale of Khun Chang Khun Phaen is often considered a Bangkok-era work, as much of the surviving text was revised in the salon of King Rama II. However, the work's origins in the Ayutthaya era are clearly seen from the traces of its original oral form, the setting in places which had disappeared by the Bangkok era, and many details of vocabulary, context, and language. The revisions in the royal salon were more superficial than usually assumed. The poetry was improved, but the plot and setting were probably unchanged.[10]

There is also debate over the dating of *Lilit phra lo*. While some parts may have been updated later, the archaic language clearly means the original work belongs to the fifteenth or sixteenth century.[11]

Wat murals deteriorate within a few decades, so any murals originally painted in the Ayutthaya era have definitely been restored, possibly several times. Like literary works, they too may have been revised during these restorations. The art historian No Na Paknam has devised methods for identifying Ayutthaya-era murals on grounds of materials, style, and conventions, and we follow his guide.

[8] Vickery, "Prolegomena"; Vickery, "Constitution of Ayutthaya."
[9] Baker and Pasuk, *Palace Law of Ayutthaya.*
[10] See Baker and Pasuk, *Tale of Khun Chang Khun Phaen*, 881–902.
[11] Bickner, *Introduction to the Thai poem.*

References

Adisorn Muakpimai, "Chantaburi" in Kajit Jittasevi (ed.), *Ayudhya and Asia: proceedings for the international workshop*, Bangkok: Research Council of Thailand and Japan Society for Promotion of Science, 1995, 163–79.

Akin Rabibhadana, *The organization of Thai society in the early Bangkok period 1782–1873*, Bangkok: Amarin, 1996.

Andaya, Barbara Watson and Leonard Y. Andaya, *A history of early modern Southeast Asia, 1400–1830*, Cambridge: Cambridge University Press, 2015.

A history of Malaysia, 2nd ed., Basingstoke: Palgrave, 2001.

Andaya, Leonard Y., "Ayutthaya and the Persian and Indian Muslim connection" in K. Breazeale (ed.), *From Japan to Arabia: Ayutthaya's maritime relations with Asia*, Bangkok: Foundation for the Promotion of Social Sciences and Humanities Textbook Project, 1999, 119–36.

Anderson, James A., *The rebel den of Nung Trí Cao: loyalty and identity along the Sino-Vietnamese frontier*, Seattle: University of Washington Press, 2007.

Anderson, John, *English intercourse with Siam in the seventeenth century*, London: K. Paul, Trench, Trübner, 1890; facsimile reprint Bangkok: Chalermnit, 1981.

Appleton, Naomi and Sarah Shaw, *The ten great birth stories of the Buddha: the Mahānipāta of the Jātakatthavaṇṇanā*, Bangkok: Chulalongkorn University Press and Silkworm Books, 2015.

Atwell, William S., "Money, and the weather: Ming China and the 'Great Depression' of the mid-fifteenth century," *Journal of Asian Studies*, 61, 1 (2002), 83–113.

Aubin, Jean, "Les Persans au Siam sous le règne de Narai (1656–1688)," *Mare Luso-Indicum*, 4 (1980), 95–126.

Aung Thein, U, "Burmese invasions of Siam, translated from the Hmannan Yazawin Dawgyi," *Journal of the Siam Society*, 5, 1 (1908), 2–82.

Baker, Chris, "Final part of the *Description of Ayutthaya* with remarks on defence, policing, infrastructure, and sacred sites," *Journal of the Siam Society*, 102 (2014), 179–210.

"From Yue to Tai," *Journal of the Siam Society*, 90, 1–2 (2002), 1–26.

"Markets and production in the city of Ayutthaya before 1767: translation and analysis of part of the *Description of Ayutthaya*," *Journal of the Siam Society*, 99 (2011), 38–71.

"Note on the *Testimonies* and the *Description of Ayutthaya*," *Journal of the Siam Society*, 99 (2011), 72–80.

"The Antiquarian Society of Siam. Speech of King Chulalongkorn," *Journal of the Siam Society*, 89, 1–2 (2001), 95–9.

"The Grand Palace in the *Description of Ayutthaya*: translation and commentary," *Journal of the Siam Society*, 101 (2013), 69–112.

Baker, Chris and Pasuk Phongpaichit, "Early modern Siam as a mainly urban society," *Modern Asian Studies*, 51, 2 (2017).

"Gender, sexuality and family in old Siam" in Rachel Harrison (ed.), *Disturbing conventions: decentering Thai literary cultures*, London: Rowman and Littlefield, 2014, 193–216.

The Palace Law of Ayutthaya and the Thammasat: law and kingship in Siam, Ithaca, NY: Cornell SEAP, 2016.

"The revolt of Khun Phaen: Contesting power in early modern Siam" in Maurizio Peleggi (ed.), *A sarong for Clio: Essays on the intellectual and cultural history of Thailand*, Ithaca, NY: Cornell SEAP, 2015, 19–140.

tr. and ed., *The tale of Khun Chang Khun Phaen*, Chiang Mai: Silkworm Books, 2010.

tr. and ed., *Yuan phai, defeat of Lanna: A fifteenth-century Thai epic poem*, Chiang Mai: Silkworm Books, 2016.

Barlow, Jeffrey G., *The Zhuang: A longitudinal study of their history and their culture*. Formerly available at https://mcel.pacificu.edu/as/resources/zhuang/, version last updated January 22, 2001. Not found now. Published by Guangxi Minorities Institute, Nanning, 2011.

"The Zhuang minority peoples of the Sino-Vietnamese frontier in the Song Period," *Journal of Southeast Asian Studies*, 18, 2 (1987), 250–69.

Bassett, D. K., "English relations with Siam in the seventeenth century," *Journal of the Malayan Branch of the Royal Asiatic Society*, 34, 2 (1961), 90–105.

Bauer, Christian, "Notes on Mon epigraphy," *Journal of the Siam Society*, 79, 1 (1991), 31–83 and 79, 2 (1991), 61–79.

"Sukhothai Inscription II: late Old Mon affinities and their implications for the history of Thai syntax," *Bulletin of the School of Oriental and African Studies*, 56, 3 (1993), 525–65.

Beemer, Bryce, "Creolization metaphors in the Southeast Asian context," *Cahiers des Anneaux de la Memoire*, 15 (2014), 331–7.

"Southeast Asian slavery and slave gathering warfare as a vector for cultural transmission: the case of Burma and Thailand," *The Historian*, 71, 3 (2009), 481–506.

Bellina, B. et al., "The development of coastal polities in the upper Thai-Malay peninsula" in Nicolas Revire and Stephen A. Murphy (ed.), *Before Siam: essays in art and archaeology*, Bangkok: River Books, 2014, 68–89.

Bellwood, Peter, "Cultural and biological differentiation in peninsular Malaysia: the last 10,000 years," *Asian Perspectives*, 32 (1993), 37–60.

"Southeast Asia before history" in Nicholas Tarling (ed.), *The Cambridge history of Southeast Asia, volume 1, part 1: From early times to c. 1500*, Cambridge: Cambridge University Press, 1999, 55–136.

Benedict, Paul, *Austro-Thai language and culture*, New Haven, CT: Yale University Press, 1976.

Bhawan Ruangsilp, *Dutch East India Company merchants at the court of Ayutthaya: Dutch perceptions of the Thai kingdom, c. 1604–1765*, Leiden: Brill, 2007.

"Kromluang Yothathep: King Narai's daughter and Ayutthaya court intrigue," *Journal of the Siam Society*, 104 (2006), 95–110.

Bickner, Robert J., *An introduction to the Thai poem "Lilit phra law" (The story of King Law)*, Dekalb, IL: Northern Illinois University, 1991.

Lilit phra law, working translation, dated November 4, 2011.

Blust, R. "Beyond the Austronesian homeland: the Austric hypothesis and its implications for archaeology" in W. H. Goodenough (ed.), *Prehistoric settlement of the Pacific, Transactions of the American Philosophical Society*, 86, Philadephia: American Philosophical Society, 1996, 117–40.

Bock, Carl, *Temples and elephants: travels in Siam in 1881–1882*, Singapore: Oxford University Press, 1986 [1884].

Boeles, J. J., "The king of Śrī Dvāravatī and his regalia," *Journal of the Siam Society*, 52, 1 (1964), 99–114.

Boisselier, Jean, *Nouvelles connaissances archéologiques de la ville d'U-Thong*, Bangkok: Fine Arts Department, 1963.

Borannasathan nai jangwat phranakhon si ayutthaya [Monuments in Ayutthaya Province], 2 vols., Bangkok: Fine Arts Department and James H. W. Thompson Foundation, 2007.

Boranratchathanin, Phraya, *Athibai phaen thi phranakhon si ayutthaya* [Description of Ayutthaya], Bangkok: Ton chabap, 2007 [1929].

Borell, Brigitte, Bérénice Bellina, and Boonyarit Chaisuwan, "Contacts between the upper Thai–Malay peninsula and the Mediterranean world" in Nicolas Revire and Stephen A. Murphy (ed.), *Before Siam: essays in art and archaeology*, Bangkok: River Books, 2014, 98–117.

Borell, Brigitte, "The early Byzantine lamp from Pong Tuk," *Journal of the Siam Society*, 96 (2008), 1–26.

Borschberg, Peter, ed., *The memoirs and memorials of Jacques de Coutre: security, trade and society in 16th-century Southeast Asia*, Singapore: NUS Press, 2014.

Bowring, Sir John, *The kingdom and people of Siam*, Kuala Lumpur: Oxford University Press, 1969 [1857].

Bras de Albuquerque, "The beginning: Malacca and Ayutthaya, 1511" in Michael Smithies (ed.), *500 years of Thai-Portuguese relations: a festschrift*, Bangkok: Siam Society, 2011, 9–14.

Breazeale, Kennon, "Ayutthaya under siege: a Portuguese account of the Burmese failure of 1549" in Michael Smithies (ed.), *500 years of Thai-Portuguese relations: a festschrift*, Bangkok: Siam Society, 2011, 37–49.

ed., *From Japan to Arabia: Ayutthaya's maritime relations with Asia*, Bangkok: Foundation for the Promotion of Social Sciences and Humanities Textbook Project, 1999.

"Memoirs of Pierre Poivre: the Thai port of Mergui in 1745," *Journal of the Siam Society*, 97 (2009), 177–200.

"Portuguese impressions of Ayutthaya in the late sixteenth century" in Michael Smithies (ed.), *500 years of Thai-Portuguese relations: a festschrift*, Bangkok: Siam Society, 2011, 50–8.

"Thai maritime trade and the ministry responsible" in Breazeale, *From Japan to Arabia: Ayutthaya's maritime relations with Asia*, Bangkok: Foundation for the Promotion of Social Sciences and Humanities Textbook Project, 1999, 1–54.

"Whirligig of diplomacy: a tale of Thai-Portuguese relations, 1613–9," *Journal of the Siam Society*, 94 (2006), 51–110.

Brereton, Bonnie Pacala, *Thai tellings of Phra Malai: text and ritual concerning a popular Buddhist saint*, Tempe, AZ: Arizona State University, 1995.

Bronson, Bennet, "The extraction of natural resources in early Thailand" in *Culture and environment in Thailand: a symposium of the Siam Society*, Bangkok: Siam Society, 1989, 291–302.

Brown, C. C., "The Malay Annals translated from Raffles MS 18," *Journal of the Malayan Branch of the Royal Asiatic Society*, 25, 2–3 (1952), 1–275.

Brown, Robert L., *The Dvāravatī wheels of the law and the Indianization of Southeast Asia*, Leiden: E. J. Brill, 1996.

Brown, Roxanne. M., *The Ming gap and shipwreck ceramics in Southeast Asia*, Bangkok: Siam Society, 2009.

Brummelhuis, Han ten, *Merchant, courtier and diplomat: a history of the contacts between the Netherlands and Thailand*, Lochem-Gent: Uitgeversmaatschappij de Tijdstroom, 1987.

Bunnowat khamchan, printed for Queen Sukhumanmalasi, Bangkok: Wachirayan Library, 1923.

Buntuean Siworaphot and Sujit Wongthet (ed.), *Aphinihan banphaburut lae pathomwong* [Miraculous ancestors and dynasts], Bangkok: Matichon, 2002.

Busakorn Lailert, "The Ban Phlu Luang dynasty 1688–1767: a study of the Thai monarchy during the closing years of the Ayuthya period," PhD thesis, SOAS, University of London, 1972.

Campos, Joaquim de, "Early Portuguese accounts of Thailand," *Journal of the Siam Society*, 32, 1 (1940), 1–27.

Carter, R. and K. N. Mendis, "Evolutionary and historical aspects of the burden of malaria," *Clinical Microbiology Review*, 15 (2002), 564–94.

Castillo, C. C., B. Bellina, and D. Q. Fuller, "Rice, beans and trade crops on the early maritime Silk Route in Southeast Asia," *Antiquity*, 90, 353 (2016), 1255–69.

Chalit Chaikhanchit, "Mueang sema khue sun klang si janasa" [Mueang Sema as the center of Si Janasa] in Sujit Wongthes (ed.), *Si janasa: rat itsara thi rap sung* [Si Canasa: A free state on the upland], Bangkok: Sinlapa Watthanatham, 2001, 125–70.

Chamberlain, James R., "A new look at the history and classification of the Tai languages" in J. G. Harris and J. R. Chamberlain (ed.), *Studies in Tai linguistics in honour of William J. Gedney*, Bangkok: Central Institute of English Language, Office of State Universities, 1975, 49–66.

"Kra-Dai and the proto-history of South China and Vietnam," *Journal of the Siam Society*, 104 (2016), 27–78.

"The Black Tai chronicle of Muang Mouay, part I, mythology," *Mon-Khmer Studies*, 21 (1992), 19–55.

Charney, Michael W., "From merchants to musketeers in Ayutthaya: the Portuguese and the Thais and their cultures in the sixteenth century" in

Michael Smithies (ed.), *500 years of Thai-Portuguese relations: a festschrift*, Bangkok: Siam Society, 2011, 72–86.

Southeast Asian warfare, 1300–1900, Leiden: Brill, 2004.

Charnvit Kasetsiri, "Ayudhya: capital-port of Siam and its Chinese connection in the fourteenth and fifteenth centuries," *Journal of the Siam Society*, 80, 1 (1992), 75–9.

"Buddhism and political integration in early Ayutthaya: 1351–1448" in Charnvit, *Studies in Thai and Southeast Asian histories*, Bangkok: Foundation for the Promotion of Social Sciences and Humanities Textbook Projet, 2015, 159–80.

"From dynastic to 'national' history: a Siam/Thailand case" in *Proceedings of the inaugural workshop of SEAMEO CHAT*, December 14–15, 2000, reprinted in Charnvit, *Studies in Thai and Southeast Asian histories*, Bangkok: Foundation for the Promotion of Social Science and Humanities Textbooks Project, 2015, 219–52.

"Origins of a capital and seaport. The early settlement of Ayutthaya and its East Asian trade" in K. Breazeale (ed.), *From Japan to Arabia: Ayutthaya's maritime relations with Asia*, Bangkok: Foundation for the Promotion of Social Sciences and Humanities Textbook Project, 1999, 55–79.

The rise of Ayudhya, Kuala Lumpur: Oxford University Press, 1976.

"The rise of Ayutthaya," PhD thesis, Cornell University, 1973.

Chatri Prakitnonthakan, *Khati sanyalak lae kan ok baep wat arun ratchawaram: The Philosophical Constructs of Wat Arun*, Bangkok: South East Asia Insurance, 2013.

"Symbolism in the design of Wat Phra Chetuphon Wimonmamgkhlaram (Wat Pho)," *Journal of the Siam Society*, 102 (2014), 1–39.

Chatthip Nartsupha, *The Thai village economy in the past*, Chiang Mai: Silkworm Books, 1999.

Chen Chingho, "Mac Thien Tu and Phraya Taksin: a survey of their political stand, conflicts, and background" in *Proceedings of the 7th IATA Conference*, Bangkok: Chulalongkorn University Press, 1979, 1534–75.

Chen Han-seng, *Frontier land systems in southernmost China*, New York: Institute of Pacific Relations, 1949.

"Chindamani" in *Wannakam samai ayutthaya* [Ayutthaya-era literature], vol. 2, Bangkok: Fine Arts Department, 1987, 433–98.

Choisy, Abbé de, *Journal of a voyage to Siam, 1685–1686*, translated and introduced by Michael Smithies, Kuala Lumpur: Oxford University Press, 1993 [1687].

Cholada Ruengruklikit, "The Thai tale of Aniruddha: popularity and variations" in Manas Chitakasem (ed.), *Thai literary traditions*, Bangkok: Chulalongkorn University Press, 1995, 170–85.

Christie, Jan Wisseman, "The medieval Tamil language inscriptions in Southeast Asia and China," *Journal of Southeast Asian Studies*, 29, 2 (1998), 239–68.

Chulalongkorn University, *The inscription of King Ramkhamhaeng the Great*, edited by Chulalongkorn University on the 700th Anniversary of the Thai Alphabet, Bangkok: Chulalongkorn University, 1984.

Coedès, George, *Recueil des inscriptions de Siam*, vol. 2, Bangkok, Siam Society, 1961.

The Indianized states of Southeast Asia, tr. S. B. Cowling, Honolulu: University of Hawaii Press, 1968.

"Une recension Pālie des annales d'Ayuthya," *Bulletin de l'École française d'Extrême-Orient*, 14, 3 (1914), 1–31.

Collins, Steven, "The discourse on what is primary (Aggañña Sutta), an annotated translation," *Journal of Indian Philosophy*, 21 (1993), 301–93.

Collis, Maurice, *Siamese White*, London: Faber and Faber, 1965 [1936].

Colquhoun, A. R., *Amongst the Shans*, New York: Scribner and Welford, 1885.

Condominas, George, *From Lawa to Mon, from Saa' to Thai: historical and anthropological aspects of Southeast Asian social spaces*, Canberra: Australian National University, 1990.

Cruysse, Dirk van der, *Siam and the West 1500–1700*, tr. Michael Smithies, Chiang Mai: Silkworm Books, 2002.

Cushman, Janet Wayne, *Fields from the sea: Chinese junk trade with Siam in the late eighteenth and early nineteenth centuries*, Ithaca, NY: Cornell SEAP, 1993.

Cushman, Richard D. (tr.), *The royal chronicles of Ayutthaya*, Bangkok: Siam Society, 2000.

Damrong Rajanubhab, Prince, *A biography of King Naresuan the Great*, tr. and ed. Kennon Breazeale, Bangkok: Toyota Thailand Foundation and the Foundation for the Promotion of Social Sciences and Humanities Textbooks Project, 2008.

Laksana kan pokkhrong prathet sayam tae boran [Nature of government in Siam from the past], Bangkok: Thammasat University Press, 1975 [1927].

Our wars with the Burmese [*Thai rop phama*], tr. Phra Phraison Salarak, Bangkok: White Lotus, 2001 [1917].

"Phraniphon khamnam" [Preface] in *Phraratcha phongsawadan chabap phraratchahatthalekha* [Royal chronicles, royal autograph edition], Bangkok: Fine Arts Department, 1999 [1912], 1–54.

"Siamese history prior to the founding of Ayuddhyā," *Journal of the Siam Society*, 13, 2 (1919), 1–66.

"The story of the records of Siamese history," *Journal of the Siam Society*, 11, 2 (1914–15), 1–20.

Davisakd Puaksom, "The pursuit of Java: Thai Panji stories, Melayu lingua franca and the question of translation," PhD thesis, National University of Singapore, 2007.

Deeg, Max, "Sthavira, Thera and '*Shaviravāda' in Chinese Buddhist sources" in Peter Skilling, Jason A. Carbine, Claudio Cicuzza, and Santi Pakdeekham (ed.), *How Theravāda is Theravāda? Exploring Buddhist Identities*, Chiang Mai: Silkworm Books, 2012, 129–63.

Dhida Saraya, *(Sri) Dvaravati: the initial phase of Siam's history*, Bangkok: Muang Boran, 1999.

"State formation in the lower Tha Chin-Mae Klong basin: the historical development of the ancient city of Nakhon Pathom" in *Culture and environment in Thailand: a symposium of the Siam Society*, Bangkok: Siam Society, 1989, 171–85.

Dhiravat na Pombejra, "A political history of Siam under the Prasatthong dynasty: 1629–1688," PhD thesis, SOAS, University of London, 1984.

"Ayutthaya at the end of the seventeenth century: was there a shift to isolation?" in A. S. Reid (ed.), *Southeast Asia in the early modern era: trade, power and belief*, Ithaca, NY: Cornell University Press, 1993, 250–72.

"Catching and selling Siamese elephants in the seventeenth century: a preliminary study," unpublished paper, 2012.

Court, company and campong. Essays on the VOC presence in Ayutthaya, Ayutthaya: Ayutthaya Historical Studies Centre, 1992.

"Javanese horses for the court of Ayutthaya" in Greg Bankoff and Sandra Stewart (ed.), *Breeds of empire: the 'invention' of the horse in Southeast Asia and Southern Africa 1500–1950*, Copenhagen: NIAS Press, 2007, 65–81.

"Life, work and gossip in the Dutch settlement: Isaack Moerdijck's *dagregister* of 1644" in *The Renaissance Princess lectures: in honour of HRH Princess Maha Chakri Sirindhorn on the occasion of her fifth cycle*, Bangkok: Siam Society, 2017.

"Princes, pretenders, and the Chinese phrakhlang: an analysis of the Dutch evidence concerning Siamese court politics, 1699–1734" in L. Blussé and F. Gaastra (ed.), *On the eighteenth century as a category of Asian history: Van Leur in retrospect*, Aldershot: Ashgate, 1998, 107–30.

Siamese court life in the seventeenth century as depicted in European sources, Bangkok: Chulalongkorn University, 2001.

"The Thasai Prince's rebellion of 1642: a forgotten event in Ayutthaya history" in *Dedications to Her Highness Princess Galyani Vadhana Krom Luang Naradhiwaas Rajanagarindra on her 80th birthday*, Bangkok: Siam Society, 2003, 145–52.

"Towards a history of seventeenth-century Phuket" in Sunait Chutintaranond and Chris Baker (ed.), *Recalling local pasts: autonomous history in Southeast Asia*, Chiang Mai: Silkworm Books, 2002, 89–126.

"VOC employees and their relationships with Mon and Siamese women: a case study of Osoet Pegua" in Barbara Watson Andaya, ed., *Other pasts: women, gender and history in early modern Southeast Asia*, Honolulu: Center for Southeast Asian Studies, University of Hawai'i at Manoa, 2000, 195–214.

Dilok Nabarath, Prince, *Siam's rural economy under King Chulalongkorn*, Bangkok: White Lotus, 2000 [1908].

Dupont, Pierre, *L'archéologie mône de Dvāravatī*, Paris: EFEO, 1959.

Evans, Grant, "The Tai original diaspora," *Journal of the Siam Society*, 104 (2016), 1–26.

Farrington, Anthony and Dhiravat na Pombejra (ed.), *The English factory in Siam 1612–1685*, 2 vols., London: British Library, 2007.

Fei Hsin, *Hsing-ch'a Sheng-lan: the overall survey of the star raft*, tr. J.V.G. Mills, revised, annotated and edited by Roderich Ptak, Wiesbaden: Harrassowitz Verlag, 1996.

Fenner, Frank, "Smallpox in Southeast Asia," *Crossroads*, 3, 2–3 (1987), 34–48.

Fickle, Dorothy H., "An historical and structural study of the Paññāsa Jātaka," PhD thesis, University of Pennsylvania, 1978.

Flood, Thadeus, "Sukhothai-Mongol relations: a note on relevant Chinese and Thai sources (with translations)," *Journal of the Siam Society*, 57, 2 (1969), 201–57.

Flood, Thadeus and Chadin Flood, *The dynastic chronicle Bangkok era: the first reign, Chaophraya Thiphakorawong edition*, vol. 1, Tokyo: Centre for East Asian Cultural Studies, 1978.

Floris, Peter, *His voyage to the East Indies in the Globe, 1611–1615: Siam, Pattani, Bantam*, Bangkok: White Lotus, 2002.

Forest, Alain, *Les missionaires français au Tonkin et au Siam (XVIIème – XVIIIème siècles). livre I, histoires de Siam*, Paris: Editions l'Harmattan, 1998.

Fouser, Beth, *The lord of the golden tower: King Prasat Thong and the building of Wat Chaiwatthanaram*, Bangkok: White Lotus, 1996.

Frederike, Caesar, "Extracts of Master Caesar Frederike his eighteene yeeres Indian Observations" in Samuel Purchas (ed.), *Hakluytus Posthumus or, Purchas his Pilgrimes*, vol. 10, Cambridge: Cambridge University Press, 2014, 88–142.

Gait, Edward, *A history of Assam*, Guwahati: Lawyer's Book Stall, 1994 [1926].

Gedney, William, "Siamese verse forms in historical perspective" in Robert J. Bickner, John Hartman, Thomas John Hudak, and Patcharin Peyasantiwong (ed.), *Selected papers on comparative Tai studies*, Ann Arbor, MI: Center for South and Southeast Asian Studies, University of Michigan, 1989, 489–544.

Gervaise, Nicolas, *The natural and political history of the Kingdom of Siam*, Bangkok: White Lotus, 1998 [1688].

Gesick, Lorraine M., "Kingship and political integration in traditional Siam, 1767–1824," PhD thesis, Cornell University, 1974.

"The rise and fall of King Taksin: a drama of Buddhist kingship" in Gesick (ed.), *Centers, symbols and hierarchies: essays on the classical states of Southeast Asia*, New Haven, CT: Yale University Press, 1983, 87–105.

Gethin, Rupert, "Was Buddhagosa a Theravādin? Buddhist identity in the Pali commentaries and chronicles" in Peter Skilling, Jason A. Carbine, Claudio Cicuzza, and Santi Pakdeekham (ed.), *How Theravāda is Theravāda? exploring Buddhist identities*, Chiang Mai: Silkworm Books, 2012, 1–63.

Giles, Francis H., "A critical analysis of Van Vliet's account of Siam in the 17th century," *Journal of the Siam Society*, 30, 2 (1938), 155–240.

Glover, Ian C., "Early trade between India and South-East Asia: a link in the development of a world trading system," Occasional Papers 16, University of Hull Centre for Southeast Asian Studies, 1989.

Glover, Ian C. and Bérénice Bellina, "Ban Don Ta Phet and Khao Sam Kaeo: the earliest Indian contacts re-assessed" in Pierre-Yves Manguin, A. Mani, and Geoff Wade (ed.), *Early interactions between South and Southeast Asia: reflections on cross-cultural exchange*, Singapore: ISEAS, 2011, 17–45.

Glover, Ian, Pornchai Suchitta, and John Villiers (ed.), *Early metallurgy, trade and urban centres in Thailand and Southeast Asia*, Bangkok: White Lotus, 1992.

Gosling, Betty, *A chronology of religious architecture at Sukhothai: late thirteenth to early fifteenth century*, Chiang Mai: Silkworm Books, 1998.

Grimm, T., "Thailand in the light of official Chinese historiography: a chapter in the 'History of the Ming Dynasty'," *Journal of the Siam Society*, 49, 1 (1961), 1–20.

Griswold, A. B. and Prasert na Nagara, "A declaration of independence and its consequences. Epigraphic and historical studies, no. 1," *Journal of the Siam Society*, 56, 2 (1968), 207–49.

"A fifteenth-century Siamese historical poem" in C. D. Cowan and O. W. Wolters (ed.), *Southeast Asian history and historiography: essays presented to D. G. E. Hall*, Ithaca, NY and London: Cornell University Press, 1976, 123–63.

"A law promulgated by the King of Ayudhyā in 1397 A.D. Epigraphic and historical studies, no. 4," *Journal of the Siam Society*, 57, 1 (1969), 109–48.

"Inscription 9. Epigraphic and Historical Studies, no. 12," *Journal of the Siam Society*, 62, 1 (1974), 89–121.

"An inscription of 1563 A.D. recording a treaty between Laos and Ayodhyā in 1560. Epigraphic and historical studies, no. 24," *Journal of the Siam Society*, 67, 2 (1977), 54–69.

"Inscription of the Śiva of Kāṃbèṅ Bejra. Epigraphic and historical studies no. 14," *Journal of the Siam Society*, 62, 2 (1974), 223–38.

"King Lödaiya of Sukhodaya and his contemporaries. Epigraphic and historical studies, no 10," *Journal of the Siam Society*, 60, 1 (1972), 21–152.

"The epigraphy of Mahādharmarāja of Sukhodaya and his contemporaries. Epigraphic and historical studies, no. 11, part 1," *Journal of the Siam Society*, 61, 1 (1973), 71–179.

"The inscription of King Rāma Gaṃhèṅ of Sukhodaya (1292 A.D.). Epigraphic and historical studies, no. 9," *Journal of the Siam Society*, 59, 2 (1971), 179–228.

"The 'Judgments of King Mǎṅ Rāy'. Epigraphic and historical studies, no. 17," *Journal of the Siam Society*, 65, 1 (1977), 137–60.

"The pact between Sukhodaya and Nān. Epigraphic and historical studies no. 3," *Journal of the Siam Society*, 57, 1 (1969), 57–107.

Groslier, B. P., "Agriculture et religion dans l'empire Angkorien," *Etudes rurales*, 53–56 (1974), 95–117.

Guehler, Ulrich, "The travels of Ludovico di Varthema and his visits to Siam, Banghella and Pegu A.D. 1505," *Journal of the Siam Society*, 36, 2 (1947), 113–50.

Guillon, Emmanuel, *The Mons: a civilization of Southeast Asia*, tr. and ed. James V. Di Croco, Bangkok; Siam Society, 1999.

Gutman, Pamela, "The Martaban trade: an examination of the literature from the seventh century until the eighteenth century," *Asian Perspectives*, 40, 1 (2001), 108–18.

Guy, John, *Lost kingdoms: Hindu-Buddhist sculpture of early Southeast Asia*, New York: Metropolitan Museum of Art, 2014.

Woven cargoes: Indian textiles in the East, London: Thames and Hudson, 1998.

Hall, Kenneth R., *Maritime trade and state development in early Southeast Asia*, Honolulu: University of Hawaii Press, 1985.

Halliday, R., "Immigration of the Mons into Siam," *Journal of the Siam Society*, 10, 3 (1913), 1–15.

Hamashita Takeshi, "Ayudhya-China relations in the tribute trade system through Ryukyu trade network" in Kajit Jittasevi (ed.), *Ayudhya and Asia: proceedings for the international workshop*, Bangkok: Thammasat University, 1995, 49–77.

Hamilton, Alexander, *A new account of the East Indies*, ed. Justin Corfield and Ian Morson, Lewiston-Queenston-Lampeter: Edwin Mellen Press, 2001 [1727].

Heeck, Gijsbert, *A traveler in Siam in the Year 1655*, tr. and ed. Barend J. Terwiel, Chiang Mai: Silkworm Books, 2008.

Hein, Don and Mike Barbetti, "Si-Satchanalai and the development of glazed stoneware in Southeast Asia," *Siam Society Newsletter*, 4, 3 (1988), 8–18.

Higham, C. F. W., "Archaeology, linguistics and the expansion of the East and Southeast Asian neolithic" in Roger Blench and Matthew Spriggs (ed.), *Archaeology and language II: archaeological data and linguistic hypotheses*, London: Routledge, 1988, 103–113.

Higham, C. F. W., *Early cultures of Mainland Southeast Asia*, Bangkok: River Books, 2002.

Higham C. F. W., K. Douka, and T. F. G. Higham, "A new chronology for the Bronze Age of northeastern Thailand and its implications for Southeast Asian prehistory," *PLoS ONE*, 10, 9 (2015), e0137542. doi:10.1371/journal.pone.0137542

Higham, C. F. W. and Rachanie Thosarat, *Early Thailand: From prehistory to Sukhothai*, Bangkok: River Books, 2012.

Hill, A. H., "Hikayat Raja-Raja Pasai. A romanised version with an English translation, an introduction and notes," *Journal of the Malaysian Branch of the Royal Asiatic Society*, 33, 2 (1990), 1–215.

Ho, Chuimei, "Export phases for Menam Basin ceramics in Thai history" in Charnvit Kasetsiri (ed.), *Sangkhalok-Sukhothai-Ayutthaya and Asia*, Bangkok: Toyota Thailand Foundation, 2002, 94–112.

Hodges, Ian, "Time in transition: King Narai and the Luang Prasoet Chronicle of Ayutthaya," *Journal of the Siam Society*, 87 (1999), 33–44.

Holm, David, "A layer of Old Chinese readings in the traditional Zhuang script," *Bulletin of the Museum of Far Eastern Antiquities*, 1 (2014), 1–45.

Hong Lysa, *Thailand in the nineteenth century: evolution of the economy and society*, Singapore: Institute of Southeast Asian Studies, 1984.

Hsieh, Shih-ching, "On the dynamics of Tai/Dai-Lue ethnicity. An ethnohistorical analysis" in Steven Harrell (ed.), *Cultural encounters on China's ethnic frontiers*, Seattle and London: University of Washington Press, 1995, 301–28.

Huffman, Franklin E., "Thai and Cambodian: a case of syntactical borrowing?" *Journal of the American Oriental Society*, 93, 4 (1973), 488–509.

Hutchinson, E. W., *1688 Revolution in Siam: the memoir of Father de Bèze, S.J.*, Bangkok: White Lotus, 1990 [1688].

English adventurers in Siam, Bangkok: DD Books, 1985.

Ishii, Yoneo, "Exploring a new approach to early Thai history," *Journal of the Siam Society*, 92 (2004), 37–42.

"Religious patterns and economic change in Siam in the 16th and 17th centuries" in A. S. Reid (ed.), *Southeast Asia in the early modern era: trade, power and belief*, Ithaca, NY and London: Cornell University Press, 1993, 180–92.

Sangha, state and society: Thai Buddhism in history, tr. Peter Hawkes, Honolulu: University of Hawaii Press, 1986.

Thailand: a rice-growing society, tr. Peter and Stephanie Hawkes, Honolulu: University Press of Hawaii, 1978.

The junk trade from Southeast Asia: translations from the Tōsen Fusetsu-gaki, 1674–1723, Singapore: ISEAS, 1998.

"The *Rekidai Hō an* and some aspects of the Ayuthayan port polity in the fifteenth century," *Memoirs of the Research Department of the Toyo Bunko*, 50 (1992), 81–92.

"The Thai Thammasat (with a note on the Lao Thammasat)" in M. B. Hooker (ed.), *The laws of South-East Asia*, vol. 1, Singapore: Butterworths, 1986, 43–203.

Iwamoto Yoshiteru, "Yamada Nagamasa and his relations with Siam," *Journal of the Siam Society*, 95 (2007), 73–84.

Iwamoto Yoshiteru and Simon J. Bytheway, "Japan's official relations with Shamuro (Siam), 1599–1745: as revealed in the diplomatic records of the Tokugawa Shogunate," *Journal of the Siam Society*, 99 (2011), 81–104.

Iwao Seiichi, "Japanese foreign trade in the 16th and 17th centuries," *Acta Asiatica*, 30 (1976), 1–18.

"Reopening of the diplomatic and commercial relations between Japan and Siam during the Tokugawa period," *Acta Asiatica*, 4 (1963), 1–31.

Jacq-Hergoualc'h, Michel, *Etude historique et critique du "Journal du Voyage de Siam de Claude Ceberet," Envoyé extraordinaire du Roi en 1687 et 1688*, Paris: L'Harmatttan, 1992.

L'Europe et le Siam du XVIe au XVIIe siècle. Apports culturels, Paris: L'Harmatttan, 1993.

Jaiser, Gerhard, *Thai mural painting*, 2 vols., Bangkok: White Lotus, 2009, 2010.

Jittrakam lae sinlapawatthu nai kru phraprang wat ratchaburana jangwatphranakhon si ayutthaya [Paintings and art objects in the crypt of Wat Ratchaburana, Ayutthaya], 2nd ed., Bangkok: Fine Arts Department, 2014.

Jory, Patrick, *Thailand's theory of monarchy: the Vessantara Jātaka and the idea of the perfect man*, New York: SUNY Press.

Jotmaihet hon: prachum phongsawadan phak thi 8 [Astrologer records: collected chronicles, part 8], Bangkok: Khurusapha, 1965.

Jotmaihet rawang ratchathut langka lae sayam khrang krung si ayutthaya [Records of diplomatic relations between Ceylon and Siam in the time of Ayutthaya], printed for the cremation of Nai Subin Sirarot, Wat That Thong, Phrakhanong, July 7, 1973.

Julathat Phayakharanon, "Bot-rian: rueang jedisathan nai suphanburi" [Learnings on religious monuments in Suphanburi], in Thai Studies Institute (ed.), *Suphanburi: prawatisat sinlapa lae watthanatham* [Suphanburi: history, art, and culture], Proceedings of a seminar, Suphanburi, November 12–20, 1987.

Julispong Chularatana, "Khwam samphan rawang sinlapa lae sathapatiyakam samai ayutthaya ton plai kap sinlapakam indo-persia" [Relation between late Ayutthaya art and architecture and Indo-Persian arts] in Sunait Chutintaranond (ed.), *Nai yuk awasan krung si mai khoei sueam* [No decline in Ayutthaya's final period], Bangkok: Sinlapa Watthanatham, 2015, 259–95.

Khunnang krom tha khwa: kan sueksa botbat lae nathi nai samai ayutthaya thueng samai rattanakosin pho so 2153–2435 [Officials of the port department, right division: study of their roles and duties in the Ayutthaya and Bangkok periods, 1610–1892], Bangkok: Chulalongkorn University, 2003.

Kaempfer, Engelbert, *A description of the Kingdom of Siam 1690*, Bangkok: Orchid Press, 1998 [1727].

Kajit Jittasevi, ed., *Ayudhya and Asia: Proceedings for the international workshop*, Bangkok: Research Council of Thailand and Japan Society for Promotion of Science, 1995.

Kelley, Liam, "Tai words and the place of the Tai in the Vietnamese past," *Journal of the Siam Society*, 101 (2013), 125–54.

Kemp, Jeremy, *Aspects of Siamese kingship in the seventeenth century*, Bangkok: Social Science Review, 1969.

"Khamchan sansoen phrakiat somdet phraphutthajao luang prasat thong" [Eulogy of King Prasat Thong] in *Wannakam samai ayutthaya* [Literature of the Ayutthaya era], vol. 3, Bangkok: Fine Arts Department, 2002, 1–55.

Khamhaikan chao krung kao [Testimony of the inhabitants of the old capital], Bangkok: Chotmaihet Press, 2001 [1924].

Khamhaikan khun luang ha wat [Testimony of the king who entered a *wat*], Bangkok: Sukhothai Thammathirat University, 2004.

Khamhaikan khun luang wat pradu songtham: ekkasan jak ho luang [Testimony of the king from Wat Pradu Songtham: documents from the palace library], ed. Winai Pongsripian, Bangkok: Committee to edit and print Thai historical documents, Office of the Cabinet, 1991.

Kobata Atsushi and Mitsuyu Matsuda, *Ryukyuan relations with Korea and South Sea countries: an annotated translation of documents in the Rekidai Hōan*, Kyoto: Atsushi Kobata, 1969.

Koenig, J. G., "Journal of a voyage from India to Siam and Malacca in 1779," *Journal of the Straits Branch of the Royal Asiatic Society*, 26 (1894), 58–201.

Kotmai tra sam duang [Three Seals Code], 5 vols., Bangkok: Khurusapha, 1994.

Kulke, Hermann, "The early and the imperial kingdom in Southeast Asian history" in D. Marr and A. Milner (ed.), *Southeast Asia in the 9th to 14th centuries*, Singapore: ISEAS, 1986, 1–22.

La Loubère, Simon de, *A new historical relation of the Kingdom of Siam*, London, 1793.

Launay, Adrien, *Histoire de la mission de Siam 1662–1811*, Paris: P. Téqui, 1920.

Le Blanc, Marcel, S. J., *History of Siam in 1688*, tr. and ed. Michael Smithies, Chiang Mai: Silkworm Books, 2003 [1692].

Lemoine, Jacques, "Thai Lue historical relations with China and the shaping of the Sipsong Panna political system," in *Proceedings of the 3rd International Conference on Thai Studies*, ANU, Canberra, July 3–6, 1984, 121–34.

Lieberman, Victor B., *Burmese administrative cycles: anarchy and conquest, c. 1580–1760*, Princeton, NJ: Princeton University Press, 1984.

Strange parallels: Southeast Asia in global context, c. 800–1830, volume 1: integration on the mainland, Cambridge: Cambridge University Press, 2003.

Lieberman, Victor B. and Brendan M. Buckley, "The impact of climate on Southeast Asia, circa 950–1820: new findings," *Modern Asian Studies*, 46, 5 (2012), 1049–96.

Lingat, R., "La double crise de l'église bouddhique au Siam (1767–1851)," *Cahiers d'Histoire Mondiale*, 4 (1958), 402–25.

"Les origines du prêt à intérêt au Siam," *Revue Historique de Droit Français et Etranger*, 28, 2 (1950), 213–35.

Luce, G. H., "The early Syam in Burma's history," *Journal of the Siam Society*, 46, 2 (1958), 123–214.

"The early Syam in Burma's history: a supplement," *Journal of the Siam Society*, 47, 1 (1959), 59–101.

Ma Huan, *Ying-yai Sheng-lan. 'The Overall Survey of the Ocean's Shores'*, tr. J. V. G. Mills, Bangkok: White Lotus, 1997 [1443].

Macgregor, A., "A brief account of the Kingdom of Pegu," *Journal of the Burmese Research Society*, 16, 2 (1926), 99–138.

Manas Chitakasem, "The emergence and development of the nirāt genre in Thai poetry," *Journal of the Siam Society*, 60, 2 (1972), 135–68.

Manat Ophakun, *Prawatisat mueang suphan* [History of Suphan(buri)], Bangkok: Sinlapa Watthanatham, 2004.

Mangrai, Sao Saimong, *The Pādaeng chronicle and the Jengtung state chronicle translated*, Ann Arbor, MI: University of Michigan, 1981.

Manguin, Pierre-Yves, "The merchant and the king: political myths of Southeast Asian coastal polities," *Indonesia*, 52 (October 1991), 41–54.

"Trading ships of the South China Sea. Shipbuilding techniques and their role in the history of the development of Asian trade networks," *Journal of the Economic and Social History of the Orient*, 36, 3 (1993), 253–80.

Manop Thawonwatsakun, *Khun nang ayutthaya* [The nobility of Ayutthaya], Bangkok: Thammasat University Press, 1993.

Marrison, G. E., "The Siamese wars with Malacca during the reign of Muzaffar Shah," *Journal of the Malaysian Branch of the Royal Asiatic Society*, 22, 1 (1949), 51–66.

Masuda, Erika, "The fall of Ayutthaya and Siam's disrupted order of tribute to China (1767–1782)," *Taiwan Journal of Southeast Asian Studies*, 4, 2 (2007), 75–128.

Mattani Mojdara Rutnin, *Dance, drama, and theatre in Thailand: The process of development and modernization*, Tokyo: Centre for East Asian Cultural Studies for Unesco, and the Toyo Bunko, 1993.

Maxwell, Thomas, "The stele inscription of Preah Khan, Angkor: text with translation and commentary," *Udaya Journal of Khmer Studies*, 8 (2007), 1–114.

Mayuri Viraprasoet, "Si janasa rue janasapura: kho sanitthan kao-mai" [New and old thoughts on Si Janasa or Janasapura] in Sujit Wongthes (ed.), *Si janasa: rat itsara thi rap sung* [Si Canasa: a free state on the upland], Bangkok: Sinlapa Watthanatham, 2002, 87–122.

McDaniel, Justin T., *Gathering leaves and lifting words: histories of Buddhist monastic education in Laos and Thailand*, Chiang Mai: Silkworm Books, 2009.

McGill, Forrest, "Jatakas, universal monarchs, and the year 2000," *Artibus Asiae*, 53, 3–4 (1993), 412–48.

"The art and architecture of the reign of King Prasatthong of Ayutthaya (1629–1656)," PhD thesis, University of Michigan, 1977.

Michel, Wolfgang and B. J. Terwiel, ed., *Kaempfer Werke IV: Heutiges Japan*, München: Iudicium, 2001.

Mills, J. V., "Arab and Chinese navigators in Malaysian waters in about A.D. 1500," *Journal of the Malaysian Branch of the Royal Asiatic Society*, 47, 2 (1974), 1–82.

Mongkut, King, "Phraratcha niphon ratchakan thi 4 rueang pathomwong" [King Mongkut on dynastic origins] in *Prachum phongsawadan phak thi 8* [Collected chronicles part 8], Bangkok: Rongphim Thai, 1918.

Muang Boran, *Chabap phetchaburi* [Phetchaburi issue], Bangkok: Akson sam-phan, 1991.

Muhammad Rabi' ibn Muhammad Ibrahim, *The ship of Sulaiman*, tr. John O'Kane, London: Routledge, 1972.

Munro-Hay, Stuart, *Nakhon Sri Thammarat: the archeology, history and legends of a southern Thai town*, Bangkok: White Lotus, 2001.

Murphy, Stephen A. and Pimchanok Pongkasetkan, "Fifty years of archaeologi-cal research at Dong Mae Nang Muang, an ancient gateway to the upper Chao Phraya basin," *Journal of the Siam Society*, 98 (2010), 49–74.

Myint, Soe Thuzar, *The portrayal of the Battle of Ayutthaya in Myanmar literature*, Bangkok: Institute of Asian Studies, Chulalongkorn University, 2011.

"*Yodayar Naing Mawgun* by Letwe Nawrahta: a contemporary Myanmar record, long lost, of how Ayutthaya was conquered," *Journal of the Siam Society*, 99 (2011), 1–24.

Nagazumi Yoko, "Ayutthaya and Japan: embassies and trade in the seventeenth century" in K. Breazeale (ed.), *From Japan to Arabia: Ayutthaya's mari-time relations with Asia*, Bangkok: Foundation for the Promotion of Social Sciences and Humanities Textbook Projet, 1999, 79–103.

Nai Suan Mahatlek, "Khlong yo phrakiat phrajao krung thonburi" [Eulogy of the King of Thonburi], 1771, at www.digital.nlt.go.th/items/show/4345.

Nai Thien, "Intercourse between Burma and Siam as recorded in Hmannan Yazawindawgyi," *Journal of the Siam Society*, 8, 2 (1911), 1–119.

"Narrative of the voyage of Abd-er-Razzak" in *India in the fifteenth century: being a collection of narratives of voyages to India, in the century preceding the Portuguese discovery of the Cape of Good Hope; from Latin, Persian, Russian, and Italian sources, now first translated into English*, London: Hakluyt Society, 1857, 1–49.

Natthapatra Chandavij, *Khrueang thuai jin thi phop jak laeng borannakhadi nai prathet thai* [Chinese ceramics from the archaeological sites in Thailand], Bangkok: Fine Arts Department, 1986.

Neijenrode, Cornelis van, "Account and description of the state of affairs in the Kingdom[s] of Siam and Cambodia (1621)," ed. Han ten Brummelhuis, unpublished manuscript, 2015.

Nidhi Eoseewong, "Ayudhya and the Japanese," 1999, at www.asianmonth.com/prize/english/lecture/pdf/10_04.pdf.

"Jak rat chai khop thueng monthon thesaphiban: khwam sueamsalai khong klum amnatdoem nai ko phuket" [From a marginal state to a provincial center: the decline of the old elite in Phuket] in Nidhi, *Krung taek prachao tak lae prawattisat thai wa duai prawatisat lae prawatisat niphon* [The fall of Ayutthaya, King Taksin, and Thai history: on history and historiography], Bangkok: Matichon, 1995, 167–225.

Kanmueang thai samai phra narai [Thai politics in the time of King Narai], Bangkok: Matichon, 1994 [1980].

Kanmueang thai samai phrajao krung thonburi [Thai politics in the time of the King of Thonburi (Taksin)], 2nd ed., Bangkok: Sinlapa Watthanatham, 1993 [1986].

"Nakhon si thammarat nai ratcha-anajak ayutthaya" [Nakhon Si Thammarat in the Ayutthaya kingdom] in Nidhi, *Krung taek prachao tak lae prawattisat thai wa duai prawatisat lae prawatisat niphon* [The fall of Ayutthaya, King Taksin, and Thai history: on history and historiography], Bangkok: Matichon, 1995, 226–69.

Pen and sail: literature and history in early Bangkok, ed. Chris Baker and Ben Anderson, Chiang Mai: Silkworm Books, 2005.

"Sangkhom lae watthanatham samai sukhothai" [Society and culture in the Sukhothai era] in Sujit Wongthes (ed.), *Phlik prawatisat khwaen sukhothai* [Overturning the history of the Sukhothai region], Bangkok: Matichon, 1997.

"Nirat nakhon sawan" in *Wannakam samai ayutthaya* [Ayutthaya-era literature], vol. 2, Bangkok: Fine Arts Department, 1987, 777–94.

Niyada (Sarikabhuti) Lausunthorn, *Panyat chadok: prawat lae khwam samkhan thi mi to wannakam roi krong khong thai* [The Fifty Jatakas: history and importance for Thai poetic literature], Bangkok: Lai kham, 2015.

Notton, Camille (tr.), *Annales du Siam*. 3 vols. Paris, Limoges, Nancy: Charles-Lavauzelle, 1926, 1930, 1932.

O'Reilly, D. J. W., "Increasing complexity and the political economy model: a consideration of Iron Age moated sites in Thailand," *Journal of Anthropological Archaeology*, 35 (2014), 297–309.

Panyat chadok [Fifty jatakas], 2 vols, Bangkok: Phetkarat, 2011.

Paschal, Eva M. "Buddhist monks and Christian friars: religious and cultural exchange in the making of Buddhism," *Studies in World Christianity*, 22, 1 (2016), 5–21.

Pasuk Phongpaichit and Chris Baker, *Thailand: economy and politics*, Kuala Lumpur: Oxford University Press, 1995.

Patcharee Lertrit, Samerchai Poolsuwan, Rachanie Thosarat, Thitima Sanpachudayan, Hathaichanoke Boonyarit, Chatchai Chinpaisal, and Bhoom Suktitipat, "Genetic history of Southeast Asian populations as revealed by ancient and modern human mitochondrial DNA analysis," *American Journal of Physical Anthropology*, 137 (2008), 425–40.

Pattaratorn Chirapravati, M. L., "Illustrating the lives of the bodhisatta at Wat Si Chum" in Peter Skilling (ed.), *The past lives of the Buddha. Wat Si Chum: Art, architecture and inscriptions*, Bangkok: River Books, 2008, 13–40.

"In search of Maitreya: early images of Dvaravati Buddha at Si Thep" in Peter Skilling and Justin McDaniel (ed.), *Buddhist narrative in Asia and beyond*, Bangkok: Institute of Thai Studies, Chulalongkorn University, 2012, Vol. 2, 97–109.

"The transformation of Brahmanical and Buddhist imagery in central Thailand, 600–800" in John Guy (ed.), *Lost kingdoms: Hindu-Buddhist sculpture of early Southeast Asia*, New York: Metropolitan Museum of Art, 2014, 221–4.

"Wat Ratchaburana: deposits of history, art, and culture of the early Ayutthaya period" in F. McGill (ed.), *Kingdom of Siam: art from Central Thailand (1350–1800 C.E.)*, Ghent: Snoeck; Bangkok: Buppha; Chicago: Art Media Resources; and San Francisco: The Asian Art Museum of San Francisco, 2005, 80–93.

Peacock, A. C. "The Ottomans and the Kingdom of Siam: relations prior to the 19th century," unpublished paper, 2015.

Penth, Hans, "On the history of Chiang Rai," *Journal of the Siam Society*, 77, 1 (1989), 11–32.

"Reflections on the Saddhamma-Saṅgaha," *Journal of the Siam Society*, 65, 1 (1977), 259–80.

Phatthiya Yimrewat, *Prawattisat sipsong chuthai* [History of Sipsong Xuthai], Bangkok: Sangsan, 2001.

Phiraphon Phitsanuphong, *Mueang si mahosot: prawatisat lae borannakhadi lem 2* [Mahosot city, history and archaeology, vol. 2], Bangkok. Fine Arts Department, 1993.

Phiset Jiajanphong, *Phra maha thammaracha kasatrathirat: kan mueang nai prawatisat yuk sukhothai-ayutthaya* [King Maha Thammaracha: politics in the history of the Sukhothai-Ayutthaya era], Bangkok: Sinlapa Watthanatham, 2003.

Sasana lae kan mueang nai prawatisat sukhothai-ayutthaya [Religion and politics in the history of Sukhothai and Ayutthaya], Bangkok: Sinlapa Watthanatham, 2002.

Phongsawadan nuea [Northern chronicles], printed for the cremation of Phraya Ratanabodi (Sa-ngiam Singholka), Bangkok: Sophon Phipatthanakon, 1931.

"Phra krasae phrabatsomdet phraphutthajao luang sop rueang rao tamra phra meru kromluang yothathep kap phraratcha phongsawadan song phraratchaniphon muea duen phruettikayon ro. so. 121" [Royal opinion on the manual of Queen Yothathep's cremation pyre and the royal chronicles, royally authored in November 121] in *Prachum jotmaihet samai ayutthaya phak 1* [Collected records of the Ayutthaya era, vol. 1], Bangkok: Office of the Prime Minister, 1967.

Phraison Salarak, Luang (Thien Subindu), "Intercourse between Burma and Siam, as recorded in Hmannan Yazawindawgyi, part II," *Journal of the Siam Society*, 11, 3 (1915), 1–67.

Phraratcha phongsawadan chabap phraratchahatthalekha [Royal chronicles, royal autograph edition], 2 vols., Bangkok: Fine Arts Department, 1999.

Phraratcha phongsawadan krung kao chabap luang prasoet [Royal Chronicles of Ayutthaya, Luang Prasoet Edition], Bangkok: Saengdao, 2001.

Phraratcha phongsawadan krung si ayutthaya chabap mo bratle [Royal chronicles of Ayutthaya, Dr Bradley edition], Bangkok: Kosit, 1964.

Phraratcha phongsawadan krung thonburi phaendin somdet phraborommaratcha thi 4 (somdet phrajao taksin maharat) chabap mo bratle [Royal chronicles of Thonburi, King Taksin the Great, Dr Bradley edition], Bangkok: Kosit, 2008 [1864].

"Phraratchaputcha khong somdet phra phetracha" [Royal enquiries of King Phetracha] in *Prachum jotmaihet samai ayutthaya phak 1* [Collected records of the Ayutthaya era, part 1], Bangkok: Prime Minister's Office, 1968.

Pieris, P. E. (tr.), *Religious intercourse between Ceylon and Siam in the eighteenth century. I. An account of King Kirti Sri's embassy to Siam in Saka 1672*, Bangkok: Siam Observer, 1908. Originally published in the *Journal of the Royal Asiatic Society*, Ceylon Branch XVIII, 54 (1903).

Pigott, Vincent, "Prehistoric copper-mining in the context of emerging craft specialization in northeast Thailand" in A. B. Knapp, V. C. Pigott, and E. W. Herbert (ed.), *Social approaches to an industrial past: the archaeology and anthropology of mining*, London and New York: Routledge, 1998, 205–25.

Pimenta, Nicolas, "Indian observations gathered out of the letters of Nicolas Pimenta, visiter of the Jesuites in India…" in Samuel Purchas (ed.), *Hakluytus Posthumus or, Purchas his Pilgrimes*, vol. 10, Cambridge: Cambridge University Press, 2014, 205–22.

Pimpraphai Bisalputra Sng, "Kan kha khrueang krabueang rawang jin samai ratchawong ching kap krung si ayutthaya samai ratchawong ban phlu luang pho so 2187–2310" [Ceramic trade between Qing China and Ban Phlu Luang Siam, 1644–1767] in Sunait Chutintaranond (ed.), *Nai yuk awasan krung si mai khoei sueam* [No decline in Ayutthaya's final period], Bangkok: Sinlapa Watthanatham, 2015, 103–68.

Pinto, Fernão Mendes, *The travels of Mendes Pinto*, ed. and tr. Rebecca D. Catz, Chicago and London: University of Chicago Press, 1989.

Pires, Tomé, *The Suma Oriental of Tome Pires*, tr. and ed. A. Cortesão, London: Hakluyt Society, 1944.

Piriya Krairiksh, "A revised dating of Ayudhya architecture," parts 1 and 2, *Journal of the Siam Society*, 80, 1 (1992), 37–55; and 80, 2 (1992), 11–26.

"Pathakatha phiset: kan kamnot a-yu khrueang sangkhalok" [Special lecture: dating Sangkhalok ware] in Charnvit Kasetsiri (ed.), *Sangkhalok-Sukhothai-Ayutthaya and Asia*, Bangkok: Toyota Thailand Foundation, 2002, 175–219.

"Prawatisat sinlapa ayutthaya" [History of Ayutthaya art] in Charnvit Kasetsiri (ed.), *Ayutthaya kap asiya. Ayutthaya and Asia*, Bangkok: Toyota Thailand Foundation, 2001, 41–92, 144–72.

Sinlapa sukhothai lae ayutthaya: phaplak thi tong plian plaeng [Art of Sukhothai and Ayutthaya: image that must be changed], Bangkok: Amarin, 2002.

"The Phra Pathon Chedi" in Kanjani La-ongsi (ed.), *Sing la an phan la noi 60 pi warunee osatharom* [This and that: 60 years of Warunee Osatharam], Bangkok: Piriya Krairiksh Foundation, 2004, 231–82.

The roots of Thai art, tr. Narisa Chakrabongse, Bangkok: River Books, 2012.

Pittayawat Pittayaporn, "Layers of Chinese loanwords in Proto-Southwestern Tai as evidence for the spread of Southwestern Tai," *Manusya: Journal of Humanities*, special issue no. 20 (2014), 47–68.

Piyada Chonlaworn, "Relations between Ayutthaya and Ryukyu," *Journal of the Siam Society*, 92 (2004), 43–63.

Podjanok Kanjanajuntorn, Supamas Duangsakun, Budsaba Uamkasem, and Ramphing Simking, "Tracing post-Dvaravati culture from space: applying remote sensing technique in West-Central Thailand," *Asian Perspectives*, 53, 1 (2014), 29–52.

Polenghi, Cesare, "Giovanni Filippo de Marini, *Delle Missioni…(1663)*: An annotated translation of the chapters on Cambodia, Siam, and Makassar," *Journal of the Siam Society*, 95 (2007), 25–72.

Polkinghorne, Martin, Christophe Pottier and Christian Fischer, "One Buddha can hide another," *Journal Asiatique*, 301, 2 (2013), 575–624.

Pornpun Futrakul, "The environmental history of pre-modern provincial towns in Siam to 1910," PhD thesis, Cornell University, 1989.

Prachum silajaruek phak thi 3 [Collected inscriptions, part 3], Bangkok: Office of the Prime Minister, 1965.

Pramin Khrueathong, *Chamlae phaen yuet krung thonburi* [Re-examining the plan to seize Thonburi], Bangkok: Sinlapa Watthanatham, 2010.

Kabot jaofa men: "orot" ratchathayat prajao tak "nadda" phraphutthayotfa [Revolt of Prince Men: descendant of Taksin and King Yotfa], Bangkok: Sinlapa Watthanatham, 2004.

Phrajao tak bueang ton [King Taksin, an introduction], Bangkok: Sinlapa Watthanatham, 2014.

Prapod Assavavirulhakarn, *The ascendancy of Theravāda Buddhism in Southeast Asia*, Chiang Mai: Silkworm Books, 2010.

Prasert na Nagara, *Khlong nirat hariphunchai: sastrajan dr. prasoet na nakhon sop kap ton chabap chiang mai* [Nirat Hariphunchai: Professor Dr Prasert na Nagara examines the Chiang Mai version], 3rd ed., Bangkok: Phrajan, 1973.

"Prawat kan sueb sai khong wong chek amat" [History of the lineage of Sheikh Ahmed] at www.ayutthayastudies.aru.ac.th/content/view/180/32/.

Pricha Setkanjanakhom, *Set phachana din phao thi jangwat phranakhon si ayutthaya* [Pottery shards from Ayutthaya], Bangkok: Silpakorn University, 1985.

Puangthong Rungswasdisab, "War and trade: Siamese interventions in Cambodia, 1767–1851," PhD thesis, Wollongong University, 1995.

Raben, Remco and Dhiravat na Pombejra, ed., *In the king's trail: an 18th century Dutch journey to the Buddha's Footprint*, Bangkok: Royal Netherlands Embassy, 1997.

Ratanapanna Thera, *The sheaf of garlands of the epochs of the conqueror: being a translation of Jinakalamalipakaranam of Ratanapanna Thera of Thailand*, tr. N. A. Jayawickrama, London: Luzak for the Pali Text Society, 1968.

Ray, Himanshu Prabha, "Early maritime contacts between south and southeast Asia," *Journal of Southeast Asian Studies*, 20, 1 (1989), 42–53.

Reid, Anthony S., "Documenting the rise and fall of Ayudhya as a regional trade centre" in Kajit Jittasevi (ed.), *Ayudhya and Asia: proceedings for the international workshop*, Bangkok: Thammasat University, 1995, 5–14.

Charting the shape of early modern Southeast Asia, Chiang Mai: Silkworm Books, 1999.

"Low population growth and its causes in pre-colonial Southeast Asia" in Norman G. Owen (ed.), *Death and disease in Southeast Asia: explorations in social, medical, and demographic history*, Singapore: Oxford University Press, 1987, 33–47.

Southeast Asia in the age of commerce, Volume 1: The lands below the winds, New Haven: Yale University Press, CT, 1988; *Volume 2: Expansion and crisis*, New Haven: Yale University Press, CT, 1993.

Revire, Nicolas, "Glimpses of Buddhist practices and rituals in Dvāravatī and its neighbouring cultures" in Nicolas Revire and Stephen Murphy (ed.), *Before Siam: essays in art and archaeology*, Bangkok: River Books, 2014, 241–71.

Reynolds, Craig J., "Religious historical writing in early Bangkok" in Anthony Reid and David Marr (ed.), *Perceptions of the past in Southeast Asia*, Singapore: Heinemann, 1979, 90–107.

"The Buddhist monkhood in nineteenth century Thailand," PhD thesis, Cornell University, 1973.

Reynolds, Frank E. and Mani B. Reynolds, *Three worlds according to King Ruang: a Thai Buddhist cosmology*, Berkeley: University of California Press, 1982.

Rhys Davids, C. A. F. and T. W. Rhys Davids, *Dialogues of the Buddha, Part III*, Sacred Books of the Buddhists, vol. 4, London: Pali Text Society, 1965.

Ribadeneira, Marcel de, *Historia del archipelago y otros reynos. History of the Philippines and other kingdoms*, tr. Pacita Guevara Fernandez, 2 vols., Manila: Historical Conservation Society, 1970.

Ringis, Rita, *Thai temples and temple murals*, Kuala Lumpur: Oxford University Press, 1996.

Rispoli, Fiorella, Robeto Ciaria, and Vincent C. Pigott, "Establishing the prehistoric cultural sequence for the Lopburi region, Central Thailand," *Journal of World Prehistory*, 26 (2013), 101–71.

Rockhill, W. W., "Notes on the relations and trade of China with the eastern archipelago and the coasts of the Indian Ocean during the fourteenth century," *T'oung Pao*, 16 (1915), 61–159.

Ronachai Krisadaolarn, *The evolution of Thai money from its origins in ancient kingdoms*, Bangkok: River Books, 2016.

Rungrot Phiromanukun, "Lum maenam chaophraya chuang lang sin ratchakan phrajao chayawaraman thi 7" [Chaophraya Basin after the reign of Jayavarman VII] in Phiphat Krajaejan (ed.), *Yuk muet khong prawatisat thai: lang bayon phuttatherawat kan khao ma khong khon thai* [A dark age of Thai history: Post-Bayon, Theravada Buddhism, advent of the Thai], Bangkok: Sinlapa Watthanatham, 2013, 122–71.

Ryley, J. Horton, *Ralph Fitch, England's pioneer to India and Burma*, London: T. Fisher Unwin, 1899.

Saichol Satyanurak, *Phutthasasana kap naeo khit thang kan mueang nai ratchasamai phrabatsomdet phraphuttha yotfa julalok (pho. so. 2325–2353)* [Buddhism and political thought in the reign of King Rama I, 1782–1810], Bangkok: Sinlapa Watthanatham, 2003.

Sak-Humphry, Chhany, *The Sdok Kak Thom inscription (K.235): with a grammatical analysis of the Old Khmer text*, Phnom Penh: Buddhist Institute, 2005.

Sakurai, Yumio and Kitagawa Takako, "Ha Tien, or Banteay Mas in the time of the fall of Ayutthaya" in K. Breazeale (ed.), *From Japan to Arabia: maritime relations with Asia*, Bangkok: Foundation for the Promotion of Social Sciences and Humanities Textbooks, 1999, 150–220.

Salleh, Muhammed Haji, "Ayudhya in Sejarah Melayu" in Kajit Jittasevi (ed.), *Ayudhya and Asia: proceedings for the international workshop*, Bangkok: Thammasat University, 1995, 126–32.

Samutphap traiphum chabap krung si ayutthaya–chabap krung thonburi lem 1 [Illustrated manuscripts of the Three Worlds, Ayutthaya and Thonburi editions, vol. 1], Bangkok: Committee on records for the celebration of the King, 1999.

San San Wai, "A study of *Saddhamma Sangaha* treatise," unpublished paper, International Conference on Burma/Myanmar Studies, Chiang Mai, July 24–5, 2015.

Santi Leksukhum, *Prang lae lai punpan pradap wat julamani phitsanulok* [*Prang* and stucco decorations at Wat Chulamani, Phitsanulok], Bangkok: James Thompson Foundations and Silpakorn University, 1996.

Temples of gold: seven centuries of Thai Buddhist paintings, Bangkok: River Books, 2000.

Santi Pakdeekham, "Silajaruek khun si chaiyarat mongkhonthep" [Inscription of Khun Si Chaiyarat Monkhonthep] in *Sapjampa phiphitaphan sapjampa jangwat lopburi* [Sap Champa Museum, Lopburi Province], Lopburi: Sab Champa Museum, 2015, 73–9.

Sarasin Viraphol, *Tribute and profit: Sino-Siamese trade 1652–1853*, revised edition, Chiang Mai: Silkworm Books, 2014 [1977].

Sarassawadee Ongsakul, *History of Lan Na*, Chiang Mai: Silkworm Books, 2005.

Satow, E. M. "Notes on the intercourse between Japan and Siam in the seventeenth century," *Transactions of the Asiatic Society of Japan*, 13, 2 (1885), 139–210.

Schafer, Edward H., *The vermilion bird: T'ang images of the south*, Berkeley and Los Angeles: University of California Press, 1967.

Schouten, Joost, "A true description of the mighty kingdom of Siam" in F. Caron and J. Schouten, *A true description of the mighty kingdoms of Japan and Siam (1671)*, ed. John Villiers, Bangkok: Siam Society, 1986.

Seabra, Leonor de, *The embassy of Pero Vaz de Siqueira to Siam (1684–1686)*, Macau: University of Macau, 2005.

Siriphot Laomanajaroen, "Naeo khit nai kan ok baep jittrakam fa phanang ubosot wat ko kaeo suttharam pradimanwitthaya kap kan sadaeng ok choeng chang" [Mural paintings in the ubosot of Wat Ko Kaeo Suttharam: iconography and craftsmanship], *Muang Boran*, 33, 1 (2007), 88–95.

Skilling, Peter, "Buddhism and the circulation of ritual in early peninsular Southeast Asia" in Pierre-Yves Manguin, A. Mani, and Geoff Wade (ed.), *Early interactions between South and Southeast Asia*, Singapore: ISEAS, 2011, 371–84.

"Dvaravati: Recent revelations and research" in *Dedications to Her Royal Highness Princess Galyani Vadhana Krom Luang Naradhiwas Rajanagarinddra on her 80th birthday*, Bangkok: Siam Society, 2003.

"L'énigme de Si Thep" in Pierre Baptiste and Thierry Zéphir (ed.), *Dvāravatī – aux sources du bouddhisme en Thaïlande*, Paris: Musée Guimet, 2009, 117–25.

"Precious deposits: Buddhism seen through inscriptions in early Southeast Asia" in John Guy (ed.), *Lost kingdoms: Hindu-Buddhist sculpture of early Southeast Asia*, New York: Metropolitan Museum of Art, 2014, 58–62.

"The advent of Theravāda Buddhism to mainland Southeast Asia" in Skilling, *Buddhism and Buddhist literature of South-East Asia: selected papers*, Bangkok and Lumbini: Fragile Palm Leaves Foundations and Lumbini International Research Institute, 2009, 104–19.

ed., *The past lives of the Buddha. Wat Si Chum: art, architecture and inscriptions*, Bangkok: River Books, 2008.

Skilling, Peter, Jason A. Carbine, Claudio Cicuzza, and Santi Pakdeekham, ed., *How Theravāda is Theravāda? exploring Buddhist identities*, Chiang Mai: Silkworm Books, 2012.

Skinner, G. William, *Chinese society in Thailand: an analytical history*, Ithaca, NY: Cornell University Press, 1957.

Smallman-Raynor, M. R. and A. D. Cliff, *War epidemics: an historical geography of infectious diseases in military conflict and civil strife*, Oxford: Oxford University Press, 2004.

Smith, George V., *The Dutch in seventeenth-century Thailand*, DeKalb: Northern Illinois University, 1977.

"Princes, nobles and traders: ethnicity and economic activity in seventeenth-century Thailand," *Contributions to Asian Studies*, 15 (1980), 6–14.

Smith, R. B., "Mainland Southeast Asia in the seventh and eighth centuries" in R. B. Smith and W. Watson (ed.), *Early Southeast Asia*, Oxford University Press, 1979, 443–56.

Smith, Stefan Halikowski, *Creolization and diaspora in the Portuguese Indies: the social world of Ayutthaya, 1640–1720*, Leiden and Boston: Brill, 2011.

Smithies, Michael, "Jacques de Bourges (c.1630–1714) and Siam" in Smithies, *Seventeenth century Siamese explorations*, Bangkok: Siam Society, 2012, 17–48.

"Portuguese as a language of communication in Southeast Asia" in Smithies (ed.), *500 years of Thai-Portuguese relations: a festschrift*, Bangkok: Siam Society, 2011, 267–76.

"Seventeenth century Siam: its extent and urban centres" in Smithies, *Seventeenth century Siamese explorations*, Bangkok: Siam Society, 2012, 1–15.

Aspects of the embassy to Siam 1685, Bangkok: Silkworm Books, 1997.

ed., *The Siamese memoirs of Count Claude de Forbin 1685–1688*, Chiang Mai: Silkworm Books, 1996.

ed., *Three military accounts of the 1688 'revolution' in Siam*, Bangkok: Orchid Press, 2002.

Smithies, Michael and Dhiravat na Pombejra, "Instructions given to the Siamese envoys sent to Portugal, 1684," *Journal of the Siam Society*, 90 (2002), 125–35.

Sng, Jeffery and Pimpraphai Bisalputra, *A history of the Thai-Chinese*, Singapore: Editions Didier Millet, 2015.

Solheim, W. G. II and M. Ayres, "The late prehistoric and early historic pottery of the Khorat Plateua with special reference to Phimai" in R. B. Smith and W. Watson (ed.), *Early Southeast Asia*, Oxford University Press, 1979, 249–54.

Sommai Premchit and Donald K. Swearer, "A translation of *Tamnān mūlasāsanā wat pā daeng*: the chronicle of the founding of Buddhism of the Wat Pa Daeng tradition," *Journal of the Siam Society*, 60, 1 (1977), 73–110.

Sorensen, P., "The Ongbah cave and its fifth drum" in R. B. Smith and W. Watson (ed.), *Early Southeast Asia*, Oxford University Press, 1979, 78–97.

Srisakara Vallibhotama, "Early urban centres in the Chao Phraya valley of central Thailand" in Ian Glover (ed.), *Early metallurgy, trade and urban centres in Thailand and Southeast Asia*, Bangkok: White Lotus, 1992, 123–30.

Isan: aeng a-rayatham [Isan: cradle of civilization], Bangkok: Matichon, 1997.

Krung si ayutthaya khong rao [Our Ayutthaya], Bangkok: Sinlapa Watthanatham, 1984.

Mueang boran nai anajak sukhothai [Ancient cities in the Sukhothai kingdom], Bangkok: Thai Khadi Institute, 1989.

"Nakhon si thammarat kap prawatisat thai" [Nakhon Sithammarat and Thai history], *Muang Boran*, 4, 3 (1998).

"Political and cultural continuities at Dvaravati sites" in D. G. Marr and A. C. Milner (ed.), *Southeast Asia in the 9th to 14th centuries*, Canberra: Australian National University, 1986, 229–37.

Sayam prathet [The country of Siam], Bangkok: Matichon, 1991.

Sternstein, Larry, "'Krung kao': The old capital of Ayutthaya," *Journal of the Siam Society*, 53, 1 (1965), 83–121.

Stott, Philip, "Mu'ang and pa: elite views of nature in Thailand" in Manas Chitakasem and Andrew Turton (ed.), *Thai constructions of knowledge*, London: SOAS, 1991, 142–54.

Struys, Jan, "*The perillous and most unhappy voyages of John Struys*...", translated by John Morrison, London 1683," *Journal of the Siam Society*, 94 (2006), 177–209.

Stuart-Fox, Martin, *The Lao Kingdom of Lān Xāng: rise and decline*, Bangkok: White Lotus, 1998.

Studies of old Siamese coins. Selected articles from the Siam Society Journal, volume X, Bangkok: Siam Society, 1961.

Suárez, Thomas, *Early mapping of Southeast Asia*, Singapore: Periplus Editions, 1999.

Suebsang Promboon, "Sino-Siamese tributary relations, 1282–1853," PhD thesis, University of Wisconsin, 1971.

Sujit Wongthes, *Khon thai yu thini* [The Thai were here], Bangkok: Muang Boran, special number, 1986.

——— ed., *Jedi yutthahatthi mi jing rue?* [Does the stupa commemorating the elephant duel truly exist?], Bangkok: Sinlapa Watthanatham, 1994.

Sumet Jumsai, *Naga: cultural origins in Siam and the West Pacific*, Bangkok: Chalermnit Press and DD Books, 1997.

Sun Laichen, "Chinese-style gunpowder weapons in Southeast Asia: Focussing on archeological evidence" in Michael Aung-Thwin and Kenneth R. Hall (ed.), *New perspectives on the history and historiography of Southeast Asia: continuing explorations*, London: Routledge, 2011, 75–111.

——— "Military technology transfers from Ming China and the emergence of northern Mainland Southeast Asia (c. 1390–1527)," *Journal of Southeast Asian Studies*, 34, 3 (2003), 495–517.

——— "Saltpetre trade and warfare in early modern Asia" in Fujita Kayoko, Shiro Momoki, and Anthony Reid (ed.), *Offshore Asia: maritime interactions in Eastern Asia before steamships*, Singapore: ISEAS, 2013, 130–84.

Sunait Chutintaranond, "Cakravatin: the ideology of traditional warfare in Siam and Burma, 1548–1605," PhD thesis, Cornell University, 1990.

——— "Cakravartin ideology, reason and manifestation of Siamese and Burmese kings in traditional warfare (1538–1854)" in Sunait and Than Tun (ed.), *On both sides of the Tenasserim range: history of Siamese-Burmese relations*, Bangkok: Institute of Asian Studies, Chulalongkorn University, 1995, 55–66.

——— "Miyanma-sayam yut nai miyanma yazawin" [Burma-Thai warfare in the Burmese chronicles] in Sunait, *Phama rop thai* [Burmese wars with the Thai], Bangkok: Matichon, 1999, 59–142.

——— *Phama rop thai: wa duai songkhram rawang thai kap phama* [Burmese wars with the Thai], Bangkok: Matichon, 1994.

——— *Songkhram khrao sia krung si ayutthaya khrang thi 2 pho. so. 2310* [Warfare at the second fall of Ayutthaya, 1767], Bangkok: Sinlapa Watthanatham, 1988.

——— "The origins of Siamese–Burmese warfare" in Kajit Jittasevi (ed.), *Ayudhya and Asia: proceedings for the international workshop*, Bangkok: Thammasat University, 1995, 87–107.

Suphawat Kasemsi, M. R., "Phra aiyakan kao tamnaeng na huamueang chabap ayutthaya" [An old registrar of official positions in provincial towns of Ayutthaya] in Winai Pongsripian and Pridi Phitphumiwithi (ed.), *Sichamaiyachan* [Two illustrious teachers], Bangkok: Ministry of Culture, 2002.

Suthachai Yimprasert, "Portuguese lançados in Asia in the sixteenth and seventeenth centuries," PhD thesis, University of Bristol, 1998.

Swearer, Donald K. and Sommai Premchit, *The legend of Queen Cāma: Bodhiraṃsi's Cāmadevīvaṃsa, a translation and commentary*, Albany: State University of New York, 1998.

Tachard, Guy, *Voyage to Siam performed by six Jesuits sent by the French king to the Indies and China in the year 1685*, Bangkok: White Orchid, 1981 [1688].

Takaya Yoshikazu, *Agricultural development of a tropical delta: a study of the Chao Phraya delta*, tr. Peter Hawkes, Honolulu: University of Hawaii Press, 1987.

Tambiah, S. J., *World conqueror and world renouncer: a study of Buddhism and polity in Thailand against a historical background*, Cambridge: Cambridge University Press, 1976.

Tamra chang chabap ratchakan thi 1 [Manual of elephants, First Reign edition], Committee for Memorial Books and Records for Celebration of the King's Age Equaling that of King Rama I in 2000, Bangkok: Ruansin, 2002.

Tamra phichai songkhram chabap ratchakan thi 1 [Manual of victorious warfare, First Reign edition], Committee for Memorial Books and Records for Celebration of the King's Age Equalling that of King Rama I in 2000, Bangkok: Ruansin, 2002.

Taylor, K. W., *The birth of Vietnam*, Berkeley, Los Angeles, and London: University of California Press, 1983.

Teeuw, A. and D. K. Wyatt, *Hikayat Patani: the story of Patani*, 2 vols, The Hague: Martinus Nijhof, 1970.

Terwiel, Barend J., "Asiatic cholera in Siam: its first occurrence and the 1820 epidemic" in Norman G. Owen (ed.), *Death and disease in Southeast Asia: explorations in social, medical, and demographic history*, Singapore: Oxford University Press, 1987, 142–61.

"The body and sexuality in Siam: a first exploration in early sources," *Manusya: Journal of Humanities*, Special Issue No. 14 (2007), 42–55.

Thailand's political history: from the 13th century to recent times, Bangkok: River Books, 2011.

Through travellers' eyes: an approach to early nineteenth century Thai history, Bangkok: Editions Duang Kamol, 1989.

"What happened at Nong Sarai? Comparing indigenous and European sources for late 16th century Siam," *Journal of the Siam Society*, 101 (2013), 19–34.

Thailand and Portugal: 476 years of friendship, 2nd ed., Bangkok: Embassy of Portugal, 1987.

Thailand in the 80s, Bangkok: National Identity Office, 1984.

Thammathibet, Prince, *Kap he ruea phraniphon jaofa thammathibet* [Boat songs of Prince Thammathibet], from www.reurnthai.com.

Than Tun, "Ayut'a men in the service of Burmese kings" in Sunait Chutintaranond and Than Tun (ed.), *On both sides of the Tenasserim range: History of Siamese-Burmese relations*, Bangkok: Institute of Asian Studies, Chulalongkorn University, 1995, 94–106.

The Travels of Ludovico di Varthema, AD 1503 to 1508, tr. J. W. Jones, London: Hakluyt Society, 1863.

Tibbetts, G. R., *A study of the Arabic texts containing material on South-East Asia*, Leiden: E. J. Brill, 1979.

Arab navigation in the Indian Ocean before the coming of the Portuguese, London: Royal Asiatic Society, 1981.

Tomosugi, Takashi, *A structural analysis of Thai economic history: case study of a northern Chao Phraya Delta village*, Tokyo: Institute of Developing Economies, 1980.

Trakulhun, Sven, "Suspicious friends: Siamese warfare and the Portuguese (c. 1540–1700)" in Volker Grabowsky (ed.), *Southeast Asian historiography. Unravelling the myths. Essays in honour of Barend Jan Terwiel*, Bangkok: River Books, 2011, 198–217.

Trongjai Hutangkura, "Reconsidering the palaeo-shoreline in the lower Central Plain of Thailand" in Nicolas Revire and Stephen A. Murphy (ed.), *Before Siam: Essays in art and archaeology*, Bangkok: River Books, 2014, 32–67.

——— ed., *Pramuan jaruek samai phraya lithai* [Review of the inscriptions of King Lithai], Bangkok: Sirindhorn Anthropological Centre, 2015.

Tun Aung Chain, tr., *Chronicle of Ayutthaya: a translation of the Yodaya Yazawin*, Yangon: Myanmar Historical Commission, 2005.

Turpin, F. H., *A history of the Kingdom of Siam and of the revolutions that have caused the overthrow of the empire up to 1770*, tr. B. O. Cartwright, Bangkok: White Lotus, 1997 [1771].

Vajiravudh, Prince, *Thieo mueang phra ruang* [Visiting King Ruang's cities], Bangkok: Ministry of the Interior, 1954 [1908].

Van Roy, Edward, "Prominent Mon lineages from Late Ayutthaya to Early Bangkok," *Journal of the Siam Society*, 98 (2010), 205–21.

——— "Safe haven: Mon refugees and the capitals of Siam," *Journal of the Siam Society*, 98 (2010), 151–84.

Van Vliet's Siam, ed. Chris Baker, Dhiravat na Pomberja, Alfons van der Kraan, and David K. Wyatt, Chiang Mai: Silkworm Books, 2005.

Vandenberg, Patrick, "The quest for the holy water: Ayutthaya's ever-changing waterways," 2010, at www.ayutthaya-history.com/files/Essay_WaterwaysI. pdf.

Vickery, Michael, "Cambodia after Angkor, the chronicular evidence for the fourteenth to sixteenth centuries," PhD thesis, Yale University, 1977.

——— "Cambodia and its neighbours in the 15th century" in Geoff Wade and Sun Laichen (ed.), *Southeast Asia in the fifteenth century: the China factor*, Singapore and Hong Kong: NUS Press and Hong Kong Press, 2010, 271–303.

——— "Piltdown 3: further discussion of the Ram Khamhaeng inscription," *Journal of the Siam Society*, 83 (1995), 103–97.

——— "Prolegomena to methods for using the Ayutthayan laws as historical source materials," *Journal of the Siam Society*, 72 (1984), 37–59.

——— "Review article: Jeremias van Vliet, *The Short History of the kings of Siam...*," *Journal of the Siam Society*, 64, 2 (1976), 207–36.

——— "Some new evidence for the cultural history of central Thailand," *Siam Society Newsletter*, 2, 3 (1986), 4–6.

——— "The 2/K.125 fragment, a lost chronicle of Ayutthaya," *Journal of the Siam Society*, 65, 1 (1977), 1–80.

"The composition and transmission of the Ayudhya and Cambodia chronicles" in Anthony Reid and David Marr (ed.), *Perceptions of the past in Southeast Asia*, Singapore: Heinemann, 1979, 130–54.

"The constitution of Ayutthaya: the Three Seals Code" in A. Huxley (ed.), *Thai law: Buddhist law. Essays on the legal history of Thailand, Laos and Burma*, Bangkok: White Orchid, 1996, 133–210.

"The Khmer inscriptions of Tenasserim: a reinterpretation," *Journal of the Siam Society*, 61, 1 (1977), 51–70.

"The reign of Sūryavarman I and royal factionalism at Angkor," *Journal of Southeast Asian Studies*, 16, 2 (1985), 226–44.

Society, economy and politics in pre-Angkor Cambodia, Tokyo: Centre for East Asian Cultural Studies for UNESCO, 1998.

Villiers, John, "Portuguese and Spanish sources for the history of Ayutthaya in the sixteenth century," *Journal of the Siam Society*, 86, 1–2 (1998), 119–130.

Volker, T., *Porcelain and the Dutch East India Company*, Leiden: E. J. Brill, 1954.

Wade, Geoff, "An early age of commerce in Southeast Asia, 900–1300 CE," *Journal of Southeast Asian Studies*, 40, 2 (2009), 221–65.

"Angkor and its external relations in the 14th–15th centuries as reflected in the *Ming Shi-lu*," unpublished paper, 2011.

"Beyond the southern borders: Southeast Asia in Chinese texts to the ninth century" in John Guy (ed.), *Lost kingdoms: Hindu-Buddhist sculpture of early Southeast Asia*, New York: Metropolitan Museum of Art, 2014, 25–31.

"Melaka in Ming Dynasty texts," *Journal of the Malayan Branch of the Royal Asiatic Society*, 70, 1 (1997), 31–69.

"Southeast Asia in the 15th century" in Wade and Sun Laichen (ed.), *Southeast Asia in the fifteenth century: the China factor*, Singapore and Hong Kong: NUS Press and Hong Kong University Press, 2010, 3–43.

Southeast Asia in the Ming Shi-lu: an open access resource, Singapore: Asia Research Institute and the Singapore E-Press, National University of Singapore, http://epress.nus.edu.sg/msl [noted in footnotes as *Southeast Asia online*, with item number].

"The *Bai-yi zhuan*: a Chinese account of a Tai society in the 14th century," paper presented at the 14th IAHA Conference, Bangkok, 1996.

"The *Ming shi-lu* as a source for Thai history – fourteenth to seventeenth centuries," *Journal of Southeast Asian Studies*, 31, 2 (2000), 249–94.

Wang Gungwu, "The *Nanhai* trade," *Journal of the Malayan Branch of the Royal Asiatic Society*, 31 (1958), 1–135.

Wannakam samai rattanakosin lem 3: Sangkhittiyawong [Bangkok era literature vol. 3: Sangkitiyavamsa], Bangkok: Fine Arts Department: 2001.

Wannakhadi samai ayutthaya [Literature of the Ayutthaya era], 3 vols., Bangkok: Fine Arts Department, 1996.

Wannasarn Noonsuk, *Tambralinga and Nakhon Si Thammarat: early kingdoms on the isthmus of Southeast Asia*, Nakhon Si Thammarat: Nakhon Si Thammarat Rajabhat University, 2013.

Wansiri Dechakhup and Pridi Phitphumwithi, *Krung kao lao rueang* [Relating about the old city], Bangkok: Sinlapa Watthanatham, 2010.

Watanyu Fakthong, "Jaruek khun si chaiyarat mongkhonthep" [Inscription of Khun Si Chaiyarat Mongkhonthep] in *100 ekkasan samkhan: sapphasara prawatisat thai lamdap thi 7* [100 key documents: essence of Thai history, no. 7], Bangkok: Thailand Research Fund, 2011, 29–53.

Webb, James L. A., "Malaria and the peopling of early tropical Africa," *Journal of World History*, 16, 3 (2005), 269–91.

Wheatley, Paul, "*Geographical notes* on some commodities involved in Sung maritime trade," *Journal of the Malayan Branch of the Royal Asiatic Society*, 32, 2 (1959), 1–139.

Nāgara and Commandery: Origins of the Southeast Asian urban traditions, University of Chicago, department of geography research paper nos. 2017–18, 1983.

The Golden Khersonese: studies in the historical geography of the Malay Peninsula to A. D. 1500, Kuala Lumpur: University of Malaya, 1961.

Wicks, Robert S., "Ancient coinage of Mainland Southeast Asia," *Journal of Southeast Asian Studies*, 16, 2 (1985), 195–225.

Money, markets, and trade in early Southeast Asia: the development of indigenous monetary systems to AD 1400, Ithaca, NY: Cornell University Press, 1992.

Wilaiwan Khanittanan, "Khmero-Thai: the great change in the history of the Thai language of the Chao Phraya Basin," *Phasa lae phasasat* [Journal of language and linguistics], 19, 2 (2001), 35–50; reprinted in S. Burusphat (ed.), *Papers from the eleventh annual meeting of the Southeast Asian Linguistics Society*, Tempe AZ, 2004, 375–91.

Winai Pongsripian, *Ajariyapucha: sapphasara prawatisat phasa lae wannakam thai* [Homage to a teacher: collected articles on Thai history, language, and literature], Bangkok: Thailand Research Fund, 2007.

"Jaruek dong mae nang mueang: moradok khwam songjam haeng mueang nakhon sawan" [Inscription of Dong Mae Nang Muang: heritage of Nakhon Sawan] in *100 ekkasan samkhan: sapphasara prawatisat thai lamdap thi 7* [100 key documents: essence of Thai history, no. 7], Bangkok: Thailand Research Fund, 2011, 5–23.

ed., *Kamsuan samut: sut yot kamsuansin* [Ocean lament: the ultimate of the lament genre], Bangkok: Thailand Research Fund, 2010.

"Phraratchaphongsawadan krung si ayutthaya chabap ho phra samut wachirayan (chabap plik mai lek tabian 222 2/k 104)" [The Wachirayan edition of the royal chronicles of Ayutthaya: the 222 2/k 104 fragment] in *100 ekkasan samkhan: sapphasara prawatisat thai lamdap thi 13* [100 key documents on Thai history, no. 13], Bangkok: Thailand Research Fund, 2012.

"Rueang phasa tai thai" [On Tai-Thai language] in Winai, *Photjananukrom kham kao nai phasa thai chabap chaloeisak* [Dictionary of old Thai words, private edition], Bangkok: Sirindhorn Anthropology Center, 2012, 9–91.

"Silajaruek wat si chum" [Wat Si Chum inscription] in *100 ekkasan samkhan: sapphasara prawatisat thai lamdap thi 1* [100 key documents of Thai history, no. 1], Bangkok: Thailand Research Fund, 2011, 39–95.

Winai Pongsripian and Trongjai Hutangkura, *Moradok khwam songjam haeng nopphaburi si lawotayapura wa duai khlong chaloemphrakiat somdet phra narai lae jaruek boran haeng mueang lawo* [Legacy of Lopburi in the eulogy of King

Narai and ancient inscriptions of Lawo], Bangkok: Sirindhorn Anthropology Centre, 2015.

Wolters, O. W., "Chên-li-fu. A state on the Gulf of Siam at the beginning of the 13th century," *Journal of the Siam Society*, 48, 2 (1960), 1–35.

History, culture, and region in Southeast Asian perspectives, Singapore: ISEAS, 1982.

"Tambralinga," *Bulletin of the School of Asian and African Studies*, 21, 3 (1958), 587–607.

The fall of Srivijaya in Malay history, Ithaca, NY: Cornell University Press, 1970.

"The Khmer king at Basan (1371–3) and the restoration of the Cambodian chronology during the fourteenth and fifteenth centuries," *Asia Major*, 12, 1 (1966), 44–89.

Wood, W. A. R., *A history of Siam: from the earliest times to the year A.D. 1781, with a supplement dealing with more recent events*, Bangkok: Chalermnit, 1959 [1924].

Woodward, Hiram W. Jr., "Seventeenth-century Chinese porcelain in various worlds," *Journal of the Walters Art Museum*, 70, 1 (2012–13), 25–38.

"Studies in the art of Central Siam, 950–1350," PhD thesis, Yale University, 1975.

"Thailand: Buddha images for worship, ceramics for export," unpublished paper, AAS 1998.

"The Jayabuddhamahānātha images of Cambodia," *Journal of the Walters Art Gallery*, 52, 3 (1994/5), 105–11.

The sacred sculpture of Thailand: The Alexander B. Griswold collection, the Walters Art Gallery, Seattle: University of Washington Press, 1997.

"What there was before Siam: traditional views" in Nicolas Revire and Stephen A. Murphy (ed.), *Before Siam: essays in art and archaeology*, Bangkok: River Books, 2014, 17–29.

Wray, Elizabeth, Claire Rosenfield, and Dorothy Bailey, *Ten lives of the Buddha: Siamese temple paintings and jataka tales*, New York and Tokyo: Weatherhill, 1972.

Wright, Michael, *Phaen thi phaen thang nai prawatisat lok lae sayam* [Maps and route-maps in the history of the world and Siam], Bangkok: Matichon, 2003.

Wyatt, David K., "Family politics in nineteenth-century Thailand" in Wyatt, *Studies in Thai history: collected articles*, Chiang Mai: Silkworm Books, 1994, 107–30.

"Family politics in seventeenth- and eighteenth-century Siam" in Wyatt, *Studies in Thai history: collected articles*, Chiang Mai: Silkworm Books, 1994, 98–106.

"Relics, oaths and politics in thirteenth-century Siam," *Journal of Southeast Asian Studies*, 32, 1 (2001), 3–65.

Thailand: a short history, New Haven, CT: Yale University Press, 1984.

Wyatt, D. K., tr. and ed., *The crystal sands: the chronicle of Nagara Śrī Dharmarāja*, Ithaca, NY: Cornell University Press, 1975.

tr. and ed., *The Nan chronicle*, Ithaca, NY: Cornell SEAP, 1994.

"The 'subtle revolution' of King Rama I of Siam" in Wyatt, *Studies in Thai history: collected articles*, Chiang Mai: Silkworm Books, 1994, 131–74.

"Translating Thai poetry: Cushman, and King Narai's 'Long song prophecy for Ayutthaya'," *Journal of the Siam Society*, 89 (2001), 1–11.

Wyatt, David K. and Aroonrut Wichienkeeo, *The Chiang Mai chronicle*, Chiang Mai: Silkworm Books, 1995.

Yamamoto Tatsuro, "East Asian historical sources for Dvāravatī studies" in *Proceedings of the 7th IAHA*, vol. 2, Bangkok: Chulalongkorn University Press, 1977, 1137–50.

"Thailand as it is referred to in the Da-de Nan-hai Zhi at the beginning of the fourteenth century," *Journal of East-West Maritime Relations*, 1 (1989), 47–58.

Zhou Daguan, *A record of Cambodia: the land and its people*, tr. Peter Harris, Chiang Mai: Silkworm Books, 2007.

Zide, A. R. K. and N. H. Zide, "Cultural vocabulary: evidence for early agriculture" in P. N. Jenner, L. C. Thompson, and S. Starotsa (ed.), *Austroasiatic Studies*, part II, Honolulu: University of Hawaii Press, 1976, 1294–334.

Index